Melodrama and Modernity

FILM AND CULTURE

John Belton, Editor

FILM AND CULTURE

A Series of Columbia University Press

Edited by John Belton

Melodrama and Modernity

Early Sensational Cinema and Its Contexts

Ben Singer

Columbia University Press

New York

Columbia University Press
Publishers Since 1893
New York   Chichester, West Sussex
Copyright © 2001 Ben Singer

Library of Congress Cataloging-in-Publication Data
Singer, Ben.
    Melodrama and modernity : early sensational cinema and its contexts / Ben Singer.
        p. cm. — (Film and culture)
    Includes bibliographical references and index.
    ISBN 0–231–11328–5 (cloth : alk. paper) — ISBN 0–231–11329–3 (pbk. : alk. paper)
    1. Melodrama in motion pictures. I. Title. II. Series.

    PN1995.9.M45 S56 2001
    791.43'653—dc21

                                                                      00–064547

Casebound editions of Columbia University Press books are printed on permanent and durable
acid-free paper.

Printed in the United States of America

c 10 9 8 7 6 5 4 3 2 1
p 10 9 8 7 6 5 4 3 2 1

Permission has been granted to reprint portions of this book derived from essays in Geoffrey
Nowell-Smith, ed., *The Oxford History of World Cinema* (Oxford, 1996); Leo Charney and Vanessa
Schwartz, *Cinema and the Invention of Modern Life* (California, 1995); *The Velvet Light Trap* 37
(Spring 1996); *Film History* 5 (November 1993); and *Camera Obscura* 22 (Winter 1990).

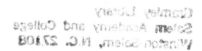

For my parents
and for Carolyn

Contents

Illustrations

Acknowledgments

———

I think of this book as a monument to miscalculation. Over a decade ago, when I began formulating a dissertation topic, I determined that the best strategy for avoiding the dreaded "ten-year plan" would be to choose a subject that was small, self-contained, exhaustible, conducive to a brief but intense burst of diligent pedantry. A study of American serial films between 1913, when they began, through about 1918 seemed to fit the bill perfectly: a brief period, an obscure body of films, few surviving prints, virtually no secondary literature, and just enough microfilm drudgery to give the project the feel of an ascetic calling.

Things did not work out quite as planned. My fundamental error was in thinking that this topic was in fact self-contained, suitable for wrapping into a neat little package. Such packaging might be possible, but only by turning a blind eye to what makes the films most interesting—their significance within larger social and intertextual contexts during a period of exceptionally rapid change in the character of modern life and melodramatic representation. Over the years, and especially during extensive postdoctoral revision and expansion, my compact micro-topic gradually mutated into a broad exploration of the meanings and interconnections of melodrama and modernity.

My study has been aided by the generosity and encouragement of many people. I owe a great deal to the mentors and friends on my dissertation committee—Robert Sklar (my adviser), Richard Allen, Tom Gunning, Charles Musser, and William Simon. I particularly would like to acknowledge Tom's altruism in reading just about everything I have ever written in film studies (beginning my senior year at college). I also thank Charlie for widening my research horizons; I stumbled across many of my most interesting images and articles while working as a research assistant on some of his Edison projects. Richard Abel and Gregory Waller, the two "anonymous" readers, offered wise suggestions for turning the manuscript into a coherent book. My early work on the serial queen phenomenon was given a major boost by Miriam Hansen's supportiveness and by Lea Jacobs's astute editorial input. Marc Steinberg, a Smith colleague in sociology, offered extremely helpful comments on my survey of modernity theory and was kind enough to scrutinize all three drafts I foisted upon him. David Bordwell showed a great deal of class in his response to a version of chapter 4 that I sent him. It has been a privilege engaging in energetic debate with such a keen devil's advocate.

Others who have shared their ideas and offered assistance include Jennifer Bean, John Belton, Tom Bottomore, Eileen Bowser, Leo Charney, Lewin Goff, Steve Higgins, Charlie Keil, Richard Koszarski, Antonia Lant, Skadi Loist, Madeline Matz, Brooks McNamara, Steve Neale, Geoffrey Nowell-Smith, Moreland Perkins, Vanessa Schwartz, Shelley Stamp, Eugene Stavis, Kristin Thompson, Paolo Cherchi Usai, and Linda Williams. Working with the team at Columbia University Press (editor Jennifer Crewe, copy editor Roy Thomas, and designer Brady McNamara) has been a pleasure.

This project was supported by the New York University Graduate School of Arts and Sciences through a Dean's Dissertation Grant and, at Smith College, by a Harvey Picker grant, along with various generous college grants for research travel and student assistance. Among the civilian population, I would like to thank Meg Ross for helping me with some arduous early filmographic research, and Rozzie Sukenik, Mark and Phyl Singer, and Lisa Farnsworth and Steed Hinkley for their hospitality during research junkets to Washington, D.C. My sisters Emily, Margie, and Anne and my good friend Jeremy Berlin encouraged me to stay the course whenever I began contemplating a career switch to motel management.

This book is dedicated to my parents, Irving and Jo Singer, who helped keep me financially afloat during years of graduate-student poverty, and to my wife Carolyn, who keeps me afloat in most other ways. Without her I would never find my keys.

Melodrama and Modernity

I don't know how my readers feel about this, but for me personally it is always pleasing to recognize again and again the fact that our cinema is not altogether without parents and without pedigree, without a past, without the traditions and rich cultural heritage of the past epochs. It is only very thoughtless and presumptuous people who can erect laws and an esthetic for cinema, proceeding from premises of some incredible virgin-birth of this art!

—Sergei Eisenstein (1944)

Introduction

M elodrama and modernity—two terms belonging high up on any list of big, vague concepts that despite their semantic sprawl, or perhaps because of it, continually reward critical inquiry. The goal of this book is to investigate some of the interconnections between the two, situating melodrama, particularly sensational melodrama in American popular theater and film between 1880 and 1920, as a product and a reflection of modernity—of modernity's experiential qualities, its ideological fluctuations, its cultural anxieties, its intertextual crosscurrents, its social demographics, and its commercial practices. This study also has a basic historical objective: it unearths two fascinating cultural phenomena—popular-priced 10–20–30 blood-and-thunder stage melodrama and early sensational film serials—that, while largely forgotten today, are crucial to an understanding of American popular culture in the decades around the turn of the century, and beyond.

It is fair to say that modernity has not been a particularly important concept in film studies, at least not until quite recently. In social theory, however, it has long been a foundational theme, motivating work by Marx, Durkheim, Weber, Tönnies, Simmel, and many others. Given its core question—What distinguishes modern Western industrial society from all others?—modernity is, not surprisingly, an extraordinarily expansive topic, encompassing an array of socioeconomic, cognitive, ideological, moral, and experiential issues. My first order of business will be to try to give some structure to this inherently diffuse body of social theory. In chapter 1, I offer an introduction to key discourses on the nature of modernity. The breakdown I propose delineates six facets: modernity as an explosion of socioeconomic and technological development (what is generally labeled "modernization"); modernity as the reign of instrumental rationality; modernity as a condition of perennial cultural discontinuity and ideological "reflexivity"; modernity as the heightened mobility and circulation of all "social things"; modernity as a milieu of social atomization and competitive individualism; and modernity as a perceptual environment of unprecedented sensory complexity and intensity. Not all of these facets are equally central to my analysis of melodrama, and my discussion takes a number of side trips to pursue specific film-historical questions not primarily hinging on issues of modernity; but in general, my analysis is interested in exploring ways in which melodrama can be regarded as a fundamentally modern cultural expression. Recent work in film studies has focused especially on the last facet, cinema's relationship to the phenomenology of the metropolis. This is an important topic, one to which I devote two chapters, but my hope is that the schematization of modernity presented here will help move the discussion toward consideration of a wider range of connections.

Next to modernity, or indeed, next to just about anything, the topic of melodrama has a much humbler intellectual pedigree. For most of the two centuries in which melodrama has been identified as a dramatic category, it has been a target of critical ridicule and derision. In 1912, for example, a couple of years after the movies had driven popular-priced stage melodrama out of urban theaters, a critic offered this merciless good riddance:

Of all the crude, slipshod, debasing, superficial, ignoble and utterly non-sensical forms of dramatic non-art, the melodrama was the worst. . . . I hope that melodrama of the ten-twenty-thirty class [i.e., popular priced — costing 10, 20, or 30 cents] is gone forever, knocked down on its head, shoveled up, dumped into the bucket and carried out to the ash heap.[1]

Even until quite recently, one could find descriptions of melodrama evoking metaphors of disease, disfigurement, perversion, and substance abuse. As a college textbook published in 1982 stated,

In the first half of the nineteenth century . . . the same blight which was afflicting playwriting in England, Germany, and France spread to American dramatists. It distorted and stunted their work to such an extent that, with few exceptions, no enduring dramatic literature was written for a hundred years. . . . The blight that perverted American dramaturgy was the love of melodrama. . . . The addiction to melodrama did not weaken until the end of the century when native playwrights, along with their European colleagues, felt the cleansing, therapeutic effects of such giants as Ibsen, Strindberg, and Chekhov.[2]

Today, such assessments strike academics as drolly shortsighted and naive, and they have become very rare (although echoes still linger outside scholarly circles).[3] What explains this academic peripety? As if in the scenario of a classic melodrama, the long-abused victim finally experienced a sudden, unexpected twist of fate. Melodrama's critical fortunes began to brighten considerably in the late 1960s and 1970s with a burst of publications in theater history and literary criticism that, for the most part, suspended aesthetic evaluation and instead concentrated on melodrama as a generic system with interesting psychosocial implications (a body of work I will discuss in chapter 5). In a more or less separate development in the late 1970s and 1980s, melodrama emerged as a major topic in film studies, becoming probably the most written about Hollywood genre. This phenomenon reflected the convergence of two influential currents in the field. On the one hand, Marxist/leftist critics began to embrace certain 1950s and 1960s family melodramas, especially the films of Douglas Sirk, as redolent quasi-Brechtian critiques of bourgeois culture. The films' focus on the dysfunctionality and materialism of the postwar American family, coupled with their tendency toward stylistic "excess," lent them a progressive cachet (made all the more alluring to critics by virtue of their supposed surreptitiousness in critiquing bourgeois capitalism from within the very Hollywood system designed to disseminate dominant ideology).[4] At roughly the same time, melodrama took on central importance as a focus of psychoanalytic and feminist film criticism and theory. Hollywood melodramas were ideal subjects for analysis: their emphasis on emotional repression and expression provided fertile ground for psychoanalytic interpretation; they often revolved around positive female protagonists and emphasized traditionally female life-issues and value systems; they invited consideration of the paradoxes posed by the existence of films catering to female audiences within a mainstream cinema that, according to the prevailing paradigm, was "tailored to the male unconscious"; and in the late eighties, as cultural studies waxed and psychoanalytic criticism waned, Hollywood melodramas offered rich possibilities for research into fan magazines, fashion tie-ins, and other intertextual arenas in which the experience of "real" female spectators could be traced.[5]

This book ventures in a somewhat different direction, examining a different type of film melodrama in a different period. My focus is on early sensational or blood-and-thunder melodrama, a variety of melodrama that enjoyed great popularity on both stage and screen in the decades around the turn of the century (and which is still very much with us, although not labeled as such). This subject caught my interest when I stumbled upon two "discoveries" that intrigued and perplexed me. The first finding made me realize just how little we still know about silent cinema. Slogging through a film trade journal on microfilm, I came across an advertisement for D. W. Griffith's *The Birth of a Nation,* released in early 1915. Recognizing that *The Birth of a Nation* was by far the most important work in American cinema in this period, I naturally assumed the film would take the trade journal by storm, monopolizing its ads, editorials, publicity items, and reviews for weeks, perhaps months, to come. I assumed that the film's original exposure would roughly correspond to its contemporary prominence in film history. A typical college textbook I recently had read covered American cinema in this period with a few paragraphs on Thomas Ince, Mack Sennett, Cecil B. DeMille, and Charles Chaplin, while Griffith was granted an entire 48-page long chapter.[6] So I knew Griffith's films were *the* monumental event of film history in the Teens. Scrolling through the microfilm, I saw another one-page ad for *The Birth of a Nation* in the week of its release, and a couple more the next week or two. And after that there was nothing much. To my surprise, Griffith's film was not at all extraordinary, at least judging from trade journal visibility. The social controversy and critical esteem the film elicited did, of course, set it apart from the average feature film, but far less than one might imagine. It was just one film in a torrent of releases.

Even now, when scholars have a greater sensitivity to the historiographical problems of canon formations, few recognize the truly astonishing magnitude of the torrent. A computation of entries in *The American Film Institute Catalog of Feature Films* indicates that nearly 5,200 feature films were produced in the United States alone between 1912 and 1920. In addition, the one-, two-, and three-reel films made in this country in those years comprised approximately 31,300 more releases. In light of such incredible numbers, one cannot help but recognize just how untenable it is to hope the films of a handful of prominent directors, representing a fraction of 1 percent of the period's output, can stand in for the vast and diverse output of American cinema in the Teens.[7]

What I *did* see a lot of as I explored the period's trade journals were a great many eye-catching double-page ads for sensational film serials like *The Perils of Pauline*, *The Exploits of Elaine*, *The Million Dollar Mystery*, *The Iron Claw*, *The Grip of Evil*, *A Lass of the Lumberlands*, *The Yellow Menace*, *The House of Hate*, *The Lurking Peril*, and *The Screaming Shadow*. Of these, only the first faintly rang a bell (probably due to the fact that the title was reused for two films made in 1947 and 1967 and has been immortalized in the Baskin & Robbins ice cream flavor "The Perils of Praline"). Not only were the ads for these films larger, bolder, more abundant and graphically interesting than anything else in the trade journals, they also promoted huge publicity schemes centered around fiction tie-ins. Hundreds, or even thousands, of newspapers across the country invited consumers to "Read It Here in the Morning; See It On the Screen Tonight!" I was also struck by the frequency with which female stars received top billing and publicity exposure. Could this be, I wondered, a cinema deliberately pitched to female spectators, a decade before the Valentino craze? This was particularly interesting since films of violence and action are seldom pitched to women. It was immediately apparent to me that the textbooks had overlooked a major and innovative facet of early American cinema.

The second moment of simultaneous revelation and bafflement triggering this project happened a few weeks later as I was sifting through the corporate papers of the Edison studio in West Orange, New Jersey, at a table a few feet away from the spot where Thomas Edison and W. K. L. Dickson had stood developing the Kinetograph almost exactly a century earlier. I came across a quality-control chart from 1915 that puzzled me. The chart divided the studio's output for that year into eight different genres: Melodrama, Drama, Historical Drama, Sob Story, Child Story, Sociological, Broad Comedy, and Light Comedy; and it evaluated films in these eight genres according to eleven criteria of quality.[8] The chart was fascinating not only because it was an index of the film studios' assimilation of techniques of industrial rationalization—a core component of capitalist modernity—but also because it marked a crisis point in film history. It was designed to help the studio executives determine whether the alarming decline in Edison film sales was due to inferior product or to a cause they considered even more unsettling: the muscling-in of feature films. What particularly intrigued me about the chart, however, was that in its generic breakdown "Melodrama" and "Sob Story" were distinguished as separate genres. The two, it seemed to me, should be more or less equivalent. The movies that instantly came to mind as I thought of examples of Hollywood film melodrama—movies like *Stella Dallas, Letter from an Unknown Woman, Written on the Wind, Imitation of Life, Peyton Place, Madam X, Back Street,* and so on—all hinged on sentimental motifs of romantic pathos and domestic tribulation. "Sob story" for me evoked the "weepie" or "tearjerker," the woman's film, the soap opera, etc. If these were not melodrama, then what was?

As I delved deeper into the trade journals looking for material on film serials, and at the same time began exploring the historical semantics of "melodrama," I came to realize that the two topics were actually more like one. Whenever genre terms were used, sensational serials, I found, invariably were referred to as melodramas. One review, for example, described the 1914 serial *Lucille Love: Girl of Mystery* as "a melodramatic melodrama, or otherwise a melodrama to the second degree."[9] What was meant by such a characterization? What made sensational serials emphatically the most melodramatic of melodramas?

Answering this question is complicated by the notorious ambiguity of the term *melodrama.* At least one scholar, exasperated by the word's inconsistent uses and connotations, has exclaimed that "melodrama as a coherent dramatic category never existed." In response, the editor of a major anthology on film melodrama dismissed that argument as just a "supercilious attempt to disprove those who have sought to establish melodrama as a genre." Reading the anthology's essays, however, and trying to follow its path from the epistolary tale of sexual malice *Clarissa* (1747) to the mystery-suspense film *Coma* (1978), via the turn-of-the-century tied-to-the-tracks stage thriller and the classical Hollywood "woman's weepie," one cannot help but sympathize, if not necessarily agree, with the naysayer's pronouncement.[10]

One way to deal with the problem of melodrama's generic slipperiness is to stop trying to understand melodrama as a genre, and instead think of it as a dramatic "mode." Linda Williams, in an interesting recent work, argues that melodrama should be designated as "a fundamental mode of popular American 'moving pictures'" since its core operation—moving us to "feel sympathy for the virtues of beset victims" and accomplishing "a retrieval and staging of virtue through adversity and suffering"—transcends any one genre or medium. This approach is undoubtedly fruitful for certain purposes. For example, it allows Williams to locate melodrama in a wider range of cultural texts, including things like television coverage of the Atlanta Olympics or the O. J. Simpson trial; and it also enables Williams to call into question the critical viability of the Classical Hollywood narrative paradigm. The problem with film analysis positing a "classical" model of orderly, goal-driven causal progression, Williams argues, is that it relegates melodramatic elements such as spectacle and excess to the periphery, as merely something extra, a deviation from the causal chain of events. Rather than being extraneous to classical narration, she stresses, melodrama is the very stuff of mainstream storytelling: "Melodrama should be viewed not as a genre, an excess or an aberration, but as what most often typifies popular American narrative in literature, stage, film and television."[11]

The fact remains, however, that melodrama is a historical object of study. Throughout the nineteenth century and at least the first quarter of the twentieth, there was something that people called melodrama. People understood what this something was; it had its own generic identity, even if its precise boundaries were often somewhat hazy. This is illustrated by the Edison chart described earlier, or by the fact that New York travel guides designated certain theaters as melodrama houses, or by thousands of newspaper reviews that used melodrama as a standard genre label.[12] It is important for us to try to delineate melodrama as a genre, rather than (or as well as) a nearly all-encompassing narrative mode, so that we can learn more about its specific historical manifestations and variations, and so that our conception of melodrama lines up, at least roughly, with that assumed in historical discourses that we wish to analyze.[13]

For the purposes of this study, a middle-ground position will be most useful. We need to situate melodrama somewhere between a specific, fixed, coherent single genre and a pervasive popular mode spanning many different genres. In chapter 2, I propose a definitional scheme that analyzes melodrama as a "cluster concept" involving different combinations of at least five key constitutive elements: strong pathos; heightened emotionality; moral polarization; nonclassical narrative mechanics; and spectacular effects. Just a couple, and perhaps even just one, of these elements might prompt the designation of a play or film as a melodrama. The meaning of the term *melodrama* is so ambiguous because there have been so many different historical combinations of these five elements.

The first two chapters, then, present conceptual frameworks for defining both modernity and melodrama. In the rest of the book, my analysis takes what might be called a "contextualist" approach. In other words, it explores ways in which a cultural object—sensational melodrama—grew out of, and existed within, a complex conjunction of social, intertextual, and commercial contexts. This framing may sound somewhat grandiose, since most history is interested in placing events within relevant contexts, establishing them as products of their time. I use the label *contextualist* simply to stress in a methodologically self-conscious way the fruitfulness of investigating an unusually wide spectrum of qualitatively disparate historical determinants.

A contextualist approach is especially appropriate and illuminating for exploring nineteenth- and early twentieth-century melodrama because the social, intertextual, and commercial forces at play at that time were part of such momentous and multifaceted historical transitions associated with the intensification of modernity. My investigation of sensational melodrama begins by considering a very broad context. Chapter 3 ("Sensationalism and the World of Urban Modernity") focuses not on melodrama specifically but on the wider phenomenon of sensationalism in popular amusement which melodrama exemplified, and on its possible connection to the new sensory environment of the metropolis. In the decades around the turn of the century, a widespread discourse emerged concerning the city as a hotbed of sensory overload. A social critic coined, in 1909, the very contemporary-sounding term "hyperstimulus" to describe the experiential quality of urban modernity. Perhaps the most vivid critique of modern hyperstimulus was communicated through images in sensationalist newspapers and satirical magazines. Expressing a dystopian imagination, they portrayed urban modernity as a series of sensory shocks and bodily perils. The chapter unearths this discourse and also examines a parallel discourse on the commercial exploitation of hyperstimulus in popular amusements. In the 1890s, a wide range of amusements, stage melodrama among them, underwent a pronounced "sensationalization," intensifying every mode of audiovisual and kinesthetic stimulation. At the same time, a number of thrilling new amusements, most notably the cinema, appeared on the scene. This phenomenon stemmed from the distinctive social demographics of modernity which allowed for the rise of a mass urban working-class audience. Social observers from the period, however, tended to stress another cause. It seemed obvious to them (as it would, a little later, to Siegfried Kracauer and Walter Benjamin) that the unprecedented sensationalism of popular amusement was somehow related to the new sensory environment of urban modernity. They saw the sensory intensification of modern amusement as an immediate reflection of the surrounding sensory intensification of the modern city. It was more than mere coincidence, they believed, that the increasing visual busyness and visceral shocks exhibited in popular amusement happened to replicate the increasing visual busyness and visceral shocks of the modern metropolis. City life promoted new forms and new intensities of vivid, action-packed, spectacle.

In recent years, a number of film scholars, drawing primarily on very brief provocative comments in essays by Kracauer and Benjamin, have embraced this idea. The argument, which has acquired the label "the modernity thesis," contends that cinema grew out of the perceptual dynamics of urban modernity. The thesis, in a nutshell, can be summed up by two assertions by Benjamin: "The mode of human sense perception changes with humanity's entire mode of existence"; and "Film corresponds to profound changes in the apperceptive apparatus."[14] In other words, the urban environment of modern capitalism brought about some kind of fundamental change in the human "sensorium," creating a pervasive new "mode of perception" which ultimately had a significant impact on the development of cinema, encouraging cinema to take shape in ways that mirrored the fragmentation and abruptness of urban experience.

While the modernity thesis may appeal to the basic assumption that artworks cannot help but reflect the social environment in which they were created, it comes up against daunting obstacles when one tries to pin down the specifics. What does it mean to say that the urban environment changed human perception? Are we talking about actual biological changes, or is the talk of perceptual transformation just figurative? Supposing we are able to make sense of that premise, is it plausible that a new mode of perception, whatever it might have entailed, actually had an impact on cinema? What were the precise mechanisms involved? How is it that an urban environment characterized by speed and complexity should foster amusements possessing similar qualities? And is the thesis actually borne out by the films of early cinema? Is it accurate to say that the films, which vary considerably in style from year to year in this early period, can be defined by qualities of dynamism and fragmentation associated with urban modernity? How does one explain

that in cinema, as in all art, works from any given period vary so widely in form and style? If urban modernity transformed something as fundamental as human perception, shouldn't all early films convey similar
formal/stylistic attributes (which they do not)? And given that movies
changed enormously between 1905 and 1915, are we to assume that
urban modernity also went through a fundamental transformation in
that brief decade (which it did not)?

These are the sorts of tough questions raised recently by David
Bordwell in a brief but incisive criticism of the modernity thesis.[15]
Bordwell complains, with some justification, that proponents of the thesis have bought into the "Benjaminian" notion of perceptual malleability far too uncritically, accepting and promoting vague, *belle lettrist* speculation as if it had the weight of empirical knowledge. Typically, one
finds the connection between modernity and movies affirmed as a matter of fact, supported by appeal to authority, that is, only by a brief
quote from Kracauer or Benjamin, as if that were enough to guarantee
the idea's validity.

Clearly, proponents of the modernity thesis have their work cut out
for them. In chapter 4 ("Making Sense of the Modernity Thesis"), I try
to address Bordwell's criticisms. The first step is to determine what is
meant by the notion of a distinctly modern "mode of perception." I
argue, venturing into the scientific literature, that there are at least four
viable ways to understand the phenomenon of sensory-perceptual
change in modernity, drawing upon neurological, experiential, cognitive, and physiological perspectives. With respect to the second premise
of the thesis—that perceptual changes actually had an impact on cinema—I trace several mechanisms proposed by Benjamin, Kracauer, and
their predecessors explaining why strong sensation in the urban milieu
should lead to an appetite for strong sensationalism in popular amusement. I also argue that key objections to the thesis—objections based on
the fact that film styles changed without corresponding change in the
urban environment, and that the rise of narrative cinema supposedly
obviated stylistic comparisons to urban modernity—rely on an overly
reductive conception of the modernity thesis. My goal is to show that,
while the modernity thesis is undeniably broad, speculative, unprovable,
and still problematic, it need not be dismissed as utterly implausible.

Chapter 5 ("Melodrama and the Consequences of Capitalism")
returns the discussion to melodrama proper and focuses on its relation
to social, rather than sensory, dimensions of modernity. Melodrama was

quite literally a product of modernity: it emerged as a distinctive dramatic form almost exactly around the year 1800. Its appearance at that time was possible only as a result of legal changes stemming from the French Revolution, a crucial watershed event marking the disintegration of the traditional order and the advent of the modern era. A number of scholars have interpreted melodrama as a cultural response to the moral insecurity and material vulnerability people felt as they faced a world no longer moored by the stable structures provided by monarchic, feudal, and religious authority. Classical melodrama filled a psychological need by offering moral certainty through utterly unambiguous designations of virtue and villainy. At the same time, melodrama's "paranoid" fixation on the relentless victimization of innocents expressed the inherent anxiety and disarray of the postfeudal, postsacred world of nascent capitalism. In this chapter I explore ways in which sensational melodrama captured the situation of social atomization and competitive individualism that classical sociologists underscored as the earmark of capitalist modernity. I conclude with a discussion of melodrama's low cultural status as an outgrowth of a culture war reflecting modern class stratification.

Although 10–20–30 popular melodrama was extinct by 1910, obliterated by the nickelodeon boom (or, more accurately, repackaged as a cinematic form), it made a lasting impression on America's cultural memory. A handful of images survive to this day, although mostly in parodic form: the terrified heroine tied to the railroad tracks; the brawny hero strapped to a log inching toward a whirring buzz saw; the mustachioed villain with black cape and silk hat exclaiming "Curses! Foiled again!" while shaking his fist at the hissing audience. As even these hackneyed images convey, the 10–20–30 was above all else an attempt to commodify strong stimulus, an attempt to package the sensory and emotional excitement of agitating suspense, startling surprise, rapid action, marvelous scenic effects, rousing hatred for the villain, and apprehensive empathy for the abused innocents. The 1909 melodrama *The Millionaire and the Policeman's Wife*, for example, showed these sensation scenes: a fight between divers at the bottom of the North River; the heroine's escape by jumping onto the roof of an elevated train; a tenement fire in which a policeman leaps from a three-story window carrying a baby; and a suspension bridge blown up by dynamite with the hero and heroine leaping from an automobile and clinging to the branches of a tree as the bridge crumbles beneath them. Remember, this is *stage* melodrama!

This emphasis on sensationalism situates melodrama within the context of modern hyperstimulus. But, as I explore in chapter 6 ("10–20–30 Melodrama: Boom and Bust"), sensational melodrama was tied to modernity in other respects, as well. To begin with, technology was at its core, both on stage and behind the scenes. On stage, sensation scenes showcased the latest marvels of the machine age, its mise-en-scène rendering (or whenever possible presenting in actuality) every conceivable emblem of the industrial era: locomotives, steamships, fire engines, submarines, automobiles, motorboats, subways, hot-air balloons, motorcycles, suspension bridges, steam hammers, pile drivers, spinning machines, etc. Modern conveyances had to appear to move through space, sometimes a great deal of space as in races-to-the-rescue ostensibly covering several miles. Such scenes, along with spectacular scenic effects representing natural forces like volcanic eruptions, waterfalls, snowstorms, explosions, fires, hurricanes, and tornadoes, required the invention of sophisticated mechanical stagecraft. Mounting a 10–20–30 melodrama was a highly organized and mechanized undertaking. It epitomized a machine-age theater, a theater inextricable from the instrumental rationality of technology. This intrinsic modern rationality was underscored by the corresponding economic rationalization of the "melodrama industry." The 10–20–30 system was built around new structures of oligopoly control, product standardization, mass production, and efficient distribution.

As fate (or, rather, as modern cultural discontinuity) would have it, stage melodrama was suddenly wiped out by a new wave of technological change and commercial rationalization: the rise of mass-market cinema. Sensational melodrama made the transition from stage to screen with remarkable ease. Lincoln J. Carter, one of the most famous and innovative producers of spectacular stage melodrama, observed (after the movies had driven him out of business), "The heroine and the hero and all the scenic effects of the melodrama have simply moved over into the films. That's all."[16] The movies essentially commandeered the genre and its entire audience. I document this transition and analyze its causes. The challenging historical question is, why did the movies demolish the 10–20–30 so quickly and decisively? One obvious explanation is economic: attending the nickelodeon cost only one-tenth to one-quarter as much as stage melodrama.[17] Another hypothesis, however, has been particularly influential in shaping our historical understanding of cinema's relationship to stage melodrama. In his classic work *Stage to*

Screen: Theatrical Origins of Early Film, published more than fifty years ago, A. Nicholas Vardac argued that movies superseded stage melodrama due to aesthetic reasons. Cinema prevailed, Vardac insisted, because its photographic verisimilitude and spatial freedom made it inherently superior as a medium for presenting "Romantic realism" (that is, for representing incredible spectacles in a convincing way). Cinematic melodrama trounced stage melodrama, Vardac argued, because it satisfied that appetite so much more effectively. The stage's scenographic artificiality and spatial constraints made it no match for the photographic realism and diegetic expansiveness of the movies. I present evidence from contemporaneous observations that suggests that Vardac's thesis was, for the most part, on target. I qualify and expand on Vardac, however, by investigating more closely the economic factors behind stage melodrama's sudden extinction, and also by discussing ways in which Vardac's argument hinged on simplistic assumptions about the basis of 10–20–30 melodrama's aesthetic appeal. His view of stage melodrama as a hapless proto-cinema, a *cinéma manqué*, overlooked the frank theatricality of stage melodrama's aesthetic of astonishment.

What happened to sensational melodrama after it made the switch from stage to screen is examined in the following chapter, "Child of Commerce! Bastard of Art!: Early Film Melodrama." I present examples of one- and two-reel melodramas from the early-cinema and nickelodeon eras (between roughly 1900 to 1913), but my primary focus is on the first wave of American serial films between 1914 and around 1920. My discussion documents the serials' low cultural status: like the 10–20–30, serial-film melodrama suffered often vehement critical disdain because of its emphasis on violent action, highly formulaic and disjointed narratives, lack of psychological depth, and appeal to a mass "lowbrow" audience whose size and commercial power troubled the guardians of culture. After analyzing the film industry's reasons for investing in the serial format, I isolate a number of core conventions of serial melodramas, such as their peculiar system of narrative overlap, their use of a coveted object (or "weenie," as it was called) as the main dramatic motivation; and the assassination of the heroine's father as the initial catalyst. The chapter concludes with a studio-by-studio chronicle of serial-film production between 1913 and around 1920.

To contemporary viewers, probably the most interesting facet of serial melodramas was their unusual emphasis on active, courageous, assertive female protagonists. Chapter 8 ("Power and Peril in the Serial-

Queen Melodrama") documents the fascination with the late nineteenth- and early twentieth-century cultural novelty of the "New Woman." The New Woman epitomized the profound cultural discontinuity of modern society; traditional ideologies of gender, essentially stagnant for centuries, became objects of cultural reflexivity, open to doubt and revision. In a range of media, but especially in serial melodramas, portrayals of female prowess functioned as a reflection of both real social change in gender ideologies and, paradoxically, of utopian fantasies of female power betraying the degree to which traditional constraints still prevailed. The films were paradoxical in another sense, as well: their emphasis on active female courage and competence was counterbalanced by graphic images of female victimization. I interpret this dynamic of power and peril as a reflection of a widespread cultural ambivalence about the flux in social definitions of womanhood. Serial-queen melodramas focused on key consequences of modernization, particularly the expansion of female mobility and circulation in the heterosocial public arena of urban modernity. This transformation was, in turn, an outgrowth of modern capitalism, since it was contingent on the rise of an urban consumer society in which the household was no longer a self-sufficient sphere of production, along with various innovations in transportation and media technology that provided the infrastructure underlying mobility and circulation.

Just as modernity ushered in unprecedented levels of individual mobility and heterosocial circulation, it also escalated the mobility and circulation of texts of all sorts. Extensive intertextuality, although perhaps not exclusive to modernity, is one of its earmarks. This idea could be elaborated in many ways, but one of the most obvious and extensive forms of modern intertextuality is mass-market advertising of cultural artifacts like cinema. Sensational serials played a pivotal role in the history of film publicity. They inaugurated a system of large-scale advertising in which marketing movies cost as much and consumed as much creative labor as producing them. Serials were by far the most heavily advertised films in the Teens, promoted through double-page magazine ads, billboards, newspaper tie-ins, prize contests, sheet music, fashion tie-ins, novelty giveaways, and all kinds of ballyhoo. Fiction tie-ins were particularly prominent in the first four or five years of serial-film production. Through this practice of close cross-medium intertextuality, movies and short stories were bound together into a larger textual entity. After surveying other forms of advertising, chapter 9 ("Marketing

Melodrama") focuses on the tie-in phenomenon. I am particularly interested in the question of whether tie-ins were more than simply an innovative form of publicity: were they also used to compensate for the unintelligibility of many films during a transitional period in which directors were still trying to figure out how to tell stories in the new narrative medium? My analysis presents a close comparison of one serial episode and its corresponding prose tie-in. The film version is utterly baffling without the prose supplement, a fact that reminds us that the dissemination of classical continuity editing and the Griffithian "narrator system" of visual storytelling was a slow and uneven process that lasted well into the late Teens.

Writing this book was another slow and uneven process, one that took about as long as the transitional era just mentioned. Much of that time was spent in the archaeological pit, toothbrush in hand, trying to uncover fragments of discourse and information and imagery buried long ago. I have tried to fill in some gaps in our knowledge of early film history, but I have also tried to show that a topic as seemingly arcane and narrow as American serial films of the Teens actually has much broader relevance. These films open onto a wide range of issues concerning the structure and history of melodrama, the sources and pathways of early cinema, and the multifaceted dynamics of modernity.

1

Meanings of Modernity

Modernity is ostensibly a temporal concept: it demarcates the period coming after the premodern or "traditional" age and before the putative postmodern era. It would seem reasonable, therefore, to venture a definition of modernity as a temporally specific span of human history. Such an approach would be fine but for the fact that there is very little agreement on which centuries that span covers.

At least since Hegel, scholars commonly have divided world history into three epochs—Antiquity, the Middle Ages, and the Modern Era.[1] This schematization marks the Renaissance as the crucial transition point between the medieval and modern eras. By this definition, then, one might date the onset of modernity as far back as the late 1300s or early 1400s. One writer actually pinpoints the death of Jeanne d'Arc in 1431 as "the sunset of the Middle Ages and the dawn of modernity."[2] Although, needless to say, such precision is dubious from a historiographic perspective, other crucial and perhaps less idiosyncratic events heralding the emergence of a new world come to mind: Gutenberg's invention of mechanical printing in 1455, the "discovery" of America in the 1490s, the Reformation beginning in 1517, the publication in 1543 of Copernicus's heliocentric theory of the solar system, or, in the same year, Vasellius's publication of the first anatomical studies based on systematic human dissection. As Habermas states, "The discovery of the 'new world,' the Renaissance, and the Reformation—these three monumental events around the year 1500 constituted the epochal threshold between modern times and the middle ages."[3] But, Habermas adds, "Only in the course of the 18th Century did the epochal threshold around 1500 become conceptualized as this beginning." This in part explains why many writers bypass the Renaissance and instead identify the onset of modernity with the moment of self-conscious recognition: the emergence of the scientific method, secular philosophy, and democratic political theory in the Enlightenment and Scientific Revolution. As Anthony Giddens writes, "Modernity refers to modes of social life or organization which emerged in Europe from about the seventeenth century onwards."[4] William Barrett elaborates, dating the transition a bit earlier: "We may take the beginning of our Modern Age to be the early seventeenth century. For that was the century that created modern science and its accompanying technology; and these two, science and technology, have become the driving forces within modern civilization."[5]

Others suggest that it is only fair to speak of modernity once the "new science" actually catalyzed major economic, demographic, and sociopolitical transformations. Only after the experimental method and breakthroughs in physics and mathematics were harnessed in practical applications—that is, only when the Scientific Revolution expanded into the Industrial Revolution of the late 1700s and 1800s—did modernity really take shape. As Krishan Kumar asserts,

Modern society is industrial society. To modernize is to industrialize. It might be possible to give some other meaning to modernity, but to do so would be perverse and misleading. Historically, the rise of modern society is intrinsically connected to the rise of industrial society. All the features that we associate with modernity can be shown to be related to the set of changes that, no more than two centuries ago, brought into being the industrial type of society.[6]

Max Nordau, in his famous 1895 assessment of the previous century, *Degeneration*, similarly argued that this period, particularly the last half of the nineteenth century, must be recognized as one like none other in the history of civilization:

All conditions of life have, in this period of time, experienced a revolution unexampled in the history of the world. Humanity can point to no century in which the inventions that penetrate so deeply, so tyrannically, into the life of every individual are crowded so thick as in ours. The discovery of America, the Reformation, stirred men's minds powerfully, no doubt, and certainly also destroyed the equilibrium of thousands of brains which lacked staying power. But they did not change the material life of man. He got up and lay down, ate and drank, dressed, amused himself, passed his days and years as he had been always wont to do. In our times, on the contrary, steam and electricity have turned the customs of life of every member of the civilized nations upside down.[7]

R. Austin Freeman, writing in 1921, echoed this stress on the extreme social upheaval of the Industrial Revolution:

The change was fundamental. Not only did it affect the conditions of industry, the lives of the workers, the means of production; not only did it change the character of the commodities used by man, the entire aspect of many parts of the country, the very character of the worker himself; it changed from the very foundations the whole fabric of society. It brought into existence new institutions of first-class importance, and rendered obsolete others which had lived on from the dawn of history. It was the greatest social revolution that had ever occurred. And the changes then set going have since continued with ever-multiplying reactions, the end of which no one can foresee.[8]

Later in this chapter we will return to this issue of modern society's extraordinary discontinuity.

Many writers, while not disagreeing with the above statements, tend to position modernity within an even briefer and more recent time frame, focusing on the decades around the turn of the century, or what one might call "modernity at full throttle." Stephen Kern, for example, isolates the period from around 1880 to the end of World War I as a watershed moment in which "a series of sweeping changes in technology and culture created distinctive new modes of thinking about and experiencing time and space."[9] These decades saw the most profound and striking explosion of industrialization, urbanization, migration, transportation, economic rationalization, bureaucratization, military mechanization, mass communication, mass amusement, and mass consumerism. Given cinema's birth amidst this context, not surprisingly this is the temporal definition of modernity that most recent film scholars have stressed in thinking about "cinema and the invention of modern life."[10]

Its highly flexible temporal boundaries, combined with its customization in so many different disciplines, make modernity an inherently broad and ambiguous term. To make matters worse, the boundaries of modernity are further muddled by its association with the term *modernism*, a complex word in its own right considering the far-flung and often contradictory aesthetic programs grouped under that rubric. While many critics perceive some kind of relationship between social modernity and aesthetic modernism, characterizations of that relationship cover the spectrum: modernism as a celebration of modernity; as a sanctuary from modernity; as a radical attack on modernity; as a mirror of the chaos of modernity; as an expression of the rationalistic order of modernity, and so on. Some critics do not even accept (or simply ignore) the premise that aesthetic modernism is intertwined with social modernity, instead advocating a program of purely formalist or reflexive modern art that investigates a given medium's essential properties.[11] From this Greenbergian perspective, the question of modernism's relation to modernity is basically irrelevant. Finally, there are the many scholars who seem to be oblivious to any distinction between modernism and modernity and use the terms interchangeably, compounding the ambiguity of both terms.

Perhaps inevitably, some degree of semantic amorphousness probably will always mark the idea of modernity. It is telling that an important recent sociology textbook devotes all of its seven hundred pages to a survey of the concept, and even at that length includes virtually nothing on the theoretical writings about modernity most often drawn upon in recent work in film studies. Siegfried Kracauer, Walter Benjamin, and Georg Simmel are barely mentioned at all: their names appear in literally two sentences.[12] If a reasonably comprehensive conceptual overview cannot be accomplished in seven hundred pages, then it is a safe bet that it cannot be done in just a few pages. Nevertheless, the brief overview that follows will yield at least a basic orientation to the concept's central themes. The goal is to offer a straightforward introduction for readers with little or no background in social theory. The facets of modernity I delineate are closely intertwined and could be divided up in different ways to yield rather different taxonomies, and other aspects altogether certainly also could be introduced. My schematization, however, will serve as a convenient framework for investigating intersections between melodrama and modernity in subsequent chapters.

Modernization The first and broadest conception of modernity points to an array of profound socioeconomic and cultural transformations that developed in a remarkably compressed time frame over roughly the last two hundred years. This essentially factual way of defining modernity generally is designated with the term *modernization*. Perhaps the central element of modernization—and, indeed, a crucial factor in all the facets of modernity that I will highlight—is the rise of mature capitalism, "the most fateful force in modern life," as Max Weber stated. Capitalism, if defined simply as the pursuit of material gain, "has been common," Weber noted, "to all sorts and conditions of men at all times and in all countries of the earth, wherever the objective possibility of it is or has been given."[13] But mature capitalism is a relatively recent phenomenon. Its defining features include a money economy; extensive (if uneven) industrialization; highly centralized and mechanized manufacture; hired labor; organized entrepreneurial investment; competitive free markets; and significant international trade. The epic socioeconomic transformations of capitalism catalyzed, or at least interacted dynamically with, a series of concomitant social phenomena. Among the most important were

- rapid urbanization and population growth;
- extensive migration and emigration;
- the rapid proliferation of new technologies and transportations;
- the rise of the nation-state, popular nationalism, and colonialism;
- the establishment of stable and predictable legal codes and institutions;
- the explosion of forms of mass communications and mass amusements as well as mass merchandising and consumerism;
- the expansion of heterosocial public circulation and interaction (epitomized by the entrance of women into public space);
- the broader implementation of efficient systems of accounting, record-keeping, and public surveillance;
- the separation of workplace and household as well as the shifting of the primary unit of production from the extended family to the factory;
- the decline of the large extended family due to urbanization and emigration as people moved to follow jobs outside the household, and due to increased use of birth control.

Although these developments differed in their precise timelines and patterns of emergence, they were all interconnected, and most reached a kind of critical mass in Europe and America near the end of the nineteenth century. Taken together, they constitute the phenomenon of modernization. In recent years, work on modernization increasingly has focused on the issue of globalization, as postcolonial, third world, and industrializing societies encounter this set of transformations.[14]

Rationality In its broadest sense, rationality is a basic human capacity, a set of cognitive abilities (use of language, symbolization, self-reflection, abstract thinking, etc.) that distinguish humans from other animals.[15] Within the context of sociology, rationality assumes a narrower meaning. A crucial argument in the work of Max Weber, and of the Frankfurt School theorists influenced by him, was that modernity entailed a new, or at least newly salient and pervasive, mode of thought governing the individual's encounter with the world. Modern rationality can be defined as a mental protocol of ascertaining and acting upon cause-and-effect relationships toward achieving a precisely defined end.[16] In other words, modernity is an era in which logical systems-building informs most avenues of human endeavor. More than in previous phases of civilization, modernity emphasizes an intellectual orientation toward deliberate calculation of efficient means for achieving concrete, clearly delimited ends. Rationality is the cognitive mindset necessary, for example, for industrial "rationalization," which meant, as the World Economic Conference of 1927 defined it, the systematic exploitation of

[all] methods of technique and organization designed to secure the minimum waste of either effort or material. They include the scientific organization of labor, standardization of both materials and products, simplification of processes, and improvements in the system of transport and marketing.[17]

Modern rationality is not entirely unprecedented (building a pyramid or aqueduct or cathedral was obviously a major logistical feat), nor does it banish irrationality or antirationality (spirituality, superstition, neurosis, warped ideology, aesthetic associationalism, random inspiration, and just plain stupidity are still very much with us), nor are the rational and the irrational mutually exclusive (the height of techno-rationality can at the same time be the height of social and ethical irrationality, as World War I and the concentration camps made so clear). Nevertheless, one need only consider the tidal wave of scientific, technological, and organizational accomplishments in the last century and a half to recognize a truly awesome expansion of systematic modes of instrumental reason.

Under capitalist modernity, bureaucracy, a system for organizing human enterprise with clearly circumscribed task specialization and chain of decision-making authority, became the dominant structure for generating goods and services. It is telling that an American business periodical published between 1900 and 1927 was simply called *System*. Glancing at its profusion of corporate organizational diagrams, industrial flow charts, and efficiency tips, one cannot help but recognize that the emergence of advanced capitalism had an enormous influence on the mindset of a great many people. Weber explored the sociopsychological consequences of rationality's reign. He argued that, while bureaucracy was not an invention of capitalism, its expansion and perfection under capitalism grew out of the ascetic diligence of Protestants motivated by perennial uncertainty about their preordained election to salvation. Although ostensibly they believed individuals were powerless to earn their salvation through worldly deeds (that would be presumptuous, since only God has the power to determine salvation), they nevertheless gained psychological comfort from the inference that the wealth they earned through arduous work in a professional calling (and through reinvestment of all earnings) was a signal that they were among God's chosen few. Later generations became stuck in the bureaucracies generated by this spirit of capitalism without any such compelling religious motivation. Trapped in "an iron cage" of rational bureaucratic administration, with no salvation associated with self-discipline, the modern employee became a "specialist without spirit," just a "small cog in a ceaselessly moving mechanism which prescribes to him an essentially fixed route to march."[18] Simmel had used this now-familiar imagery a number of years earlier: "The individual has become a mere cog in an enormous organization of things and powers which tear from his hands all progress, spirituality, and value in order to transform them from their subjective form into the form of a purely objective life."[19]

The blue-collar equivalent of bureaucracy was Taylorism or Fordism, rational systems of manufacturing based on the minute analysis and division of labor. Marx's concept of alienated labor shared with Weber's critique of bureaucracy the central observation that modernity had brought about an impoverishment of experience as rational systems compelled each worker to perform just a small, monotonous, personally meaningless part of the production process.[20]

Cultural Discontinuity The spread of rationality is inextricably linked to another major aspect of modernity: the moral and ideological instability of a postsacred, postfeudal world in which all norms, authorities, and values are fragile and open to question. The rise of the empirical scientific method, philosophical skepticism, and liberal political theory contributed to what Weber termed the disenchantment (or "demagification") of the world. The mores, customs, superstitions, supernatural beliefs, spells, and rituals that governed and gave shape to people's lives in traditional societies diminished in the face of the new discoveries and intellectual protocols of science and reason. Modernity in this sense denotes the rise of secularism and a corresponding deflation of the influence of religious and political mythologies. Alfred de Musset, writing in the 1840s, captured the spirit of this situation:

Alas! Alas! Religion is vanishing. . . . We no longer have either hope or expectation, not even two little pieces of black wood in a cross before which to wring our hands. . . . Everything that was is no more. All that will be is not yet.[21]

Writing at the same time, the French historian Larmartine declared:

These times are times of chaos; opinions are a scramble; parties are a jumble; the language of new ideas has not been created; nothing is more difficult than to give a good definition of oneself in religion, in philosophy, in politics. . . . The world has jumbled its catalogue.[22]

Enlightenment philosophers had believed that reason—logic, justice, science—would replace religion and monarchic autocracy as the basis for social order and cultural stability. This proved a naive hope, however, for the very mode of critical inquiry central to reason bred moral and intellectual uncertainty. The void left by the world's disenchantment was filled not by the solid ground of fixed truths uncovered by reason, but rather by the quicksand of philosophical doubt, constant scientific revision, and relentless technological and social change. Far from establishing a world of certitude, continuity, and order, the Enlightenment yielded a condition of perpetual uncertainty, discontinuity, and instability. Giddens observes the irony of what he refers to as modernity's essential "reflexivity":

When the claims of reason replaced those of tradition, they appeared to offer a sense of certitude greater than that provided by preexisting dogma. But this idea only appears persuasive so long as we do not see that the reflexivity of modernity actually subverts reason, at any rate where reason is understood as the gaining of certain knowledge. . . . We are abroad in a world which is thoroughly constituted through reflexively applied knowledge, but where at the same time we can never be sure that any given element of that knowledge will not be revised.[23]

Historically, social theorists have tended to regard this continuous discontinuity with ambivalence. There is no question that the political, scientific, and technological fruits of the Enlightenment greatly improved the material well-being of many people in the West, but technological developments come at an awfully heavy cost (advanced warfare, mechanistic dehumanization, environmental degradation, urban congestion and stress, etc.). On a moral level, there is obviously much to be said for emancipation from the bonds of oppressive traditionalism, but at the same time the discontinuity and reflexivity of modernity created an unsettling condition of moral relativism and nihilism, a state of "transcendental homelessness," as Lukács put it.[24] Even Nietzsche, while celebrating the death of God, conveyed the anxiety created by the "madly thoughtless shattering and dismantling of all foundations, their dissolution into a continual evolving that flows ceaselessly away, the tireless unspinning and historicising of all there has ever been."[25] Many social theorists emphasized the negative consequences of the loss of cultural moorings in modern life. As Émile Durkheim stressed with the notion of "anomie," the normlessness of modernity fostered a cycle of moral ambiguity, restless desire, frustration, and existential meaninglessness.

Mobility and Circulation While undoubtedly the rise of empirical science, philosophical skepticism, and political critique all contributed to the corrosion of moral, ideological, and spiritual cohesion, it should be borne in mind that science and philosophy were discursive arenas in which only a small intellectual elite actually participated. If a fragility of traditional norms, authorities, and values did indeed affect society as a whole, the engine of social change probably had somewhat less to do with the trickling down of Big Ideas than with concrete demographic, socioeconomic, and technological forces that directly influenced the everyday life of entire populations. The primary catalyst of social discontinuity, in other words, was the global rise of capitalism and the unprecedented social mobility and circulation that it generated.

Already by the middle of the nineteenth century, barely a decade or two after the introduction of steam-powered engines in transportation, the forces of capitalist trade had created a worldwide network of interconnections. As Marx and Engels observed in 1848: "The need of a constantly expanding market for its products chases the bourgeoisie over the whole surface of the globe. It must nestle everywhere, settle everywhere, establish connections everywhere."[26] This phenomenon would escalate even more rapidly in the second half of the century (and, of course, has continued unabated ever since). Modern transportation and communications technologies exploded traditional relationships between time and space, resulting in "the annihilation of distance" and "the shrinkage of the world."[27] As a consequence of time-space compression, modernity saw a radical expansion in the mobility and circulation not only of commodities but of whole populations and, indeed, of every conceivable "social thing." "By social things," Pitirim Sorokin wrote in 1927,

I mean anything, material or spiritual, which is created or modified by conscious or unconscious human activity: newspaper news, or Communist ideology, or a chopped stone implement, or an automobile, or bobbing of hair, or birth control, or money, or cultivated land—all are social things according to this definition.[28]

With the emergence of new technologies of communication and conveyance, every social entity—people, ideas, values, images, objects, styles, techniques, customs, texts, etc.—could be scattered with rapid diffusion and on a great scale far beyond the very limited spheres of exposure characteristic of traditional agrarian life. As Sorokin put it,

While in the past there was necessary a period of several hundreds or thousands of years for the diffusion of a definite value (custom, belief, ideology, religion) within a rather limited area or for its penetration from one group to another one, now this diffusion is achieved within a few months, or for the whole world within a few years.[29]

Modern mobility and circulation entailed the unprecedented diffusion, interpenetration, and hybridization of people and all other social things as they spread out within and across cultures via the media, trade, tourism, migration, and other forms of social contact. In contrast with the relative isolation, uniformity, and continuity of traditional societies, modernity was distinguished by its fluid and chaotic mixture of social objects and subjects.

Modernity saw a great increase in both "horizontal" mobility (i.e., geographic mobility involving migrations from nation to nation, country to city, city to city, neighborhood to neighborhood), and "vertical" mobility (i.e., socioeconomic mobility involving changes in profession, status, class, affiliation, and associated changes in mentalities and constructions of identity). While the latter is difficult to quantify, the scale of the former type of mobility can be surmised by statistics on, for example, railways. According to figures cited by Nordau, in 1840 railway routes in Europe covered three thousand kilometers; in 1891 there were 218,000 kilometers. In that period, the number of travelers in Germany, France, and England alone rose from 2.5 million to 614 million.[30]

Statistics on several modes of communication, cited by Sorokin, are equally telling.[31] For example, the total number of telegrams dispatched on Earth in 1860 was just under five and a half million; in 1913 the number was 500 million. "Interurban" telephone calls showed a similar increase: in 1896, 69 million such calls were made; in 1913 the figure was 691 million. A comparison of the number of letters and parcels mailed per head-of-household in 1875 and in 1913 (tables 1.1 and 1.2) also illustrates modernity's effect on the circulation of ideas and things.

Table 1.1
Letters Mailed per Head of Household (* = 1880; ** = 1916)

	1875	1913	% Increase
Austria	7	47	671
Belgium	11	39	354
England	37*	96**	259
France	15*	49**	326
Germany	13	80	615
Italy	4	15	375
Japan	1.6	29**	1,813
Russia	0.5	81	600
Sweden	5	32	640
Unites States	23*	89**	386
British India	0.7	3	429
Egypt	0.7*	4	571
The Congo	0.0005	0.1**	20,000

Table 1.2

Parcels Mailed per Head of Household (* = 1880; ** = 1916)

	1875	1913	% Increase
Austria	10	60	600
Belgium	18	105	583
England	45	128	284
France	23*	91**	396
Germany	16*	113**	706
Italy	8	44	550
Japan	1.6	35	2,188
Russia	0.77	11.5	1,494
Sweden	5	42	840
United States	29*	164**	566
British India	0.7	3.3	471
Egypt	1.04*	6	577
The Congo	0.001	00	—

These statistics are useful not only because they capture the increasing circulatory dynamism of modernity, but also because they remind us that the phenomenon was predominantly a European and American one. Colonial societies showed rates of increase equivalent to those of industrial countries, but the volumes were of a completely different order. Nevertheless, one could argue that colonized societies, by the very nature of colonialism as a form of sociocultural penetration, experienced modern cultural upheaval just as powerful as that of the West.

Nordau presented similar statistics on postal communication, with an earlier comparison period starting in 1840. "This year has not been arbitrarily selected," he explained. "It is about the date when that generation was born which has witnessed the eruption of new discoveries in every relation of life, and thus personally experienced those transformations which are the consequences."[32] In 1840 the British postal service delivered 277 million domestic letters; in 1891 the number was 1,299 million letters, an increase of 469 percent. The increase was 634 percent in France, from 94 million to 595 million. Worldwide international mail—i.e., letters from all countries sent to other countries—showed an even more impressive rise, demonstrating the global scope and intricacy of social circulation in modernity. In 1840, 92 million letters crossed international borders; in 1891 over 2.75 billion (2,759 million) international letters were dispatched, an increase of 2,999 percent.

Books constituted another vehicle for the circulation of ideas, advertisements, and other social things. In Germany 1,100 new book titles were published in 1840. Fifty years later, the number had risen to 18,700, an increase of 1,700 percent. Statistics on newspapers (table 1.3) tell the same story:

Table 1.3
Number of Newspapers in Print

	1840	1891	% Increase
England (1846)	551	2,255	409
France	776	5,182	668
Germany	305	6,800	2,230

All of these statistics affirm the fact that the circulation of social things, on a global scale, was an absolutely paramount feature of capitalist modernity.

The cultural discontinuity of post-Enlightenment reflexivity and the extraordinary circulation and mobility of capitalist society fed off of and intensified each other. The result was a prevalent conception of modernity as an epoch of ceaseless change, instability, fragmentation, complexity, and chaos. This is the conception articulated so well in an oft-quoted passage by Marx and Engels:

Constant revolutionizing of production, uninterrupted disturbance of all social relations, everlasting uncertainty and agitation distinguish the bourgeois epoch from all earlier ones. . . . All fixed, fast-frozen relations, with their train of ancient and venerable prejudices and opinions, are swept away; all new-formed ones become antiquated before they can ossify. All that is solid melts into air, all that is holy is profaned.[33]

Sorokin wrote in the same vein:

We live in a mobile age, in an age of shifting and change. . . . [Modern] societies remind one of a mad merry-go-round in which men, objects, and values incessantly move with a mad rapidity, shift, turn round, clash, struggle, appear, disappear, diffuse, without a moment of rest and stability.[34]

The core idea was that modernity was, above all else, an epoch of intense social dynamism.

Individualism The phenomena of cultural discontinuity and social mobility also fostered new conceptions of the individual and new qualities of social interaction. Modernity commonly has been associated with the rise of the individual. Not that there was no such thing as distinct individuals or personalities in premodern times, but the modern subject, or "sovereign individual," to use the term coined by John Locke often adopted as shorthand for this line of thought, is different in certain fundamental respects. The subjectivity of sovereign individuals—their sense of identity and place in the world with respect to status, rank, position, purpose, mode of life, etc.—was no longer a given, no longer predetermined by birth into a particular status, religion, or community, or by feudal obligations and ties to a particular parcel of land, by vocational ties to a family trade passed from generation to generation, by kinship customs or similar bonds seemingly preordained by divine will and immutable tradition. The individual, in the premodern order of things, was closely tied to these sorts of fixed and unquestioned social parameters. Modern individuals may be no less products of social context, but there is a great difference in the degree of social *pre*determination, predictability, and reflexive awareness of potential alternative life courses. By the eighteenth century, many people were able to envision real possibilities of social, geographic, and economic mobility for themselves in ways that would not have been seen as reasonable in centuries past.

A number of ideological currents converged to form a new conception of the centrality of the individual. Renaissance humanism laid the groundwork by placing Man at the center of the Universe (even as Copernicus denied Earth that privilege). The Reformation and Protestantism, while still subordinating the individual to the will of God, nevertheless cultivated individualism by giving personal conscience a direct relationship with God, bypassing and defying the religious institutions of the Church. Enlightenment thinkers then questioned the existence of God, and celebrated Man's scientific and logical powers to master nature and harness knowledge to achieve substantive Progress. Enlightenment philosophy, epitomized by Descartes and Locke, focused on the rational, thinking, conscious subject as the steadfast, indivisible core of epistemological certainty. Enlightenment political and economic theory, and the American and French revolutions, created conceptions of the empowerment of the common man through doctrines of democracy, individual rights, private property, and laissez-faire (in both libertarian and economic senses). Of course, the development of individualism was experienced at different times and tempos according to gender, race, ethnicity, etc., but on a broad level, a new ideology clearly was in the air.

This sea change in ideological conceptions of the individual set the stage for, and became intimately tied to, the rise of capitalism. Capitalism itself undoubtedly had a powerful impact on the status of the individual. For one thing, modern individuals (at least, adult white males), unlike premoderns, became "formally free." Whatever the reality of material compulsion, they were at liberty to sell their labor on the market, entering into contracts independently and voluntarily. As Marx wrote in 1867,

Labor power can appear upon the market as a commodity only if, and so far as, its possessor, the individual whose labor power it is, offers it for sale, or sells it, as a commodity. In order that he may be able to do this, he must have it at his disposal, must be the untrammeled owner of his capacity for labor, i.e., of his person.[35]

Individuals' ownership of their own labor power—a phenomenon obviously crucial to capitalist production dependent upon the flexible availability of hired labor—altered the social nature of the individual. Rather than being bound by inherited trappings, the individual became, at least nominally, volitional, self-determining, and "untrammeled" by formal constraints. Even within economic structures built around the exploitation of labor, individuals were granted a kind of independence as "free agents," sellers of a commodity over which they had sole control.

The rise of the money economy and the consolidation of large amounts of capital by manufacturers, coupled with the existence of formally free labor, led to a much more intricate division of labor than ever before. As more and more goods and services became commodities on the market, it increasingly became no longer necessary for a member of a family group or other communal entity to be a jack-of-all-trades, performing all the tasks required to secure subsistence. Individuals were able, for the first time, to narrowly specialize their talents and offer their own commodities on the market. This functional differentiation cultivated individualism by creating more diverse life experiences, in contrast to tribal or feudal society in which the daily activities governing most people's lives (working the land, for example) were more or less homogeneous. More fundamentally, individualism stemmed from the personal autonomy made possible by the money economy. The ability to acquire material necessities in the marketplace freed the individual from dependence on family, tribe, or commune. As Simmel noted in 1900: "The dissolution of the family is the result of the relative self-sufficiency of the individual members, and the latter is possible in a money economy which can give them a subsistence even if they fully specialize their particular one-sided talents."[36]

Simmel stressed the paradox of this autonomy: the individual became less dependent on others but, at the same time, much more dependent on an enormous network of other people who were relied upon to provide all sorts of material necessities. The crucial distinction for Simmel, one with profound implications for the quality of human interaction, was that capitalism separated the individual from *specific* others, specific people with whom there were long-standing personal, human, "subjective" relationships (e.g., members of the family, or this particular barrelmaker whose goods would be acquired through face-to-face barter exchange).[37] Capitalism replaced specific others with a network of merchants with whom transactions were generally "objective" (governed solely by rational calculation of money values), impersonal (the merchant's whole person was irrelevant to the transaction), and nonspecific (all things being equal, any merchant providing the desired commodity could fulfill the function as well as any other). The individual's relationship to the actual producer of the commodity was even more detached and bereft of human qualities; indeed it was usually completely nonexistent, a state of affairs that fostered what Marx referred to as commodity fetishism.[38]

Modern capitalism redefined the basic social unit from the group to the individual. Individual independence did not entail literal self-sufficiency, but rather self-sufficiency contingent on the provision of material necessities via the marketplace. Independence also implied social atomization or separation. The individual was separated from the family, tribe, or commune (or at least, from their productive labors) and also separated from other free agents in the capitalist economy. That latter situation could be described as an emotional separation, in the sense that subjective, personal human ties and feelings no longer factored (at least not necessarily) into the process of acquiring material goods. The separation was also literal in the sense that, with the rise of commodification, the individual had no direct contact with the vast majority of the people who produced those material goods.

Perhaps above all else, capitalist individualism implied pervasive competition for personal material advancement. As Adna Ferrin Weber insisted in 1899, capitalism promoted the aberration of "exaggerated individualism . . . the essentially egoistic, self-seeking and materialistic attitude."[39] This was also an aspect accentuated by Ferdinand Tönnies in his 1887 book *Gemeinschaft und Gesellschaft*, a particularly influential work, among several in the nineteenth century conceptualizing the social and psychological ramifications of the transition from primitive, feudal, agrarian society to urban capitalist society.[40] In Tönnies's ideal-type formulation, *gemeinschaft* (translated as "community") denoted a social order that was communal and cooperative, governed by a sense of unity and fellowship that grew out of kinship ties, traditional mores, folkways, common religious beliefs, and emotional bonds to homeland. Its economic life was noncompetitive, motivated primarily by an interest in simply achieving subsistence. Should any surplus materialize, it would be shared communally.

With the emergence of modern capitalism and urban life, *gemeinschaft* gave way to *gesellschaft* (translated as "society," or "association"), a social order, and frame of mind, shaped by an economic life based on universal competition, a money economy, contractual relations, wage labor, the commodification of goods and services, and a profit-motivated system of exchange among totally independent and self-interested parties. If in *gemeinschaft* everyone was in some sense kindred, in capitalist *gesellschaft*, everyone was above all else looking out for themselves, with no appreciable sense of affinity or fellowship with others. Tönnies articulated the argument in a straightforward manner:

In Gesellschaft, every person strives for that which is to his own advantage. The relation of all to all may therefore be conceived as potential hostility or latent war. . . . Business people . . . try to get the better of the other. . . . They are forced to crowd each other out or to trip each other up. The loss of one is the profit of the other, and this is the case in every individual exchange. . . . This constitutes general competition.[41]

The destruction of communal feeling may have stemmed from capitalism in general but, as many social critics stressed, it was exacerbated by the anonymity and impersonality of urban society. Writing in 1903, Simmel commented on the social coldness of city people and suggested that it went beyond mere indifference: "If I do not deceive myself, underlying this outer reserve . . . is a slight aversion, a mutual strangeness and repulsion that will break into hatred and fighting instantly upon closer contact, however caused."[42] John A. Hobson also blamed urbanization for the disintegration of shared identity and moral cohesion, noting the irony that this cultural fragmentation should happen most rapidly in the city, the very center of institutional apparatuses designed to shape common ideas and identities:

In spite of the machinery of political, religious, social and trade organizations in large towns, it is probable that the true spiritual cohesiveness between individual members is feebler than in any other form of society. . . . As the larger village grows into the town, and the town into the ever larger city, there is a progressive weakening of the bonds of moral cohesion between individuals.[43]

The modern metropolis changed the fabric of life. Although many social critics appreciated the city's anonymity as an antidote to the stifling provincialism of traditional society, they recognized a painful trade-off: urban individualism bred anticommunal aloofness and social antipathy.

Sensory Complexity and Intensity A final conception of modernity also concentrates on the consequences of urban life, but from a different angle, focusing less on the social dynamics of the urban environment than on its sensory-perceptual dynamics. This concern is often traced back, via Kracauer and Benjamin, to Baudelaire, whose essay "The Painter in Modern Life" (written in 1859) was among the first to express a phenomenology of urban experience. Baudelaire explicitly invoked the word "modernity" to capture a new world of fleeting impressions: "By modernity, I mean the ephemeral, the fugitive, the contingent." On one level, this wording anticipates the theme of continuous discontinuity discussed earlier. Just as Nietzsche spoke of a "continual evolving that flows ceaselessly away" and Marx and Engels exclaimed that "all new-formed [relations] become antiquated before they can ossify; All that is solid melts into air," Baudelaire associated modernity with the experience of a constant present tense that is always changing and always new—hence his interest in the cultural phenomenon of fashion, the quintessence of modernity's perpetual spinning and unspinning. But whereas Nietzsche and Marx employed images of ephemerality more or less metaphorically, to describe social change spanning years and decades, Baudelaire emphasized the more immediate phenomenal flux of the bustling metropolis. The flaneur, immersed in the visual and aural distractions of the big city, meandering in search of anything novel, arousing, engaging, experienced the metropolis as an ever-fluctuating stimulus field of constant immediacy.

In a similar vein, many social observers in the decades around the turn of the century took as the earmark of modernity an experiential milieu—a specifically urban one—that was markedly quicker, more chaotic, fragmented, and disorienting than in previous phases of human culture. Amid the unprecedented turbulence of the big city's traffic, noise, billboards, street signs, jostling crowds, window displays, and advertisements, the individual faced a new intensity of sensory stimulation. The metropolis subjected the individual to a barrage of powerful impressions, shocks, and jolts. This conception of modernity as a fundamentally different register of subjective experience is connected, obviously, to the socioeconomic phenomena of modernization. However, rather than simply pointing to the range of technological, demographic, and economic changes of advanced capitalism, the modernity-as-stimulus approach accentuates the ways in which those changes transformed the texture of everyday life. It should also be noted, without getting mired in debates about the relationship between modernity and postmodernity, that this dimension of modernity anticipates many portrayals of postmodernity stressing "immediacies, intensities, sensory overload, disorientation, the melee of signs and images."[44]

Modernization, rationality, discontinuity, mobility, individualism, and stimulation—I will be returning to these six facets of modernity throughout this study as I analyze the social, cultural, ideological, intertextual, and commercial aspects of sensational melodrama. As one might expect, arguments about modern transformations in the perceptual environment—the modernity-as-stimulus model—are particularly relevant to the escalation of sensationalism in popular amusements like 10–20–30 melodrama and cinema. It is this connection that chapters 3 and 4 examine. Chapter 5 then explores the suggestive coincidence between the birth of melodrama and the emergence of capitalist modernity. Melodrama invites interpretation as both an allegory of capitalist *gesellschaft* and a compensatory response to the "transcendental homelessness" of modern society. Before pursuing those ideas, however, we need to pin down what we mean by "melodrama." The next chapter undertakes that task.

2

Meanings of Melodrama

While several overviews have noted its semantic ambiguity, the term *melodrama* seems to have adopted a more or less stable meaning in contemporary film studies. *Melodrama* as it generally is used today refers to a set of subgenres that remain close to the heart and hearth and emphasize a register of heightened emotionalism and sentimentality. But this was not at all the common usage in the early years of the film industry (or even much later, as Steve Neale has discovered in his excellent exhaustive research into the use of the word in trade journals in the 1950s).[1]

It is telling, for instance, that the word *melodrama* is never once used in a 1910 magazine article entitled "The Tear-Drenched Drama," which discussed what would seem to be the direct theatrical antecedent to Hollywood's woman's weepie. "The drama of heart-ache," Alan Dale observed, caters to "the rapacity of women for the love-woe. . . . Marriage and its many variations being the biggest factor in the feminine life, women take a breathless interest in woebegone stories that delay it, or render it impossible, or offer it as the result of terrific struggle."[2] Dale's synopsis of one such drama, *The Awakening of Helena Richie*, reads like the synopsis of a classical Hollywood domestic melodrama:

The heroine lived a life of unwedded marriage with a gay deceiver who, in the eyes of the world, was her brother. When the guileless people of Old

37

Chester, Pennsylvania, were present, Helena Richie was a formal and coldly affectionate sister to the man; when they were alone she would spring into his arms and fervently tell him how much she loved him! Later on, of course, her "past" was discovered by the "strait-laced" people of the village, who had "early Victorian" ideas unlike those of Helena, who talked about "living her own life" in her own way. She had adopted a boy whom she grew to love. When her "past" was revealed the good gentleman who had assigned the boy to her care felt it his duty to remove the lad. She was not a fit person to be entrusted with the care of children. Her lover, who had an adult daughter of his own, betrayed a marked disinclination to marry Helena. . . . . At this point the tears were shed lavishly. After scenes of pointless agony, in which Helena's soul underwent all sorts of contortions and gyrations, her "awakening" took place, and when she said good-bye to the little boy, in the unhappy "big" act, of course there wasn't a dry eye in the house.[3]

By contemporary generic rubrics, this story is melodrama pure and simple, an almost archetypal example. It anticipates many of the narrative conventions that would define Hollywood melodramas of the 1930s and 1940s: centering around a sympathetic heroine, it deals with the pathos of misplaced love and obstructed marriage, generational friction and the pressures of filling an impossible maternal space (Helena's relationship with her lover's daughter), the dignity and difficulties of female independence in the face of conventional small-mindedness and patriarchal stricture, and, above all else, the pathetic nobility of self-sacrifice. The fact that "The Tear-Drenched Drama" should nowhere even mention the word *melodrama* suggests the term's dominant connotations may have shifted since the decades around the turn of the century. This is not to say that extreme pathos, domestic duress, and romantic distress had no place in popular melodrama a century ago—on the contrary. But it does suggest that in that period's common conception of melodrama, the sentimental side may have been somewhat overshadowed by other aspects.[4]

Attempts to define melodrama can take a few tacks. One approach is to highlight a primary defining element that manifests itself in various ways throughout all the genre's many permutations, or in other words, to discern an underlying foundation that structures the genre's array of surface attributes and conventions. The essential element perhaps most often associated with melodrama is a certain "overwrought" or "exaggerated" quality summed up by the term *excess*. Although the currency of this notion in film criticism stems from several sources, one important one was Geoffrey Nowell-Smith's brief essay "Minnelli and Melodrama" (1977).[5] Nowell-Smith argued that the genre was subject to a kind of textual "conversion hysteria." Melodrama foments psychic energies and emotions which the narrative "represses," blocks from full expression, gratification, or resolution, because they are fundamentally incompatible with the demands of dominant patriarchal ideology. As a consequence of this repression on the narrative level, the undischarged emotions, "which cannot be accommodated within the action, subordinated as it is to the demands of family/lineage/inheritance" (by which Nowell-Smith presumably means emotions like Oedipal or homoerotic drives), are diverted or "siphoned off." Like neurotic symptoms, they find an outlet through other channels of expression—especially spilling into nonnaturalistic mise-en-scène and swelling music. In Sirk's 1950s family melodramas, for example, the mise-en-scène is conspicuously oversaturated with glaring colors, overstuffed with too much furniture and too many mirrors, and overdetermined with props that are often "too symbolic," too obvious in their sexual implications (such as the ubiquitous phallic oil rigs in *Written on the Wind*, or, in the same film, the five-year-old boy intently getting his jollies on a rocking horse just as the protagonist is informed that he is impotent).

While the premise that texts can manifest symptoms just like human psyches may not seem quite as compelling today as it did twenty years ago, the basic idea of a connection between melodrama and expressionist excess is widely accepted. The idea can be extended in useful ways to incorporate other aspects of the genre. To begin with, melodrama obviously showcases emotional excess. Hollywood melodramas are brimming with characters on the verge of hysteria and collapse, or at least by characters suffering extreme emotional duress. Classical melodrama—melodrama based around a truly evil villain that victimizes an innocent, purely good soul—portrays emotional excess in the villain's expressions of hatred, envy, jealousy, spite, or malice. Traditionally, particularly in stage melodrama, these emotions were conveyed through codified modes of histrionic "overacting" that further accentuated the quality of excess.

Melodrama also activates various kinds of excess in the spectator's visceral responses. A good Hollywood melodrama is one that makes you cry, or one that arouses strong sentiment, particularly powerful feelings of pathos. Melodramatic excess is a question of the body, of physical responses. The term *tearjerker* underscores the idea that powerful sentiment is in fact a physical sensation, an overwhelming feeling.[6] Over and above the poignant emotion of pathos, melodrama thrives on stimulating the sensation of agitation—for example, the physical, visceral thrill created by situations of acute suspense. Classic cliffhangers (like *North By Northwest*, with its literal cliffhanging, or virtually any contemporary action film), or situations in which the protagonist is unaware of imminent peril (such as in *Rear Window* when Lisa searches Thorwald's apartment as he is putting his key in the door to enter), or race-to-the-rescue sequences with life-and-death deadlines (a powerful subgenre since Griffith's day), are designed to create a nervous charge in the spectator, a kind of sensory excess.

Melodrama triggers another variety of agitation as well: the agitation that comes from observing extreme moral injustice, the feeling of distress, of being profoundly disturbed or outraged when we see vicious power victimizing the weak, usually involving some kind of bodily violence. A waif being battered (as in *Broken Blossoms*), an animal being abused (*Lassie Come Home*), or a mother having her baby torn away from her by a group of puritanical busybodies (for example, *The Mother and the Law*, *Way Down East*, *The Awakening of Helena Richie*): such scenes are designed to generate unbridled agitation, a mode of visceral excess in the spectator. One could add to this the sensation of intense hatred. Classical melodrama, particularly on stage, gave the audience the cathartic pleasure of the very purest, unequivocal kind of hatred, repulsion, or disdain for the villain. Melodrama was designed to arouse, and morally validate, a kind of primal bloodlust, in the sense that the villain is so despicable, hated so intensely, that there was no more urgent gratification than to see him extinguished. It was this aspect of melodrama's visceral and emotional excess that prompted Ludwig Lewisohn, writing in *The Nation* in 1920, to associate the genre with the primal brutality of the mob:

[For the average American] his highest luxury is the mass enjoyment of a tribal passion. War, hunting, and persecution are the constant diversions of the primitive mind. And these that mind seeks in the gross mimicry of melodrama. Violence, and especially moral violence, is shown forth, and the audience joins vicariously in the pursuits and triumphs of the action. Thus its hot impulses are slaked. It sees itself righteous and erect, and the

object of its pursuit, the quarry, discomfited or dead. For the great aim of
melodrama is the killing of the villain. . . . The villain, whether tribal
enemy, mere foreigner, or rebel against the dominant order, is always rep-
resented as an unscrupulous rake. He attacks the honor of native women,
and thus—especially if his skin is a tinge darker—there is blended with
the other motives of pursuit the motive of a vicarious lynching party of the
orthodox kind. The melodrama of this approved pattern brings into vicar-
ious play those forces in human nature that produce mob violence in peace
and mass atrocities in war. Nations addicted to physical violence of a sim-
pler and more direct kind have cultivated the arena and the bull ring.
Those who desire their impulses of cruelty to seem the fruit of moral energy
substitute melodrama.[7]

As we will see in chapter 5, the association between melodrama and "the
mob" informed much of the criticism against it, although usually the
simple fact of the mass's enjoyment of melodrama, irrespective of any
bloodlust, was enough to secure its ill repute.

* * *

Along with excess, another concept merits consideration as the essential
core of melodrama. In an ambitious essay, Lea Jacobs has suggested that
at the heart of melodrama is the element of "situation."[8] *Situation* is a
rather difficult concept to narrow down, but it could be defined as a
striking and exciting incident that momentarily arrests narrative action
while the characters encounter a powerful new circumstance and the
audience relishes the heightened dramatic tension. Situation often
entails a startling reversal or twist of events that creates a dramatic
impasse, a momentary paralysis stemming from a deadlock or dilemma
or predicament that constrains the protagonist's ability to respond
immediately. Action might be temporarily suspended when characters
are stunned by shocking news (the villain who has been trying to kill the
heroine is really her uncle who has stolen her inheritance!), or faced with
a deadly peril (the hero looks with alarm as the buzz saw draws ever
nearer), or fixed in a deadlock among counterbalancing forces (the hero
is in a triangular gun standoff threatening death for all if anyone tries to
shoot first—a situation used, for example, in *Pulp Fiction*). Situation
involves a considerable amount of suspense—suspense about how the
deadlock will be broken, how the protagonist will get out of the plight.
Victorian stage melodrama literalized the aspect of arrested action in the
form of the tableau, in which actors froze in an arrangement that stark-

ly revealed the dramatic conflict among opposing parties. A contemporary counterpart might be the tense immobility just before the commercial break in a TV soap opera when characters register facial reactions to some kind of bombshell or stiffen in pensive contemplation of
the current interpersonal state of affairs. The notion of situation also
evokes the serial film's cliffhanger climaxes where narrative action is suspended not only while the wide-eyed protagonist assesses a grave peril
but indeed for a full week until the next episode resolves the predicament.

The importance of situation as a peculiar earmark of melodrama is
indicated by the frequency with which the term appeared, sometimes in
quotation marks, in discussions of melodrama. As a critic maintained in
1907: "What people have always come first to care for [in melodrama]
is dramatic situation. . . . They [are] eager to see something happen; they
want to have their emotions stirred, their blood quickened. . . . There is
an abundance, an inordinate abundance, of situation."[9] A 1914 essay
called simply "Ten-Twenty-Thirty" similarly remarked, "There must be
a 'situation' . . . two wills clashing together; words that lead and parry,
words with a 'punch' behind them."[10] A critic writing in 1919
bemoaned the fact that, "At present the method adopted [in writing
melodramas] would appear to be that some person conceives an abom-
ination known as 'a situation': the more ludicrous and revolting it be the
more he treasures it."[11]

While the notion of situation provides a valuable conceptual lens
for examining melodrama, and while it is clearly applicable to a great
many melodramatic moments, one might question whether it can be
generalized as the genre's essential defining element.[12] One problem is
that it is a very broad and malleable concept and the boundary between
a bona fide situation and a more "ordinary" level of dramatic incident is
rather hazy. Situation may be a distinguishing feature of melodrama, but
one could argue that it is the foundation of many other kinds of stories
as well. To this objection one could reply, probably with some justification, that there is indeed a qualitative difference in the intensity of situation in melodrama. Perhaps a more difficult problem has to do with
the question of whether situation is in fact a necessary component of *all*
melodrama. Does it pertain equally well to both classical melodramas
and Hollywood family melodramas and women's pictures of the
1930s–1950s? What if a narrative does not contain an urgent climax
involving a shocking reversal or revelation, or a deadlock, or a tem-

porarily immobilizing deadly peril? While Hollywood melodramas may have high points of strong emotion and swelling music, some might maintain a more even dramatic tenor, or contain dramatic peaks that are not sudden, startling, tense, or perilous enough to deliver the kind of swift, powerful impact distinctive of a *situation.*

Jacobs is mindful of the need to relate the concept of situation not only to classical melodrama but to Hollywood melodrama as well. There is a connection, she suggests, in that the female protagonists of Hollywood melodrama are characteristically caught in no-win dilemmas that prevent them from effecting meaningful positive change in their lives. Drawing on an observation by Thomas Elsaesser, Jacobs notes that, "Melodrama tends to generate impasses in which the characters are trapped and find it difficult to take action, to make choices, or to move directly towards some goal."[13] The connection Jacobs proposes highlights the element of arrested or suspended action, action made difficult to implement. There would seem to be a difference, however, between Jacobs's original conception of situation as a brief, climactic local instant of arrested action and the much more diffuse condition of frustration or futility spanning almost the entire plot of a typical Hollywood melodrama. An example of the latter would be the premise of *Written on the Wind* as described by Elsaesser: "Dorothy Malone wants Rock Hudson who wants Lauren Bacall who wants Robert Stack who just wants to die."[14] As I understand her argument, Jacobs would consider this scenario an example of situation because of the narrative impasse portrayed—the characters' inability to fulfill their desires. The definition of situation appears to have slipped from meaning something roughly equivalent to a "thrill"—a highly focused charge of narrative excitement—to meaning something more like an entire scenario. Both classical melodrama and Hollywood melodrama present human crises, but the crises are "situational" in different ways. In the latter, they tend to be more general life crises whose causes span relatively long periods in the protagonist's personal history. Although the films may be punctuated with moments of crisis (for example, people falling down grand stairways as in *Written on the Wind, Gone with the Wind,* or *La Signora Di Tutti*), in general the situations in Hollywood melodramas do not quite match the definition of a situation as an intense, climactic plight that is crystallized in a flash and, after a moment of suspense, broken to allow another thrill to develop. Although a very productive critical tool, it remains an open question whether the concept of situation is able to function as a common denominator or essential element linking all forms of melodrama.

* * *

An alternative approach toward a definition of melodrama is more piecemeal and hence less prone to the difficulty of fitting everything under one umbrella. Rather than looking for a single essence or foundation, I prefer to analyze melodrama as a "cluster concept," that is, to view melodrama as a term whose meaning varies from case to case in relation to different configurations of a range of basic features or constitutive factors. If a word has a set range of applicable features, the meaning of the word in any given instance will depend on precisely which features come into play, and in what combinations.[15] Charting melodrama's genealogy has proven so problematic, and the literature on melodrama is so inconsistent, because over the last two hundred years the genre's basic features have appeared in so many different combinations. An early attempt to define melodrama as a cluster concept was made by William S. Dye in a 1919 dissertation: "In reality, no one form of melodrama exists today. . . . A fair definition would include many characteristics, not all of which might be found in any one play. The definitions might with truth state that either singly or in combination [a range of] elements are to be found in melodrama."[16] Dye goes on to list more than a dozen typical features of melodrama.[17] I will focus on five key constitutive factors (some of which have already been touched on), although certainly more could be justified, as Dye's breakdown suggests.

Pathos The presentation of strong pathos (i.e., the elicitation of a powerful feeling of pity) is, of course, a common element of melodrama, particularly as it is understood in contemporary film studies. Aristotle defined pity as "a sort of pain at an evident evil of a destructive or painful kind in the case of somebody who does not deserve it, the evil being one which we might imagine to happen to ourselves."[18] This is an insightful definition. The first part aptly describes the experience of pathos as a kind of visceral physical sensation triggered by the perception of moral injustice against an undeserving victim. The second part touches on the sense in which pathos requires identification, which, by extension, leads to the notion that pity often (or always?) involves an element of self-pity. Eric Bentley made this observation very directly: "The tears shed by the audience at a Victorian melodrama come under the heading of a good cry. . . . The phrase 'having a good cry' implies feeling sorry for oneself. The pity is self-pity. . . . Most pity is self-pity. We are identified with those others who are threatened; the pity we feel for them is pity for ourselves."[19] This conception affirms the degree to which the power of pathos derives from a process of emotional identification or, perhaps more accurately, of association, whereby spectators superimpose their own life (melo)dramas onto the ones being represented in the narrative. Melodrama is so moving because it hits home. (Offering support for this notion, students in my melodrama class have often reported that the first thing they did after our screening of *Stella Dallas* was to rush back to their dorm rooms to call their mothers to say how much they love them and to thank them for all their sacrifices.)

Overwrought Emotion Overlapping the strand of pathos to a very large degree, but not entirely, is melodrama's interest in overwrought emotion and heightened states of emotive urgency, tension, and tribulation. As a 1914 screenwriting manual says, "in melodrama . . . all emotion is passion."[20] While the representation of pathos generally involves this kind of dramatic intensity, not all instances of highly charged emotion necessarily involve pathos. For example, the intense emotions portrayed in daytime TV soap operas (jealousy, compassion, envy, greed, spitefulness, lust, etc.) often involve a melodramatic register of overwrought feeling (particularly as amplified by soap opera codes of acting and camerawork) without necessarily depicting the kinds of martyrdom, miscommunication, or helplessness characterizing pathos. A cinematic example might be the scene in the Sirk version of *Imitation of Life* in which the Meredith daughter (Sandra Dee) confronts her mother (Lana Turner) with anger/frustration/resentment/disappointment about the fact that she (Mom) was always too busy with her acting career to really be there for her as a conventionally nurturing mother. This outburst is followed by the mother's own self-defensive reaction of anger/frustration/resentment/disappointment. The scene is melodramatic in its expression of raw emotion, the overcoming of repression in a supercharged climax of full articulation, but there is nothing especially pathos-inducing about the scene.

Moral Polarization An aspect of melodrama invariably mentioned by turn-of-the-century critics is an extreme moral polarization between good and evil—a moral absolutism and transparency in which, in the

blunt phrasing of the 1914 manual cited above, "the hero and the heroine are very, very good; the villain and the adventuress are very, very
bad."[21] Melodrama's worldview is simplified; everyone's ethical status is
immediately legible. As a critic commented in 1907,

> *The crowd behind the footlights hisses [at the villainness]. . . . She is very
> wicked, and the wicked are to be held in derision. That is to say, in melo-
> drama. In real life it is often difficult to distinguish between the wicked
> and the elect; but here,—why her very name is Zidella St. Mar. Can any
> good come out of Zidella? [Melodrama offers] dear familiar sentiments of
> primitive black and white morality.*[22]

Another critic writing about a decade later reiterated the motif of black
and white moral clarity: "In melodrama black is black and white is
white; and the black is of coal-like hue and the white akin to driven
snow; there are no half-tones in the coloring."[23] The clarity of melodrama's moral dichotomy stemmed from "a normal sympathy for virtue
and hatred for vice [that] wants to express itself,—a sympathy which in
real life is often puzzled by circumstances, but which here finds all lines
sharply drawn, all actions clearly labeled upon the stage."[24] Melodrama's
interest in moral intelligibility reflected, as this writer suggested, a fundamental human impulse, but it was also an impulse inflected by history. Many recent scholars (as I discuss in chapter 5) have interpreted
melodrama's insistence on moral affirmation as a symptomatic response
to a new condition of moral ambiguity and individual vulnerability following the erosion of religious and patriarchal traditions and the emergence of rampant cultural discontinuity, ideological flux, and competitive individualism within capitalist modernity. Melodrama expressed the
anxiety of moral disarray and then ameliorated it through utopian moral
clarity.

Nonclassical Narrative Structure A fourth aspect of melodrama has
to do with what one might call its nonclassical narrative mechanics.
Compared with the classical narrative's logical cause-and-effect structure, melodrama has a far greater tolerance, or indeed a preference, for
outrageous coincidence, implausibility, convoluted plotting, deus ex
machina resolutions, and episodic strings of action that stuff too many
events together to be able to be kept in line by a cause-and-effect chain
of narrative progression. This is a dimension of melodrama that bourgeois critics traditionally have found particularly objectionable. As

Boston newspaper reviews complained about an 1891 production of *The Wolves of New York*: "Inconsistency and incongruity play very prominent parts in this play. . . . Plot is conspicuous only by its almost utter absence. . . . The spectator goes home with but a vague idea of the plot which he has seen."[25] Rollin Lynde Hartt reiterated this gripe in 1909: "Conceived as a play, [melodrama] involves non sequiturs, discrepancies, contradictions; it makes your head swim. . . . No one cares if there are too many scenes. Nobody cares if the scenes won't hang together."[26] In the same vein, Harry James Smith noted in 1907:

To attempt to give an account of the plot would be useless. The more you examine it, the less there is. There is an abundance, an inordinate abundance, of situation, . . . but when you try to work out the interrelations you are doomed to failure. It would take a higher intelligence to answer all the hows and whys. . . . If your mind is sophisticated enough to insist on logic, it is bound to be left in some confusion.[27]

A British touring manager in the late Teens carped:

Modern melodrama is a shapeless, formless thing. . . . Your melodramatist is ignorant of the rudiments of play-making. The absence of construction in most of his efforts is amazing: no form, no coherence; a story that lags, falters half-way, dodges down blind alleys. . . . A main theme that will carry the play through from beginning to end is hard to find. Without a backbone, wobble is inevitable.[28]

And, lest there be any doubt about melodrama's deviation from the classical model, Henry Tyrell bemoaned in 1904:

In the bright lexicon of the melodramatic playwright, there are no such words as "motive," "character," or "logical development"; but "scene," "startling situation," "appalling peril and heroic rescue" are writ large. His world is indeed a strange one, where the impossible is of everyday occurrence; where miracles come and hunt people up to participate in them; where it is biff! bang! a constant series of phenomena, without preparation or proper sequence.[29]

All these critics point to a melodramatic tendency toward episodic construction resulting from a greater concern for vivid sensation (or "situation") than for narrative continuity. Continuity and "sustained elaboration" was relatively unimportant in melodrama since, as Hartt put it: "Each new shocker obliterates its predecessor, and it is precisely this brevity of perspective that makes a series of unrelated episodes more facile of interpretation. . . . Make scene depend upon scene and you cruelly overtask the Neolithic mentality."[30] Although with a somewhat milder presumption of stupidity, Smith similarly noted the melodrama audience's short attention span and anticontemplative nature:

Whatever situation is proposed must come to its culmination rapidly, directly, and by means which require no thought in order to be fully grasped. There can be no real plot structure here: only episodes; the situations presented simply become more and more startling as the play nears its conclusion.[31]

Melodrama, Smith stressed, constituted an aesthetic of astonishment, an aesthetic whose focus on rapid, powerful impressions worked against measured causal progression. A variation on this notion has become familiar to recent scholars in the form of "the cinema of attractions." Indeed, Smith made an overt connection between popular melodrama and early cinema. It was no coincidence, he suggested, that the other amusements preferred by the melodrama audience—vaudeville and "penny-in-the-slot arcades" (i.e. movie peep-show kinetoscopes)—were similarly "disjointed and scattering in [their] make-up."

Sensationalism   The final constitutive factor of melodrama I propose follows from the one just described. Crucial to a great deal of popular melodrama was sensationalism, defined as an emphasis on action, violence, thrills, awesome sights, and spectacles of physical peril. This may have been the term's key denotation around the turn of the century—and presumably the one intended for Melodrama in the 1915 Edison quality-control chart mentioned in the introduction. As Frederic Taber Cooper noted in a 1906 article entitled "The Taint of Melodrama": "Ask the next person you meet casually how he defines a melodramatic story, and he will probably tell you that it is a hodge-podge of extravagant adventures, full of blood and thunder, clashing swords and hair's-breadth escapes."[32] Christopher Strong, writing in 1912, declared: "The paranoic who wrote the plays did so because he didn't know Art from Hank; he *did* know that people like *action*, so he gave them more action (and of the same sort) than you would find in an asylum full of delirium tremens fiends and St. Vitus's dance artists."[33] Melodrama's classic iconography, as described by an essayist in 1908, included: "Trap-doors, bridges to be blown up, walls to be scaled, instruments of torture for the persecuted heroines, freight elevators to crush out the lives of the deserving characters, elevated trains to rush upon the prostrate forms of gagged and insensible girls."[34] A *Harper's Weekly* essayist put it concisely in 1890: "Melodrama . . . must reek with gore."[35] The equating of melodrama with action and violence was reiterated once again in 1919 by Pennsylvania's chief film censor: "One speaks of melodrama as meaning that it in some way is devoted to the exploitation of crime; there is a good deal of crime in it—a murder or two, some robbery and all sorts of violence and everything of that kind. That is the basis of a melodrama."[36]

At the heart of the sensationalism of classical melodrama was not simply action and violence but also a peculiar mode of scenic spectacle that tried to combine amazing sights with credible diegetic realism. As William S. Dye wrote in 1919,

Melodrama . . . is a play of . . . dire distresses, of hazardous situations, of thrilling rescues, of theatrical and sensational clap-trap, of suspense and surprise. . . . Throughout all, there is a liberal use of mechanical and electrical effects that run the gamut from a representation of a thunder shower with real rain to a train wreck, a burning steamboat, or an automobile accident, and heroes and heroines are rescued in the nick of time from burning buildings or pulled from the very teeth of huge circular saws in real log-sawing machines, while villains are strapped to switchboards and light through the bodies the great white ways of cities.[37]

In chapter 6 I will explore in depth sensational melodrama's efforts at spectacular scenographic realism. In the meantime, a brief excursus on melodrama and realism will help avoid some of the confusion that often surrounds the issue.

* * *

Discussions of realism and melodrama can get rather convoluted because several different senses of the word begin to stumble over one another. In many ways, melodrama is patently antirealist—and critics never tired of deriding it as "glaringly false-to-life," "lacking any true realism," and so on. Here, realism would denote something basically akin to "naturalism"—the depiction of ordinary quotidian reality, with an attempt to portray fully developed, psychologically multidimensional "real" characters experiencing "real" situations.[38] Popular stage melodrama occupied the other end of the spectrum—its sensational situations were strikingly out-of-the-ordinary, characters were one-dimensional ethical stand-ins, plot twists were highly implausible, acting was grandiosely artificial, etc. As a critic commented in 1904, "Of any effective analysis of . . . character motives the yellow drama is utterly and grotesquely incapable."[39] A critic writing in 1912 concurred: "Melodrama went on the general principle of taking what was diametrically opposed to actual life and playing that falsity up with all the feverish activity of a lunatic asylum."[40] Melodrama offended the aesthetic sensibilities of cultured theatergoers, who preferred works by Ibsen and others in "the modern school of [drama], the repressed-quietude-of-realism sort."[41] "What is wrong with the melodrama of today," complained a critic in 1919, "[is that playwrights do not] endeavor to make it at least an approach to a reflection of life and reality."[42] Melodrama was, according to a 1906 essay, "a series of happenings that would be impossible in real life, [which] makes you look upon life through defective lenses that magnify and distort reality to the verge of caricature."[43]

With this background, it might appear incongruous that melodrama around the turn of the century was often referred to as "the realistic class of plays."[44] This phrase points to the fact that melodrama immediately conjured up the aspiration toward spectacular diegetic realism. That kind of realism, for which A. Nicholas Vardac proposed the term "Romantic realism," aimed at credible accuracy in the depiction of incredible, extraordinary views. A 1916 publicity article entitled "Risks Life for Realism," describing a scene in a film serial in which a car drives across a 35-foot chasm at 60 mph, proclaimed, "It will give a thrill to the story, and that is what we are after, realism with a big 'R.'"[45] In chapter 6 I try to refine this conception of realism by distinguishing between two varieties of spectatorial apprehension, which I call *apperceptive realism* and *absorptive realism*. For now, it will suffice simply to underscore that sensational melodrama was preoccupied with diegetic realism in general, which involved both efforts at verisimilar mise-en-scène and the use of real objects on stage—real horses, real fire engines, real pile drivers, real water, etc. This sort of realism, not surprisingly, did not assuage proponents of naturalism. As Alan Dale argued in 1899, "Life is generally neglected in melodrama for the sake of a real lamp post, a noisy fire engine, or a mimic storm. . . . Real fire engines and unreal men and women make no appeal to the fastidious."[46] An 1894 review of *A Nutmeg Match* could barely suppress its contempt:

[This melodrama] was evidently written to appease the yearning among playgoers for a drama with a real steam pile-driver in it. It was intended to supply a long-felt want such as those that had been satisfied by the introduction of real fire engines, real patrol wagons and real locomotives as stage properties. The author's task was to take a pile-driver and write a play around it. . . . Now all the good people who were pining for a real pile-driver on the stage and declaring that they would never be truly happy till they had found one there should go and see A Nutmeg Match. *For others, the show possesses only a minor interest. The story is that of a good man and a bad man, who are enemies and rivals. The bad man is about to demolish the good man with the pile-driver when a good girl comes along and saves the good man's life.*[47]

For proponents of naturalism, spectacular diegetic realism was just superficial surface realism. It diverted attention from subtler, more interesting things like character psychology.

Despite melodrama's unabashed fascination with superficial spectacular realism, a considerable amount of criticism upholds melodrama as a genre possessing a kind of profound, beneath-the-surface realism. As Thomas Elsaesser noted in 1972, "Even if the situations and sentiments defied all categories of verisimilitude and were totally unlike anything in real life, the structure had a truth and a life of its own."[48] This third conception of realism shares with traditions of Platonic philosophy and Marxist aesthetics (among others) the presumption that true reality is not to be located in surface appearances. It can be found only at a deeper level, in the underlying forces governing surface phenomena. This approach to melodrama points to its power to expose important underlying dimensions of experience. For example, even though its characters lack psychological depth, melodrama has been championed for its capacity to reveal the reality of the psyche. Melodrama overcomes repression, giving full expression to the magnified passions, the intensities of love and hate residing deep (or not so deep) within us all. Peter Brooks has elaborated this notion most fully, but an earlier concise articulation is from Eric Bentley:

I am arguing, up to a point, that melodrama is actually more natural than Naturalism, corresponds to reality, not least to modern reality, more closely than Naturalism. . . . The melodramatic vision is in one sense simply normal. It corresponds to an important aspect of reality. It is the spontaneous, uninhibited way of seeing things. . . . Melodramatic acting, with its large gestures and grimaces and its declamatory style of speech, is not an exaggeration of our dreams but a duplication of them. In that respect, melodrama *is the Naturalism of dream life. . . . Melodrama is not so much exaggerated as uninhibited. In* The Interpretation of Dreams *Freud says that neurotics, like children, "exhibit on a magnified scale feelings of love and hatred for their parents." . . . Any nonmagnified feelings represent an ideal standard, and what we all have are the magnified feelings of the child, the neurotic, the savage.*[49]

In a somewhat different vein, melodrama may be said to reveal a basic existential truth about the human condition. As Clayton Hamilton observed in 1911:

[In] melodrama . . . the incidents determine and control the character. In both tragedy and comedy, the characters control the plot. . . Life is more frequently melodramatic than tragic. . . . Much of our life—in fact, by far the major share—is casual instead of causal. . . . Nearly all the good or ill that happens to us is drifted to us, uncommanded, undeserved, upon the tides of chance. It is this immutable truth—the persistency of chance in the serious concerns of life and the inevitable influence of accident on character—that melodrama aims to represent. . . . Since the purpose of the drama—like that of all the arts—is to represent the truth of life, the theatre must always rely on melodrama to complete its comment on humanity.[50]

Melodrama has persisted as a dramatic mode because, in a fundamental sense, it succeeds in expressing "the truth of life," capturing a crucial existential truth, an aspect of life that affects everyone—namely, that, ultimately, we are all governed by random forces of happenstance. We are all flotsam and jetsam adrift in the "tides of chance." In literature this perspective is particularly evident, as Elsaesser recognized, in Dickensian melodrama:

What seems to me important in this form of melodrama . . . is the emphasis Dickens places on discontinuity, on the evidence of fissures and ruptures in the fabric of experience, and the appeal to a reality of the psyche—to which the notions of sudden change, reversal and excess lend a symbolic plausibility.[51]

The universal force of chance and discontinuity may be a metaphysical constant, but it is also one with a sociohistorical trajectory. It loomed large during the rise of modernity, an era defined by cultural and personal discontinuity, and it possessed particular pertinence for the working class that comprised melodrama's core audience. Hartt, in 1909, argued that there was a basic affinity between melodrama and the volatile nature of working-class life.

In the Grand [i.e., 10–20–30], pray notice, there are many who have had first-hand—or at least second-hand—acquaintance with the melodramatic. From among [them] come firemen, policemen, seamen, and those who gain their bread in trades replete with danger and daring. Meanwhile the tenement street has its daily melodramas, such as they are,—melodramas of crime, drunkenness, and frightful vice, though generally lacking the completeness that would fit them on the stage. . . . The life of the people gives a tremendous reality to the melodramatic.[52]

In other words, incongruous as it may sound, sensationalism actually contains a considerable degree of realism. Melodrama's sensation scenes of course surpassed those of ordinary experience (few members of the audience had dagger fights on the bottom of the East River, or hurtled off the Brooklyn Bridge after their automobile exploded), but the events portrayed nevertheless correlated, even if only loosely, with certain qualities of corporeality, peril, and vulnerability associated with working-class life.

* * *

The contrast between blood-and-thunder sensational melodrama—the melodrama of spectacular diegetic realism—and Hollywood family and maternal melodrama could not be more marked. Sensational melodrama had no interest in exploring emotional nuances in the portraiture of female martyrdom, disillusionment, repression, anxiety, resignation, and frustration. If the family melodrama can be described as a form in which, as Sirk said, everything happens "inside"—within a zone that is doubly "inside," concentrating on the interior spaces of the home and the heart—sensational melodrama was distinct in its externalization, its insistence that everything happen on the outside.[53] It virtually eradicated any characterological complexity, emotional entanglement, or sentiment in favor of a focus on physical action and violence. Sensational melodrama externalized psychology by proclaiming obvious, unequivocal dispositions of villainy, virtue, and valor. At the same time, it externalized its focus of diegetic interest, avoiding the private sphere in favor of an adamantly nondomestic mise-en-scène of criminal dens, submarines, lumber mills, diamond mines, munitions factories, racetracks, abandoned warehouses, gothic mansions, military front lines, rooftops, airfields, highways, and railways.

As this contrast suggests, melodrama's nature as a cluster concept means that the genre's key constitutive factors can appear in any number of different configurations. One might have two completely distinct combinations—sharing none of the same elements—yet both warranting the label melodrama. Presumably, sometimes all five elements would manifest themselves within the same text, but more commonly, only a few of the factors combined to form particular varieties of melodrama. Hollywood melodramas of the studio-system era generally involved just two of the basic elements: pathos and emotional intensification. In fact, many Hollywood melodramas hinged on the absence of the element most accentuated in classic stage melodrama—i.e., moral polarization between good and evil. Hollywood melodramas focused not on the battle between good and evil characters, but rather on the pathos of situations of moral antinomy in which two or more morally good (or at least nonvillainous) characters find that their interests are fundamentally incompatible. The poignancy of *Stella Dallas*, for example, derives from the fact that one sympathizes with the mother and recognizes her goodness at the same time as one sympathizes with the daughter and recognizes the validity of her embarrassment about her mother's poor taste. The antinomy involves the incompatibility of two ethical imperatives: preserving the maternal family versus allowing the daughter to achieve the upward mobility for which she is so obviously suited. Sirk's *Imitation of Life*, in a similar way, involves the pathos of having to choose between two morally good but irreconcilable options: preserving the mother-daughter bond between Annie and Sarah Jane versus allowing Sarah Jane to escape the injustices of racial bigotry. A secondary (although, as mentioned earlier, somewhat less pathetic) antinomy opposes Lora Meredith's professional freedom as an ambitious actress against her maternal presence in the home—both morally positive but, in the film's logic, contradictory values. *Written on the Wind* also exemplifies the Hollywood melodrama's eschewal of moral polarization. Kyle Hadley, the volatile husband—the person responsible for the wife's suffering—is not vilified and punished, but rather pitied as a victim of alcoholism, depression, and bad parenting. Similarly, the suffering and loneliness of the Rock Hudson character Mitch Wayne (due to unrequited love for his best friend's wife) cannot be blamed on any sinister force, but rather results from his own moral code that compels him to honor the sanctity of marriage.

These examples illustrate the degree to which the melodramatic element of pathos often presupposes the exclusion of the melodramatic element of moral polarization. In contrast, action-oriented melodramas often reverse this formula: they present moral polarization without pathos. For example, serial-queen melodramas like *The Perils of Pauline* (1914) and *The Hazards of Helen* series (1913–1917), which I investigate in chapter 8, pit nefarious villains against plucky, athletic heroines that are entirely good but in no way pathetic. Because of their heroic agency, or at least their eagerness for risky adventure, the serial-queens' physical victimization never seems to translate into pathos, as it does in a melodrama like *Broken Blossoms* where the imbalance of power is more grossly lopsided and not activated by a voluntarily risk-taking heroine. As a rule, in action melodramas, villains victimize protagonists— through abduction, torture, and every form of imperilment—but if the victimization serves to showcase the protagonists' bravery and resilience, they do not really come across as victims. There is no intimation of weakness or pity, as there is in a pathetic melodrama where the protagonist suffers physical abuse and emotional distress without the power to fight back or respond without profound self-sacrifice.

My argument here differs with one made by Linda Williams. She writes:

Melodrama . . . offers some combination of pathos and action. . . . The important point is that action-centered melodrama is never without pathos and pathos-centered melodrama is never without, at least some, action. The dialectic of pathos and action is a crucial feature of all melodrama. . . . The study of melodrama has often suffered from the misperception that it was one or the other of these poles. Melodrama's greatest interest as a form is in the dialectic between them.[54]

I would certainly agree that a great deal of melodrama interweaves pathos and action. *Way Down East*, which Williams analyzes, is an excellent example: there is superabundant pathos in the guiltless heroine's victimization and self-abnegation, and an impressive dose of action in the climactic waterfall-rescue sensation scene. Williams is astute, furthermore, in stressing that pathos and action serve the same function in the sense that they both establish moral legibility. It is through situations both pathetic and/or active that virtue and villainy are designated. The two are also related as triggers of affective arousal. As Alan Reynolds Thompson remarked in 1928, with reference to *Uncle Tom's Cabin*:

We should not be surprised that the emotional instability that permits sen-
timentality makes it possible for the same spectator to feel at the same play
a lust for blood and horror. The liberated pendulum of passion swings
from the one to the other, and unreasoning sympathy for a victim demands
unreasoning hatred for an oppressor.[55]

Pathos and action both share a power to swing "the liberated pendulum
of passion."

However, I think it is an overstatement to assert that melodrama
must necessarily incorporate both pathos and action. One need only
think of any James Bond action thriller. I suppose one could say, with a
bit of a stretch, that James Bond is a victim inasmuch as he is the target
of attacks by villains intent on killing him, but his predicaments certainly never elicit anything that legitimately could be called pathos. The
British playwright and essayist Richard Steele, writing in *The Tatler* in
1710, articulated the key distinction:

Gallant men who are cut off by the sword move our veneration rather
than our pity, and we gather relief enough from their own contempt of
death to make it no evil [since it] was approached with so much cheerful-
ness, and attended with so much honor. [However,] when we let our
thought wander from such noble objects, and consider the havoc which is
made among the tender and the innocent, pity enters with an unmixed
softness, and possesses all our souls at once.[56]

We pity the perennially powerless who endure pain through no fault or
action of their own. But hardship, abuse, punishment, even death, do
not generate pathos if the victim enters into dangers voluntarily, or
exhibits sufficient strength, skill, and fortitude of will to allow for the
possibility of recuperation, retaliation, or glorification.[57]

* * *

It is important to recognize that just as one can have melodrama without pathos, one might also have pathos without melodrama. Although
most narratives that elicit strong pathos are melodramas, they are not
necessarily so. An example that comes to mind is Visconti's *Death in*
Venice. The drama of a dying man longing for, and mourning the loss
of, youth, beauty, and impossible erotic plentitude, and particularly the
final scenes in which he tries to disavow his decay through a grotesquely unsuccessful dandifying makeover, could not possibly be more
poignant and pathetic. Like sentimental melodrama, *Death in Venice*

revolves around the pathos of desire for unrealizable love, the pathos of enduring pain caused by forces beyond control, of loss that can never be regained, of the irreversibility of time.[58] Nevertheless, I doubt anyone would categorize the film as part of the melodrama genre, or even as an example of a "melodramatic mode."

Why isn't *Death in Venice* a melodrama? This is a difficult question to answer. To some extent, it may have to do with the naturalism of Dirk Bogarde's performance style. While clearly his character is experiencing emotional turmoil, his expression of emotion (even as underscored by the emotiveness of the Mahler soundtrack) does not seem overwrought or excessive relative to his situation. Another explanation, following Thompson (who follows Clayton Hamilton), might assess the "universality" of the character's duress. For these critics, a defining feature of melodrama is that it preoccupies spectators with immediate sensational crises that have no broad implications beyond the specific narrative situation. The spectator is wrapped up in suspenseful agitation about whether Pauline will escape the buzz saw. Tragedy, on the other hand, supposedly provokes issues and identifications that have philosophical or spiritual weight and universal meaningfulness. Tragedy— and they would see *Death in Venice* as an example—prompts contemplation about the nature of the human condition. As Hamilton put it, tragedy "reveals some phase of the absolute, eternal Truth," that which has relevance to humanity as a whole, not just to the specific characters depicted. While this hypothesis merits further analysis, it is not immediately convincing because it obviously rests on a number of questionable assumptions (for example, about the universality of human nature, about the existence of something called Truth, or about the impossibility of extracting broad sociopsychological significance from melodramatic plights).[59]

A third possible explanation pertains to the complexity of character psychology. Robert B. Heilman proposes the distinction that melodrama characters are "whole" or "monopathic": they are defined by one-sided, unified, unchanging psychological attributes, and the problems that beset them derive from external forces. Tragedy, on the other hand, is built around protagonists who are "divided" or "polypathic," conflicted, torn between contradictory impulses and imperatives; and the problems they experience derive from drives within themselves.[60] Although *Death in Venice* centers around a problem that is, strictly speaking, external and beyond control (human ephemerality, the impossibility of reversing time, the painful lure of unattainable beauty), the protagonist's situation definitely sets off a complex range of internal anxieties, fears, passions, doubts, and conflicting impulses. It may be the complexity, ambiguity, and delicacy of characterization that keeps *Death in Venice* from being a melodrama. But then again, considering Hollywood melodrama's structure of moral antinomy mentioned earlier, it is perhaps an oversimplification to suggest that melodramas cannot also feature the characterological complexity of divided protagonists. Sarah Jane in *Imitation of Life* is clearly anguished by her conflicting impulses as a daughter who loves her mother, and as a young woman refusing to acquiesce to a pernicious system of racial injustice. Why a film like *Imitation of Life* is a melodrama, but a film like *Death in Venice* is not, remains an open question.

* * *

Despite some lingering ambiguities, melodrama, I have argued, is a highly variable but not utterly amorphous genre. It contains works constructed out of many different combinations of a set of primary features: pathos, emotionalism, moral polarization, nonclassical narrative form, and graphic sensationalism. Whereas most film studies work on melodrama has focused on the first two of these elements, the chapters that follow concentrate on a form of melodrama that potentially combines all five elements, but at minimum absolutely requires two—moral polarization and sensational action and spectacle. Before examining the nature and history of sensational melodrama in popular-priced theater and cinema, we begin, in the next two chapters, by exploring melodrama's context in a broad sense, focusing not on melodrama specifically but on the phenomenon of modern sensationalism in general.

3

Sensationalism and the World
of Urban Modernity

The rise of urban modernity was an awesome phenomenon. Cities
had always been busy, but they had never been as busy as they
became just before the turn of the century. A wave of urbanization made
the modern city considerably more crowded, chaotic, socially heterogeneous, and stimulating than ever before. The urban population in the
United States quadrupled between 1870 and 1910, from just under 10
million to over 42 million. (In other words, it doubled in size every
twenty years or so.) Metropoli like New York and Chicago grew even
faster. (See fig. 3.1.) Commercial activity exploded, with the U.S. gross
national product growing a remarkable 550 percent between 1870 and
1910. Urbanization and commercialization caused a new density of
downtown congestion. The rapid expansion of electric trolleys (whose
track mileage in the Northeast increased almost 350 percent in the
1890s alone) exacerbated traffic in city streets already crowded with
pedestrians, horses, wagons, and, toward 1910, automobiles (see figs.
3.2 and 3.3). The perceptual complexity of navigating traffic was aug-
mented by new strategies of visual solicitation. The Outdoor
Advertising Association of America estimated that the amount spent on
commercial billboards and signs increased 1,750 percent between 1900

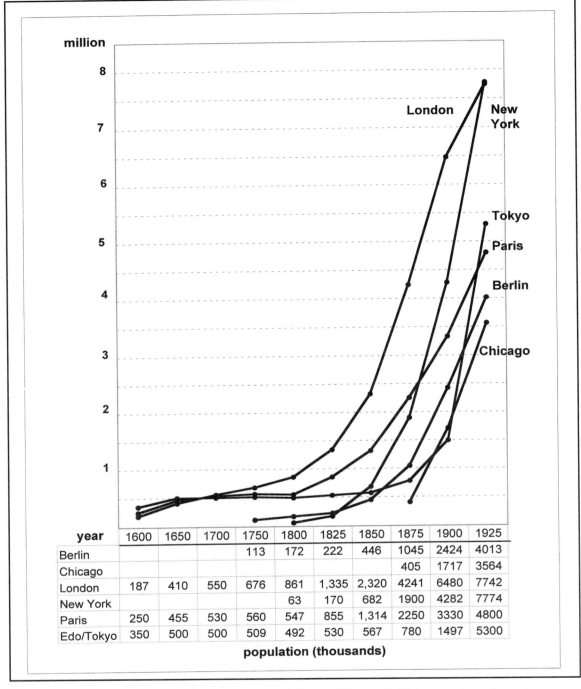

year	1600	1650	1700	1750	1800	1825	1850	1875	1900	1925
Berlin				113	172	222	446	1045	2424	4013
Chicago								405	1717	3564
London	187	410	550	676	861	1,335	2,320	4241	6480	7742
New York					63	170	682	1900	4282	7774
Paris	250	455	530	560	547	855	1,314	2250	3330	4800
Edo/Tokyo	350	500	500	509	492	530	567	780	1497	5300

population (thousands)

Fig. 3.1 Urban Population Growth in Selected Cities, 1600—1925. (Data from Chandler and Fox, *3000 Years of Urban Growth*)

and 1921 (see figs. 3.4, 3.5, 3.6 and 3.7). A sense of disorder and fragmentation was heightened by a new level of social heterogeneity as far-flung immigrant groups poured into the cities and women enjoyed greater freedom to circulate unchaperoned in public.[1]

Georg Simmel pointed to an important aspect of the transformation in his famous 1903 essay "The Metropolis and Mental Life" by noting that urban modernity entailed an "intensification of nervous stimulation." According to Simmel, modernity transformed both the physiological and psychological foundations of subjective experience:

The rapid crowding of changing images, the sharp discontinuity in the grasp of a single glance, and the unexpectedness of onrushing impression: These are the psychological conditions that the metropolis creates. With each crossing of the street, with the tempo and multiplicity of economic, occupational and social life, the city sets up a deep contrast with small town and rural life with reference to the sensory foundations of psychic life.[2]

Fig. 3.2 Post Office Square, Boston, 1904. (From Warner, *Streetcar Suburbs*)

Fig. 3.3 Opening day, Siegel and Cooper's department store, Sixth Avenue and 18th Street, New York City, c. 1900. (From Zeisloft, ed., *The New Metropolis*, 1899)

One need only look at early "actuality" footage of Manhattan, Berlin, London, or Paris—not to mention smaller cities like Lyons, France, or Harrisburg, Pennsylvania—to be convinced of Simmel's assertion, if not as an encapsulation of all aspects of modern experience, then at least of a significant part of it.[3]

Social observers in the decades around the turn of the century were fixated on the idea that modernity had brought about a radical increase in nervous stimulation, stress, and bodily peril. The motif of sensory violence appeared in a wave of articles on "the plague of city noises," warning of "the deleterious effect of the constant shock of . . . the continual rattle, roar, and screams which assault [our] ear drums at nearly all hours of the day and night."[4] Henry Adams's description of urban life, written in 1905, similarly stressed the sensory upheavals of modernity:

Fig. 3.4 42nd and Broadway, New York City, 1898. (From Zeisloft, ed., *The New Metropolis*, 1899)

Forces grasped his [modern man's] wrists and flung him about as though he had hold of a live wire. . . . Every day Nature violently revolted, causing so-called accidents with enormous destruction of property and life, while plainly laughing at man, who helplessly groaned and shrieked and shuddered, but never for a single instant could stop. The railways alone approached the carnage of war; automobiles and fire-arms ravaged society, until an earthquake became almost a nervous relaxation.[5]

Writing in 1912, Henry Woolston, a sociologist from City College of New York, summed up "the urban habit of mind" in a similar vein, highlighting the impact of both social and audiovisual (over)stimulation:

Urban life is marked by its heightened stimulation. When many people are brought close together contacts are multiplied and reactions are greatly increased. Men are assailed at every sense by the presence of their neighbors. The sound of footsteps and hoof-beats, the rattle of wagons and rush of cars, the clang of bells and hoot of whistles, the stroke of hammers and

Fig. 3.5 42nd and Broadway, New York City, 1909. (Bettmann Collection/Corbis)

Fig. 3.6 Fifth Avenue and 23rd Street, New York City, c. 1900. The building at center is now the site of the Flatiron Building. (Courtesy H. J. Heinz Co., Pittsburgh)

whir of machinery, cries of children and peddlers, strains of music, shouts and laughter swell into a dull roar as the city wakes to its day's work. One who watches the torrent of people pouring through the boulevards of Paris, or who struggles for a foothold in the rush at Brooklyn Bridge, becomes aware of innumerable prods at his attention. The crowd sets the pace. The individual must hurry with it or be pushed aside. Such excitement deeply stirs the nervous system. . . . Constant mingling on the crowded streets, in shops and factories, in parks and theaters; frequent public gatherings, religious and political; repeated meetings at unions, clubs, and social functions, all tend to heighten mental stimulation.[6]

A New York social reformer named Michael Davis coined an apt and surprisingly mod-sounding term to describe the new metropolitan environment (as well as the sensational amusements it fostered). Modernity, he declared in 1911, was defined by "hyperstimulus."[7] This preoccupation with the sensory intensity of urban life can be found in every genre and class of social representation in this period—from essays in aca-

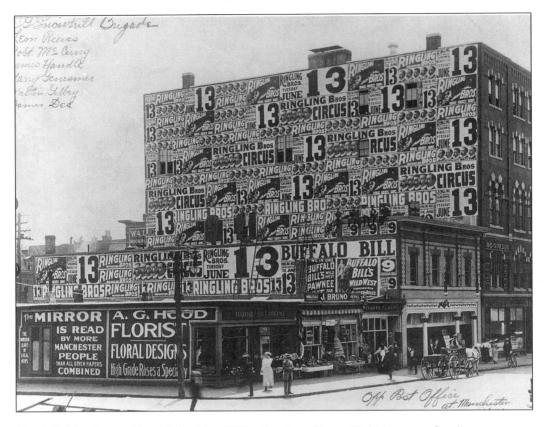

Fig. 3.7 Manchester, New Hampshire, 1911. (Courtesy Circus World Museum, Baraboo, Wisconsin)

demic journals, to aesthetic manifestos (such as Felippo Tommaso Marinetti's and Fernand Leger's), to middlebrow commentaries (such as the ubiquitous discussions of neurasthenia), to cartoons in the illustrated press—both in comic magazines such as *Puck, Punch, Judge,* and *Life* and popular sensational newspapers like the *New York World* and *New York Journal.*[8]

The illustrated press offers a particularly vivid trace of the culture's fixation on the sensory intensity of modernity. Comic magazines and sensational newspapers scrutinized the chaos of the modern environment with a dystopian alarmism characterizing much of the period's discourse on modern life. Many cartoons depicted modern life as inherently unnatural and unhealthy. They particularly criticized the degree to which the tempo of life had become more frenzied, sped up by new forms of rapid transportation, the pressing schedules of modern capitalism, and the ever-accelerating pace of the assembly line (figs. 3.8, 3.9). Many others represented the new landscape of commercial solicitation as a horrific assault on the senses (figs. 3.10, 3.11). Such images portrayed the kind of modern aberration described by Walter Lippmann in 1911: "The eastern sky ablaze with chewing gum, the northern with toothbrushes and underwear, the western with whiskey, and the southern with petticoats, the whole heavens brilliant with monstrously flirtatious women."[9] Other images, portraying dense, chaotic mobs of pedestrians (fig. 3.12), conveyed the degree to which, as Benjamin put it, "fear, revulsion, and horror were the emotions which the big-city crowd aroused in those who first observed it."[10]

A 1909 illustration in *Life* represented New York City as a frantic onslaught of sensory shocks (fig. 3.13). The combination of multiple spatiotemporal perspectives in a single, instantaneous view conveys the fractured perceptual polyvalence of urban experience. The multi-perspectival composition is curiously suggestive of Cubism, although it predates it by several years. The formal similarities between this illustration and the Cubist aesthetic suggest that they may have reflected a common source in the perceptual transformations of modernity.[11]

A number of illustrations dealt specifically with the harsh transformation of experience from a premodern state of balance and poise to a

EFFICIENCY

Fig. 3.8 "Efficiency." (*The Masses* 9 [July 1915])

Fig. 3.9 "Saving (?) Time." (*Life*, September 19, 1907)

Fig. 3.10 Untitled capitalist cityscape. (*Punch*, September 6, 1890)

modern crisis of discomposure and shock. A 1900 cartoon in *Life* (fig. 3.14), for example, contrasted a sixteenth-century pastoral scene with a twentieth-century view of a trolley car bearing down on terrified pedestrians. In the background, billboards advertise a sensational newspaper called *The Whirl* and Sunday movie shows of boxing movies. The contrast with the serenity of the "savage's" life in the past accentuated the true savagery of the metropolitan present.

The collision between two orders of experience—premodern and modern—also figured in numerous images representing actual collisions between horse-drawn carts (the traditional mode of transportation) and their modern-day replacement, the electric trolley (figs. 3.15, 3.16). Such pictures conveyed an anxiety about the perilousness of life in the modern city and also symbolized the kinds of nervous shocks and jolts to which the individual was subjected in the new environment.

By far the dominant dystopic motif around the turn of the century

Fig. 3.11 "How We Advertise Now." (*Punch*, December 3, 1887)

highlighted the terrors of big-city traffic, particularly with respect to the hazards of the electric trolley. A plethora of images representing streams of injured pedestrians, piles of "massacred innocents," and perennially gleeful death figures focused on the new dangers of the technologized urban environment (figs. 3.17, 3.18, 3.19, and 3.20). The text accompanying fig. 3.20 read: "The merciless trolley car has added another victim to its list of massacred innocents and still runs on unchecked. Thousands of citizens have protested and a united press has assailed the pitiless trolley monopoly without result. The slaughter still goes on. What will Brooklyn do about it?"

Sensational newspapers had a particular fondness for "snapshot" images of pedestrian deaths (figs. 3.21, 3.22, 3.23). This fixation underscored the sense of a radically altered public space, one defined by chance, peril, and shocking impressions rather than by any traditional conception of continuity and self-controlled destiny. Unnatural death, needless to say, had been a source of fear in premodern times as well (particularly with respect to epidemics, famine, and natural disasters), but the violence, suddenness, randomness (and, in a sense, the humiliating public character) of accidental death in the metropolis appear to have intensified and focalized this fear. The specter of unlucky victim Isaac Bartle seems to have infiltrated the modern consciousness. As an 1894 article in the *Newark Daily Advertiser* reported:

Isaac Bartle, a prominent citizen of New Brunswick, was instantly killed at the Market street station of the Pennsylvania Railroad this morning. His body was so horribly mangled that the remains had to be gathered up with a shovel and taken away in a basket. . . . He was ground into an unrecognizable mass under the wheels of a heavy freight engine. The engine struck Mr. Bartle in the back and dragged him several yards along the track, mangling his body in a horrible manner. Almost every bone was broken, the flesh was torn away and distributed along the track, and so

Fig. 3.12 "A Quiet Sunday in London: Or, the Day of Rest." (*Punch* March 20, 1886)

Fig. 3.13 "New York City: Is It Worth It?" (*Life*, May 6, 1909)

Fig. 3.14 "Broadway—Past and Present." (*Life*, April 26, 1900)

Fig. 3.15 "Horse Smashed Cable Car Window." (*New York World*, February 21, 1897)

completely was the body torn apart that the coins and knife in the trousers pocket were bent or broken, and the checkbook, pocketbook, and papers were torn in pieces.[12]

Although there is no question that descriptions such as this were motivated in large part by the fact that grotesque sensationalism sold newspapers, they manifest something more: in its meticulous attention to the physical details of accidental death, the Isaac Bartle item seems to convey a distinctive hyperconsciousness of environmental stress and physical vulnerability in the modern city.[13] The chaos of the city instilled life with a nervous edge, an uneasy feeling of exposure to random injury (although, naturally, some would have experienced the visceral tensions of urban stress more acutely than others). As the editor of *The Outlook* magazine mentioned in 1900, "The Spectator is not unduly timorous, but he confesses that in these days of haste he often gets a little nervous in the city streets lest something may happen to somebody."[14] This writer describes a pervasive vague anxiety, but navigating the traffic and crowds of the metropolis also triggered more jolting reflex reactions and nervous impulses, flowing through the body, as Benjamin described it, "like the energy from a battery." It is interesting that illustrations of accidents almost always employed a particular presentational schema: they were obliged, of course, to show the victim at the moment of deadly impact, but along with this they almost always showed a startled bystander looking on in horror, his or her body jolted

Fig. 3.16 "Trolley Car Hits a Truck and Motorman Is Thrown and Badly Hurt." (*New York World*, December 6, 1896)

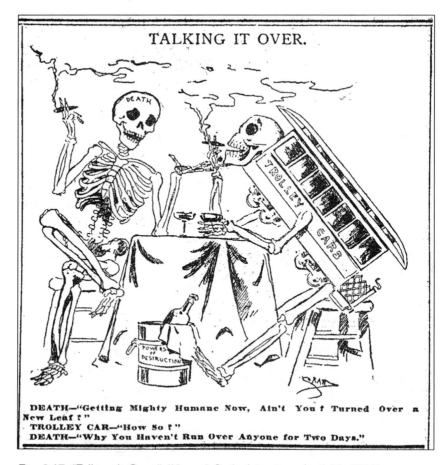

Fig. 3.17 "Talking It Over." (*Newark Daily Advertiser*, April 30, 1894)

into a reflex reaction. Such illustrations thus stressed not only the dangers of big-city life but also its relentless nervous shocks.

The popular fear of trolley hazards did eventually subside. One sees a dropping off of this theme in the sensational press around 1903 and 1904. But just as the public apparently was getting used to trolley traffic, another peril—the automobile—followed on its heels and assumed an equivalent position as the central motif of modernity's dystopic imagination. The 1913 illustration "When Unlicensed Chauffeurs Are Abroad" (fig. 3.24), among numerous others, portrayed a state of affairs in which, as Benjamin put it, "moving through traffic involves the individual in a series of shocks and collisions."[15] Indeed, the image criticized

IN THE WAKE OF A CABLE CAR.

Fig. 3.18 "In the Wake of a Cable Car." (*Life*, May 2, 1895)

-NOON HOUR - BROADWAY -

Fig. 3.19 "Noon Hour—Broadway." (*New York World*, March 8, 1896)

modernity on two fronts: overtly, it decried the hazards and jolts of modern traffic; implicitly, it cast aspersions on the expanded presence of women outside the domestic sphere. The picture presented a soon-to-be stereotypical image of women as bad drivers and, at the same time, in representing only female pedestrians, offered a variation on a common paternalistic admonition about the vulnerability of unaccompanied women in the big city. (See also figs. 3.25 and 3.26.)

Aside from traffic hazards, three other motifs that pervaded turn-of-the-century newspapers suggest the depth of the popular fixation on the new dangers of modern life. The first portrayed deaths of workers mangled by factory machinery. One can get a good idea of this motif from a few sample titles and subheadings from the *Newark Daily Advertiser* in 1894: "Whirled to Instant Death: His Body Caught in Rapidly Revolving Belts and Crushed Against the Ceiling at Every Revolution," and "Horrible Death of a Street-Cleaner: His Head Twisted Almost Off by a Sweeping Machine."[16] This keen attention to graphic accidental death in the workplace, like the traffic death stories, posed modern technology as a monstrous assault on life and limb. It stressed a hazardous dimension of modern life that, not coincidentally, was suffered most acutely by the working class that made up the sensational press's core readership.

Another motif, also focusing on modern working-class experience, concentrated on a broad variety of deaths relating to various hazards of

Fig. 3.20 "The Brooklyn Horror." (*The Standard*, May 4, 1895)

The street-car companies have "deliberated" for several months over numerous fenders submitted and will probably "deliberate" several months longer. In the meantime—

Fig. 3.21 Untitled (death rides on trolley roof). (*Newark Daily Advertiser*, April 19, 1894)

Fig. 3.22 "Another Trolley Victim." (*New York World*, April 5, 1896)

tenement life—ranging from brutal attacks by crazed neighbors to deaths involving novel facets of tenement architecture (fig. 3.27). Newspaper stories in this genre sometimes emphasized a sense that uncontrollable, almost supernatural, dangers lurked everywhere in the urban environment. One item, for example, described the agonizing death of a little girl whose skull was pierced by a rusty steel rod. The account noted: "Where the rod came from, or how it received enough force to make the wound that it did is a mystery. The child was at play

A WOMAN KNOCKED DOWN BY A CABLE CAR AND DRAGGED
TWENTY FEET BY HER HAIR

Fig. 3.23 "Woman Knocked Down by a Cable Car." (*New York World*, May 6, 1896)

in the yard when the rod, propelled by an unseen force, crashed down through the branches of a cherry tree, penetrating the girl's skull. The little girl died in great agony this morning."[17] In the modern environment, death could drop from the sky, inexplicably.

Falls from great heights also preoccupied sensational newspapers (figs. 3.28, 3.29). At first glance, this genre may seem the most "purely" sensational, having little to do with anxieties about modern life. But in several respects, such illustrations overlapped with the others. All the deaths by falling, except for suicide leaps, were workplace accidents and thus conveyed a general sense of the perils of proletarian labor. Even the

Fig. 3.24 "When Unlicensed Drivers Are Abroad." (*San Francisco Post* [1913]; reprinted in *Cartoons* 4 [1913])

Fig. 3.25 "The Lives of the Hunted." (*Life*, October 22, 1903)

suicides can be read as implicit indictments of modern life, especially since they often involved modern transportations as the immediate agents of physical obliteration (in illustrations, for example, showing a man plunging from a building onto the tracks of an oncoming train [fig. 3.30]). Some of these falls also underscored the tyranny of chance in the modern environment and the random dangers of tenement life. A typi-

Fig. 3.26 "*Life*'s Guide to the Suburbs—Where to Walk." (*Life*, October 17, 1907)

Fig. 3.27 "Child Choked by a Transom." (*New York World*, April 5, 1896)

Fig. 3.28 "Perilous Night Work on Sky Scraper." (*New York World*, November 29, 1896)

FELL TEN STORIES TO HIS DEATH.

Fig. 3.29 "Fell Ten Stories to His Death." (*New York World*, November 15, 1896)

Fig. 3.30 "Plunged in Front of an 'L' Train." (*New York World*, May 18, 1896)

cal example is an image of a little boy about to be squashed to death by
house painters plummeting off a broken scaffolding (fig. 3.31).[18]

The portrayals of urban modernity in the illustrated press seem to
have fluctuated between, on the one hand, an antimodern nostalgia for
a more tranquil time, and on the other, a basic fascination with the hor-

rific, the grotesque, and the extreme. The illustrated press's images were, paradoxically, both a form of social critique and, at the same time, a form of commercialized sensationalism, a part of the very phenomenon of modern hyperstimulus the images decried. In both these aspects, the illustrated press traded in bombast. This is not surprising, since the press had an obvious commercial interest in portraying the world in a drastic light. After all, hue and cry and thrills, not uneventful quotidian real-

Fig. 3.31 "A Falling Man Kills a Boy." (*New York World*, May 9, 1896)

ism, sold copies.

Beyond the commercial logic of sensationalism, however, these representations, in their superabundance and intensity, seem to convey a critical fixation, a sense of anxious urgency in documenting and dissecting an awesome social transformation. At the heart of this fixation was a cultural uneasiness surrounding the onset of urban modernity. It was a culture that on some level had not yet fully adjusted to the sensory upheavals of urban modernity; or at least, it was a culture that for some reason felt a strong need to represent itself as such. The images of modern chaos were those of social observers who were feeling the "shock of the new" firsthand. Today, urban modernity is the cultural norm, fully ensconced for over a century. At the turn of the nineteenth century, for some people at least, life in the metropolis still felt somewhat unnatural and unnerving. The premodern millennium had yet to fade into a quaint abstract concept; it was still a vital and tangible memory, one that constantly accentuated the novelty and upheaval of the new reality. Ortega Y Gasset aptly described this situation: "The tempo of modern life, the speed with which things move today, the force and energy with which everything is done, cause anguish to the man of archaic mould, and this anguish is the measure of the imbalance between his pulse-beats and the pulse-beats of the time."[19] The critical fixation on modernity underscores if not the "anguish," then at least the sensitivity of a generation trying to express the feeling of such an imbalance.

* * *

As one might expect, the discourse on the sensory overload of urban modernity inevitably led to a parallel discourse on the escalation of sensationalism in popular amusement. It did not take long for critics to perceive a correlation between the hyperstimulus of the metropolis and popular amusement's increasing emphasis on powerful sensations and thrills. Their logical assumption was that they had something to do with each other. The environment of urban modernity, they surmised, had a significant impact in shaping hyperkinetic entertainments.

The 1890s presented a crucial watershed in the history of popular entertainment. An array of commercial amusements greatly intensified an emphasis on spectacle, sensationalism, and astonishment. On a more modest scale, these elements had often shaped amusements geared toward working-class (and occasionally multiclass) audiences, but the new prevalence and power of immediate, gripping sensation defined a fundamentally different epoch in popular entertainment. Modernity ushered in a commerce in sensory shocks. The *thrill* emerged as the keynote of modern diversion.

The thrill took many forms. Beginning around 1895, as we just saw, sensational newspapers began flooding their pages with high-impact illustrations of anything strange, sordid, or shocking. Amusement parks were, for all intents and purposes, an invention of the 1890s. The Midway at the 1893 Columbian Exposition in Chicago featured an impressive Ferris wheel—the world's first—along with a Snow and Ice Railway, in which a train of linked bobsleds careened down a 400-foot chute of artificially made ice. The Coney Island amusement complex opened in 1895, and other parks specializing in exotic sights, disaster spectacles, stunning electric illumination, and thrilling mechanical rides soon proliferated across the country (see figs. 3.32, 3.33). These concentrations of audiovisual and kinesthetic sensation epitomized a distinctly modern intensity of *manufactured* stimulus.[20] So did a variety of mechanical daredevil exhibitions such as "The Whirlwind of Death" and "The Globe of Death," in which a car somersaulted in midair after hurtling off a 40-foot ramp. The editors of *Scientific American*, who in 1905 cast a bemused eye on the expanding field of dangerous automotive stunts, aptly summarized the essential objective: "The guiding principle of the inventors of these acts is to give our nerves a shock more intense than any hitherto experienced" (see fig. 3.34).[21] A competing spectacle, for a dubious "hazardous terrific" automobile stunt that seemingly violated the laws of physics, boasted of "Out-Thrilling All Other Thrillers—A New Astounding Sensation." In this stunt and others, the phenomenon of female daredevils amplified the novelty (see figs. 3.35 and 3.36).

Vaudeville, which also emerged as a major popular amusement in the 1890s, encapsulated the new trend toward brief, forceful, and sensually "busy" attractions, with its eclectic series of stunts, slapstick, song-and-dance routines, trained dogs, female wrestlers, and the like. Gaudy burlesque shows and "dime museums" (housing sundry curiosities, freak shows, and occasionally short blood-and-thunder dramas) took on greater prominence around this time.[22] Popular-priced stage melodrama underwent a particularly striking shift in emphasis around the turn of the century (as we will explore more fully in chapter 6). Whereas earlier melodrama had highlighted the pathos and moralizing oratory of innocent victims and their brawny champions, melodrama grew more

Fig. 3.32 Water Slide at Sea Lion Park, Brooklyn, N.Y., 1895. (Courtesy Library of Congress)

Bisby's Spiral Airship, Long Beach, Cal.

Fig. 3.33 Bisby's Spiral Airship, Long Beach, Calif., c. 1898. (From Cartmell, *The Incredible Scream Machine*)

and more synonymous with violent action, stunts, and exciting spectacles of catastrophe and physical peril based on elaborate mechanical stagecraft. A New York critic, writing in 1903, described melodrama as "a series of adventures calculated to give anyone except a hardened boy the echoes of delirium tremens."[23]

The trend toward vivid, powerful sensation saw one of its most robust manifestations in the rise of cinema. From very early on, the movies gravitated toward an "aesthetics of astonishment" both in terms of its form and subject matter. The thrill was central, for example, to the early spectacle-centered "cinema of attractions" as well as to powerful suspense melodramas such as Griffith's 1908–1909 Biograph thrillers and action serials of the Teens built around explosions, crashes, torture contraptions, elaborate fights, chases, and last-minute rescues and escapes (examined in chapter 7). A key aim of these films was to generate sensations of visceral agitation and awe, triggered not only by the thrilling and sensational spectacle but also by techniques of crosscutting and accelerated editing that amplified the sensation of suspense. Vachel Lindsay, writing in 1915, declared that "such spectacles gratify the

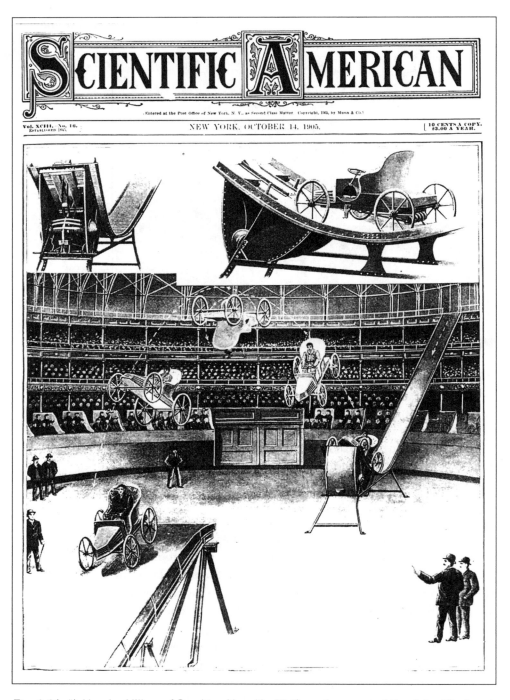

Fig. 3.34 "A Hundred Ways of Breaking Your Neck" (from the cover of the *Scientific American*, October 14, 1905). The fine text originally located at the bottom of the cover read: "The 'Whirlwind of Death,' an aptly named apparatus which has killed one performer and in which an automobile is made to turn a somersault before it touches the ground."

Fig. 3.35 Poster for the "Double Forward Somersault." (Courtesy Circus World Museum, Baraboo, Wisconsin)

incipient or rampant speed-mania in every American."[24] A generation of young European critics embraced the stimulating dynamism of American films. As Gabriele Buffet wrote in 1917 in the modern art journal *391*, "Above everything else, the American film is active, and does not waste itself in useless representations or in pantomime. . . . The plot is advanced by a succession of facts of direct significance. Fisticuffs, kisses, falls, chases!"[25] The modernist avant-garde celebrated cinema's dynamism and discontinuity. Marinetti and other Futurists hailed cinema as an exciting "jumble of objects and reality thrown together at random."[26] Dada artists frequently alluded to cinema as the ultimate form of visual impact and chaotic fragmentation. Dada had a natural affinity to cinema since, as Benjamin put it, both were "an instrument of ballistics [hitting] the spectator like a bullet."[27] For the French Surrealists, sensational serials "marked an epoch" by "announcing the upheavals of the new world." They recognized the mark of modernity both in the

Fig. 3.36 Poster for The Sisters La Rague daredevil stunt. (Courtesy Circus World Museum, Baraboo, Wisconsin. Image reproduced with the permission of Ringling Bros.—Barnum & Bailey Combined Shows, Inc.)

sensational subject-matter of the *cine-feuilletons* ("crimes, departures, phenomena, nothing less than the poetry of our age") and in the film medium's power to convey speed, simultaneity, visual superabundance, and visceral shock.[28] Soviet directors studied Hollywood's sensationalism and refined montage editing as a means to assault the spectator with a series of high-impact jolts. The goal of cinema, Eisenstein declared in 1925, was to "smash skulls with kino-fists!"[29]

* * *

What caused this broad-based phenomenon of sensationalization? The rise of commercial sensationalism undoubtedly stemmed to a large extent from the rapid growth of a massive urban working class in the last quarter of the nineteenth century. The new proletariat was predisposed toward startling and violent spectacle, however one might attempt to explain that predisposition. As journalist Robert Wagner put it in 1920,

"Rough workers . . . like things that go bang."[30] So too, increasingly as the nineteenth century came to a close, did a new generation of white-collar amusement-goers, the product of modern capitalism's great bureaucratic expansion. The post-Victorian middle class, and particularly the burgeoning lower middle class, was inherently more receptive to sensual and spectacular amusements than previous generations governed more thoroughly by the moral austerity of the Protestant establishment. The surge in popular sensationalism in the decades around the turn of the century was an immediate response to the new demographics of the amusement marketplace.[31]

But this socioeconomic explanation was not generally the one stressed by those who tried to understand the phenomenon while it was happening around them. Period observers were much more inclined toward a kind of zeitgeist argument. The broad escalation of sensational amusement was clearly a sign of the times, they argued, or more specifically, a symptom of the emergence of urban modernity. As the urban environment grew more and more intense, so too did the sensations packaged in the form of commercial amusement. As modernity transformed the texture of random daily experience, synthetic, orchestrated experience necessarily followed suit. Commercial sensationalism, many critics believed, was simply the aesthetic counterpart to sensory overload in the capitalist metropolis. The commercialization of the thrill was a reflection and expression—as well as an agent—of the heightened stimulation of the modern environment.

Recent scholars have tended to valorize Kracauer and Benjamin as the sources of this theme, but it is important to recognize that the association between urban modernity and vivid entertainments was a stock intellectual motif by the time Kracauer and Benjamin elaborated it, one that was more or less complete and ready "off the shelf" to be plugged into essays in cultural criticism. The basic insight was already being articulated as early as 1911, when a German critic named Hermann Kienzl declared that movies were the prime expression of the new metropolitan experience. "The psychology of the cinematographic triumph," Kienzl proclaimed, "is metropolitan psychology. The metropolitan soul, that ever-harried soul, curious and unanchored, tumbling from fleeting impression to fleeting impression, is quite rightly the cinematographic soul."[32] In a similar but less celebratory vein, Michael Davis used his term "hyperstimulus" to characterize the aesthetic of vaudeville. That entertainment, he complained, was symptomatic of "the excitement of the city and the mental disintegration induced by the kaleidoscopic stimuli of New York life." In its vivid, disjointed, fleeting spectacle, vaudeville mirrored "the experience afforded by a street-car ride, or any active day in a crowded city."[33]

An American journalistic literary critic named Burton Rascoe, writing in 1921, similarly situated cinema within the new environment of audiovisual bombardment and distraction:

There is scant repose for the retina of the modern man either in the towns or the cities on account of the increase in frequency of the appeal to sight. Huge gothic headlines which appeared for the first time during the war have remained as lurid and startling, even though the events to which they now call attention are neither catastrophic nor of particular interest to large numbers of people. Signboards vie with each other in color and design and in frugality of words necessary for conveying the sales idea. On the aural side the nervous strain of the American city resident is not less great. . . . The movies are merely contributions to the mass effect of conditions which tend toward . . . the nervous derangement of the modern American. . . . To attain the hold they have upon Americans, the movies have had to compete in blatancy with posters, billboards, the newspaper headlines and magazine advertisements, the picture papers and the electric signs.[34]

Kracauer incorporated the general idea five years later, in his famous essay "The Cult of Distraction." Amusements based on disconnected, busy, powerful impressions, or "distraction," reflected the modern experience: "[Such shows are] meaningful . . . as a reflection of the uncontrolled anarchy of our world. . . . In pure externality, the audience encounters itself. Its own reality is revealed in the fragmented sequence of splendid sense impressions. . . . Shows which aim at distraction are composed of the same mixture of externalities as the world of the urban masses."[35] The aesthetic of shallow thrill and sensory stimulation, Kracauer observed, paralleled the texture of urban, technological experience.

Benjamin picked up on this idea a decade later, in 1936, in a footnote to "The Work of Art in the Age of Mechanical Reproduction." "The film," he asserted, "corresponds to profound changes in the apperceptive apparatus—changes that are experienced on an individual scale by the man in the street in big-city traffic, on a historical scale by every present-day citizen."[36] He elaborated on this theme three years later, in

"On Some Motifs in Baudelaire":

Moving through traffic involves the individual in a series of shocks and collisions. At dangerous intersections, nervous impulses flow through him in rapid succession, like the energy from a battery. . . . Whereas Poe's passers-by cast glances in all directions which still appeared to be aimless, today's pedestrians are obliged to do so in order to keep abreast of traffic signals. Thus technology has subjected the human sensorium to a complex kind of training. There came a day when a new and urgent need for stimuli was met by the film. In a film, perception in the form of shocks was established as a formal principle. That which determines the rhythm of production on a conveyor belt is the basis of the rhythm of reception in a film.[37]

Cinema's rapid tempo and audiovisual fragmentation, Benjamin stressed, matched the velocities and shocks of modern life.

Now, fast-forward some fifty years. Since about the late 1980s, when an unprecedented interest in early cinema began to intersect with renewed interest in Kracauer and Benjamin, this idea of a close connection between the sensory environment of urban modernity and the emergence of sensational amusements has been enjoying a renaissance. The appeal of this concept derives partly from the hope that, after the exhaustion of *Screen*-style film theory and the pendulum's swing to hard-nosed empirical film history, it seems to offer the possibility of a commodious middleground of theoretically informed history and/or historically informed theory. The argument is beginning to draw strong criticism, however, from scholars who think that it relies on premises that are vague, implausible, and counterfactual. The following chapter tries to shed light on the conceptual structure of the thesis and assesses its potential usefulness for understanding the forces that shaped early cinema.

4

Making Sense of the Modernity Thesis

Already my eyes and my ears too, from force of habit, are beginning to see and hear everything in the guise of this rapid, quivering, ticking mechanical reproduction. I don't deny it; the outward appearance is light and vivid. We move, we fly. And the breeze stirred by our flight produces an alert, joyous, keen agitation, and sweeps away thought. . . . Outside there is a continuous glare, an incessant giddiness: everything flickers and disappears. . . . All this furious haste is not natural, all this flickering and vanishing of images; there lies beneath it a machine that seems to pursue it, frantically screaming.

— Pirandello, *Shoot! The Notebooks of Serafino Gubbio, Cinematograph Operator* (1915)[1]

In the late 1980s a number of film scholars began drawing upon Kracauer's and Benjamin's suggestive remarks on modernity and cinema, and upon the seminal figures, especially Baudelaire and Simmel, who influenced the Weimar critics. Over the 1990s something akin to a school of thought coalesced (I am tempted to call it the New York

School since most of its contributors lived there at the time they began working in this vein); or, if calling it a school is too grandiose, at least a fairly cohesive focus of inquiry has taken shape. What unites recent work by Guiliana Bruno, Leo Charney, Anne Friedberg, Tom Gunning, Miriam Hansen, Lynne Kirby, Lauren Rabinovitz, Mark Sandberg, Vanessa Schwartz, and others is an interest in unearthing or rethinking cinema's emergence within the sensory environment of urban modernity, its relationship to late nineteenth-century technologies of space and time, and its interactions with adjacent elements in the new visual culture of advanced capitalism.[2] This research program has yielded what David Bordwell, in his impressive recent book *On the History of Film Style*, calls "the modernity thesis."[3] While this label sounds overly monumental, given the enormous scope of debates about modernity in sociology and philosophy, it will suffice as well as any.

Proponents of the thesis agree with many early social critics that cinema, and adjacent forms of spectacle, "marked an epoch." Cinema is the quintessential product of fin-de-siècle society. It stands out as an emblem of modernity. But what does it mean to say that cinema is, or was, an emblem of modernity? In and of itself, it is a vague contention, so I will try to be specific in laying out what the idea entails.

The modernity thesis, as I understand it, has three main components, three suppositions that, in various combinations, proponents of the thesis have tended to weave together. First, there is simply the idea that in certain salient respects cinema is *like* modernity. The modernity thesis stresses key formal and spectatorial similarities between cinema—as a medium of strong impressions, spatiotemporal fragmentation, abruptness, mobility—and the nature of metropolitan experience. Both are characterized by the prominence of fleeting, forceful visual attractions and contra-contemplative spectatorial distraction. As Gunning writes:

Attractions trace out the visual topology of modernity: a visual environment which is fragmented and atomized; a gaze which, rather than resting on a landscape in contemplation, seems to be pushed and pulled in conflicting orientations, hurried and intensified, and therefore less coherent and anchored. . . . The attraction in film consists of a specific relation between viewer and film that reveals aspects of the experience of modernity.[4]

Thus, the first component of the modernity thesis posits a relationship of resemblance. Movies and movie-viewing resemble the subjective experience of urban modernity.

But more is involved than mere resemblance. "We are dealing here," as Gunning suggests, "not only with equivalences and interpretations, but with actual intersections among the diverse manifestations of modernity."[5] In other words, the modernity thesis is interested in understanding cinema as a *part* of modernity, that is, as a significant element of modernity in dynamic interaction with a range of adjacent similar phenomena. These include, among others, new technologies (e.g., the railroad, the telegraph, the photograph, electric illumination), new entertainments (e.g., the panorama and diorama, the amusement park, the world exhibition, the yellow press, the wax museum, the morgue), new architectural forms (e.g., the panopticon, iron-and-glass construction), new visual displays (e.g., the billboard, the shop window, the illustrated press), new social spaces (e.g., the boulevard, the arcade, the department store), new social practices (e.g., *flâneurie*, shopping, unchaperoned female mobility, widespread tourism, systematized surveillance), and new (or newly rampant) environmental obstacles (e.g., crowds, traffic, congestion). All these phenomena emerged, or greatly intensified, in the extraordinary historical moment spanning the decades around the turn of the century. This second component of the modernity thesis, in short, positions cinema within relationships of contextual contiguity and interaction.

The third component of the modernity thesis, and the most controversial, is the argument that cinema—either cinema in general or particular forms stressing overt stimulation, like "the cinema of attractions" or sensational melodrama—was a *consequence* of modernity. This idea posits a relationship of causality. Although proponents of the thesis have said relatively little about the precise mechanisms by which modernity created cinema, or at least encouraged it to develop in the way it did, the general assumption is that the intensity of modern experience generated in individuals a psychological predisposition toward strong sensations, reflecting profound changes in the "perceptual mode" prevailing in modern society. A corollary assumption would be that perceptual modernity somehow influenced the creative process so that filmmakers were inclined, consciously or subliminally, to express in film style the tempos and shocks of modern life. Benjamin states the idea quite directly:

> *During long periods of history, the mode of human sense perception changes with humanity's entire mode of existence. The manner in which human sense perception is organized, the medium in which it is accomplished, is determined not only by nature but by historical circumstance, as well. . . . Film corresponds to profound changes in the apperceptive apparatus—changes that are experienced on an individual scale by the man in the street in big-city traffic, on a historical scale by every present-day citizen.[6]*

Let us call this the "history of perception" argument.[7]

The gist of the history-of-perception argument is that modernity caused some kind of fundamental change in the human perceptual apparatus, or "sensorium," as Benjamin and others called it. Immersion in the complex, rapid-fire environment of the metropolis and industrial capitalism created a distinctly modern perceptual mode. The city's bombardment of heterogeneous and ephemeral stimuli fostered an edgy, hyperactive, fragmented perceptual encounter with the world. This proposition feeds into the modernity thesis perhaps most directly by providing a middle, human, link in the causal relationship between modernity and movies. Instead of the rather vague thesis, "Modernity somehow shaped the movies," it allows for the slightly less vague thesis, "Modernity somehow shaped human perception, which then somehow shaped the movies."

There has been some disagreement about whether all three components of the modernity thesis (cinema as like, as a part of, and as a consequence of, modernity) are essential. Bordwell argues that the modernity thesis cannot help but embrace the problematic third notion of causality. The idea of some sort of causal relationship between modernity and movies is problematic because it seems "too linear," too simplistic in its tight correlation between society and its artistic creations. Bordwell challenges the notion of a causal connection by noting that many movies simply did not behave the way they were supposed to— their style, he contends, failed to reflect the supposed intensity and fragmentation of urban modernity. I will return to this objection later. As for the question of whether the causal strand of the thesis is indispensable, Tom Gunning maintains that it need not be. He stresses that cultural histories of cinema in modernity are above all else explorations of the first two ideas—film's resemblance to and contextual interaction with other elements or aspects of the metropolitan environment.[8]

Bordwell counters that any such exploration of the elements and aspects of the modern environment automatically assumes (if not by necessity then at least by normal inference) that the things being juxtaposed stem from, or are manifestations of, a set of common causal forces (such as urbanization, technology, capitalism, etc.). Otherwise, why go to the trouble of juxtaposing them? We might detect certain surface similarities among various elements and aspects, but if they lacked any common determining factors or sources, the juxtaposition would have no deeper explanatory value. To use a zoological analogy, one might note the similarity between the long necks of giraffes and those of ostriches, and observe that the animals inhabit the same environment and perhaps even interact with each other; but this juxtaposition is of no consequence and lacks knowledge value unless it is informed by some sort of causal argument about how their common environment promoted similar anatomical adaptations.[9]

I am inclined to agree with Bordwell that there is no getting around the causal supposition. However much they may wish to avoid the pitfall of facile teleology, proponents of the modernity thesis should be able to offer justifications, even if only hypothetical ones, for comprehending cinema, or certain types of cinema, as at least partially an outgrowth of urban modernity. At the very least, they could cite the causal arguments articulated by Kracauer, Benjamin, and others (which I will detail later in this chapter). Although their expositions were often rather sketchy, this first generation of modernity theorists did hypothesize a set of psychosocial mechanisms linking urban modernity and what Benjamin described as the "new and urgent need for stimuli" met by cinema.

* * *

In order to understand cinema as an outgrowth of perceptual modernity, first we must make sense of the notion of a new mode of perception. "We might begin," Bordwell rightly suggests, "by asking what is meant by 'perception' or 'vision.'" He continues:

If such terms are shorthand for "thought" or "experience," the position becomes vague, if not commonplace. But advocates of the position certainly talk as if there is not only a history of ideas, beliefs, opinions, attitudes, tastes, and the like but also a history of how people take in the world through their senses.[10]

Bordwell argues that it is spurious to claim that urban modernity triggered some sort of profound transformation in the perceptual apparatus. The human perceptual equipment, he points out, is hardly malleable enough to undergo major biological changes to correspond to every sudden change in the lived environment. That would be equivalent to the thoroughly discredited Lamarckian theory that traits acquired to help individuals adjust to a short-term environmental state-of-affairs become part of the next generation's genetic inheritance, bypassing the much longer-term process of natural selection. Bordwell writes:

In what sense can we talk about short-term changes in perception, that intricate mesh of hard-wired anatomical, physiological, optical and psychological mechanism produced by millions of years of biological selection? If vision has adapted itself in a few decades to collective experience and the urban environment, we have a case of Lamarckian evolution. . . . This conclusion is highly implausible.[11]

It is hard to disagree on this point. It would indeed be unwise to base the modernity thesis on a notorious scientific dead end. Whether or not recent scholars have been so foolhardy is open to debate,[12] but in any case, the pressing question is, if we rule out a Lamarckian explanation, are there other ways to make sense of the history-of-perception thesis? If that question can be answered in the affirmative, one of the two key pillars of the modernity thesis will be allowed to stand. Once that premise is in place, then the somewhat wobbly second pillar—the argument that the new perceptual mode actually influenced cinema—will have to be supported.

There are, I propose, at least four viable ways to understand the phenomenon of perceptual change in modernity. It is not necessary to choose among the four models, as they could coexist in varying combinations and degrees of influence. The first model returns us to the question of the mutability of biological wiring. If one divests it of the claim relating to genetic inheritance, the idea of short-term perceptual malleability resulting from environmental stimulation is not all that ludicrous after all (as the recent proliferation of strange, *Caligari*-esque mobiles hanging above baby cribs in yuppie homes attests). One of the most important breakthroughs in recent neurobiology has been the discovery of "neural plasticity," particularly plasticity in the perceptual apparatus. As the *MIT Encyclopedia of the Cognitive Sciences* (1999) states:

In the last few years, visual neuroscience, which aims to understand how our visual system works, [has been] undergoing fundamental changes in approach. Visual neuroscience is beginning to focus on the mechanisms that allow the cerebral cortex to adapt its circuitry and learn a new task. . . . Instead of the hardwired cortical structures implied by classical work . . . we may be confronted with significant neural plasticity, that is neuron properties and connectivities that change as a function of visual experience.[13]

A 1994 article in *Science*, also concerning plasticity in vision, explains:

Neural circuitry in sensory areas of the cerebral cortex is intricately organized, evoking the impression of an elegantly hard-wired machine that performs stereotyped computations on sensory input. Recent experiments, however, have shown that this circuitry is subject to dramatic plastic changes. Topographic organization can be altered by . . . chronic performance of a sensory task . . . by changes in the behavioral context in which a stimulus is presented, and by direct manipulation of the sensory environment. Plasticity thus appears to be a common feature of the adult cortex and may be closely linked to the behavioral ability to respond flexibly to the environment.[14]

One could not hope for a pithier encapsulation of the basic premise of the history-of-perception argument: perception is reorganized in response to a new sensory environment. Studies in rats, cats, monkeys, and humans all show that the brain's neural architecture and chemistry are significantly altered by environmental context. Researchers have proven that exposure to "enriched" environments (for rats, those involving extensive contact with other rats, runways, and toys) markedly increases the number of synapses per neuron and thus the intricacy of interconnections within and between regions of the brain.[15] As one would expect, the growth is most evident in the parts of the brain that govern perceptual, cognitive, and behavioral tasks demanded by a particular environment. For example, cats raised in artificial environments containing nothing but vertical lines showed morphological change in the part of the visual cortex devoted to apprehending vertical orientation; and blind humans who read Braille (which is read with the left hand) showed neural growth specifically in the corresponding part of the brain.[16] Perceptual neuroplasticity is by no means limited to the critical period of infant development or to recovery from brain injury; the normal adult brain also responds morphologically to differential experience and training. As the aforementioned encyclopedia of cognitive science states, "A growing body of evidence reveals a remarkable degree of mutability of function in primary sensory cortex that is not limited to the first months of life but extends throughout adulthood."[17]

It may be overstatement to call such changes "fundamental" or "radical" reorganizations of perception (such terms would seem more apt if, say, we were to gain the capacity to see infrared light or hear with the sonic range of dogs), but the changes are significant, nonetheless. Most research on the practical cognitive and behavioral effects of neural plasticity has compared enriched-condition rats to impoverished-condition rats. "EC" rats consistently outperform "IC" rats in experiments measuring learning, memory, exploratory behavior, object interaction, task facility, problem-solving, and escape from predation.[18] Probably more pertinent for our purposes are findings of perceptual improvements in a wide range of perceptual tasks, including, among other things, visual acuity, hue discrimination, velocity estimation, and acoustic pitch discrimination, all related to changes in cortical topography.[19]

The crucial question is whether these perceptual tasks—and others that will be identified with further research—are the ones that play a role in the distinctive "mode of perception" supposedly generated by urban modernity. Are the perceptual processes that are subject to neuroplasticity the same ones that are activated by immersion in the metropolis? And is the urban environment, or the sensations and actions triggered by it, actually powerful and consistent enough to generate significant neural plasticity? These remain open questions. Research into the conditions and effects of neural plasticity is still in its infancy, but it holds promise for cultural historians interested in the perceptual consequences of the lived environment.

* * *

A second conceptualization of a modern perceptual mode is perhaps the most straightforward. It does not presuppose any alteration of the sensory apparatus. Rather, it simply suggests that the normal apparatus, or certain aspects of it, were activated much more extensively in the environment of urban modernity. The new "mode" describes a qualitative, not a structural, change in perception. To speak of a new mode of perception is to underscore its new subjective texture. For example, it is safe to assume that a key qualitative modification of perception caused by metropolitan experience would involve patterns of eye movement as the individual faces diverse stimuli. Simmel noted that urban vision was distinguished by "the rapid crowding of changing images, the sharp discontinuity in the grasp of a single glance, and the unexpectedness of onrushing impression."[20] Although I have not found any empirical studies of eye movement in complex real-world environments, one can assess Simmel's description by monitoring personal experience. Recently, I made a summertime day-trip to downtown Boston—an environment very different from my relatively calm home in Northampton, where much of my time, during the summer break at least, is spent in low-stimulus environments (at my computer, in my backyard, on a deserted college campus, cleaning my dogs' ears, etc.). As I walked along one of the busiest commercial streets, which was typically noisy and crowded with shoppers, loitering teenagers, traffic, store displays, parked cars, lampposts, parking meters, and so on, it struck me that my perceptual encounter with the world around me did indeed feel markedly more fragmented, busy, and dispersed than normal. What I became most aware of was the increased activity of my eyes: the much greater frequency of saccades (rapid, jerky movements as the eyes jump from one point of fixation to another), the zigzag spatial discontinuity of the different points of fixation, and the relative prominence of abrupt, automatic, stimulus-driven saccades over those following more directed pathways of intentional visual search.

Although this erratic, haphazard, fleeting form of divided attention is no different from ordinary vision on a biological level, one could argue that it is qualitatively different enough to merit being called a distinct perceptual mode. Mode of perception, in this case, would be equivalent, simply, to perceptual experience. This formulation stresses that the qualities of perceptual activity can change significantly in accordance with the sensory environment. It is unclear to me how Bordwell addresses this version of the history-of-perception argument. Is this what he has in mind when he writes, "If such terms [as "mode of perception"] are shorthand for 'thought' or 'experience,' the position becomes vague, if not commonplace"? If so, it is unfortunate, since the idea requires careful evaluation, not an out-of-hand dismissal. Alternatively, perhaps Bordwell sees this pattern of vision as being subsumed under the "habits-and-skills" interpretation he proposes (which I am about to discuss). A third possibility is that he simply sidesteps the most elementary conception of perceptual change.

* * *

Bordwell himself offers a third interpretation of the history-of-perception thesis. Perhaps what is really being pointed to when people talk about changes in the perceptual apparatus, he suggests, are historical changes in the habits and skills used to scan the world and process perceptual information into salient categories. While our hard-wiring may (or may not) remain unchanged, the things we are conditioned to pay attention to, the strategies we use in scrutinizing those things, and the sense we make of them, can and do change as we adapt to different environments. Bordwell writes, "Since [the Lamarckian explanation] is highly implausible, should we not rather speak of changes in *habits and skills*, of cognitively monitored ways of noticing or contextualizing information available in new surroundings?"

This reframing seems fair enough. Someone crossing a road in New Amsterdam in 1650 might be inclined to stroll across casually, eyes cast downward watching for mud puddles and chamber-pot slops, on the subliminal assumption that any horse-drawn carriage traveling along the road would move too slowly to pose much of a threat, or would be noisy enough to announce its presence well before the possibility of a collision. Someone crossing the same street in Manhattan in 2000, however, might automatically look left, then glance right, then quickly left again, and only then venture off the sidewalk, with eyes and ears still on high alert for speeding taxis and silent-but-deadly bicycle messengers. The two pedestrians share the same biological capacity to acquire, process, and react to sensory information about the world. The only difference is that the particular information they receive about their environments prompt appropriately different actions.

Bordwell's position is basically the same as one articulated in 1928 by Nels Anderson and Eduard Lindeman, two New York–based sociologists, in a discussion of "the city as dynamic stimulus":

A change in human nature is essentially a change in behavior, attitudes, or in the operation or form of human institutions—a cultural as distinguished from a biological modification. To use specific sociological terms, it is an accommodation rather than an adaptation, the [latter] word used to describe change in the biological or physical realm. Biologically, man changes slowly, if at all, but the environment is always changing, and he is forced to make some adjustment to it, to re-orient himself—usually a cultural or behavior change. The rate of change in the environment is often very great and obviously greater than that for organisms. . . . As a setting

in which human organisms live, the city makes . . . demands which com-
bine to form a stimulating environment to which man can adjust himself
only by learning new modes of behavior.[21]

Among the new modes of behavior the metropolis demands, Anderson
and Lindeman suggested, are "habits of urgency and speed," a general
"intensity of countenance and rapidity of pace," and increased tolerance
of being "physically impinged upon" by others. "The human organisms
which become adjusted to [the city's] demands, or that survive the best,
are those capable of responding in some organized fashion to the
increase in rapidity and intensity of stimuli."

This emphasis on acquired habits and skills offers an important
avenue of approach for analyzing how the perceptual apparatus might
operate differently in different cultural-historical contexts. Indeed, some
of Benjamin's observations about the effects of urban modernity fit very
well within this framework. Consider, for example, his remark that,
"Whereas Poe's passers-by cast glances in all directions which still
appeared to be aimless, today's pedestrians are obliged to do so in order
to keep abreast of traffic signals. Thus technology has subjected the
human sensorium to a complex kind of training." Benjamin describes a
heightened vigilance, alertness, and speediness necessary for "making
the light" and avoiding injury in modern traffic. The skills and/or habits
of walking quickly and "keeping one's eyes peeled" are more or less
intentional (even if not deliberately thoughtful) activities. Probably the
most plausible interpretation of Benjamin's reference to the complex
training of the sensorium is that he is stressing the degree to which sur-
vival in the metropolis requires behavioral adjustment and cognitive-
perceptual reorientation through acquired skills and habits guiding
interaction with the environment.

However, one need only take a look at another street-crossing comparison—the one depicted in fig. 3.14, "Broadway—Past and
Present"—to see that this recasting of the issue cannot encompass the
entire history-of-perception argument. While the skills-and-habits
approach is valuable, its main shortcoming is that it does not seem to
get at the heart of what Benjamin stressed about the *bodily*, visceral
experience of urban modernity—the shocks and nervous restlessness
triggered by audiovisual chaos and erratic, fleeting stimuli. What is
needed is a *physiological* formulation of the history-of-perception argument.

* * *

This fourth, physiological, version can draw upon a wealth of data amassed by experimental psychologists in the fields of "environmental psychology" and "sociophysiology" concerning the subjective effects of urban life, sensory overstimulation, overcrowding, navigating traffic, living next to airports, working on speeded-up assembly lines, and similar mostly aversive environmental stimuli. Stressful experiences of this sort activate an array of neurophysiological events mediating arousal and alertness. More specifically, when the brain perceives a threatening stimulus, it activates the autonomic nervous system (particularly the "sympathetic" or excitatory part of the system), which signals the adrenal and other endocrine glands to start secreting epinephrine (adrenalin), norepinephrine, cortisol, and other hormones that then trigger a second wave of responses. Breathing rate increases. The heart pumps faster and more forcefully, increasing cardiovascular output to five times that of the heart during rest. Blood vessels constrict, narrowing the channel to increase blood pressure. Blood is shunted away from the digestive tract, kidneys, and skin (hence the blanching associated with shock or fear) in order to increase the volume of blood reaching parts of the body more crucial for dealing with emergencies: the muscles, lungs, and brain. The lungs increase capacity. Muscle tension increases. The pupils dilate. Perspiration increases, and hence so does the skin's electrical conductivity (a standard measurement of stress level). The mouth, nose, and eyes become dry as apocrine glands decrease their secretion of saliva, mucus, and tears. Gastrointestinal motility becomes irregular. The metabolism speeds up to about twice the normal rate in order to rush glucose and other energy-giving nutrients into the bloodstream. Insulin is blocked, stopping the storage of nutrients in fat cells. Mentation and alertness increase, as revealed by brain waves measured by electroencephalograph (EEG).[22]

The visceral sensations caused by some or all of this series of physiological events are what we subjectively experience as jumpiness, nervousness, shock, fright, suspense, excitement, thrill, and feelings of that sort. Although the term *stress response* entered common usage after 1950, following an influential work by Hans Selye, physiological research on stress can be regarded as another "invention" of fin-de-siècle modernity. Adrenalin and its excitatory hormonal effects were discovered in 1898 and confirmed by two scientists in 1910. After a series of animal experiments between 1910 and 1914 (for example, what happens, neurologically, when you put a barking dog next to a constrained cat?), Walter B.

Cannon introduced the now familiar concept of a "fight or flight" reflex.[23]

When Benjamin talked about "profound changes in the perceptual apparatus" and "nervous impulses flow[ing] through [the body] in rapid succession, like the energy from a battery," it seems likely that he was referring to neurophysiological events associated with the stress response. This response involves a great deal more than simply adjustment in habits and skills, and there is no suggestion of any sort of sudden change in hard-wiring. What changes, rather, are the kinds of charges that the hard-wiring carries. For Benjamin and others, it is legitimate to talk about perception having a cultural history since in urban modernity the texture of subjective experience undergoes a transformation (as also noted in the second version of the argument), and this transformation is in part a physiological one. Benjamin's premise is that an appreciably greater occurrence of nervous "fight or flight" sensations marked modernity as an era of relative visceral disequilibrium. No one would go so far as to claim that perceptual life in the capitalist metropolis contained nothing but shocks and jolts and sensory overload (there were slow times of day, empty side streets, and dull suburbs then as now), or deny that premodern society occasionally involved a high degree of environmental stimulation (festivals, fairs, marketplaces, etc.), but overall, in modernity the individual faced a more hectic, intense, and unpredictable array of audiovisual and social stimuli than ever before, and the consequences reverberated throughout the mind and body.

A potential pitfall in this physiological interpretation is that "stress" strikes one as a harsh word, seemingly too aversive and extreme to cover much of what recent scholars have highlighted regarding the sensory experience of modernity. What about the flaneur strolling voyeuristically through the arcade, or the distracted pleasure-seeker at the glitzy picture palace? Gunning's discussion of the proliferation of attractions in the modern milieu lays particular emphasis on "a new culture of consumption which arouses desire through an aggressive visuality": "Besides the arcades themselves, attractions appear in the other devices of display thrown up by the developing consumer culture. World fairs, the department store (and its shop windows), the billboard, and the amusement park all exploited visual attractions, creating the context in which early cinema shaped itself."[24] While all these forms of spectacle emphasized "aggressive," attention-grabbing display, the goal, after all, was to evoke curiosity, pleasure, and desire, not to punish people with nervous shocks and stress responses. The stress-response interpretation may relate to the noxious dimensions of the modern environment, but can it cover the alluring ones?

This is less of a problem than it first appears, since it is largely a semantic issue. Medical research, and popularizations of it, naturally focus on the injurious aspects of stress. Consequently, "stress" has come to be equated with "distress." But that conflation is misleading, since the physiological phenomena comprising the stress response are not at all specific to aversive stimuli. From a physiological perspective, all forms of sensory excitation—both unpleasant or pleasant, shocking or inviting, fear-inducing or curiosity-inducing—are essentially the same: they trigger the same series of bodily reactions described above: hormonal secretion, increased cardiovascular and respiration rates, pupillary dilation, changes in brain-wave patterns and galvanic skin resistance, and so forth. Attraction and aversion occupy opposite ends of the affective continuum, but otherwise they are not opposites at all: they are two versions of the same physiological condition. Another way of stating it is that both distress and "eustress" are forms of arousal. "Arousal" has positive connotations that mirror the negative ones of "stress." Both are forms of pronounced psychophysiological excitation. Lennart Levi, a Swedish researcher who compared adrenalin secretion triggered by pleasant and unpleasant stimuli, conveys this bi-hedonic model of stress with an inverted-U diagram (fig. 4.1).[25]

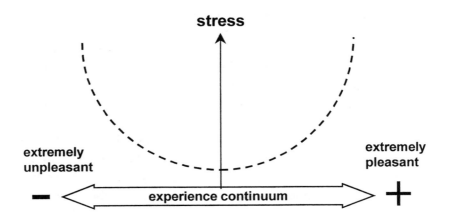

Fig. 4.1 Physiological Response: Pleasant and Unpleasant Experience (adapted from Levi 1972; see also note 26, this chapter).

The physiological version of the history-of-perception argument posits that the rise of urban modernity nudged experience upward along both sides of the curve. Modernity multiplied and intensified both pleasant and unpleasant forms of arousal. Even relatively ubiquitous and routine urban stimuli would have had distinct excitatory physiological effects. This was discovered in two different research traditions. In the Soviet Union, Pavlov's successors analyzed the physiological signature of the "orienting reflex," also called the "orientation reaction" or "what-is-it? reflex" (i.e., the body's automatic call-to-attention/alertness upon sensing a novel stimulus).[26] In America the "new experimental aesthetics" of the 1960s spearheaded by D. E. Berlyne analyzed increases in electrodermal and electroencephalographic activity caused by looking at pictures with high degrees of complexity, incongruity, novelty, surprisingness, size, or brightness.[27]

* * *

At one point in his critique of the modernity thesis, Bordwell seems as if he might even be receptive to a physiological formulation of the history-of-perception thesis. He writes:

The history-of-vision proponent may reply [in response to the Lamarckian objection] that biological evolution is irrelevant to claims about the new modes of perception in modernity. I am not so sure. . . . The point of departure for many of these theorists—the confusion a person feels when adrift in the modern city—does seem phenomenologically convincing. If you come from a small town, a day in Times Square or Piccadilly Circus can leave you with a feeling of sensory overload. But we might hypothesize that this confusion has an evolutionary explanation. Over several million years, humans evolved in a savanna environment, with its open spaces, unobstructed views of danger and shelter, and the possibility of easily retreating some distance from other humans. We have not had sufficient time to adapt (in the strong, biological sense) to the challenges of life in any city, ancient, medieval, or modern. The densely packed industrial city, as an environment for which we were not made, should seem particularly threatening. An explanation along these lines would treat the perceptual skills that help us cope with this environment as acquired through experience, with all the ephemerality and all the variations among individuals that any such learned skills display.[28]

Although I find Bordwell's lead-in to this discussion dubious,[29] there seems to be at least one important point of agreement. Bordwell finds "phenomenologically convincing" the notion that urban modernity may be associated with feelings of sensory overload and distraction. Bordwell accepts as a real phenomenon the "Uncle Josh" or "Rube" reaction portrayed in myriad cartoons, vaudeville acts, and early films around the turn of the century, and in this 1896 description:

Observe the confusing and almost stupefying effect on the inhabitant of the way-back rural district when he visits the city for the first time. He is the butt of every joke, not necessarily because he has a faulty sensorium (in this respect he may be, and often is, far better off than those who laugh at him); his trouble is that he has no skill in selecting and discarding among the million sights and sounds that rush in upon his consciousness.[30]

Like this writer, Bordwell approaches sensory overload as a challenge to be dealt with through adjustment in habits and skills. To paraphrase this line of reasoning: if humans have not yet adapted (in the strong, biological sense) to the metropolitan environment, then there is all the more impetus for us to learn to adapt to city life (in the narrower sense) by acquiring perceptual skills that help us cope with the new environment. This is quite true, and I would not wish to contradict it. However, it is important not to ignore what would seem to be an obvious question raised by the phenomenon of sensory overload: what does the experience involve on a physical level? Sidestepping the bodily experience of sensory arousal and focusing only on changes in habits and skills neglect an important aspect of perceptual transformation brought on by urban modernity.

One reason Bordwell places emphasis on a habits-and-skills version of the history-of-perception thesis (aside from the fact that it serves as a viable alternative to an untenable quasi-Lamarckian position) is because that version appears (at first glance, at least) to weaken the modernity thesis's contention that the experience of urban modernity was so powerful and pervasive that it actually had an impact on cinema. If many people learned how to cope with urban stimuli by acquiring certain strategies for dealing with complex environments, then the metropolis must not have been all that overwhelming, after all. According to this line of thought, the city would not perennially have been perceived as chaotic, stressful, and distracting because people—eventually even Uncle Josh—simply got used to it; they habituated. Of course, some people might have learned the relevant coping skills better than others, but that variation among individuals simply reinforces the fact that urban modernity was not a force pervasive and decisive enough to have a significant impact on cultural expressions like cinema.

While I definitely endorse the habits-and-skills interpretation, I do not think that in and of itself it is able to provide an adequate account of the experiential consequences of urban modernity. Nor do I see it as contradicting the modernity thesis. There is no question that some degree of adaptation and habituation helped people cope with the urban environment, but it is unclear just how much, since many urban stimuli, by their very nature, seem to preclude complete habituation. For example, as Ludwig Weber noted in 1918:

Noise is a problem, particularly in the metropolis, because sounds constantly vary so that there is no chance to adapt to them. It is sometimes pointed out that even outside the metropolis a lot of people lead long and healthy lives even though they live in environments filled with sounds and noise, for example, the miller and similar professions. But in those cases one is dealing mostly with steady, monotonous sounds that are easy to get used to. The difference with urban noise is the constant change, the sudden and unpredictable startling effect of always-different sounds.[31]

To be sure, city dwellers may become less sensitive to noise, but only to a certain extent (and perhaps not very much at all).[32] The basic aversive qualities of environmental stressors prevent full habituation. It is very difficult to habituate to a car alarm or honking horn, to people talking next to you, or to the muffled rap music issuing from personal headphones across the aisle from you on a bus. Stress researchers have isolated three variables determining the likelihood that a given environmental stimulus will generate stress: its predictability, its controllability, and (where applicable) its spatial clarity. While personality dispositions, past experience, and life-cycle stage influence how unwanted stimuli are appraised by individuals (different people have different tolerances), in general, stimuli that are unexpected, not controllable, and confusing or chaotic are likely to cause stress.[33] Needless to say, urban life multiplies just such stimuli.

Supposing, however, that we accept the fact (and it is indeed a fact) that city dwellers do develop some very effective adaptations, habits, and skills to help them cope with the complex urban environment. Does this fact weaken the modernity thesis? The argument would be that it is implausible to regard the sensory intensity, shock, and fragmentation of urban modernity as a significant influence on cinema if coping mechanisms served to mitigate those qualities in the perceptions of habituated urbanites. If people adapted and habituated to the sensory busyness of city life, and if the city was therefore not really perceived as a hothouse of shock and sensory overload, then it is problematic to assert that cinema grew out of the urban experience of shock and sensory overload. The point is well taken, but it overlooks the fact that it was precisely those adaptations to city life, those new habits of mind, which Anderson and Lindeman described as "habits of urgency and speed" and an "intensity of countenance and rapidity of pace" that could be expected to exert an influence on, or generate a preference for, stimulating entertainments like cinema. Adaptation to the tempos and intensities of urban life would have been more likely to enhance, rather than diminish, the qualities of urban experience encouraging cinematic dynamism.

* * *

Thus far, I primarily have been defending the first pillar of the modernity thesis: the premise that urban modernity brought about tangible changes in perception. But that is just half the problem. Supposing, for the sake of argument, we accept the first premise; we now face a second hurdle. The pressing question is, did the putative perceptual changes really affect the movies, and if so, how? It is generally taken for granted that cultural expressions reflect their social context, but this correlation is much trickier when what is at issue are formal-stylistic properties of artworks rather than social ideologies and topical allusions contained within artworks. How is it that an urban environment characterized by complexity, speed, fragmentation, and abruptness should foster amusements possessing similar qualities?

The first point to be made in addressing this question, which I state not as an excuse but as a basic fact of academic inquiry, is that it is not imperative that we fully understand the mechanisms at work in order to justify arguing the modernity thesis. The connections between a society and its cultural-aesthetic expressions are extraordinarily complex and elusive. Inability to pin them all down need not preclude observation of what appear to be significant correlations between the social and artistic spheres, or in this case, between the history of sensation and the history of commercial sensationalism. That said, let us consider some hypotheses—in particular, those made by the first generation of modernity theorists. Kracauer, Benjamin, and their predecessors sketched out several psychosocial mechanisms to explain the relationships between the experience of urban modernity and the sensory texture of modern amusement.

The basic hypothesis involves the notion of a general reconditioning or recalibration of the individual's perceptual capacities and proclivities to correspond to the greater intensity and rapidity of stimuli. Both the physiological and cognitive/behavioral changes discussed above presumably contributed to this synchronization, in which the senses shifted into a higher gear of nervous arousal to keep pace with the geared-up world. Whatever the underlying conditioning process may have been, the key point is that the modern individual somehow internalized the tempos, shocks, and upheavals of the outside environment, and this generated a taste for hyperkinetic amusements. As Simmel noted:

The psychological foundation of the metropolitan personality type is the intensification of nervous stimulation, which results from the rapid and ceaseless change of outer and inner stimuli. . . . A secret restlessness [and] helpless urgency . . . originates in the bustle and excitement of modern life. . . . There emerges today the craving for excitement, for extreme impressions, for the greatest speed in its change.[34]

In 1912 Howard Woolston also stressed the connection between modern environmental stimulation and the appetite for "powerful shocks," and he made the connection to popular amusements even more overt:

Urban life is marked by its heightened stimulation. . . . Such excitement deeply stirs the nervous system. The natural result of city life is increased nervousness. The restless current in which men are immersed produces individuals who are alert, active, quick to seek new satisfactions. The recreation of city dwellers is perhaps as true an index of their characteristic reactions as can be found. The most popular amusement of large towns today is furnished by saloons, dance halls, variety theaters, and moving picture shows. Coney Island, with its "chutes" and "bumps," "loops of death" and "circular swings," "ticklers," peep shows, bars, and assorted gastronomic marvels, is a favorite resort for thousands of young New Yorkers. There is "something doing every minute."[35]

This argument—that stimulating amusements corresponded to the perceptual conditioning of modern life—is what Benjamin alluded to when he maintained that film, conceived of as a medium of shocks, emerged to meet "a new and urgent need for stimuli."[36]

Such assertions are, of course, only anecdotal, and it is hard to imagine what sorts of empirical studies would confirm or disconfirm them, but one small ethological study from the late 1960s is at least suggestive. A scientist from the Primate Research Center of the University of Wisconsin, Madison (not to be confused with the Department of Communication Arts), studied two groups of rhesus monkeys, one group captured from natural-habitat jungle areas and the other procured from busy urban bazaars in India. The urban environment was assumed to be more highly stimulating, with more opportunities for varied perceptual and motor experiences. The monkeys were compared for visual curiosity responses to stimulus displays of varying complexity (eight simple gray cubes on a black wood board; a battery of eight empty rat cages; and a toy train with some colored toys moving on a circular track three feet in diameter). The study found that the urban monkeys spent considerably more time looking at the complex displays. Earlier studies found a similar difference with respect to manipulatory and exploratory responses to novel objects. The researcher concluded that the findings supported the hypothesis that, "The manipulatory, exploratory, or curiosity behavior of an individual is to a great extent determined by the complexity level of the individual and of the stimulus situation confronted; an individual with greater perceptual and motor experiences is supposed to interact maximally with stimuli of higher complexity values."[37] The study supports the notion that the urban environment brought about perceptual changes that attuned the individual toward complex stimuli.

A number of writers expanded on this argument by noting a paradox. The "craving for excitement" may have reflected the cranked-up cadence of modern conditioning, but at the same time, it could be interpreted as a symptom of sensory burnout caused by too much stimulation. According to Simmel, the two conditions were intertwined in modern society: "There exists a deep inner connection between too close a captivation with things and too great a distance from them which, with a kind of fear of contact, places us in a vacuum. We knew for a long time that we were suffering equally from both of them."[38] As a host of physicians specializing in neurasthenia (or "modern nervousness") insisted, excessive sensory stimulus eventually exhausted and incapacitated the sensory apparatus. The idea was that human nerves were subject to physical wear and tear, becoming weaker, duller, and progressively less responsive when exposed to too many stimuli. Max Nordau's assessment of the injurious effects of the complexity of modern life typified the common view. After inventorying the escalation of mobility and social circulation (as cited in chapter 1), he asserted:

All these activities, even the simplest, involve an effort of the nervous system and a wearing of tissue. Every line we read or write, every human face we see, every conversation we carry on, every scene we perceive through the window of the flying express, sets in activity our sensory nerves and our brain centers. Even the little shocks of railway travelling, not perceived by consciousness, the perpetual noises, and the various sights in the streets of a large town . . . cost our brains wear and tear. . . . Fatigue and exhaustion . . . are the effect of contemporary civilization, of the vertigo and whirl of our frenzied life, the vastly increased number of sense impressions and organic reactions, and therefore of perceptions, judgments and motor impulses . . . forced into a given unit of time.

One result of sensory stress and exhaustion, Nordau contended, was a tendency to "crave for stimulus, for a momentary artificial invigoration, or an alleviation of painful excitability."[39] Simmel articulated a very similar argument. "Over-excited and exhausted nerves," he asserted, led to deadened sensation, a condition he referred to as the "blasé" or "jaded" attitude:

The blasé attitude results first from the rapidly changing and closely compressed contrasting stimulations of the nerves. . . . [Such stimulation] agitates the nerves to their strongest reactivity for such a long time that they finally cease to react at all. . . . Through the rapidity and contradictoriness of their changes, harmless impressions force such violent responses, tearing the nerves so brutally hither and thither that their last reserves of strength are spent; and if one remains in the same milieu they have no time to gather new strength. An incapacity thus emerges to react to new sensations with the appropriate energy. . . . The essence of the blasé attitude consists in the blunting of discrimination. This does not mean that the objects are not perceived, but rather that the meaning and differing values of things, and thereby the things themselves, are experienced as insubstantial. They appear to the blasé person in an evenly flat and gray tone; no one object deserves preference over any other. [See fig. 4.2] [40]

This rhetoric may strike contemporary readers as quaint hypochondria, but the general idea was borne out by stress research beginning a half century later. As Hans Selye, the founder of modern research into stress, stated in 1950: "Even a fully inured organism cannot indefinitely main-

Fig. 4.2 "Picturesque America." (*Life*, June 25, 1908)

tain its adaptation when continuously exposed to a potent systemic stressor agent. . . . The adaptability or 'adaptive energy' of the organism is eventually exhausted. The time at which this breakdown of adaptation occurs is usually referred to as the 'stage of exhaustion.' "[41]

Sensory exhaustion led to escalating sensationalism, the argument claimed, since stronger and stronger audiovisual impacts were needed simply to break through the blunted sensorium. In popular amusements, the demand for thrills escalated as blasé perception required increasingly intense impressions. Woolston summed up the idea concisely; after listing an array of popular recreations (quoted above), he concluded, "All these have a tendency to stimulate a jaded attention by a succession of brief, powerful shocks that arouse the tired organism to renewed activity."[42] Burton Rascoe, writing in 1921, also implicated cinema within this syndrome of deadened sensation and ever-more-powerful countermeasures:

The modern man's sensitivity . . . is blunted by the excessive . . . appeal to sight . . . and noises which assail his ears. . . . The net result of these terrific drains upon the senses and upon the vital energy necessary to resist these drains [is] . . . an unresponsiveness to any visual or aural impressions which are not violent, badly organized, and sensational. The movies are merely contribution to the mass effect of conditions which tend towards either the nervous derangement of the modern American or to his complete imperviousness to anything which is fine, delicately organized, poised, and harmonious.[43]

Often this hypothesis was supplemented with a slightly different characterization of the blasé attitude. Blunted sensation may have stemmed in part from organic fatigue—an inability to muster adequate reaction—but it also reflected the organism's attempt to protect itself by filtering out extreme stimuli. As Simmel stated, "The metropolitan type of man . . . develops an organ protecting him against the threatening currents and discrepancies of his external environment which would uproot him."[44] As Rascoe similarly suggested, "His sensitivity to sound is blunted by . . . the protective mechanism of the body [which] tends to make him impervious to the less distracting of these noises. Otherwise, he would go to pieces under the extraordinary demands made upon his nervous system."[45] Pitirim Sorokin wrote in the same vein in 1927:

A trait of contemporary Western psychology . . . is an increase in the insensitiveness of our nervous system. Our nervous system [would] be wrecked completely if it were sensitive to all the innumerable phenomena which surround us in our permanent mobility. It could not have stood physiologically if it did not develop an insensitiveness toward many stimuli. They are so numerous and so changeable that it is a matter of necessity to be

insensitive in regard to many of them. . . . Our nervous system, for the
sake of its preservation, has become thicker or less sensitive.

Following the familiar inflationary logic, and anticipating Benjamin's reference to "a new and urgent need for stimuli," Sorokin blamed this protective insensitivity for producing "the necessity of sensations."[46]

Benjamin also explored a somewhat different conception of self-protection from shocks. He drew upon a theory laid out by Freud in "Beyond the Pleasure Principle" concerning the function of anxiety as an adaptive defense against traumatic shock. Studying victims of shell shock from World War I, Freud observed that a severe traumatic breakdown occurred only among soldiers for whom the frightful event was totally unexpected. Those who, on the other hand, had anxiously prepared for the shock by fixating on it, by mentally rehearsing it over and over again, or, in other words, by getting used to it in small, controlled doses, did not suffer major breakdowns. In this context, Freud believed, anxiety was self-protective, since the individual could defend himself against the traumatizing potential of shock. "The more readily consciousness registers shocks," he wrote, "the less likely they are to have a traumatic effect. . . . The ego subjects itself to anxiety as a sort of inoculation, submitting to a slight attack of the illness in order to escape its full strength."[47] Benjamin applied this hypothesis to the film experience: the shocks of the film functioned as a kind of preparation or immunization against the shocks of the modern environment.

The acceptance of shocks is facilitated by training in coping with stimuli. .
. . The film is the art form that is in keeping with the increased threat to
his life which modern man has to face. Man's need to expose himself to
shock effects is his adjustment to the dangers threatening him. . . . Film
serves to train people in those sorts of perceptions and reactions which are
necessary for any interaction with [technological] apparatuses—apparatuses
es whose role in the lives of such people are increasing almost daily.[48]

The spectator's sensory interaction with the rapidly changing film image, Benjamin hypothesized, improved the capacity to cope with the rapid stimuli of the modern world. It provided a sort of sensory calisthenics in a controlled setting in which the individual would be primed and ready for stimulation.

Although Benjamin did not discuss it, one could extend the hypothesis by suggesting that the cinema offered an environment in which crowds could congregate in a highly structured context. As I mentioned earlier, three factors most crucial in turning potential stressors into actual stressors are predictability, controllability, and spatial clarity. If, on the spectrum of crowd formations, the mob lies at one end—since mobs are, by definition, uncontrollable, unpredictable, and spatially chaotic—the audience lies at the other. Audiences are crowds that have been tamed by established rules of behavior, clear territorial definitions of personal space, and unified attentional focus. According to Benjamin's logic, the audience experience might help individuals cope with crowds falling elsewhere on the spectrum, just as exposure to film's audiovisual intensity and discontinuity helped them cope with other shocks of the metropolis.

A final idea explaining the connection between urban modernity and cinema held that sensationalism functioned as a compensatory response to the impoverishment of experience in modernity. Distractions and thrills offered a momentary escape from the anxious and meaningless hustle and tedium of alienated labor in the modern factory and bureaucratized office. As Kracauer wrote, "The tension to which the working masses are subjected is . . . greater and more tangible [than in the provinces]—an essentially formal tension which fills their day fully without making it fulfilling. Such a lack demands to be compensated."[49] Simmel had made a similar argument as early as 1896. In an essay on the Berlin Trade Exhibition, he observed, "It seems as if the modern person wishes to compensate for the one-sidedness and uniformity of what they produce within the division of labor by the increasing crowding together of heterogeneous impressions, by the increasingly hasty and colorful change in emotions."[50] Kracauer's debt to Simmel (and to a broader discourse) is evident here, but Kracauer was more sensitive to the argument's inherent irony. The compensatory thrills of popular amusements reproduced the very register of hyperstimulus that vitiated modern experience to begin. Alienated labor and urban experience "demands to be compensated," Kracauer stated, "but this need can only be articulated in terms of the same surface sphere which imposed the lack in the first place. . . . The form of entertainment necessarily corresponds to that of enterprise."[51] Ludwig Weber had made the same point in 1918:

The increase of stimuli in the metropolis, . . . the restlessness of modern life which forces one to continually hurry [and face] obvious competition that intensifies . . . responsibility, tension and worry . . . creates constantly new and grotesque forms of pleasure. . . . Only the steady increase of stimuli guarantees the longed-for pleasure or the temporary release from the tensions and worries. "Theater, concerts, even gambling and excess should do away with the lively impressions caused by the responsibilities of business, which stick in the mind, and should bring rest, but instead bring just new excitations."[52]

Pirandello's 1915 protagonist captured perhaps most vividly the irony that popular sensationalism both compensated for and, at the same time, mimicked the disjointed texture of modern life:

The rest that is given us, after all the clamor and dizziness, is so wearying, so stunning and deafening, that it is no longer possible for us to snatch a moment for thought. With one hand we hold our heads, with the other we wave in a drunken sweep: "Let us have a little amusement!" Yes. More wearying and complicated than our work do we find the amusements that are offered us.[53]

The compensation hypothesis presumably loops back into the blasé attitude–sensory exhaustion hypothesis: sensational amusement is just one more ingredient contributing to the inflationary curve of strong sensation.

* * *

These first-generation hypotheses attempting to explain why cinema should have reflected urban modernity are far from being problem-free, and there is much work to be done to assess their viability or to explore other hypotheses altogether. I will defer that work and instead turn to an issue that could short-circuit the entire enterprise. All of the hypotheses become irrelevant if film style did not in fact reflect modernity after all, or if the putative formal-stylistic congruence between movies and modernity was extremely uneven, closer at some points than at others without any corresponding change in the conditions of modernity.

Critics of the modernity thesis, especially Bordwell and Charlie Keil, object that the argument is much too blunt-edged to yield any useful insights into the actual aesthetic development of film. Their criticism is partly an expression of disappointment about the general direction the modernity thesis tends to steer historical work on early cinema—away from highly nuanced formal-stylistic analysis and toward broader generalizations about the medium (supposedly attractive to scholars who do not have the stomach for painstaking early-cinema research, but who see a Culturalist popularization of it as promising a new Grand Theory to cling to after the implosion of subject-position theory left them stranded).[54] The basic objection, however, hinges on a logical question: if a particular mode of perception supposedly dominated fin-de-siècle modernity, and it supposedly expressed itself in the artistic sphere through stylistic elements that replicated the qualities of urban abruptness and fragmentation, how does one explain the fact that films exhibited such stylistic variation? The abruptness of editing is often cited as a basis for cinema's perceptual modernity, but many early films had relatively little editing, or none at all. The problem does not go away if one instead cites "attractions" ("small doses of scopic pleasure adapted to the nervous rhythm of modern urban reality")[55] as the key stylistic marker of perceptual modernity. Some films contained strong attractions, others did not. And if the "cinema of attractions" was gradually superseded, or forced "underground," by the rise of classical narration beginning around 1907, are we to assume, following the thesis's logic of cultural reflection, that urban modernity underwent a corresponding transformation? Given that the experiential texture of modernity was, for all intents and purposes, the same in the first and the second decades of the twentieth century, how does one explain the fact that films from the two decades differed so much? Indeed, the key element that changes in the second decade—the emergence of narrative and of editing conventions designed to make visual stories engrossing and easy to follow—might be viewed as running counter to the modernity thesis's emphasis on cinematic shock, astonishment, and discontinuity.

These are important questions, expressing precisely the kind of skepticism that Big Ideas like the modernity thesis need to face. However, in their attempt to highlight causal inconsistencies in the modernity thesis, these critics ascribe to the modernity thesis—and themselves seem to embrace—a very naive conception of historical determinism in which a phenomenon (cinema) can have only one source or influence (modernity) which can only claim validity if it can be shown to hold sway in any and all instances. No proponents of the modernity thesis purport to isolate the *only* historical force governing cinema. It goes without saying that a great many forces shape cultural artifacts like cinema (although, to be fair, the criticism is not undeserved, given that articulations of the thesis generally have made little effort to include such qualifications, or acknowledge potential counter-arguments or alternative explanations). Movies were responsive to developments in cinematographic technology, stylistic and generic cycles, industry practices, shifts in cinema's social functions, and so on.[56] All the modernity thesis aims to do is to add "environmental context" or "sensory experience" to that list. If some films do not fit well with the modernity thesis (for example, a slow film with minimal editing, simple scenery, and subdued acting), we can assume it is because other determinants took precedence. There is little point in speculating on relative degrees of influence among all the determinants (assuming we can even identify them), but it is fair to say that proponents of the modernity thesis think it is worthwhile to explore the possibility that the emergence of urban modernity—arguably the most momentous social transformation in human history—had some degree of impact on an art form that developed within that context (while, at the same time, documenting the extent to which writers in that period gravitated toward the same hypothesis).

Charlie Keil warns that "certain tendencies within the modernity thesis risk sacrificing the fine-grained sense of historical change early cinema study has been cultivating over the past fifteen years." There may be some validity to this concern, but ultimately I think it is a false alarm, since there is nothing inherent in the modernity thesis that should dissuade scholars from pursuing close-analysis histories of film style, and there is every reason to think that such a valuable research program will continue to thrive. The modernity thesis enhances rather than competes with close-analysis approaches. As Bordwell and Keil stress, however, the two do not always jibe. When that happens, we should not automatically assume that nimble close analysis automatically discredits the lumbering generalizations of the modernity thesis. Sometimes a "fine-grained sense of historical change" can miss the bigger picture. For example, a central argument in both Bordwell and Keil's critiques concerns the transition from the cinema of attractions to classical narrative cinema. Keil writes:

The conceptual terms of the modernity thesis fail to adequately accommodate the changes early cinema undergoes during the transitional period. . . . The transitional period ushers in modified formal operations . . . designed to facilitate audience comprehension of increasingly complicated narratives, but surely they would mitigate the degree of perceptual shock associated with the cinema of attractions. Assuming the continued prevalence and

strongly determinant quality of modernity within the culture when cine-
ma makes its shift toward more conventional narrative modes, one is hard
pressed to understand how such a shift could occur.[57]

The problem with this argument, aside from the simplistic determinism mentioned above, is that it shackles the modernity thesis to the
most limited definition of the cinema of attractions (i.e., a specific period in early-cinema history, before around 1906, in which a presentational style prevailed) and establishes a false dichotomy between attractions (defined more broadly as any element prompting sensory excitation) and the cinema of narrative integration. To reiterate a point that
has been made innumerable times already, attractions were not rendered
extinct by the onset of narrative integration; rather, arousing spectacle
became an important component of narrative film. Moreover, there is
no reason to think that the emergence of "formal operations" designed
to improve narrative comprehension and effectiveness would have mit-
igated the impact of attractions. On the contrary, it is more likely that
classical narration amplified the stimulating capacity of attractions by
endowing them with strong dramatic and emotional significance. A
shot of a speeding locomotive may be arousing, but it is all the more so
if the locomotive is carrying the protagonist who is racing to stop the
villain from putting a ring on the finger of his childhood sweetheart and
ruining her life through a mock marriage. Moreover, classical editing
opened up a whole new dimension of visual rapidity and visceral excitation, as Griffith's race-to-the-rescue melodramas illustrate so well.[58]

Critics of the modernity thesis contend that it is disproved by either
(1) the fact that changes in film style did not necessarily reflect parallel
changes in the modern environment, or (2) the putative fact that the
transition to narrative cinema obviated comparisons between film and
urban modernity. Both of these arguments rely on an overly reductive
conception of the thesis. Neither is the modernity thesis monolithically
"grand" (it does not impose urban modernity as the only force shaping
cinema), nor is it rigidly localized (it need not be tethered to cinema's
first decade). The forms that attractions took changed and expanded
with the transition to the cinema of narrative integration, but the medium was no less likely to invite comparisons to urban modernity—in
fact, the large majority of early observations to that effect date from after
the transition.

* * *

I have presented in this chapter some of the original assertions of a link between movies and modernity, but I have no doubt that scholars have barely scratched the surface of this historical discourse. The assertions must be approached critically—not immediately taken at face value as faithful records of actual experience. They represent deliberate rhetorical postures toward modernity, not some sort of pure expression of its effects. More work needs to be done to interpret underlying motivations and implications. Nevertheless, the discourse did not arise magically out of nothing, emerging with no basis in actual perceptions of the modern state of affairs. We must acknowledge, and take seriously, the frequency with which early moviegoers (at least those who wrote about their experiences) described cinema as a medium of powerful fleeting impressions, kinetic speed, novel sights, superabundant juxtaposition, and visceral stimulation, and therefore as a medium in which people perceived a striking resemblance to modern urban experience.

As scholars continue thinking about these expressions, and about the modernity thesis in general, two branches of inquiry need to be pursued. The first, involving scientific and empirical analysis, asks: "Is it true? Did urban modernity really change modes of perception? And if so, were movies really influenced as a result?" This is the branch I have focused on here. I have made the case that the hypothesis of perceptual change is plausible, and that the arguments refuting the notion that modernity might have influenced film style are flawed. The second branch of inquiry, involving cultural history and discourse analysis, asks "What does it mean? Whether or not modernity really changed perception and influenced cinema, why were the themes of urban hyperstimulus and cinematic dynamism so prevalent? Why did early twentieth-century writers gravitate toward the modernity thesis, rather than socioeconomic explanations, in trying to understand the escalation of popular sensationalism? What social and psychological functions were served by the discourse on the sensory upheavals of urban modernity and their supposed reflection in cinema?" Perhaps the greatest challenge we face will be to understand how the phenomena revealed by these two branches of inquiry interrelate and inflect one another.

5

Melodrama and the
Consequences of Capitalism

M elodrama was, in a quite literal sense, a product of modernity. While its basic elements—moral dichotomy, violence, spectacle, "situation," pathos, etc.—are as old as theater itself, melodrama proper, melodrama specifically labeled as such and recognized as a codified set of structures and motifs, emerged almost precisely around 1800, appearing first in France and copied immediately in England, America, and elsewhere. The genre was already taking shape in the 1790s, in a spectacle bearing the oxymoronic label *pantomime dialoguée*, but 1800 is generally accepted as the beginning of the form because it was then that the term was first applied to a new type of thrilling popular drama, and also because a particularly important example—Guilbert de Pixerecourt's *Coeline ou l'Enfant du Mystère*—appeared in that year. *Coeline* was a tremendous commercial success, produced almost 1,500 times. Along with Thomas Holcroft's 1802 *A Tale of Mystery* (an equally successful British adaptation of Pixerecourt's play), it served as a template defining the genre.[1]

What was it about the beginning of the nineteenth century that fostered melodrama? One crucial causal factor is easy to identify. Melodrama coalesced in France at that time because only then was its existence legally permissible. Prior to 1791, theaters in France were under strict government regulations that prohibited dialogue in the dramatic productions of all but a handful of officially sanctioned theaters.[2] Popular theaters had to settle with pantomime shows built out of nonverbal elements: music, dance, gesture, costume, scenery, etc. Stories relied on spectatorial foreknowledge of current events and folk tales (a strategy also employed in early cinema), along with signs and banners (precursors of silent cinema's intertitles), which helped clarify basic information (although probably most spectators were illiterate).[3] The French Revolution transfigured the theatrical landscape. In January 1791 the bourgeois National Assembly did away with the old system of government regulation, legalizing dialogue in all theaters. With that gag removed, many producers began to integrate dialogue into the pantomimes they had been offering (hence the term *pantomime dialoguée*). This lineage helps account for melodrama's characteristic appeal to the eye and its emphasis on simple dramatic conflicts and stock characters.

Melodrama thrived in part because its ideological dynamics were so well suited to the period. The liberal-democratic ferment catalyzing the French Revolution and codified in "Declaration of the Rights of Man and of the Citizen" of 1789 encouraged dramatic scenarios affirming the new social principles.[4] By demonizing venal, abusive aristocrats, melodramas reflected the revolutionary shift in political and ideological power. It expressed, as Thomas Elsaesser has observed, "the struggle of a morally and emotionally emancipated bourgeois consciousness against the remnants of feudalism."[5] This formulation is complicated somewhat by the fact that the bourgeoisie traditionally has disdained melodrama as a product of lowbrow vulgarity. It would be more apt to say instead that melodrama manifested the powerful new *populist* consciousness. Melodrama was a cultural expression of the populist ideology of liberal democracy, even if the bourgeois champions of that ideology did not have populist aesthetic sensibilities.

To a certain extent, melodrama can be regarded as an index of actual popular empowerment after the French Revolution. Its psychosocial context was more complicated, however. For many people, the social upheavals of modernity—the erosion of traditional feudal and religious authority and the rise of modern capitalism—were more anxious, unsettling, and oppressive than they were empowering. Melodrama conveyed the stark insecurities of a modern life in which people found themselves "helpless and unfriended" in a postsacred, postfeudal, "disenchanted" world of moral ambiguity and material vulnerability. From this perspective, melodrama was less about an emergent liberal populism than about the anxieties of a society experiencing unprecedented moral, cultural, and socioeconomic disarray.

This view of melodrama as an expression of the instability and insecurity of the transition to modernity—and, correspondingly, as an expression of the need to "resolve" the disarray through a utopian myth of divine protection—has been developed by a number of scholars since about the late 1970s. Peter Brooks's *The Melodramatic Imagination* (1976) is most often cited, but it is important to acknowledge that Brooks's symptomatic reading of melodrama echoed and expanded on insights already articulated by Eric Bentley in 1964, Michael Booth in 1965, Robert Heilman in 1960 and 1968, David Grimsted in 1968 and 1971, and Thomas Elsaesser in 1972 (and later elaborated by Martha Vicinus, Laura Mulvey, Christine Gledhill, Judith Walkowitz, and others).[6] Indeed, as I will discuss shortly, the underlying conception of melodrama as a hunger for resacralization has been articulated with some frequency since at least the early years of the twentieth century.

Melodramatic conflicts gave dramatic shape to the adversities and insecurities of the modern world. Scenarios in which good people experience duress from forces beyond their control resonated with the urban masses. Poverty, class stratification and exploitation, job insecurity, workplace hazards, heartless contractual systems of housing and money-lending—these and similar components of the new capitalist social order, which represented such a striking contrast to the feudal gemeinschaft that had governed life for many centuries, played prominent roles in the narratives of classical melodrama. As Grimsted notes: "The worst clichés of melodrama in the late nineteenth century—the heroine tied to the railroad tracks or the family about to be tossed into the snow for lack of mortgage money—were telling symbols for the latent fears in a society characterized by rapid technological change and widespread home ownership on time payments."[7] Walkowitz similarly observes the social foundations of the insecurity conveyed in melodrama:

In both form and content, melodrama was an appropriate genre for working-class audiences, evoking the instability and vulnerability of their life in the unstable market culture of the early nineteenth century, where traditional patterns of deference and paternalism had been eroded. Below the surface order of reality lurked a terrible secret that could erupt unexpectedly with violence and irrationality. The melodramatic narrative acted arbi-

trarily in its very structure calling into question the operation of law and justice. Melodramatic plots overwhelmingly reinforced the sense of destiny out of control.[8]

A number of scholars have suggested that the anxiety of modernization derived not only from the basic mechanics of the capitalist system, symbolized by unemployment (for all intents and purposes, a modern phenomenon) and the possibility of being thrown out of one's home for nonpayment, but also, more generally, from what Lukács referred to as the "transcendental homelessness" of modernity. Modernity eroded the stability, certainty, and simplicity of traditional religious faith and patriarchal tradition. The emergence of melodrama was a symptom of this loss of social and psychological moorings. As Brooks writes:

Melodrama . . . appears to be a peculiarly modern form. . . . The origins of melodrama can be accurately located within the context of the French Revolution and its aftermath. This is the epistemological moment which it illustrates and to which it contributes: the moment that symbolically, and really, marks the final liquidation of the traditional Sacred and its representative institutions (Church and Monarch), the shattering of the myth of Christendom, the dissolution of an organic and hierarchically cohesive society. . . . It comes into being in a world where the traditional imperatives of truth and ethics have been violently thrown into question, yet where the promulgation of truth and ethics, their instauration [restoration] as a way of life, is of immediate, daily, political concern.[9]

By this interpretation, melodrama allegorized the modern situation in which the age-old safety nets of cosmic faith, feudal protection, and communal cohesion were fast falling apart.

Classical melodrama reacted to modernity in a somewhat paradoxical but nevertheless common psychological binary response. On the one hand, melodrama portrayed the individual's powerlessness within the harsh and unpredictable material life of modern capitalism; on the other, it served a quasi-religious ameliorative function in reassuring audiences that a higher cosmic moral force still looked down on the world and governed it with an ultimately just hand. As Brooks elaborates, "Melodrama starts from and expresses the anxiety brought by a frightening new world in which the traditional patterns of moral order no longer provide the necessary social glue. It plays out the force of that anxiety with the apparent triumph of villainy, and dissipates it with the eventual victory of virtue."[10] With its exaltation of virtue and ultimate poetic justice, melodrama offered a kind of compensatory faith that helped people cope with the vicissitudes of modern life.

This function of melodrama has long been recognized. As Clayton Hamilton noted in 1911:

Much of our life—in fact, by far the major share—is casual instead of causal. . . . Nearly all the good or ill that happens to us is drifted to us, uncommanded, undeserved, upon the tides of chance. It is this immutable truth—the persistency of chance in the serious concerns of life and the inevitable influence of accident on character—that melodrama aims to represent. . . . We derive a solid comfort from our certainty that the virtue of the heroine is inviolable. At every moment she is chaperoned by destiny. . . . Virginity is its own defense and virtue shields itself with spiritual armor. . . . Life as it exists is not so ordered. . . . We look about us and it seems that there is neither right nor reason in the inappealable decrees of destiny. But meanwhile the noble art of melodrama stands up scornful before many spears and confronts the iniquity of fate. . . . Melodrama answers one of the most profound of human needs: it ministers to that motive which philosophers term the will to believe. It looks at life—as Paul enjoined humanity to look at it—with faith and hope. So when the toilers in our sweatshops attend the ten, twenty, and thirty cent theatres, they escape into a region where faith is not an idle jest and hope is not an irony; and thereafter, when they reassume the heavy and the weary weight of all their unintelligible world, they may smile backward in remembrance of that momentary dream-world in which destiny was just and kind and good.[11]

An essayist writing in 1910 in the British journal *The Nation* pursued the analogy between melodrama and religion even more overtly:

There is a state of mind in which it is proper to visit a melodrama, as there is a state of mind in which it is proper to go to church. . . . On this stage nothing is in doubt. . . . You expect from the melodramatist a firm and unquestioning morality, a well-tried plot, an inevitable end. His message has the certainty of orthodox preaching. . . . The curtain is his surplice, the cheers of the gallery his ordination. He stands in an apostolic succession, and you may predict of him . . . that he will question none of the councils and prevaricate over none of the articles. In his pulpit there is no heresy. Virtue will always triumph. . . . You go to the solemn perform-

*ance not because you look for novelty, but because you are comfortably cer-
tain of its absence. It is a ritual, and you love it because it stirs in your
breast the older loyalties, the surer faiths of our race.*[12]

Rollin Lynde Hartt, writing in 1909, further underscored melodrama's
purpose to bolster faith in a stable moral order, an ideological bedrock
able to ward off the anxiety of "transcendental homelessness":

*[The melodrama audience] demands . . . an extreme simplicity and per-
spicuity of idea, a stripping of truth to the bone. I say truth advisedly.
However wild and unrepresentative the incident, and however crude the
depiction of character, the underlying notions must consist solely of plati-
tudes,—or, to put it more genially, of fundamental verities. . . . The glory
of melodrama is that it preaches nightly a gospel that gives the mere plati-
tudes of morals a glaring, thrilling intensity that finds the heart and sets it
leaping.*[13]

The main difference between these early versions of the idea and
those ventured more recently by Brooks and others is that the latter
stress a more specific historical symptomology. The contemporary spin
interprets the hunger for moral stability and intelligibility as a reflection
of a post-Enlightenment, postsacred, postfeudal world, or in short, a
reflection of modernity. This idea may have been implicit in the early
versions, but they were not so concerned to argue that melodrama
reflected the modern condition in particular. They implied a broader
human desire for the comforting myth of benign Providence, moral legibility, and poetic justice. The recent version, focusing on psychological
consequences of social change, may be more thought-provoking for
contemporary scholars, but given that people in all places, at all times,
undoubtedly have gained psychological comfort from the belief that
destiny rewards the virtuous and punishes the bad, the early version has
the advantage of being more sensitive to a wider, transhistorical dimension of melodramatic myth.

Melodrama's fusion of anxiety and wish-fulfillment is particularly
evident in the centrality of chance. Chance wreaks havoc on the lives of
the protagonists, accentuating their vulnerability within an unpredictable world. But, conventionally, it is also chance, rather than causal
action on the part of the protagonists, that brings about the villain's
demise and saves the day. The villain might be struck by a bolt of lightning, or fall into a grain silo, or be buried under an avalanche, or, as in

The Perils of Pauline, suddenly be killed by a disgruntled henchman without any dramatic preparation whatsoever. Through chance, bad things happen to bad people, and good things happen to good people. In the 1906 Vitagraph film *The 100 to One Shot; or, A Run of Luck*, for example, a poor family is being evicted from their farm because they have fallen behind on the rent. The son goes to the city, pawns his last possessions, and, stumbling on a hot tip, bets it all at the racetrack. He wins big and rushes home just as the heartless landlord is expelling his aged parents. Melodrama thus affirmed the certainty of a kind of cosmic moral adjudication. Justice was meted out by a higher power that never failed to reward the humble and good and eradicate or reform the greedy, lustful, and corrupt.

In classical melodrama, protagonists are unable to stop villainy through their own actions. Taking the causal agency of retribution out of their hands was apt for several reasons. By maintaining the protagonists' dramatic powerlessness, melodrama was able to function as a parable of modern anxiety. It also let them keep their hands morally clean (they were able to heed the commandment "thou shall not kill" in a way they could not if they themselves had eradicated the villain). Above all, making forces of nature and fate the agents of moral retribution served a psychological need. It reassured audiences that, ultimately, they were not transcendentally homeless, after all. Although the world's demagification, combined with the harsh realities of capitalism, fostered moral and material insecurity, classic melodrama's clear-cut moral dichotomies and ineluctable poetic justice affirmed that some sort of Providence still reigned. Melodrama granted an ethical simplicity and legibility that made the world more secure, if not socially or economically then at least psychologically.

* * *

The ameliorative aspect of melodrama often seems grossly overshadowed by its anxious or paranoid dimension. Moral legibility is evident throughout, but punishment and reward only appear at the very end of the play. Stage melodramas typically had four acts, with four scenes each, so the imbalance between villainy and retribution was substantial. The imbalance was particularly pronounced in serial-film melodramas, which ran over sixteen weeks or so. The protagonists endure assaults week after week with nary a hint of poetic justice until the last five minutes of the last episode. The villain just keeps on launching one abduction or assassination attempt after another.

Such an imbalance conveys not just a sense of moral and material insecurity, but a whole modality of interpersonal interaction introduced (or greatly amplified) by the advent of modern capitalism. As I noted in chapter 1, nineteenth-century social theory was fixated on the phenomenon of competitive individualism as a historical development closely linked to the transition from traditional to modern urban society. In 1844, for example, Engels observed a pervasive social atomization in urban modernity:

We know well enough that the isolation of the individual—a narrow-minded egotism—is everywhere the fundamental principle in modern society. But nowhere is this selfish egotism so blatantly evident as in the frantic bustle of the great city. The disintegration of society into individuals, each guided by his private principles and each pursuing his own aims, has been pushed to its furthest limits in London. Here indeed human society has been split into its component atoms.[14]

Marx and Engels reiterated this theme four years later, stressing (with ironic ambivalence) the power of bourgeois individualism to demolish age-old patterns of human cohesion:

The bourgeoisie, wherever it has got the upper hand, has put an end to all feudal, patriarchal, idyllic relations. It has pitilessly torn asunder the motley feudal ties that bound man to his "natural superiors," and has left remaining no other nexus between man and man than naked self-interest, than callous "cash payment." It has drowned the most heavenly ecstasies of religious fervor, of chivalrous enthusiasm, of philistine sentimentalism, in the icy waters of egotistical calculation.[15]

Capitalism reconfigured society as a chaotic conglomeration of competing individual interests. It also created a world in which social antipathy was never far beneath the surface and needed only a minor catalyst to erupt into out-and-out hostility. As Ferdinand Tönnies argued:

In gesellschaft, every person strives for that which is to his own advantage. . . . The relation of all to all may therefore be conceived as potential hostility or latent war. . . .

Everybody is by himself and isolated, and there exists a condition of tension against all others. . . .

Rational will [calculated maneuvering and exploitation] has always been permitted against enemies, has even been considered praiseworthy. But only gesellschaft *makes such a condition general and necessary. . . . Its elementary relationships . . . become not only a possible source of hostility, but a source in which hostility is natural and merely veiled (and consequently highly probable, requiring only slight provocation to cause an outbreak). . . .*

[Gesellschaft] consists of free persons who stand in contact with each other, exchange with each other and cooperate without any gemeinschaft *or common will among them. . . . These numerous external contacts, contracts, and contractual relations only cover up as many inner hostilities and antagonistic interests.*[16]

John A. Hobson, in his 1894 book *The Evolution of Modern Capitalism*, similarly perceived pervasive adversarial hostility as the earmark of the capitalist social structure: "Anti-social feelings are touched and stimulated at every point by the competition of workers with one another, the antagonism between employers and employed, between sellers and buyers, factory and factory, shop and shop."[17]

It is intriguing that this strand of social theory developed at roughly the same time as the rise of popular melodrama. It might be helpful to describe a sequence from a typical early serial-film melodrama to see how sensational melodrama dramatizes a world in which competition, advanced to the point of social hostility, prevails as a consequence of the "every-man-for-himself" (or, more accurately, "every-man-against-all-others") basis of capitalist modernity.

The plot of *A Woman in Grey*, produced in 1919, is incredibly convoluted, in keeping with melodrama's nonclassical narrative mechanics (which was greatly exacerbated in serial films by the need to keep stories going for three or four months of weekly episodes, with each episode requiring at least one or two climactic sensation scenes). The bare-bones setup is this: Ruth Hope is a poor but virtuous young woman who is actually heiress to an immense fortune. She and her beau Tom Thurston battle an oily mustachioed villain, J. Haviland Hunter, who alternately wants to kill Ruth, kidnap her, steal from her a secret code leading to a treasure trove, or wrench off her hand a large piece of jewelry covering a scar that he thinks will expose Ruth as an escaped murderer. To make matters more complicated, there is a completely separate second villain, the lawyer Gordon. He originally had helped Ruth undergo an identity change through plastic surgery when she was falsely accused and convicted of murder. Now, as repayment, he wants to have his way with her. He repeatedly kidnaps Ruth after she spurns his advances.

Toward the end of episode nine, Tom Thurston finds a note written by Gordon ordering a brutish old henchman to kidnap Ruth and take her to an abandoned mansion that the henchman and his vile hag of a wife are using as a hideout. The old man binds and gags Ruth and drags her into the abandoned building and, to keep her still until Gordon arrives, straps her to a bed in a room in which there just happens to be hanging from the ceiling a massive stone block with an impaling rod projecting out of it. He orders his wife not to toy with the quarry, and hits her when she repels his admonition. The hag (fig. 5.1) pretends to acquiesce, but when her husband goes off to take a nap, she pushes the bed right under the massive block and spike and puts a candle under the pulley rope that is keeping it up. Ruth flails helplessly as the candle proceeds to burn through the braids of the rope (fig. 5.2). Meanwhile, boyfriend Tom arrives and enters the hideout, and the villain Hunter is also hot on the trail. Tom looks through a keyhole and, in a POV shot,

Fig. 5.1 The hag from *A Woman in Grey* (Serico, 1919–20; frame still enlargement from video).

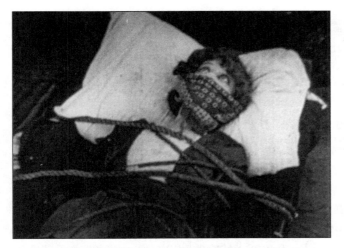

Fig. 5.2 Ruth in peril. (Three frame still enlargements from *A Woman in Grey*; Serico, 1919–20)

sees Ruth and the block that is about to impale and squash her. Just as Tom is about to break down the door, the old hag pulls a lever and he falls through a trap door into a basement dungeon, which, we find, is already occupied by a crazed savage who has been chained to the wall for years. The episode ends with the sight of the hag laughing grotesquely as Ruth squirms helplessly in terror and the rope continues to burn and snap.

Episode ten opens with the serial's characteristic temporal overlap and dubious narrative rewriting. We see the terrified Ruth, but we also now see the villain Hunter climb through the window and taunt Ruth as the rope burns down to its last strands. Tom arrives and looks through the keyhole. The POV shot now shows Hunter on the scene, trying to wrench the bracelet off Ruth's hand (fig. 5.3). The hag pulls the lever and Tom falls thirty feet into the dungeon. As the villain Hunter continues to attack Ruth, the massive block finally falls, crashing through the floor into the dungeon. It misses Ruth and Hunter because, for some reason, they are no longer directly under the block. A charitable

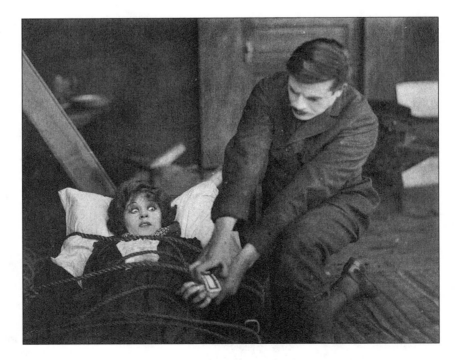

Fig. 5.3 Publicity still for *A Woman in Grey*. (From Lahue, *Bound and Gagged*)

reading would surmise that during his attack Hunter had inadvertently moved the bed on which Ruth was tied; but since that is not established, it is probably more likely that the film simply hopes viewers will be too excited by the thrilling events to remember the spatial details of the previous episode's cliffhanger crisis. Awakened by the crash, the henchman comes in and brawls wildly with Hunter. Meanwhile, down in the dungeon, the crazed savage jumps around, excited at having a new playmate to maim and kill. Intertitles indicate that the nasty old couple keep the savage as a kind of human disposal system. After the old man knocks out Hunter with a hammer, he and the hag look down the huge hole in the floor and delight in the plight of their "new boarder" Tom. (The extreme high-angle/low-angle POV shot reverse shot is a wonderful stylistic flourish.) Meanwhile, Ruth remains bound, gagged, and petrified. The villain Hunter regains consciousness, but now he is also tied up and can only move his head. However, this does not stop him from resuming his attack on Ruth and trying to remove her bracelet by chewing away at her flesh with his teeth.

At first glance, it may seem absurd to endow this lurid, overheated little sequence with the weight of symptomatic meaning by reading it as an allegory of capitalist modernity. Obviously, its objective was to get the primarily lowbrow and juvenile audience that patronized blood-and-thunder melodrama hollering and stamping with excitement. It must be conceded, furthermore, that as long as there have been stories, there have been stories about hostile competition between hero and villain, about coveted objects, about sexual extortion. Audiences and readers in a wide range of sociohistorical contexts have found such themes gripping. To a large extent, the sequence's dramatic appeal must be viewed as universal and historically nonspecific.

That fact, however, need not stymie more specific symptomatic interpretation. I think Martha Vicinus has the right formulation when she suggests that, "Melodrama is best understood as a combination of archetypal, mythic [elements] and time-specific responses to particular cultural and historical conditions."[18] There is something about the action in this sequence—something about the extraordinary ferocity and polyvalence of the antagonism—that reverberates, inviting interpretation as a distillation of the interpersonal dynamics distinctive of its epoch. It is impossible to overlook the rabid intensity and omnidirectional ubiquity of the malevolence. As figure 5.4 diagrams, the heroine is assaulted by the villain Gordon (via his brutish henchman, whom

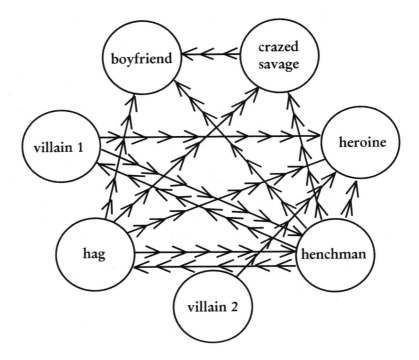

Fig. 5.4 Character relationships in *A Woman in Grey* as revealed through arrows showing targets of aggression.

Gordon domineers), by the main villain Hunter, and by the hag; the hag and the husband are starkly unpleasant toward each other; the hag does violence to the hero, who is also threatened by the crazed savage; the henchman and the hag abuse the crazed savage by keeping him chained in a dungeon.

Whether or not a sequence of such omnidirectional antagonism could have found expression in a cultural context other than modernity, it undoubtedly resonated with special power within modern capitalist society. The sequence manages to make perceptible, through the defamiliarizing capacity of melodramatic exaggeration, a situation of competitive individualism run rampant. Sensational melodramas like *A Woman in Grey* capture the essence of social atomization and all-against-all antagonism. Everyone is in competition with everyone else.

This subtextual representation of capitalist modernity is particularly interesting in film serials, since in serials the social atoms invariably were agitated, as in capitalism, by competition for sole possession of a coveted material object (in this case, papers leading to a hidden fortune) that, like money, symbolized power and wealth. (The convention of structuring narratives around the back-and-forth exchange of a fetish object, or "weenie," is discussed in chapter 7.) It is worth noting, moreover, that, just as the rise of capitalist gesellschaft was predicated on the disappearance of traditional patriarchal authority (be it the head of the household, the leader of the clan, the feudal lord, or God), in serial-film melodramas the frenzy of hostile competition was triggered, without fail, by the murder or incapacitation of a father figure (a convention also detailed in chapter 7). In serial-film melodrama, as in modern society as a whole, the rise of rampant individualism and antisocial will coincided with the downfall of benign paternalism.

Sensational melodrama's narrative gesellschaft would have had particular meaning for a society that was still adjusting to modernity. For many people in the nineteenth and early twentieth centuries, the aggressive individualism of modern social and economic life was not yet a transparent and unremarkable fact of life. It still registered as something relatively new and strange, something disquieting. Urbanization, which intensified class and ethnic divisions and a general tone of impersonality, was an exponential ongoing phenomenon. The trials of gesellschaft might have been felt most strongly among the millions of urban immigrants who previously had known nothing but agrarian village life. However, any worker caught up in the new machinery of exploitation and profiteering, and who faced the erratic waves of unemployment peculiar to industrial society, would have been sensitive to the harsh underpinnings of capitalist modernity. To a large extent, these were the people for whom sensational melodrama was geared, and for whom it might have resonated as the reflection of a new reality.

* * *

Any consideration of melodrama's relation to the social context of modern capitalism must point out the degree to which melodrama grew out of, and persisted to accentuate, cultural divisions basic to the capitalist structure of class stratification. It is, of course, no historical revelation to point out that sensational melodrama was a popular amusement catering especially to the urban working class—that much generally is taken for granted. However, it is important to document the way in which the cultural division expressed itself, both in order to establish that what we take for granted is correct and matches what was taken for granted by earlier generations, and in order to highlight just how distasteful the middle class found popular melodrama and its clientele.

From its earliest days, melodrama was affiliated with a working-class audience. As a critic writing in 1914 observed:

It is not surprising that the French Revolution should have given birth to the melodrama as we know it. "I write," said Pixerecourt, "for those who cannot read." For the first time they and the barely well-to-do become powerful patrons of the stage.[19]

Inexpensive playhouses specializing in melodramas mushroomed in the early 1800s, giving the area in Paris where they were clustered the nickname the "Boulevard du Crime."[20]

Melodrama's class affiliation changed little over the next century. While there were strains of melodramatic spectacle in the "legitimate" productions of Dion Boucicault and David Belasco (tempered by refined sentiment and milder violence), for the most part melodrama was culturally segregated and stigmatized as a proletarian amusement. A 1911 review in the *San Francisco Weekly* described melodrama's audience as "the grubbers after mere existence."[21] A 1909 magazine essay suggestively entitled "The Mellowdrammer" (mimicking a lower-class accent) proclaimed: "The melodrama is the primary form of entertainment with the Other Half. In every city of any importance it has several homes. All smell equally bad and contain much the same sort of people and exactly the same sort of piece."[22] The author, Porter Emerson Browne, described the audience as comprised mainly of gossipy shop-girls with mouths full of gum, weasely young men with well-watered hair and yellow suspenders embroidered with green shamrocks, and fat immigrants with respiratory problems. The essay was full of useful advice for prospective white-collar slumming expeditions:

When you approach the box-office, don't say, "Have you, perhaps, a good aisle-seat, somewhere in the first few rows, that is not already disposed of?" Nay! Nay! The proper way to phrase your query is: "Wotter yuh got down front, Bill? . . . Huh? . . . De sekind row? Awright. Gimme it."[23]

In the same year, Hartt described the context of popular melodrama in very similar terms: "Reduce the conventional theatre to a state of dog-eared shabbiness; borrow a whiff or so of the Dime Museum's [i.e., freak show's] aroma; and fill the house with office-boys, bell-boys, messengers, common laborers, factory-girls, shop-girls, waitresses, and 'generals.'"[24] A few years later, in 1914, Arthur Ruhl reinforced this image, stating that the 10–20–30 audience was comprised of "fat women in wilted shirt-waists; flippant girls chewing gum; boys and men who, one vaguely feels, ought to be at work somewhere."[25]

The well-to-do found cheap melodrama distasteful not only because of a basic aversion to lower-class types but also owing to an aversion to melodrama's aesthetic aberrations: "Turbulent contortions of grammar, large chunks of decomposed rhetoric, spasms of emotion that have noting to do with what has gone before or what is to follow, revolvers, hisses, saw mills . . . villains in riding breeches and black moustachios, country girls suddenly found in opium dens . . . ; these are the awful messes which melodrama puts forth."[26] A British columnist writing in 1919 posed the rhetorical question: "Is it conceivable that any audience with the smallest pretension to taste or education could be moved to anything but ridicule or contempt by the average melodrama production of today?"[27] The obvious answer was articulated by a writer in the *Atlantic Monthly* a decade earlier: "The majority of us scoff at the popular melodrama as a matter of course."[28] The problem, according to Hartt, was that melodrama was geared to the "Neolithic mind":

Melodrama is not got up for psychologists. Its devotees care nothing for the portrayal of the inner life, save in its crudest, most ferocious manifestations. They want "sump'n doin.' " Strip the action, therefore, of all those interpretative, significant, philosophic touches that make it human. Give it go. Give it noise and bluster as it goes. Let it career madly in a cloud of dust and with sparks flying. And make it simple. . . . Reduce character, incident, structure, and ideas to their lowest terms, enabling the Neolithic mind (and such is the Grand's) to comprehend.[29]

Hartt goes on to explain that the proletarian's interest in melodramatic thrills resulted from the fact that "only the glaringly sensational gets through their armor of stupidity to leave a vivid impression."

The Neolithic mind was not just obtuse, it was also thought to be vulgar and degenerate. A haughty letter to the drama critic of the *American Magazine*, a middle-class monthly, claimed to represent an antimelodrama coalition:

This is a plea for help from the A.V.M., meaning the American Victims of Melodrama. Consider it an urgent request to be represented as opposed to this onslaught of melodramatic stuff, this reeking, bloody, villain-pursued-her . . . sort of stuff. . . . We are sick of this sort of play, weary of their mechanical construction, of the conventional villain, hero and heroine, of their artificial human interest, of their trashy romance and cheap excite-ment.[30]

Melodrama, in short, was at the center of a culture war, one that essen-tially was also a class conflict. Of course, the well-to-do fashioned their own varieties of spectacle in forms of upscale melodrama, such as David Belasco's two-dollar Broadway shows, and in pageantry, high-class vaudeville, opera, and grandiose Shakespearian productions.[31] But these amusements were less violent and generally less invested in the excite-ment of "thrills for thrill's sake." Melodrama emerged "from below" to express, and to redress through myth, the common person's material vulnerability and "ideological shelterlessness" in modern capitalism (to use Kracauer's variation on Lukács).[32] It dramatized the social atomiza-tion of capitalist gesellschaft, and remained a reflection of the cultural divisions of a stratified society.

6

Ten—Twenty—Thirty Melodrama: Boom and Bust

While stage melodrama offered many pleasures—cathartic pathos, moral affirmation, abundant comedy, and so on—what distinguished it most markedly from other dramatic forms was its aspect of excitation, its display of violent action, gripping suspense, startling surprise, and remarkable spectacle. This emphasis on excitation tied melodrama to urban modernity on a qualitative level—both involved "hyperstimulus"—and, consequently, also on a practical level. The ambitious scenic effects that were melodrama's specialty were achieved through new technologies of mechanical-electrical stagecraft. The connection between melodrama and technology also expressed itself in diegetic motifs. Melodrama's action-adventure stories were designed to showcase the wonders of modern technology. As Horace Kallen observed in 1910: "Of all dramatic forms, [melodrama] has to keep pace with the march of the times. Telegraphy, the telephone, the automobile, the air-ship, the rapid-fire gun, and the North Pole are made familiar to the public by means of the melodramatic stage long before they could be brought concretely to the public attention by other means."[1] "Melodramas are transitory . . . ," Kallen concluded, evoking Baudelaire's definition of modernity as "that which is ephemeral, fugitive, contingent."

If melodrama was transitory, expressive of cultural discontinuity by virtue of its exploitation of new technologies, it was even more so in its commercial history. In the 1890s and early 1900s, the 10–20–30 industry enjoyed a boom, flourishing in huge theaters all across the nation and making its oligarchic group of playwrights and producers very rich. Like all truly modern enterprises, its industrial organization had become highly rationalized and centralized. Ten-twenty-thirty melodrama was a commodity, produced, transported, and marketed through efficient, predictable systems of operation. But that was not enough to protect it from the vicissitudes of modern capitalism. Just two or three years after its peak around 1907, 10–20–30 melodrama was all but extinct, killed off, with incredible rapidity, by the movies. The 10–20–30 was destroyed, in other words, by a quintessentially modern transformation in market forces, technologies, and cultural habits. Marx's characterization of modern capitalism as the "constant revolutionizing of production, uninterrupted disturbance of all social relations, everlasting uncertainty and agitation" comes to mind. It is ironic that an art form so concerned with expressing the essential instability and vulnerability of life under modern capitalism should have itself become such a vivid casualty of capitalist discontinuity.

This chapter focuses on 10–20–30 melodrama during its heyday, examining its conventions and chronicling its fatal crisis during the nickelodeon boom. I then turn to the immediate historical question at hand: what explains stage melodrama's sudden obliteration (or perhaps more accurately, its cannibalization) by the movies? My analysis both supports and criticizes the answer put forward by A. Nicholas Vardac in his pioneering work *Stage to Screen: Theatrical Origins of Early Film*. Chapter 7 then charts sensational melodrama after its transformation into a cinematic form.

The first thing to note in understanding the historical trajectory of sensational melodrama is that it underwent a major reconfiguration in the final decades of the nineteenth century. The shift involved not so much a new combination of elements as a quantum leap in the emphasis placed on one element in particular: blood-and-thunder sensationalism. Moral opposition, pathos, extreme emotion, and structural incoherence all remained prominent aspects of the genre, but starting around 1890 graphic action and intense spectacles of danger became more and more important as melodrama's crucial attraction. "Sensation scenes," such as burning buildings, explosions, and shipwrecks, had been an ingredient in stage melodrama since the early 1800s, and Dion

Boucicault's 1860 production of *Colleen Bawn* was particularly influential, according to a critic writing in 1883, in "introducing a new graphic school of melodrama, which has since been dubbed the sensational; in this the actor and the author are subordinated to the painter, carpenter, and property man, and the situation is made to depend upon scenic instead of imaginative effects."[2]

Near the turn of the century, however, scenic effects and perilous stuntwork grew more and more realistic, ambitious, and astonishing. And whereas earlier melodramas might have had one climactic spectacle, turn-of-the-century melodrama piled thrill upon thrill. The entire focus and tenor of melodrama underwent a fundamental shift. As Archibald Haddon observed in 1905: "A startling change has come over the tone and spirit of melodrama. The simple, demonstrative human element no longer appeals. Touring dramas, nowadays, are not properly constituted unless every scene is a shriek, every title a yell."[3] A newspaper review of *The Queen of the White Slaves*, also from 1905 (and presumably written by a press agent), supports Haddon's contention:

Those who like sensation piled upon sensation with no let-up from the very beginning until the very end will find [this melodrama] admirably suited to their taste. It is a play of thrilling and sensational incidents, events and climaxes . . . with little extraneous matter. . . . Each [scene] ends with a thrilling rescue, or timely foiling of villainy, or some other episode that meets with the entire approval of the audience.[4]

Desmond MacCarthy reiterated the perception of a change in 1914 (although by this time most sensational melodrama was to be found in the movies): "The development of recent melodrama has been away from high moral sentiments and towards catastrophes and ingenious thrills. Noble harangues are no longer essential; the adventures, not the virtues of the hero and heroine are important, and mechanism has almost ousted morality."[5]

Essentially episodic in design, the standard 10–20–30 melodrama had four acts, with fifteen to twenty scenes, most ending in some kind of thrilling "situation" or scenic effect. Lincoln J. Carter's 1906 play *The Eye Witness*, for example, showed on stage:

A daring leap by a huge automobile over a partially opened jack-knife bridge spanning the Chicago River; then a girl is rescued from the lake in which the hero is seen to dive after her and cut away the weights fastened to her by the villain in his dastardly attempt to murder her; as a hair-rais-

ing finish, a great cyclone scene in which houses are wrecked, trees uproot-ed and the villain finally killed by a shaft of lightning.[6]

Theodore Kremer's 1906 play *Bertha, the Sewing Machine Girl* included a four-way race between two automobiles, a locomotive, and a bicycle, as well as a motorboat race, fire engines speeding toward a burning building, and various torture scenes.[7] Charles Blaney's *The Girl and the Detective* (1908) climaxed in a variation on the classic buzz-saw peril: "The hero is flung by the villain on the table of a steam hammer and, while he lies there prone, a huge pig of iron, at white heat, swings into position and descends."[8] In *Edna, the Pretty Typewriter*, a 1907 melo-drama by Owen Davis, the heroine jumps from the roof of a building to the top of a moving elevated train. Another scene depicted a race between real automobiles (placed on a treadmill while an immense panorama backdrop moved rapidly in the opposite direction). The abducted heroine leaps from the villain's car into the hero's, at which point the hero's car, pushed beyond its limits, blows up in a fiery explo-sion (fig. 6.1).[9]

Fig. 6.1 Poster illustration for *Edna, the Pretty Typewriter*, 1907. (*Literary Digest*, August 10, 1912)

TYPICAL SENSATION SCENES

Material in this section has been gathered primarily from clippings in the Harvard Theatre Collection, along with clippings at the Billy T. Rose Theater Collection, New York Public Library; poster blueprints in the New York Historical Society; and descriptions in Goff, "The Popular-Priced Melodrama in America," and Booth, *Victorian Spectacular Theatre.*

A real balloon inflated with gas carrying three passengers rising above a crowd at the Crystal Palace and descending in the English Channel; rescue by lifeboat with eight oarsmen: in *The Ruling Passion*, Charles Brougham (1882).

Two train wrecks; a snowstorm in Piccadilly Circus; a mob breaking real glass bank windows; a burning building: in *Pluck*, Henry Pettitt and Augustus Harris (1882).

Horse-drawn wagons carrying 250 children on an excursion; troops in Burma escaping on rafts down a river—real water used in tanks: in *Our Silver Wedding*, author not determined (1886).

A river with real water, real swans, houseboats, steam-powered motorboats, racing skiffs; a rainstorm with real water: in *Dark Secret*, James Willing and John Douglas (1886).

A real fire engine, drawn by real horses, crossing the stage at "full speed," using treadmills, smoke bombs, and a rolling panoramic backdrop: in *The Still Alarm*, Joseph Arthur (1887).

Two locomotives racing side by side; a steamboat explosion on the Mississippi; a view of Niagara Falls from a suspension bridge: in *The Fast Mail*, Lincoln J. Carter (1889).

A real buzz saw cutting through real planks of wood—and almost the hero: in *Blue Jeans*, Joseph Arthur (1890).

A storm at sea, with sailors furling huge sail; an advancing steamship (coming toward the audience); a collision between two ocean liners; a tornado; a bird's-eye view of Chicago: in *The Tornado*, Lincoln J. Carter (1892).

A real pile driver: in *A Nutmeg Match*, William Haworth (1893).

A heroine swinging by rope across a chasm to save hero from dynamite explosion; heroine saving a racing horse from a burning stable; a horse race in which "half a dozen thoroughbreds tear across the stage abreast": in *In Old Kentucky*, Charles T. Daley (1893).

A quarry with four giant steam drills in active operation; dynamite blasting of massive boulders; a mammoth derrick hoisting tons of rock; an actual ten-horse-power lifting engine, working with live steam: in *A Flag of Truce*, Horace Mitchell (1894).

Underwater fight to the death between hero and villain in diving suits: in *The White Heather*, Henry Hamilton and Cecil Raleigh (1897).

A full-sized railway ferryboat; wreck of the battleship *Trenton* at Samoa: in *Under the Dome*, Lincoln J. Carter (1897).

A locomotive approaching "at terrific speed" from miles away until its fenders projected over the orchestra pit; the streets of Chicago during the Great Fire, with fire engines in full operation; panoramic views of the city's ruins; villain throwing hero off skyscraper; views of the World's Fair: in *The Heart of Chicago*, Lincoln J. Carter (1897).

A runaway locomotive (with a smoke-belching engine) surrounded by movie screens (!) showing the passing landscape: in *Chattanooga*, Lincoln J. Carter (1898).

A naval battle; the bombardment of Manila: in *Remember the Maine!*, Lincoln J. Carter (1898).

An Alpine avalanche that sweeps the villain to his death: in *Hearts Are Trumps*, Henry Hamilton and Cecil Raleigh (1899).

A prairie on fire: in *The Flaming Arrow*, Lincoln J. Carter (1900).

An ocean liner on fire; a race-to-the-rescue on real horses: in *Lost in the Desert*, Owen Davis (1901).

A locomotive racing through a forest fire: in *The Ninety and Nine*, Ramsay Morris (1902). (See figs. 6.2 and 6.3.)

A fight on telegraph wires; aerial views of Paris: in *The Dangers of Paris*, E. Hill Mitchelson and Charles Langdon (1902).

A burning fireworks factory; the approach and landing of a ferry-boat: in *The Searchlights of a Great City*, author not determined (1902).

Hero adrift in mid-ocean on a raft, and a battleship approaching to save him; a collapsible cell that almost crushes the hero to death and does kills a villainous henchman: in *The Queen of the White Slaves*, Owen Davis, under pseudonym Arthur J. Lamb (1903).

An ascending hot-air balloon; a flood: in *Just Struck Town*, Lawrence Russell (1903).

A canoe going over rapids: in *Through Fire and Water*, Charles A. Taylor (1903).

Heroine tightrope-walking a laundry line hung between a cliff and a lighthouse, while villains try to shoot her and cut the cord (fig. 6.4): in *Lighthouse by the Sea*, Owen Davis (1903).

An ascending hot-air balloon in which hero and villain do battle and villain is hurled overboard: in *Hearts Adrift*, Langdon McCormick (1903).

A human chain through a manhole to save a child trapped on sub-way tracks as a train barrels toward her: in *Child Slaves of New York*, Charles Blaney (1903).

A locomotive departing from the station; a steamship; a dam burst and the ensuing flood: in *The Flood Tide*, Cecil Raleigh (1903).

Ruins, fires, after the San Francisco earthquake; demolition of buildings; city of tents at Golden Gate park: in *While Frisco Burns*, Lincoln J. Carter (1905).

A motorboat race on the Harlem River; a leap for life from a burning building; a sweatshop; an iron maiden torture contraption; a chase involving autos, bicycles, and a locomotive: in *Bertha, the Sewing Machine Girl*, Theodore Kremer (1906).

A trolley racing across a suspension bridge; a yacht drawing toward a dock, with a panoramic view of New York harbor: in *The Burglar's Daughter*, Owen Davis (1906).

A race between a train and a real automobile: in *Bedford's Hope*, Lincoln J. Carter (1906).

Heroine tied to mill wheel at the foot of a crashing waterfall: in *Tennessee Tess: Queen of the Moonshiners*, John P. Ritter (1906).

A human bridge of girl athletes between two tenement buildings; heroine escapes over it; an on-rushing subway train: in *Chinatown Charlie*, Owen Davis (1906).

An automobile leaping over an open drawbridge; an underwater rescue scene in which hero cuts weights that were fastened to the heroine by the villain; a furious cyclone: in *The Eye Witness*, Lincoln J. Carter (1906).

An automobile exploded by dynamite while crossing the Brooklyn Bridge during a blinding snowstorm; the passengers sent hurtling through the air into the water: in *Nellie, the Beautiful Cloak Model*, Owen Davis (1907).

Heroine jumping from the roof of a building to the top of moving train; a car chase, heroine leaping from one car to the other; an explosion: in *Edna, the Pretty Typewriter*, Owen Davis (1907).

Heroine pinioned to the blades of a huge windmill; a leaky boat at sea during a raging storm; the big locomotive yard at Grand Central Station; various other Manhattan locales: in *Since Nellie Went Away*, Owen Davis (1907).

A daring jump from roof to roof across an alley; an ocean liner demolished by an explosion; police boats making rescues: in *A Chorus Girl's Luck in New York*, Owen Davis, under the pseudonym John Oliver (1907).

Hero stuck under steam hammer as white-hot iron descends: in *The Girl and the Detective*, Charles Blaney (c. 1908).

A fight between divers at the bottom of the North River; a heroine's escape by jumping onto the roof of an elevated train; the Tarrytown Bridge blown up by dynamite; hero and heroine leaping from automobile and clinging to branches of a tree as the bridge crumbles beneath them; a tenement fire in which a policeman leaps from a three-story window carrying a baby: in *The Millionaire and the Policeman's Wife*, Owen Davis (1909).

Four airplanes in combat; battle in the trenches with bursting shells, air raids, bombs dropping, buildings collapsing: in *An American Ace*, Lincoln J. Carter (1918).

At the heart of popular melodrama, as the examples in the inset reveal, was an effort to portray situations and environments that challenged the physical and spatiotemporal boundaries of the indoor stage. Eschewing tame indoor settings, melodrama situated its dramatic crises outdoors: at racetracks, quarries, canyons, oceans, and so on. Scenic effects conjured great spatial expanse and apparent rapid movement through that expanse—movement either in depth (for example, as a battleship or locomotive raced closer toward the audience, or as a town gradually disappeared from the vantage point of an ascending balloon) or in lateral perspective (for example, as a cityscape flew by in the background as a fire engine raced across town). Forces of nature loomed large in melodrama: fires, floods, storms, explosions, tornadoes, blizzards, avalanches,

Fig. 6.2 Scene from stage production of *The Ninety and Nine*, 1902. (Photo by Byron, The Byron Collection, Courtesy Museum of the City of New York)

and the like amplified the crises of victimization. Stuntwork further intensified the portrayal of physical danger: characters swung by ropes from ledge to ledge, tightrope-walked across telegraph wires, dove off cliffs into the ocean, moved inches away from real buzz saws or pile drivers, and so on.

The 10–20–30 exploited, and pioneered, the latest innovations in stagecraft technology. The big effect in Lincoln J. Carter's *Bedford's Hope*—a race between a train and an automobile—was, according to the *New York Morning Telegraph*, "the triumph of modern ingenuity." The article included this account by Carter:

There are seven moving panoramas and ground profiles, several feet apart on independent rolls, all moving in one direction at rates of speed varying from two miles an hour to twelve. In this way the foreground moves rapidly, the middleground slower, and the far distance still slower. The train

Fig. 6.3 Poster for *The Ninety and Nine* stage production, 1902. (Courtesy Museum of the City of New York)

Fig. 6.4 Poster illustration for *Lighthouse by the Sea*, 1903. (*American Magazine*, September 1914)

and automobile move in the opposite direction at the rate of fourteen miles per hour, although it seems to be twice that from the front. . . . There are many thousands of pounds of steel and iron in the construction, and it takes a twenty horse-power motor to move the main shaft, from which minor shafts run to control the entire thing. It is built with the nicety of mechanical accuracy of a watch, a locomotive, or a printing press. You may notice also that it makes no noise. . . . How do I manage to run my race scene twice as long as any race scene has ever before been run? My panoramas are only 78 feet long and keep repeating . . . but there are three main panoramas and they all move at different speeds. That makes it possible to run twenty-five complete revolutions without duplicating any scene.[10]

While far from foolproof (as I will discuss), this technology was often very effective in arousing excitement. One review of *Bedford's Hope* reported that, "The house shrieked with delight when the automobile finally forged ahead of the train. The scenery went one way, while the automobile and train went the other, and the audience went wild."[11] Another review, from the *Toledo Blade*, described the same scene (in which the hero's car chases the train carrying the villain, who is rushing to sell a gold-mine deed he has stolen from the heroine): "It had the audience on the verge of nervous prostration. . . . The auto creeps up on the train, and inch by inch passes it, while the audience rise in their seats and shout themselves hoarse."[12]

* * *

This kind of sensational melodrama was not simply a marginal, small-time popular entertainment. In its commercial structure, and in its expansion into large theaters throughout every American city, "cheap melodrama" had become big business. Popular-priced theater circuits and syndicates coalesced on a national scale in the late 1890s, which stabilized the business by systematizing the financing, booking, promotion, and mass production of large-scale touring shows. Expenses and profits became extremely predictable. This rationalization of the melodrama industry provided a context of financial security necessary for the production of increasingly labor- and capital-intensive sensational spectacles. According to playwright Owen Davis,

The average business of these theaters was definitely fixed at about three thousand five hundred dollars a week [about $65,000 today]. The fluctuations of business were nominal. . . . All we had to do was to see that our weekly running expense came to five hundred dollars less than our share of the take, then multiply this by forty, as the houses were open forty weeks a year, and we had a profit of twenty thousand [$371,000] a year from each show.[13]

Davis (fig. 6.5), the most prolific 10–20–30 playwright, claimed (with, no doubt, some exaggeration) that for the 1906–1907 season he had written twenty-three new melodramas and, at the same time, had at least ten revivals touring.

The 10–20–30 melodrama business was essentially a factory system, with plays "mass-produced" according to standard formulas. The business was dominated (at least in the eastern states) by an oligopoly made up of the Stair and Havlin circuit of popular-priced theaters and a handful of major producers and producer-playwrights. A. H. Woods was the most important producer. Davis was a Harvard graduate who had taken a course with psychologist (and classical film theorist) Hugo Münsterberg.[14] Theodore Kremer and Charles Foster (before his death in 1895) were the key playwrights. Hal Reid, Charles Blaney, Lincoln J. Carter, and Charles Taylor, among others, were major producer-playwrights. The Stair and Havlin circuit was formed in 1900 when E. D. Stair, who controlled houses in Toledo, Cleveland, and other northern

Fig. 6.5 The most prolific of
the prolific, playwright Owen
Davis. (*American Magazine*,
September 1914)

lake cities, joined forces with John H. Havlin, who had a chain of theaters in Cincinnati, St. Louis, and other cities. They expanded their territory rapidly: a 1903 article in the *Brooklyn Daily Eagle* indicates that by that time Stair and Havlin controlled the bookings for roughly 150 popular-priced theaters from Maine to California, with a central office in New York.[15] Considering the small size of the oligopoly that controlled it, popular-priced melodrama was a very lucrative industry. The shows rotating on the Stair and Havlin circuit alone (not counting smaller circuits and independent productions) generated a yearly net profit (going by Davis's comment above about per-production profits) equivalent to almost $56 million in today's money.

Cheap melodrama's heyday came to an abrupt halt with the meteoric rise of the nickelodeon in 1907–1908. In the spring of 1908 the *New York Dramatic Mirror* ran a series of five articles on what it called "the theatrical nightmare of 1907–08," beginning with a piece entitled "What Is the Cause? A Great Falling Off in Patronage of the Popular-Price Theatres." While most commentators in this series were reluctant to acknowledge that the rise of the movies was the key factor behind the problem (they instead used the forum as an opportunity to call for the "elimination of the blood-spilling melodrama" and a "return to the good old melodrama of our fathers"), one writer did admit that "the popular price houses have been hit very hard by moving pictures."[16] By November 1908 there seemed little doubt about it: an article in the *New York Dramatic Mirror* reported that melodrama, "especially of the wild and woolly kind," was suffering badly; there were significantly fewer productions, and for those that were mounted, attendance had fallen off at least 50 percent—"all attributed to the picture houses."[17] Dramatic critic Walter Prichard Eaton, writing a year later, also noted that "popular melodramas, since moving pictures became the rage, have decreased fifty percent."[18] In New York City, according to an article in *Success* magazine published in the spring of 1910, the movies had pushed out or taken over every melodrama theater in the city—almost a dozen in all:

Were you aware of the fact that . . . the blood-curdling, hands-up-or-I'll-shoot melodrama has all but disappeared from our midst? . . . Twelve months ago there were eleven melodrama houses in New York which were frequented by patrons of "Lottie the Poor Saleslady," "The Millionaire and the Policeman's Wife," "Bertha the Sewing Machine Girl," and other dra-

matic tidbits of similar construction and equally bizarre names. Today there is not a melodrama theater in our biggest city. Motion pictures are being presented in all of the eleven, and at the present writing there are in all the United States only a few second-rate theaters catering to the old blood-and-thunder trade. Motion picture films, it has been found, can tell a story of Mephistophelian villainy . . . quite as well as, if not better, than can a troupe of indifferent actors; and Patsy and Mamie can get their fill of chortles and thrills for half what they paid in the old days. With the disappearance of a demand for their wares and a corresponding uselessness of a supply, the providers of melodramatic entertainments have been forced to enter other fields. In a year, through the influence of motion pictures, melodrama with all its people has become little more than a memory.[19]

Dozens of other articles from the period confirmed cinema's extraordinary displacement of popular-priced melodrama.[20] Newspaper advertising also provides evidence of the phenomenon. According to Lewin Goff,

A survey of the newspaper advertisements in the Brooklyn Daily Eagle *for the years 1902 and 1910 almost tells the story of the rise and decline of the popular-priced melodrama. The advertisements from 1903 to 1909 become gradually more glaring and bold, particularly for the Grand and the Folly Theaters. By 1909 the ads for these two theaters alone covered almost an entire page. Through the year 1910, however, they diminished sharply in size and gradually were found only in the more insignificant parts of the theater page.*[21]

The crisis was not restricted to melodrama alone. Movies were cutting into most theatrical amusements. A survey of the touring theatrical companies mentioned in the *New York Dramatic Mirror* in a given week finds their number plummeting from an all-time high of 420 companies in 1904 to 337 in 1908, 236 in 1910, 95 in 1915, and a mere 25 in 1918.[22] Popular-priced melodrama was the hardest-hit theatrical commodity of all. Lacking big-name stars, famous playwrights, or prestigious titles, it was a generic product easily replaceable by the movies. By 1911 or 1912, sensational melodrama had all but disappeared in urban theaters, although it may have limped along on provincial circuits for another decade or so.[23]

A few producers, such as Lincoln J. Carter, tried to compete with the movies by launching, or trying to launch, more ambitious superspectacles. In 1911, and then again in 1913, Carter announced the imminent production of a spectacular new play whose big effect would be a cattle stampede (sometimes described as involving 5,000 cattle, sometimes 10,000). The *Columbus Journal* reported that "Mr. Carter had made countless little models of steers worked upon gearing and which were fixed so they seemingly approached the audience."[24] As far as I can determine, the production never materialized. In 1918, however, Carter did succeed in getting backing for *An American Ace*, an attempt to revive sensational melodrama by capitalizing on wartime patriotism. The play was not well received.

As early as 1910, Stair and Havlin lost hope of ever resuscitating stage melodrama and regeared their theater circuit toward popular-priced vaudeville. A. H. Woods, the 10–20–30's biggest producer, was also compelled to redefine his business. A 1918 article stated that, "He took his profits out of the Theodore Kremer–Owen Davis melodrama and put them into 'the two dollar game,' meaning the production of plays of better literary quality and looser morality." He quickly become the "purveyor in chief of bedroom farces." Owen Davis underwent a remarkable conversion into a "serious" dramatist. By the early 1920s he was being compared with Eugene O'Neill, and in 1923 won a Pulitzer Prize for his drama *Icebound*.[25]

Melodrama did not disappear altogether, however. Some producers adapted to the new situation by switching over to "drawing room" melodrama with few if any spectacular sensation scenes. Ostensibly more upscale, and certainly more talkative, these milder melodramas were geared for middle-class audiences, which had yet to abandon the theater for the movies. Producer William A. Brady described the new formula in 1915:

Keep the background of wealth and social supremacy always in view. There must be no pauperism, no misery or want, no rags, no tenements, no murky nights on the swirling river—not so much as a suspicion of any of the old material. Whatever happens, the glamour must be directly in evidence all the time. . . . Dress your characters in the latest modes, give them the veneer of apparent good breeding, no matter how thin, and then go as far as you like with the criminal element. . . . The principal change in melodrama's status is that where formerly the public swallowed it plain, it must now be triple gold plated.[26]

While it is unclear whether this strategy was financially successful, such plays were for the most part critical failures. Critics disdained legitimate theater's slippage into middlebrow banality and indeed expressed a surprising nostalgia for "those noble old rough-house" melodramas that did not try to put on airs and hide their true identity. Clayton Hamilton, for example, wrote in 1911: "Lately, there has appeared in our theatres a new type of the sort of melodrama that is ashamed of itself—which, while not pretending to be tragedy, pretends to be a serious study of contemporary social problems. . . . The new melodrama will never rival the glory of the old until it sloughs off all sophistication and disguise."[27] George Jean Nathan, writing in 1917, ridiculed the new "indoor" melodrama:

The melodrama of our youth was based largely upon the theory that the most momentous crises in life occurred always in the vicinity of railroad tracks or at the foot of Pier 30, North River. The melodrama of the present-day geniture is based to a similar degree upon the theory that the most important eventualities in life come off always in the vicinity of long writing tables standing in the center of libraries in private houses and having on them a push button. Melodrama, in short, has moved indoors. . . . Melodrama is essentially a thing of "exteriors." Move it under a roof and into "interiors" and it becomes effeminate, maidenly—a thing to curve the spine and benumb the pulse. . . . Harvard has spoiled the old melo-pieces by squirting into them pseudo economic and social problems, by affectedly unsplitting their infinitives and by treating them, in general, to a dosage of sophomore fine writing.

Nathan drove his point home by comparing typical prop lists for old-style versus new-style melodramas:

In the old days: Act 1: Small rifle for soubrette lead. Revolvers and carbines for juvenile lead and leading heavy. Dagger for character heavy. Rifle for character lead. Wire across stage to be dropped when telephone wires are cut down. Small telegraph instrument. Bludgeon for leading heavy. Blackjack for Irish comic. Slug-shot for negro comic. Bag of nuggets and money-belt for juvenile lead. Brass knuckles for second heavy. Red fire and flash-torch for fire effect. Key to lock door. Axe. Thin boards to make door to be battered in by axe. Half pail of water behind water-tank to come through piping at climax. Brace of pistols and rope for female juvenile lead. Act 2: Ropes, boat-hook and axe for juvenile lead and second juvenile. Bolt to attach to door. Poniard for third heavy. Revolver for utility and "billy" for soubrette lead. Smoke pots. Gong bell. Life-preserver and large crab. Fire-net. Imitation of crying baby and nursing bottle with milk for eccentric character woman. Package of documents. Wallet. Six packages of stage money. Circular saw. Machinery connected with saw. Revolver for juvenile lead. Two sticks nailed together to make loud noise when used to strike with: one for Jew comic, one for Chinese comic. A chicken and an egg for Negro comic. Skyrocket. Two stuffed clubs. Bottle marked "chloroform." Kerosene lamp made so it can be upset and smashed. Keg marked "dynamite" and fuse. Wind machine and storm effects. Italian disguise for juvenile lead. Chair with legs sawed half-way through so they will break readily when crashed on leading heavy's back. Hook-and-ladder truck. Steam fire-engine. Act 3: Brace of pistols for juvenile lead. Revolver and riding whip for leading heavy. Musket for female juvenile lead. Mining implements. Wine and beer glasses, cigars. Peddler's disguise for juvenile lead. Dice and dice-box. Pack of playing cards containing five aces. Searchlight. Two bloodhounds. Stiletto for female heavy. Trick bottle to break. Clasp-knife and gag for second heavy. Window panes covered with isinglass; a box of glass to make noise when window is broken. Two imitation bricks for Irish comic. Long rope with noose. Colored fire. Gun and hand cuffs for second juvenile. American flag. . . .

Today: A revolver (unloaded). A writing desk.[28]

* * *

Why did cheap melodrama give way to the movies? Without question, economic factors were crucial in melodrama's shift from stage to screen, particularly in light of the relative poverty of melodrama's primary audience. The movies cost a nickel instead of the 25 to 75 cents charged by melodrama theaters. (The difference in ticket prices was substantial: a nickel in 1910 was equivalent to about 95 cents today; thus 25 to 75 cents would be equivalent to about $4.75 to $14.00.) William Lyon Phelps, a Yale English professor, summed up the situation in a 1916 talk: "The 'movies' have driven . . . melodrama from the stage, and the reason is simple. . . . Why should you pay two dollars to see *Nellie, the Beautiful Cloak Model* or *Wedded, But No Wife* when you can see the same thing for five cents?"[29]

Walter Prichard Eaton, writing a month earlier, was equally sure of the economic causality:

The type of cheap, sentimental melodrama exemplified by that classic Nellie, the Beautiful Sewing Machine Girl *[sic] used to be called Third*

Avenue melodrama. Over on Third Avenue, and elsewhere in similar districts throughout the country, it has been supplanted now by the movies, which offer exactly the same sort of rubbish for a much smaller price.[30]

Movies were a better deal than stage drama not only for spectators but for theater managers and producers, as well. They could realize greater profits with movies, even with the much lower ticket prices. Producing stage plays was a risky and expensive proposition, requiring large sums of capital to build sets and pay actors, stage carpenters, and technicians. Lincoln J. Carter's *An American Ace* reportedly required fifty-five stagehands to run the show. While this was extraordinary, it suggests how labor-intensive the stage-melodrama industry was. By the turn of the century, most theater managers did not produce their own shows (the stock-company system of in-house production largely faded away in the 1880s), instead relying on traveling companies. With this system, they generally were obliged to split profits fifty-fifty with the touring show's producer, and then had to fork over up to a third of their remaining share to the centralized booking agency that served as the middleman between theaters and touring-show producers.[31] Theater managers were happy to do away with this system; renting films for exhibition was much less complicated and costly. Moreover, with films, exhibitors could run many more shows per day (ten to twelve, instead of just one or two stage shows), and movies could be exhibited year-round. Most melodrama (and other dramatic) theaters were boarded up during the summer, the traditional theatrical off-season. Movies helped theater owners maximize profits by doing away with that dead time.

The question remains, however, to what extent the aesthetic preference of audiences, rather than simple economic pragmatics, is responsible for killing stage melodrama. As a 1912 article in *McClure's* stated with distinct assurance, "The moving picture has supplanted the old form of 'mellerdrammer,' the greater intensity of its realism appeals to popular audiences."[32] This assertion parallels the central argument of Vardac's classic study *Stage to Screen*, a key reference point for any consideration of the cinema's intertextual origins. Focusing on aesthetic factors to the almost total exclusion of economic ones, Vardac argued that the cinema grew out of the demand for a combination of Romantic spectacle and pictorial realism, that is, for incredible sights presented with credible diegetic realism. Cinema "made its appearance," Vardac asserted, "in response to the insistence of social pressure for a greater pictorial realism in the theatre."[33]

Interestingly, Vardac's argument took as its point of departure an idea about melodrama's relation to modernity. Like a great many historians of art, literature, and popular culture, Vardac observed that a predilection for diegetic realism informed virtually all arts and amusements in the nineteenth century. Why was realism the crucial nineteenth-century aesthetic? Vardac suggested that the public's craving for realism was an expression of the "modern objective and scientific point of view" fostered by the Enlightenment. "Can the motion picture," Vardac speculated in his introduction, "be considered as the ultimate aesthetic expression of a cycle of realistic-pictorial theatrical production which had been a part of the rebirth of the objective spirit in the middle of the eighteenth century and which was to mature through the nineteenth-century age of invention?" (xviii). He elaborates:

The spirit which dominated the nineteenth century arose from the intellectual upheavals of the eighteenth. . . . Realistic rebellion and intellectual inquisition were breeding. The universe was questioned and dissected and its fabric examined. The modern objective and scientific point of view was in the process of birth. Its most immediate and sensational manifestations may indeed have been in the political arena, with revolutions flaring upon two continents within a matter of decades, but the power of this new spirit, pervading the eighteenth-century horizon, found a ready reflection in aesthetic areas as well. In the arts of the theatre this spirit . . . stimulated the growth of a new realism in staging and acting. As the objective or scientific point of view dominated society, finding its outlet in the flood of scientific invention of the nineteenth century, the cycle of realistic theatrical presentation . . . marched in close step." (xvii)

Vardac unfortunately did not offer an adequate explication of why the objective spirit of Enlightenment rationality should have manifested itself as a taste for spectacular realism. It is quite a leap to suggest that the desire to unearth the laws of science through empirical analysis somehow generated a desire to see theatrical renderings of sensational train wrecks.

Fortunately, Vardac's enticing but vague framing of melodrama as a product of Enlightenment rationality is not crucial to the book's main argument about cinema's displacement of stage melodrama. Cinema, Vardac contended, emerged at just the moment when stage melodrama had gone as far as it could to satisfy the Romantic realist aesthetic (how-

ever one explains the period's zeal for realism). Just when stage melodrama was straining hardest to simulate locomotive crashes, raging
infernos, auto chases, ocean grottoes, rushing waterfalls, erupting volca-
noes, and so on, film came along and offered it all more vividly, with an
intrinsic photographic realism that made the stage's scenic and mechanical contrivances appear embarrassingly artificial. Film ousted stage
melodrama, according to this argument, because audiences immediately recognized that film was an inherently superior medium for showing
a series of incredible sights in a realistic way. The theater's attempts at
spectacular realism had never been particularly successful, he suggested.
However hard stage melodrama strove to be "cinematic" (to use Vardac's
post hoc characterization), it came up against insurmountable limitations in its ability to present awesome environments and stunning feats
in a convincing way. After the shift from gas lighting to less forgiving
bright electric stage lighting, and especially in provincial theaters that
lacked the dimensions and facilities for full-blown scenic effects, the
patently artificial sets and props (stock painted flats, for the most part)
deflated illusionistic absorption. Even in the larger melodrama theaters,
mechanical and electrical devices often malfunctioned. Many productions tried to intensify realism by using real objects on stage (real horses, real automobiles, real pile drivers, real trees, real water, etc.), but
against the backdrop of two-dimensional painted-canvas sets and props,
this attempt at realism created an incongruity that simply heightened an
awareness of the overall scenic artificiality. Stage melodrama also had
difficulty keeping up with tumultuous action: it tried to change scenes
rapidly, or switch back and forth between settings to create suspense,
but its conventional techniques of rearranging flats, revolving sets, and
shifting spotlights achieved only awkwardly what film could do much
more easily and effectively through editing. "There is clear indication,"
Vardac wrote, "of a highly cinematic conception being limited and
debased in its production by the traditional staging devices" (24). As
soon as cinema appeared, he suggested, audiences recognized its superiority as a medium for realistic, rapid-fire sensations. Unable to compete
with film as a medium for spectacular diegetic realism, stage melodrama
quickly faded away.

Judging from period sources, Vardac for the most part appears to
have been right on target. One finds numerous indications that stage
melodrama's attempts at sensational realism were falling flat. A 1906
review of *Bedford's Hope* commented that

Some weakness is sure to present itself in nearly every one of the first half-hundred performances. . . . Perhaps the automobile would not appear at the right time, or one of the panoramas would stick, or move at less speed than was required, or the smoke from the train would not be emitted regularly. Every performance developed some weakness.[34]

In the same year, a review of *Bertha, the Sewing Machine Girl* reported: "Mishaps to some of the intended effective mechanical climaxes marred several incidents, and an extremely shaky fire engine in act three thoroughly destroyed the realism of the scene. . . . The various mechanical effects, particularly the motor boat episode and the fire scene, will be more effective when they work smoothly."[35] A 1903 review of *Queen of the White Slaves* mocked stage melodrama's inability to render a convincing illusion of deep space using small painted flats for supposedly distant objects: "When the hero is placed on a raft in mid-ocean the gallery last night began to worry. It was a ticklish position, but never fear! An ocean liner several sizes smaller than the hero and his planks hove into view! Saved! Saved!"[36] In 1907, Harry James Smith, reporting on his slumming expedition to a 10–20–30 production called *'Neath the Shadow of the Gallows*, recounted: "In the distance is heard a faint toot-toot, and at the same time across the farthest trestle puffs a locomotive. It must be miles away, it looks so small. [A girl sitting nearby says to her friend,] "Gee, look at that train! Ain't it the cutest?"[37] And Porter Emerson Browne's 1909 description of a typical 10–20–30 production stressed the show's scenographic absurdity:

The hero is tied to the railroad track; but just before he is about to be run over by the lightning express (which acts like a Long Island Limited), along comes the heroine on a hand car and saves his life just as the train dashes past at the rate of two miles an hour. To show that he is not unappreciative, the hero walks over a great precipice on the character woman's clothes-line, and hanging by his toes from a tree that looks like a cross between a persimmon and a huckleberry bush, snatches the heroine from certain death at the hands of the villain and his assistants. He likewise pulls her out from beneath a crosscut saw, drags her from under the whirling wheels of a canvas automobile just as she is about to be ground to death, races eighty miles in plain view of the audience in the marvelous time of two minutes and twenty-three seconds, on an ex-cab-horse, and turns off the current just as the villainess, who has cut the trolley wire, is about to inject hypodermically a couple of thousand volts into the heroine's prostrate form.[38]

In 1918, *An American Ace* met with this tepid review:

> *The beginning of the aerial battle, with the whir of the American machine going higher and higher until it seemed to be directly above the head of the audience, was exciting, and there was just one glimpse of a tiny airplane and a rolling country below, which satisfied the imagination. After that, the fighting fliers ran into clouds which were much too gross in texture, and the planes failed to work smoothly. Most of the action took place in a small circle bounded by palpable canvas, which gave a much more compelling suggestion of a fish pond than a bit of sky.*[39]

Although Vardac appears to have been largely unaware of it (since his research did not extend into general periodicals), a host of critics witnessing stage melodrama's demise firsthand accounted for the phenomenon in precisely the same terms Vardac would later put forward: film melodrama beat stage melodrama on aesthetic grounds. As a writer in the *Independent* stated in 1910: "It is a mistake to suppose that [the movies'] amazing popularity is due altogether to their low price of admission. On the contrary, the cinematograph has some advantages not only over the cheap [melodrama] shows which it at first rivaled, but over any previous form of dramatic art."[40]

Scores of writers pointed to a range of aesthetic advantages enjoyed by the film medium. They accentuated film's powerful diegetic realism—its ability to situate dramatic action in real-world settings—and noted film's superiority in capturing movement, depth, and spectacle. They also recognized the radical novelty of film's power to move instantly from scene to scene, to crosscut back and forth between scenes, and to show different vantage points within a scene. The *Independent*'s critic summed up these cinematic advantages with remarkable astuteness:

> *The abolition of the painted scenery of the backdrop gives to the [film] drama a sense of reality, a solidity, that it never had before. The mountains and clouds do not now show spots of threadbare canvas. The tumbling waves do not throw up a dust. The rock and trees do not shiver at the touch of the actors. . . . The modern manager limits his playwrights to three or four changes of scenery on account of expense and the time it takes to set them. But for the cinematograph there are no such restrictions. . . . The setting may be changed in the twinkling of an eye, or it may be gradually shifted to follow the actors without jar or rumble. The moving*

scenery of Wagner's "Parsifal" and the treadmill of the racecourse play,
which aroused the admiration of our fathers, seem to us absurdly crude
and clumsy. The divided stage, with its broken partition end-on to the
spectator, may also be sent to the lumber room. The moving picture has it
in its power by alternating scenes to show us what is going on simultane-
ously in two different places, inside and outside a house, for example, or in
adjoining rooms. [Film] can vary at will the distance of the stage, giving
us a closer view at critical moments. . . . The artist foresee[s] our desire
and suddenly the detail is enlarged for us until it fill[s] the canvas.[41]

The general press quickly recognized cinema's special affinity for melodrama. In a 1907 *Harper's Weekly* article, "The Nickel Madness," one of the earliest general-periodical articles on the movies, Barton W. Currie noted the "melodramatic" vigor of the accelerated pacing and spectacle made possible by film editing: "Is it any wonder that the lovers of melodrama are delighted? . . . Melodrama is served hot and at a pace the Bowery theatres can never follow. In one place I visited, a band of pirates were whirled through a maze of hair-raising adventures that could not have occurred in a Third Avenue home of melodrama in less that two hours."[42] The temporal compression made possible through editing was perfectly suited to the melodrama's principal objective of delivering "punch."

Critics were most impressed by the greater illusion of reality creat-ed by the photographic medium of film. As a writer in *The World Today* put it in 1908, "The pictures have a curious semblance to reality, and when thrown on the screen are supposed to be motographs of actual life."[43] Frank Woods, "The Spectator" in the *New York Dramatic Mirror*, employed similar phrasing in 1909: "We have the illusion that we are looking at the photograph of an actual event in real life."[44] Both state-ments are interesting in their sophistication, suggesting a mode of real-ism that hinges on a consciousness of the medium's photographic basis—they do not say "movies show us real life," but rather "movies show us photographs of real life." More typically, writers stressed a more direct and powerful illusion of reality, based on a suspension of disbelief that maximizes emotional and kinesthetic absorption. As a writer in *Photo-Era* elaborated in 1908, whereas with stage melodrama the spec-tator never loses an awareness that "this is but representation," film's realism created a much deeper illusion of being in front of real events actually unfolding:

I believe I am old enough, hard, traveled and experienced enough to sepa-rate the false from the true in experience, life or books as the majority of my fellows. I know how motion pictures are made, where they are made and for what purposes. Yet I am free to say that the photoplay I once saw of a kidnapping of a little child made me fairly writhe, and I could hardly wait to get home from the theater . . . to my own little man to see that he, too, wasn't a victim. The intense realism comes in the natural surround-ings—so utterly different from the scenes of the best staged play ever put on the boards. When you see a ruffian on the stage drag a kidnapped child across a stage rock and then slam him up against a stage door, made of canvas and that yields to his weight, you may be mildly excited, but your senses tell you all the time, "This is but representation." But when you see a real ruffian take a real child and drag him over real rocks and through real water—real because photographed from life—you live that scene, and your emotions are correspondingly greater.[45]

A number of critics resisted this idea that film was inherently more illusionistic by pointing to film's flatness, grayness, and muteness. But for many, the aesthetic consequences of film's diegetic realism were pro-found and compelling. There was a widespread sense that film had made stage melodrama look ridiculously artificial in comparison. George Bernard Shaw stressed the point in 1915:

[Film] reduces the would-be deceptive realistic scenery of the spoken drama to absurdity. . . . The illusion of theatrical scenery has always been itself an illusion: everyone who has rehearsed a play containing outdoor scenes knows how the first rehearsal with the scenery produces a disheartening and ridiculous disillusion, whereas the film . . . transports the spectator to the very place that has been photographed. Against the competition of such powers of actual representation the theater can do nothing except with indoor scenes.[46]

A 1917 article in *The Century* similarly emphasized the impossibility of achieving a convincing illusion of reality when real objects and actors were surrounded with mere painted flats:

One cannot without absurdity burn a house or wreck a train in the the-ater. . . . And so far as his scene transcends what can be actually set upon the stage, just so far will the contrast between his actors, who are in truth flesh and blood, and their environment, which is not what it seems, but only light and paint and canvas, become more patently incongruous.[47]

Writing in 1914, Eaton perceived not only that cinema had killed stage melodrama, but that its emergence as the principal medium of spectacular realism would indirectly foster modernist developments in theater:

Because the camera can be carried so easily far afield, to show mountains and gorges, rivers and caverns, deserts and jungles, which all people love to look upon and which the pasteboard stage of the theater can never hope to depict with a thousandth part of the camera's realism, it is more than likely that the old-fashioned spectacular play will fall more and more into disrepute, and the drama will more and more concentrate upon modern realistic plays with an intellectual drift, or upon poetry and that form of scenery which is not realistic but consciously artificial, calculated to achieve a decorative or suggestive effect. The old-fashioned popular melodrama has already disappeared from the stage, and reappeared upon the movie screen.[48]

But not everyone was always so ready to concede cinema's superiority as a medium for realism. Eaton, always up for a good argument, particularly against himself, concluded elsewhere that all the talk about film realism was overblown, since films merely employed the same artificial stagecraft as theatrical melodrama:

The assumption that because "the camera can go anywhere" therefore the motion picture plays have opened a new world vista has proved to be nonsense, and instead of an enlarged art, we are getting a feeble and old-fashioned type of "real pump" realism. The desert is a stretch of sand in California. A Moorish village is built out of painted wood; the walls of Babylon suggest the rear view of a Revere Beach [Boston] or Coney Island amusement park, where you see the wooden props and the bits of tin. Fake, fake, fake! What does it matter whether a Moorish village is built at Fort Lee or on the stage of the Belasco Theater? . . . Possibly the camera can go anywhere, but the fact remains that it doesn't. The writer for the screen has no more chance of authentic realism than the writer for the oral stage.[49]

But Eaton was far outnumbered in the critical discourse. The obvious consensus was that, as Vardac would eventually argue, it was cinema that made stage melodrama look "fake, fake, fake!"[50]

* * *

As abundant and unequivocal as the contemporaneous critical discourse is in supporting the thesis that stage melodrama failed because of its relative inadequacy as a vehicle for Romantic realism, Vardac's thesis may obscure as much as it illuminates. It is simultaneously apt and misleading. Just how misleading depends on how one interprets Vardac's underlying conception of "pictorial realism" with respect to the nature of spectatorship. Discussions of diegetic realism can get rather muddled because the term can convey at least three rather different assumptions about the spectator's relation to the image or mise-en-scène.

One sense of diegetic realism is more or less equivalent to "naturalism." It is a quasi-documentary mode of verisimilitude that focuses on the representation of ordinary phenomena as they occur in lived experience. At issue are both subject matter and style. The subject matter must represent "actual" scenes, scenes that really occurred, or at least scenes that give the impression that they *could* really have occurred in the course of ordinary experience. At the same time, the style must present scenes in a manner that replicates empirical observation or mimics perceptual reality, keeping to a minimum any subjective or expressionistic devices that may render scenes less lifelike in outward appearance. This mode or realism is not at all like Romantic realism, in which the phenomena, while conveyed realistically in terms of style, are supposed to be extraordinary and amazing in subject matter, presenting events that are well beyond the scope of mundane quotidian experience.

A second sense of "realism" entails that a spectator perceives that a given aesthetic construction renders the world with a high degree of verisimilitude or convincing detail. At first this may sound similar to the first definition, but it differs in that it does not rule out the extraordinary events of Romantic spectacle (or mythological and cosmic/supernatural scenes, etc.). This sense of realism differs from the first with respect to the kinds of subject matter it presents. But another issue is more crucial in defining it—an issue involving the spectator's posture toward the depicted scenes. While the depiction solicits from the spectator a recognition or appreciation of the work's lifelikeness, the verisimilitude does not create a strong feeling of diegetic immersion in the represented space. The spectator perceives that, as a consequence of certain aesthetic techniques deployed by the creator, the scene looks "realistic." However, the spectator remains "outside" the work, not wrapped up in the illusion of reality. I will use the term *apperceptive realism* to denote this spectatorially detached mode of realism. One could also use the term *photographic realism*, but the term is not ideal since it is only metaphoric when used to describe theater, painting, or other nonphotographic forms of representation.

In its strongest sense, realism implies a mode of "illusionism" in which the spectator experiences a powerful sense of absorption in the diegesis. With this mode, which I will refer to as *absorptive realism*, spectators are said to suspend disbelief and imagine they are witnessing an event happening in front of them in the real world. Needless to say, extreme illusionism, in which the spectator actually mistakes the representation for reality, is seldom if ever achieved. But the feeling of presence as an onlooker in a highly convincing diegesis is much stronger with absorptive realism than with apperceptive realism. Absorptive realism, which one might also call diegetic illusionism, is what typically has been regarded as the goal of effective commercial filmmaking. From early on, viewers and critics perceived, as a writer in 1917 put it, "The moving picture is primarily a device for visualizing imaginary action as actually taking place."[51]

Vardac argued that "pictorial realism" was the ultimate goal of stage melodrama. It is not clear, however, what he meant by this. While he definitely did not have the first sense of realism—naturalism—in mind, there is little in his discussion to indicate whether he thought of pictorial realism in terms of apperceptive realism or absorptive realism. Given Vardac's argument that movies beat melodrama at its own game, and given the pervasive critical emphasis on cinema's absorptive powers, I am inclined to think Vardac's pictorial realism was essentially equivalent to absorptive realism. But it is not crucial that we make a determination one way or the other. However Vardac conceived of pictorial realism, his fundamental assumption was that realism was melodrama's crucial and defining goal. This premise prompts Vardac to belittle melodrama as just a hapless *cinema manqué*, groping toward effects that were, as he put it, "properly cinematic."

* * *

This teleological view of stage melodrama as simply a primitive, "debased" proto-cinema, striving for realism but never graduating beyond "sham, toylike devices," hinges on an overly simplistic conception of stage melodrama's aesthetic foundations and of the mode of theatrical spectatorship it called into play.

For many spectators of popular stage melodrama, the conspicuous mechanical contrivance of stagecraft may not have been a glaring deficiency but rather one of the amusement's key attractions. As with many forms of artistic illusion, an apperceptive aesthetic of medium-aware-ness, a fascination with what technique and artifice can do, operated alongside an aesthetic of absorptive realism.

An association between melodrama and illusionism, or absorptive realism, had long been stressed, particularly by bourgeois critics who made fun of the gullibility and stupidity of working-class and provincial audiences. Popular audiences were often said to be duped, like children or simpletons, by stage melodrama's illusionism. Rollin Lynde Hartt, for example, asserted, "It is beyond the power of the Neolithic mind [of the 10–20–30 spectator] to distinguish between the visible representation and the thing it claims to represent."[52] Porter Emerson Browne provides another example:

In the vernacular, the melodramatic audience is a "warm" house to play to—it "eats" a "show." And why not? It's real to them; as real as is life itself—and sometimes even more real than life itself. . . . To it, the exag-gerated, affected acting and mannerisms and enunciation of the players; the dull tawdry absurdity of the scenery; the glaring inconsistencies in both production and text; the utter lack of logic; the hopeless impossibility of sit-uation, convey only the impression of actual things that actually exist, of events actually happening before its very eyes. Melodramatic audiences are the children of the theatre.[53]

But perhaps it was Browne and his colleagues who were under a misap-prehension. There is no reason to think popular audiences were duped by the stage's realist devices. Nor were they necessarily disappointed or bothered by a persistent awareness of the stage's mimetic inadequacy. Stage melodrama's aesthetic appeal derived in part precisely from the frank artificiality of its devices and settings. Its pleasures were based on the flux between absorptive realism (or perhaps only apperceptive real-ism) and the enjoyment of overt theatricality.

The stereotypical image most often used to convey the condition of overabsorbed spectatorship is that of the audience member so wrapped up in the fictional world that he cannot help but shout out at the actors—spontaneously blurting out warnings to the heroine or curses to the villain. As Browne recounts the typical 10–20–30 show:

A boy in the gallery unexpectedly and embarrassingly saves the lives of both of them [hero and heroine] just as they are about to drink an allo-pathic dose of deadly poison that has been prepared for them by the vil-

lain, by yelling, in shrill and excited treble: "Hey, youse! Don't swally dat on yuh life! I seen de guy wit' de black hair put knockout drops in it!"

What this image of spectatorial gullibility overlooks is that raucous interactivity between audience and stage was a ritual part of the melodrama experience. As Browne himself stated, "The audience from gallery to orchestra joins in hungrily hissing the villain."[54] The "gallery gods" who interrupted the show by standing up and yelling catcalls probably did not do so because they were overly immersed in the narrative diegesis, but rather because the performance presupposed a constant disruption of diegetic absorption. The interaction between audience and actors (it went both ways—most notably, when the villain broke out of the diegesis to curse back at the audience with raised fist) could not help but accentuate the audience's awareness of the concrete theatrical setting and of the overtly presentational quality of the performance (fig. 6.6).

Audiences did not go to a stage melodrama just to be transported into a convincing Romantic other-world. They went also to enjoy a mode of rowdy, vocal, "distanced" (yet very involved) spectatorship. Allowing plenty of room for rambunctiousness was a key provision in the implicit contract between audiences and producers. As Owen Davis stated, "You must create a situation at which the audience must shout and yell at the end of each act. Melodramatic audiences like to whoop and hurrah, so you've got to give them an opportunity."[55] John Hollingshead, a London theater producer in the late nineteenth century, described the ritual uproar during a performance of *Oliver Twist* at the Vic:

Nancy was always dragged around the stage by her hair, and after this effort, Sykes always looked up defiantly at the gallery, as he was doubtless told to do in the marked prompt-book. He was always answered by one loud and fearful curse, yelled by the whole mass like a Handel Festival Chorus. The curse was answered by Sykes by dragging Nancy twice round the stage, and then like Ajax, defying the lightning. The simultaneous yell then became louder and more blasphemous. Finally, when Sykes, working up to a well-rehearsed climax, smeared Nancy with red ochre, and taking her by the hair (a most powerful wig) seemed to dash her brains out on the stage, no explosion of dynamite invented by the modern anarchist, no language ever dreamed of in Bedlam, could equal the outburst. A thousand enraged voices which sounded like ten thousand, with the roar of a dozen

Fig. 6.6 The Bowery Theatre, New York City, 1878. (Clipping, unidentified newspaper, Harvard Theatre Collection)

escaped menageries, filled the theatre and deafened the audience, and when the smiling ruffian came forward and bowed, their voices in thorough plain English expressed a fierce determination to tear his sanguinary entrails from his sanguinary body.[56] *[See fig. 6.7.]*

From such accounts, one infers that the creation of absorptive illusion was not the preeminent objective. The communal shattering of illusion was probably just as crucial, if not more so, to the experience of attending a melodrama.

This question of audience participation may be something of a side issue, however, since Vardac's argument does not concentrate on the relationship between the audience and the actors, but rather on the relationship between the audience and the quasi-realistic scenography. Was stage melodrama's scenographic artificiality an aesthetic liability, as Vardac contended? Clearly, as the passages I have quoted indicate, many people did view the awkwardness and phoniness of the painted flats as a major shortcoming. But the artificiality was surely also a source of pleasure. For some spectators, apperceptive and/or absorptive diegetic realism may have been less important than the pleasure taken in the aesthetic contrivance of the spectacle. Over and above the "surreal" or

Fig. 6.7 *Oliver Twist*, stock poster, c. 1870. (Courtesy Harvard Theatre Collection)

"poetic" qualities possibly created by the scenography's colorful transposition and estrangement of reality, Romantic realist spectacle probably also evoked pleasure in appreciating what scenic effects could be accomplished using the tricks of stagecraft. The sight of an ascending hot air balloon or a canoe going over rapids was probably engaging less because it allowed audiences to suspend their disbelief and imagine they were witnessing an event occurring in the real world, or because the effect approached photographic realism, than because it prompted delight that such a sight could even be rendered, however inexactly, within the constraints of the medium. In terms of dramatic narration or enunciation, stage melodrama presented a mode of "discours," not "histoire." It did not try for "invisible" representation; rather, the narrational agent declared loudly, "Hey, look what we're doing up here!" A consciousness of the stagecraft mechanisms at work—horses galloping on a treadmill; the rolling painted backdrop simulating movement through space, and so on—involved a different kind of pleasure than apperceptive realism or diegetic illusionism. It is the pleasure of the trick; a "how to" interest in the medium's materials and its representational potentials.

The use of real objects on stage may have involved another kind of thrill, as well. Vardac argued that the juxtaposition of real objects against painted flats just made matters worse, accentuating the phoniness of the entire setup. But that interpretation may miss the point, at least to some extent. The sight of a real horse at full gallop on a treadmill, or of real water, real fire engines and automobiles, real pile drivers, and real buzz saws, and so on, was exciting not because (or not *just* because) it gave the illusion of another time and place beyond the theater, but rather because of the anti-illusory novelty of objects brazenly out-of-place within the real theater space. This diegetic break tended to annoy critics schooled in bourgeois codes of representation. As Olivia Howard Dunbar complained: "The ecstasy experienced by persons of a certain degree of simplicity in recognizing on the stage a familiar object or character has never been explained. . . . It has often been apparent that audiences betrayed a keener delight in the introduction into a play of a cow or a horse than in the exploits of the most accomplished actor."[57]

The incongruity between the indoor stage and the real-world objects that clearly belonged elsewhere—belonged out-of-doors, in coal mines, farm yards, racetracks, highways—must have created a thrill, an uncanny pleasure in seeing such a vivid "category mistake." This kind of sensation is still exploited today: the spectacle of a real downpour on stage in the mid-1980s made a major hit out of a critically panned Broadway adaptation of *Singin' in the Rain*. Similarly, one of the appeals of "monster truck" shows in New York City is the opportunity to see Madison Square Garden transformed into a backwoods bog, with tons of mud covering the same floor the Knicks play on. This sort of theatrical pleasure derives not only from the illusion of being transported to another world but also from a heightened awareness of the nondiegetic time and place of the real theatrical setting.

One gets a sense of the delight created by the paradoxical anti-illusionistic quality of conspicuous realism from an 1890 review of the New York premiere of *Blue Jeans*, a Joseph Arthur melodrama that had an important influence on the direction 10–20–30 melodrama would take in the next twenty years. The critic wrote:

The great sensation of Blue Jeans *is the buzz-saw, but that is the last act and I must work up to it. Realism is conspicuous in every act. There is a real barn built upon the stage, and a real girl (no, she is not real; there are none such in real life) climbs the ladder and daubs real red paint on the bare boards, and whisks the paint off the brush into the face of a man who stands below the ladder. This latter touch of realism is received with flattering applause which is very gentle compared to the shouts that go up when this unreal girl pulls a string and lets a shower of real grain down upon the head of the man . . . and a pan of dish-water is thrown on two men who happen to be in the way. . . . In the second act, we have a real brass band, a real live calf, a real dead calf, and a real live horse with overalls on his front legs to keep the flies off. . . . Then there is a peach-tree in full blossom, with blossoms that fall in showers whenever it is touched. Bob Hilliard shakes the tree over June, and she says "Shake it again," so that the audience may see how inexhaustible is the supply of loose blossoms. . . . The fourth and last act shows us the Buzz Saw going at full speed. To show that the saw is as real as the buzz, it is made to cut thick boards into lengths, and cold shivers pass over the audience as it settles itself down to enjoy what it thinks, I will not say hopes, may be a real tragedy. . . . With a fiendish smile upon his face, [the villain] points to the buzz-saw, winks at the audience and places the unresisting form of Hilliard within a few feet of the cruel wheel. He is being drawn nearer and nearer his doom, and we expect every moment to see the buzz-saw do to the prostrate actor what King Solomon intended to do to the disputed baby, when June breaks through the door and grabs him away from certain death just*

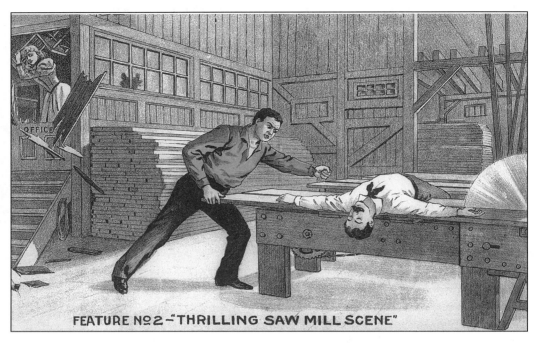

Fig. 6.8 Poster for *Blue Jeans*, c. 1895. (Courtesy Debra Clifford, Vintage Poster Works: www.vintageposterworks.com)

Fig. 6.9 Stage production of *Blue Jeans*, c. 1890. (Courtesy Museum of the City of New York)

Fig. 6.10 Advertisement for 1917 film version of *Blue Jeans*. (*Motion Picture News*, December 8, 1917)

before he is split in twain. Can the art of playwright further go? No it cannot, if we are to judge by the breathless excitement of the audience during this scene and the applause which followed it.[58]

It is clear that this kind of realism never purported to provide a window onto the world. It was extremely self-conscious, soliciting the delight of a highly medium-aware audience (see figs. 6.8, 6.9, and 6.10).

The audience's reaction to the spectacle of physical peril in *Blue Jeans* is particularly telling: the thrill was not that the protagonist would be killed by the saw, but rather that Robert Hilliard, the actor playing the protagonist, might be injured. It was an awareness that the stunt was risky, that something might go wrong, or the timing might be off, that agitated spectators. They feared for the actor's flesh, not the protagonist's. This form of spectacular realism shifts the frame of attention from a believable diegetic realm, the frame one would expect realism to foster, to the material circumstances of the theater. Indeed, this is the precondition for the spectacle's effectiveness as a thrill.

This fact is illustrated very clearly in A. H. Wood's account of tinkering with the engineering of a thrill to make it more powerful:

There was a news account of how a brave fireman rescued a girl from the top of a burning building by guiding her across a stretch of telephone wires to safety on another roof. When the rescue was dramatized, however, it fell flat. Its basis was all right, we were sure; but somehow the whole thing did not project the desired sensation. We originally used a heavy wire with a protecting guide wire above for the heroine to escape over. So we figured it out that the thing looked too easy, and hence was robbed of the longed-for thrill. We go a finer wire and tried out the scene. It was not right yet. Probably the height of the wire from the ground did not seem sufficiently great. We raised the wire and faked the scenery so that the height seemed twice as great. Still the effect failed. We abolished the upper guide wire, to which the rescuer clung, thus making the feat more difficult; but the thrill was still found to be lacking. We had the flames from the blazing building shoot out over the wires and threaten the escapers with the double peril of fire and electric shock from the wires, off which the insulation would be in imminent danger of being burned—and still the spine out in front [i.e., the collective audience, ready for its spine-chilling thrill] was not affected as it should have been. In this way we spent our time pondering over the secret of the thrill that was steadfastly eluding us, until one day the stage manager suggested that we had overlooked the main thrill-element of the rescue. "It ain't the flames or electric shock or danger of falling naturally that'll thrill the audience," he argued: "but the fear that the wires'll break under the actors' weight and hurl them to the ground below." We saw in a flash that he was right. We had a couple of wires hang down on the poles, as if they had already broken, and at the beginning of the fire and just before the rescue scene, we had a man stationed inside the burning house slyly snap one of the telephone wires and let it fall to the ground with the usual hissing sound. The effect was instantaneous. The spines realized that the remaining wires might snap at any moment! And they poured their silver tribute into the box office.[59]

This thrill only became truly a thrill when the producers were able to convince the audience there was in fact some real danger that the real actors could fall and suffer real broken bones if they plummeted onto the stage floor. The effect was sensational not because it reproduced a convincing diegesis but, in a certain sense, precisely because it did not. To achieve the thrill, the illusion had to be obstructed and the material theatricality of the spectacle underscored.

Interestingly, a similar situation obtained in the cinematic successors to sensational stage melodrama, which also strove for "Realism with a big R."[60] Publicity materials for serial melodramas of the Teens constantly stressed the injuries risked or suffered by the real-life stars during shooting. Producers invariably claimed that for the sake of realism stunts were rarely faked.[61] To promote the idea that serials showed real actors imperiled by real physical dangers (and to foster the new "star system"), producers used the actors' names for the protagonists (as I will detail in chapter 9).

Also as with stage melodrama, spectacular realism in the movies could have an ironically anti-illusionistic effect: it broke the illusion by drawing attention to the sophisticated contrivance of its stunts and special effects. A writer in *The Editor* admonished prospective screenwriters:

Not long ago, directors were still going to the trouble and expense of smashing a couple of trains into kindling wood. They expected their audiences to quake in horror. Instead every one was wondering how much it cost to stage a fake wreck. None but the most guileless was fooled. Such attempts at realism merely give rise to questions not bearing on the subject at hand. The imagination is set going in the opposite direction. . . . All this striving after realism is such a waste of effort. . . . If a director wishes to create a life-illusion, his methods must not be so obvious as to destroy that illusion. This is exactly what realism does.[62]

Underlying this statement is an aesthetic bias toward bourgeois naturalism and against sensational melodrama. But beyond that, it suggests a more basic conviction that any use of the film medium that obstructs diegetic absorption is a misuse, a violation of the medium's true calling.

A belief in the paramount importance of absorptive realism may have informed Vardac's conception of the cinema—and stage melodrama. Or perhaps Vardac was only interested in affirming the importance of apperceptive realism to cinema's—and stage melodrama's—representation of spectacular action. Either way, Vardac's characterization of stage melodrama as simply an inadequate proto-cinema—a clumsy cinema "wannabe"—slights an artform whose aesthetic foundations were undoubtedly more complex. Certainly, audiences enjoyed the increased sensationalism of real, albeit "canned," train wrecks and explosions rather than unconvincing theatrical simulations. But stage melodrama provided different kinds of pleasures. It is worth bearing this in mind not only to do justice to stage melodrama's aesthetic distinctiveness, but also because it returns us to the historical question of how and why the movies wiped out popular-priced stage melodrama, tilting the balance between economic and aesthetic determinants. If 10–20–30 melodrama did indeed offer distinct pleasures, pleasures other than those cinema could provide more effectively, it may suggest that stage melodrama's rapid obliteration was due less to the audience's recognition of its aesthetic inadequacy than to the significant economic advantages that movies exploited.

However one chooses to place the emphasis, there is no question that by around 1909 fans of sensational melodrama with a little bit of pocket money and free time most likely would have strolled past the old 10–20–30 theater they used to patronize and instead headed for one of the many nickelodeons that had sprung up all over town. There they could count on finding virtually the same kind of thrills, perhaps even better executed in certain respects, for considerably less money. The rapidity with which the 10–20–30 disappeared suggests that the large majority of its audience was content to make the switch from stage to screen. Some habitués of stage melodrama no doubt were sorry to see the movies usurp the 10–20–30's niche, but even less happy about this development were the many film industry and cultural critics who had hoped the cinema would aspire to "something better" than "mere mellerdrammer." Ultimately, their hopes would be satisfied to at least some degree—a middlebrow cinema did gradually emerge in the Teens—but, as the next chapter shows, a robust and persistent strain of sensational melodrama would always be there as a counterbalance.

7

"Child of Commerce! Bastard of Art!": Early Film Melodrama

The movies usurped the 10–20–30's niche during the nickelodeon boom of 1907–1909. Popular melodrama entered a new phase, a phase of unprecedented mass distribution by means of a modern technology of mechanical reproduction. Repackaged in a new medium— silent, black-and-white, canned—sensational melodrama was transformed. More striking, however, was the degree to which it remained the same.

"I wonder if you realize," wrote a moviegoer from Duluth, Minnesota, to the *Moving Picture World* in 1910, "that the plots of many of [the nickelodeon's] little plays are nothing more than picturized versions of 'Nick Carter' and 'Diamond Dick' stories."[1] A few months earlier, the *New York World*, the city's largest newspaper, had printed an editorial lodging the same complaint. The *New York Dramatic Mirror* responded to the *World*'s accusation in a rather curious way. One might have expected the *Mirror* to point to the obvious irony that Pulitzer's *World*, the first and most sensational yellow newspaper in the country, was in no position to shake its finger. Rather, the trade journal rebutted the attack by denying the validity of the dime novel comparison and instead arguing that what the movies really emulated was 10–20–30 stage melodramas. This was essentially an empty retort since 10–20–30 and dime novel melodramas were cut from the same cloth and were widely regarded as equally disreputable. One can only assume that the *Mirror* had concluded that the best rebuttal strategy was simply to muddy the waters. The response did go on to distance movies from 10–20–30 melodrama somewhat (maintaining that movies appealed to a wider audience, and that not all films were melodramas), but it is significant that the *Mirror* could not deny the initial complaint that the movies were, to a large extent, just a new variety of sensational melodrama.[2]

Early film melodramas were, of course, not simply carbon copies of stage melodramas. At the very least, their necessary brevity and silence meant that certain components could not carry over from stage to screen. One was comedy. On stage, according to an observer in 1907, "the melodrama is full of comedy; it is sure to follow every scene of pathos or violence."[3] Film melodramas tended to place much less emphasis on episodes of comic relief displaying the antics of ethnic types, hoboes, country rubes, scrappy urchins, and the like. The reasons for this are probably both narrational and pragmatic. Films generally tried to maintain a more consistent dramatic tenor throughout the narrative as opposed to stage melodrama, which almost always alternated between serious and comic scenes. In stage productions, comic shticks served as an upstage distraction during scene changes going on behind the painted backdrop or curtain. As stage melodrama's scenic effects grew more and more sensational and complicated, these diversions became absolutely necessary to avoid dead time between scenes. In film, however, comic scenes were no longer needed for this purpose and, in any case, a one- or two-reel film (with each reel running about fifteen minutes) had much less room for such material than a three-hour play.

The time constraint, along with the cinema's lack of sound dialogue, also meant that film melodramas placed less emphasis on the kind of protracted oratorical posturing of the histrionic acting associated with 10–20–30 productions (fig. 7.1). Stage melodrama's grand proclamations of resolute heroism, innocent desperation, and arch villainy (with built-in pauses for boisterous audience responses) did not carry over into movie melodrama, or at least did so only in abbreviated and transmuted form. Film critics did complain that the "melodramatic" style of acting (employing exaggerated stances based on a standardized semiotics of pose and gesture) was all too prevalent in the movies, but more naturalistic techniques gradually became conventional.[4]

"I WILL SAVE YOU FROM THEM FOUL FIENDS WHO IS STRIVIN' TO ENCOMPUSS YOUR ROON."

Fig. 7.1 "I Will Save You!" (*Everybody's Magazine*, September 1909)

Whatever the stylistic and structural differences between stage melodrama and film melodrama, there is no question that movies succeeded in capturing the essence of sensational melodrama. Movies delivered abundant rapid action, stimulating violence, spectacular sights, and the thrills of physical peril, abductions, and suspenseful rescues. On a narrative level, film melodramas relied on similar story lines emphasizing pure villainy and heroism catalyzed by the villain's jealousy and/or greed and often relying on extraordinary coincidences, sudden revelations, and unexpected twists of circumstance. In what follows I offer a small sampling of one- and two-reel films between 1901 and 1913 before turning to a more detailed discussion of serial films from 1914 to around 1920. The survey does not purport to be systematic, comprehensive, or studio-balanced; it simply presents some typical examples conveying the close intertextual connections between sensational stage melodramas and the films that took their place.

* * *

The earliest film melodramas were too brief to allow developed stories, but nevertheless they emulated stage melodrama in their use of artificial stagecraft to render sensation scenes. Pathé's *Un Drama au Fond de la Mer* (1901), for example, used a background of painted flats to depict an underwater view of a sunken ship set against the descent of two divers to an ocean floor scattered with bodies and treasure. Vardac would have disapproved of the unabashed artificiality. The film consists of a single incident of melodramatic violence: motivated by greed, one diver attacks the other from behind, cuts his air hose, and grabs the treasure. The victim staggers around and collapses as the murderer ascends. Richard Abel notes that the same spectacle was featured in an 1897 British melodrama entitled *The White Heather* (it also appeared in *The Millionaire and the Policeman's Wife*, 1909, and no doubt in several other stage melodramas, as well).[5] Another Pathé film, *L'Encendiare* (1905), brought together numerous melodramatic elements: a spectacular sensation scene, a wild chase, bodily peril, unjust victimization, and a last-minute rescue of sorts. A gypsy couple and their baby live in a makeshift hut. The husband falls asleep while smoking a pipe and accidentally sets fire to a haystack. Numerous shots of the burning haystack provide a sensation scene. Thrilling action comes in the form of a chase as an angry mob tries to capture the supposed arsonist. After a series of shots highlighting real settings and objects (a locomotive, a bridge, several walls, a shallow pond through which the man wades), the mob seizes the man and hangs him from a tree. When the mob disperses, the wife saves her husband by cutting the ropes with a scythe.

The Curfew Must Not Ring Tonight, a 1906 British film directed by Alf Collins for Gaumont, featured an action climax borrowed directly from David Belasco's 1895 Civil War melodrama *The Heart of Maryland.* Billed as "A Romance of the Days of Cromwell," the film portrays the capture, trial, and sentencing-to-death of a Royalist hero. He will be executed when the curfew bell rings that night. His lover risks her life to save him: she climbs up the perilous vines of the high tower and grasps onto the bell clapper to stop it from striking the bell. She swings violently back and forth, hitting the walls of the bell, and succeeds in silencing the death knell. Cromwell, furious that the bell did not ring, starts beating the pathetic deaf bell-ringer. The heroine cannot bear to see this and comes forward to confess her crime. Cromwell is so impressed by her courage that he pardons the Royalist, and the couple is happily reunited.[6]

Edwin S. Porter's *Life of an American Fireman* (Edison, 1903) may be regarded as a melodrama since it was built around two sensation scenes—a thrilling race of fire trucks and a treacherous rescue of a woman and child trapped in a burning building. *The Great Train Robbery* (1903) expanded on the motifs of sensational melodrama by showing a violent binding-and-gagging, a daring robbery, three shocking murders, a racing locomotive, a hot pursuit on horseback, and a final gunfight killing all the bandits. Porter's 1906 film *The Trainer's Daughter; Or, A Race for Love* moved even closer to the classic melodramatic form, employing the conventional triangle of ingenue, favored beau, and jealous villain, and climaxing in a thrilling scene involving the young woman's courageousness. Jack owns a racehorse; wealthy Delmar owns the entire stable. Jack and Delmar wager on the next day's race. The ingenue, whom both men desire, overhears and pledges to give her hand in marriage to the winner. Delmar soon realizes that his horse has no chance against Jack's. That night, Delmar and a henchman try to drug Jack's horse, but they are interrupted by Jack's jockey. Delmar beats the jockey unconscious and hides him in a deserted house. The next day it appears that Delmar will win by default since Jack's horse has no one to ride it. At the last minute, the jockey staggers in and reveals Delmar's villainy. The ingenue, still bound by her promise, decides to ride in the jockey's place to avoid an awful matrimonial fate. The race provides an opportunity for both suspense and thrilling action. She rides fearlessly and beats Delmar's horse by a nose. Racetrack melodramas were a common subgenre of sensational stage melodrama on both sides of the Atlantic in the decades around the turn of the century. The plot of Porter's film closely resembles that of *A Race for Life*, a 10–20–30 melodrama by Theodore Kremer that toured for several years beginning in 1904. An identical narrative was used in 1911 in a film entitled *The Girl and the Motor Boat*, the only difference being that the race involved speedboats instead of horses.[7]

According to a review in *Variety*, Pathé's 1907 film *The Female Spy* showed "unlimited action," but was "chaotic in its development." Echoing a familiar complaint against melodrama, the critic stated that, "The situations do not hold together in an easily followed line, but are scattered, what book reviewers call 'episodic.'" The review does not include a synopsis, but does mention a melodramatic sensation "in which the captured woman spy is dragged by her hair across the fields behind a wild horse."[8] Abel's description based on a surviving print adds that the female spy is the daughter of a Cossack chieftain. She gives vital information to her lover, a young Tartar leader. For this treason, the father has her stabbed to death by a half dozen men and then dragged back to the Tartar's encampment. In a failed attempt at a last-minute rescue, the lover chases after the body across the fields.

Variety's review of a 1907 Western melodrama entitled *The Bad Man* also mentions a "wealth of incident." After being defeated by a "tenderfoot" (i.e., an Easterner) in a fight over the favors of a pretty railroad station clerk, the villain, bent on robbery, attacks the romantic couple. In classic melodramatic form, "The tenderfoot is tied to the railroad track, while the woman is bound hand and foot to the table within the telegraph office. She escapes in time to effect her lover's release and the two embrace as the express rushes past."[9]

D. W. Griffith is widely regarded as probably the finest director of melodramas in the feature film era. *The Birth of a Nation, The Mother and the Law, Broken Blossoms, Way Down East, Orphans of the Storm, Hearts of the World*, and other films are extraordinary in their mastery of the mechanics of melodramatic pathos, moral injustice, and sensationalism. Griffith honed his skills as a melodrama specialist during the first phase of his career at Biograph. In the plot synopses published in *Biograph Bulletins*, it is evident that his earliest films, from his directorial debut in July 1908 to about February 1909, gravitated heavily toward blood-and-thunder melodrama. Although one would have to view the actual films to confirm their sensational quality, the synopses suggest that of the roughly seventy films released during those seven months, about half (or two-thirds if one excludes comedies) contained some combination of extreme moral polarity, abduction, assault, brawling, brutality, binding-and-gagging, murder, and "infernal machines" (intricate death-delaying contraptions used to prolong suspense). The third film of Griffith's career, *The Black Viper* (released in July 1908), illustrates this blood-and-thunder orientation. Its narrative contains brutality against a woman, a brawl, a binding-and-gagging, an attempted murder, two rushes-to-the-rescue, hazardous rolling boulders, another brawl, a fall off a roof, and a stabbing death:

A brute becomes enamored of Jennie, a pretty mill-girl whom he rudely accosts as she is on her way home from work. He is repulsed and in return violently attacks her, knocking her down and kicking her, as Mike her sweetheart rushes to the rescue, giving the cur a sound thrashing. Later in the evening Mike and Jennie go for a stroll but the viper, meanwhile has gone to his usual haunt and informed his gang of the episode, soliciting their assistance in wreaking vengeance. In a wagon they follow Mike and Jennie and, at a lonely place in the road, seize and bind Mike, throwing him into the wagon, but Jennie escapes. They drive off with him to the foot of a rocky cliff up which they carry him. Jennie has given the alarm, and a rescue party at once starts in another wagon. They reach the foot of the cliff where the viper's gang are about half way up, who roll large rocks down to prevent their ascent. The gang reach the top of the cliff with Mike and a terrific fight ensues, ending with their both rolling from the roof to the ground below. Here the struggle is renewed and Mike succeeds in gaining possession of the Viper's dagger and lays him out, just as Jennie and her friends appear, the approach of whom has frightened off the viper's gang.[10]

Biograph's synopsis clearly conveys Griffith's reliance on a preexisting intertextual reservoir of thrilling incidents familiar from 10–20–30 melodramas and dime novels.

In a similar vein, *The Fatal Hour* (August 1908), described as "a stirring incident of the Chinese White Slave Traffic" and "exceedingly thrilling," contains two violent abductions of women by a Chinese villain and his henchman, the binding and gagging of a female detective, an infernal machine (the pistol in front of which the detective is tied will fire when the hands of a clock reach twelve), and a "wild ride" to the rescue. It should also be noted that, in typical melodramatic fashion, the story hinges on a chance occurrence: the police apprehend the henchman and learn the location of the imperiled detective after the henchman is injured in a streetcar accident.[11]

One of Griffith's most suspenseful melodramas is *The Cord of Life*, released in late January 1909. A Sicilian "worthless good-for-nothing scoundrel" demands money from his cousin but is emphatically rebuffed. Determined to get back at him, the villain waits until the cousin and his wife briefly leave their baby unattended in their fifth-floor tenement room. Darting into the apartment, he puts the baby in a basket, ties a rope to it, dangles the basket out the window, and closes the window on the rope so that when anyone opens it the baby will fall to its death. He then goes off to track down the husband. Just as he is about to stab him in the back, a policeman grabs the villain and places him under arrest. Indignant, and eager to agitate his cousin, the malefactor boasts about what he has done with the baby. Griffith creates powerful suspense by crosscutting between the husband racing home and the wife, who has returned and repeatedly approaches the window to hang out some clothes to dry but gets distracted each time. The husband finally bursts in, needless to say, just as the wife is starting to open the window. They are in a quandary as to how to rescue the baby without opening the window. Eventually, the husband lowers the upper panel of the window and precariously hangs head down, held by the feet, to lift the baby back inside. *Biograph Bulletins* assures that "while the subject is intensely thrilling, it is totally devoid of gruesomeness." This disclaimer is significant, for it signals a policy change at Biograph that almost certainly resulted from the launching of the Motion Picture Patents Company in late December 1908, and the institution of the National Board of Censorship in March 1909. Biograph sought both to avoid censorship problems and to make good on the MPPC's rhetoric about the cinema's moral "uplift." After releasing in January and February a few blood-and-thunder films that had already been in production, Griffith shifted his focus to sentimental and didactic melodramas about noble sacrifice and moral reawakening, in addition to pastoral romances, comedies, and other dramas palatable to censors, reformers, and multiclass audiences. Race-to-the-rescue thrillers like *The Drive for a Life* (April 1909) and *The Lonely Villa* (June 1909) occasionally were thrown into the mix, but the films were never vulgar or sordid and seldom violent. If violence was depicted, it was carefully framed as part of a moral lesson.[12]

The Kalem Company, with its heavy emphasis on railroad westerns and Civil War stories, had something close to an all-melodrama production policy (although it did make comedies, too). Kalem is particularly notable as the first studio to build virtually all its melodramas on the heroics of courageous young women, thus setting a precedent for the "serial queens" discussed in the next chapter. The studio produced a *Girl Spy* series in 1909, and dozens upon dozens of one- and two-reel weekly releases followed, all adhering to the "plucky girl" formula before Kalem went out of business in early 1917. *The Open Switch*, released March 1913, typifies Kalem's railroad melodramas in its simple moral polarity, graphic action, and female agency:

Grace Lane, the daughter of the operator at Ferndale, is in love with Billy Warren, the engineer on the local train. Jim West, a rough character employed as section foreman in the yards, endeavors to force his attentions on Grace and is roundly thrashed by Billy. West plans to ditch Billy's train. Grace discovers him tampering with the switch and runs for help, but he overtakes her and ties her near the tracks. During the struggle his revolver slips from his pocket unnoticed and when he leaves to watch Billy's train dash to destruction, Grace struggles with her bonds, secures the revolver and fires at the telegraph wires. She succeeds in breaking one of the glass insulators and a broken wire falls within her reach. With her hands still tied, she taps the end of the wire on the rail, crossing the circuit that operates the telegraph instrument in her father's station. Grace's father, receiving the warning, flags Billy's train in the nick of time and releases the girl, none the worse for her harrowing experience. After a desperate struggle with West, Billy leads him of to jail.[13]

Beginning in November 1914, Kalem streamlined its marketing of railroad thrillers by incorporating them all within the *Hazards of Helen* series, which ran for 119 weekly episodes until March 1917.

Kalem's Civil War melodramas (and some set during the Mexican Revolution and Boer War) were very similar, showcasing various kinds of thrilling spectacle and female stuntwork. *War's Havoc*, released two weeks after *The Open Switch*, is representative of this subgenre. The young heroine serves as a spy for the Confederate army (adhering to a curious convention in silent Civil War films that the protagonist side with the Confederacy). Inside enemy territory, she cuts the wires to a Federalist telegraphy station and shoots its operator. She then hijacks a train and puts it on a collision course with a train carrying Federalist troops amassing for an attack. The trains collide on a bridge with a spectacular explosion. The heroine jumps off the train and into the river below. In all of this, she is assisted by a faithful slave (fighting for the Confederacy!).[14]

Kalem also made numerous melodramas showcasing the courage and wit of "girl detectives" and "girl reporters," such as *The Girl Reporter's Big Scoop* (September 1912) in which the heroine goes undercover as a maid to spy on a band of robbers. She masters flash-photography chemistry to catch them in the act. Some of Kalem's output translated to film the most classic chestnuts of 10–20–30 melodrama, such as *Saved by the Telephone* (June 1912), *A Sawmill Hazard* (December 1912), and *The Wheel of Death* (June 1912), in which villains strap the hero to the massive paddle wheel of a Mississippi riverboat.

* * *

Sensational melodrama remained a prominent genre as the feature film emerged in the early Teens (a fact that should be borne in mind in light of the tendency to oversimplify the feature film as an emblem of the film industry's gentrification). But it was in serial films that the genre really flourished. While sensational melodrama was just one genre among many in regular short subjects and feature films, with serials it was virtually the *only* genre. With few, if any, exceptions all film serials were sensational melodramas. They covered a range of subgenres (such as detective, western, gothic, patriotic, and working-girl melodramas), but they all concentrated on violence and intense action—abductions, entrapments, brawls, hazardous chase sequences, and last-minute rescues—in narratively stark conflicts between a heroine or hero-heroine team and a villain and his criminal accomplices. Film serials represent an immediately recognizable and iconographically faithful descendant of the 10–20–30 and its literary cousins.

As titles like *The Perils of Pauline* (1914), *The Exploits of Elaine* (1915), *The House of Hate* (1918), *The Lurking Peril* (1920), *The Perils of Thunder Mountain* (1919), and *The Screaming Shadow* (1920) make obvious, serials promised thrills (see fig. 7.2). Ellis Oberholtzer, Pennsylvania's cranky head censor in the Teens, described the serial as, "in the main made up of shooting, knifing, binding and gagging, drowning, wrecking and fighting. . . . It is crime, violence, blood-and-thunder, and always obtruding and outstanding is the idea of sex."[15] A 1919 article in *Photoplay* stressed the melodramatic dynamism of serials and remarked on their connection to lowbrow literary antecedents:

Action, action and yet more action! Situations if they come along, yes, but never worked out! . . . A famous serial writer said recently that serials consisted of action without psychology. It might be stated more simply by calling them action without padding. Something is always happening in a serial. Often the direct motive is lacking for this action, but serial audiences do not mind. They are not analytical. They want conflict and the serial producers feed it to them in reel lengths. . . . Serials are The Modern Dime Novels! They supply the demand that was once filled by those blood curdling thrillers. . . . Melodrama! Of course it's melodrama.[16]

In a similar vein (as I noted in the introduction), the *New York Dramatic Mirror* described an episode of Universal's 1914 serial *Lucille Love, Girl of Mystery* as "a melodramatic melodrama, or otherwise a melodrama to the second degree." About another episode, the reviewer stated:

It is, of course, improbable, impossible, out of the question, and any other synonyms that stand for "can't be done," but the film disregards these questions of credence lightly in its more ardent quest for action—constant

Fig. 7.2 Publicity still from *The Perils of Thunder Mountain*, 1919. (*Motion Picture Magazine*, September 1920)

action. . . . The plot is one of those "tear up the cheee-ild" affairs.
Knowing that an assault on an unprotected girl is likely to provoke the
attention; realizing that a strenuous brawl will please a large number of
people . . . the producers have proceeded to picture it. . . . The result is a
selection of hysterical action bound together by loose ties of unity.[17]

"Tear up the cheee-ild" alludes to a stock parody of popular stage melodrama spoofing the acting as being so bad that the villain flubs the line
"Give me the child or I'll tear up the papers!" The reference indicates the
degree to which contemporary viewers recognized serials as a reincarna-
tion of earlier stage melodrama. A promotional review for *The Shielding
Shadow* (Pathé, 1916) emphasized their common focus on showcasing
realistic sensation scenes:

There are numerous spectacular events, an especially big one in each
episode. Nothing has been spared to make them realistic. In the first
episode there is a ship burned at sea. It is not a miniature, but a real
schooner that is destroyed, and the effect is startling to say the least. "Into
the Depths," the second release, has a gruesome but thrilling scene, an
octopus dragging a man into the sea. For realism this incident has never
been surpassed. The fire scenes at the theater in the third episode and the
earthquake in the fourth are also very spectacular and well done.[18]

As one might expect, guardians of social propriety tended to regard
sensational serials as the lowest form of cheap amusement. Ellis
Oberholtzer insisted in 1920 that, "The most hurtful and the most noxious and altogether objectionable kind of a crime picture that we have
on the screen at the present is the serial picture—there is no question
about it. The serial is the old dime novel made into a picture. . . . There
is nothing more deplorable than those crime serials, and yet I do not
know how to get rid of them."[19] Just how low the serial's low cultural
status was is conveyed by instances in which even producers who specialized in serials spoke of them in a demeaning way. Carl Laemmle,
whose Universal studio was very heavily invested in serial production,
saw fit to reassure exhibitors that his studio's feature film offerings were
"not marred by a 'serial-ish tone.'"[20] (See fig. 7.3.)

An even more remarkable instance came from George B. Seitz,
Pathé's serial czar, in a curious 1916 trade journal article entitled "The
Serial Speaks." It opened with these lines:

I am the serial. I am the black sheep of the picture family and the reviled

Fig. 7.3 Advertisement for *The Diamond from the Sky*, 1915. (*Moving Picture World*, August 21, 1915)

of critics. I am the soulless one with no moral, no character, no uplift. I am ashamed. . . . Ah me, if only I could be respectable. If only the hair of the great critic would not rise whenever I pass by and if only he would not cry, "Shame! Child of commerce! Bastard of art!"[21]

It is rare indeed for a promotional article in the Teens to lapse, however briefly, from the film industry's perennial mantra: "We are attracting the better classes. We are uplifting the cinema. We are preserving the highest moral and artistic standards." Probably few readers ever took such affirmations as anything more than perfunctory reassurances to a cultural establishment that approached the cinema with an unpredictable mixture of hostility and meddlesome paternalism. Nevertheless, it is unusual, and telling, that a studio mouthpiece should see fit to abandon the "uplift" conceit altogether. Clearly, it was impossible even to pretend that the serial played any part in the cinema's putative rehabilitation. The serial's intertextual background doomed it to disrepute.

Serials stood out as "the black sheep of the picture family" at a time when mainstream elements in the film industry were trying to broaden the market by making innocuous middlebrow films suitable for heterogeneous audiences in the larger theaters being built at the time. Rather than catering to "the mass"—a supposedly classless general audience fancied by the emerging Hollywood institution—serials were made for "the masses," the predominantly working- and lower-middle-class and immigrant audience that had supported the incredible nickelodeon boom. Oberholtzer again offered a sharp assessment of the serial's reputation and milieu:

The crime serial is meant for the most ignorant class of the population with the grossest tastes, and it principally flourishes in the picture halls in mill villages and in the thickly settled tenement houses and low foreign-speaking neighborhoods in large cities. Not a producer, I believe, but is ashamed of such an output, yet not more than one or two of the large manufacturing companies have had the courage to repel the temptation to thus swell their balances at the end of the fiscal year.[22]

Oberholtzer's characterization of serials as dangerous rabble trash was obviously motivated by the classist snobbery of the conservative bourgeoisie to which he belonged. He undoubtedly pigeon-holed serials and their audience too narrowly. Serials were probably seen, at some time or another, by spectators from all classes, and their sensationalism quite likely appealed to disparate audiences.

Nevertheless, there is little question that the intertextual field of sensational melodrama to which serials belonged was most closely tied to the working-class audience. As a critic in *Variety* noted about the 1916 serial *The Yellow Menace*, "The impression that these installments create is that the picture was produced with an idea of catering to the popular taste. The story thus far is 'mellerdrammer' of the most rabid type."[23] Almost never screened in large first-run theaters, serials were a staple of small neighborhood theaters and cheap second-run downtown houses. Some of these theaters, clinging to the less expensive "variety program" well after the ascendance of the feature film, showed episodes from as many as five different serials each week, usually along with slap-stick comedies and westerns.[24] Serials evidently were associated with cheap theaters and working-class audiences in England as well the United States. A writer in the *New Statesman* in 1918, observing that British moviegoers paid much higher ticket prices than Americans, noted an exception to this rule: "Only in those ramshackle 'halls' of our poorer streets, where noisy urchins await the next episode of some long since antiquated 'Transatlantic Serial' does one notice the proletarian invitation of twopenny and fourpenny seats."[25]

On both sides of the Atlantic, "noisy urchins" raised hell during the screenings. As Oberholtzer stated with chagrin, "The very announce-ment that such and such a picture, such as *The Brass Bullet*, 'will be shown in this house next Tuesday' has been enough to set young America wild—to howl and shout."[26] This vocal, rowdy mode of spec-tatorship, particularly among youths, resembled the rambunctiousness of 10–20–30 audiences. The "gallery gods" had found a new stomping ground. The resulting clamor, anathema to highbrow sensibilities because of its association with a long tradition of disorderly working-class conduct in popular amusements, was in fact one of the serials' sell-ing points. A trade journal advertisement for a 1917 Pearl White serial reprinted a telegram that the Pathé Exchange had received from the manager of the Bijou Theatre in Wilmington, North Carolina. It read: "Showing *Fatal Ring* Here Today—Audience cheering so loud can be heard on tenth floor of Murchison Building and at a distance of one block down the street!"[27] (See fig. 7.4.) This was a far cry from the tame decorum that contemporary scholars describe as the earmark of a new "homogenized" audience in the early Teens, a time when the film indus-try was attempting in various ways to create a mass audience in which

Fig. 7.4 Trade journal ad for *The Fatal Ring*, 1917. (*Motion Picture News*, October 27, 1917)

differences in class, ethnicity, and community no longer affected the film-viewing experience.[28] Although the rowdiness associated with serials was probably primarily a function of juvenile (as opposed to class or ethnic) identity, it reminds us that the paradigm of homogenized spectatorship never prevailed entirely.

Serial producers were perennially on the defensive. One fairly common rhetorical strategy was to maintain that those who scoffed at serials were actually secret serial-lovers. The aforementioned 1919 *Photoplay* article illustrates this tack:

There are some picture fans who will dish up for you all the old arguments about serials. They will tell you that they are silly, ridiculous, illogical, make a fool out of the audience, and stretch the imagination way beyond its proper degree of elasticity. They want to see good features with one thousand feet out of the allotted 5000 devoted to close-ups of the star smiling, or crying, or admiring a rose. Then they sneak over to Third Avenue or Main Street and sit enthralled through an episode of the latest serial.[29]

The reference to Main Street pointed to neighborhood theaters. "Third Avenue" suggested the low-rent locale of second- or third-run houses but, more specifically, it alluded to a bastion of 10–20–30 melodrama. New York's Third Avenue Theater was a famous popular-priced melodrama house. Sensational melodrama in general often was called simply "Third Avenue melodrama."

A more common defensive strategy employed by serial producers was to disavow the connection between their films and the lowbrow address of other serial melodramas. A trade journal advertisement for Vitagraph's 1916–17 serial *The Secret Kingdom*, for example, announced in bold print that it was "the only serial ever offered that meets the taste of all classes—a delight to audiences that heretofore have refused to accept serial productions." The claim was motivated by a desire to attract bookings beyond the usual neighborhood theaters, and perhaps also by an upwardly mobile social mindset among producers. At the same time, the ad reassured small-theater exhibitors that the serial's supposed refinement in no way dampened "all the thrills, the tense interest, the mystery, the death-taunting situations that crowd adventure-lovers into your theater."[30] Nonetheless, it is doubtful that this or other serials (with a few exceptions) managed to break through the social and theatrical barriers. As a Pathé executive recalled, "At the time when the pioneer serials like *The Perils of Pauline, The Adventures of Kathlyn,* and *The*

Million Dollar Mystery were being issued, the attitude of the majority of the larger theaters was one of undisguised contempt."[31]

A third strategy employed by serial producers to defend their product and woo theater owners involved a display of earnest self-criticism. In this rhetorical ploy, producers would admit that the films had not been as respectable as they should have been and promised that serials would shape up right away, or at the very least adhere more closely to basic conventions of narrative logic. A glance at statements by serial producers and distributors in the 1919–20 and 1920–21 editions of *Wid's Year Book* reveals how rote this rhetoric became:

The serial must, is and will change for the Better.—Sidney Reynolds, Supreme Pictures

We have passed through the era of cheap melodramatic serials with inconsistent plots and impossible situations.—Joe Brandt, National Film Corp.

I feel certain that the time has come for a breaking away from the old standards and the elevation of this class of films to a higher level.— William Fox

Today the serial is playing in better class houses than heretofore. . . . [When serials are well made,] then and only then will the best theaters who have never run serials before be willing to show serials.—Harry Grossman, Grossman Pictures

Serials will be better and higher class. They will have to be, because they are going into the big theaters which heretofore thought serials were not the proper diet for their patrons.—Carl Laemmle, Universal

We have consistently improved the quality of our serial stories and their production to the point where the product is thoroughly acceptable in the best class of theaters today. [But our] serials have just as big an appeal to the popular-priced houses as has the former type of blood-and-thunder serials.—Paul Brunet, Pathé Exchange

I long ago ceased to make serials as they are commonly known. In the past, the serial has been a series of sensational incidents strung together by the thinnest sort of plot which was constructed merely as a background for stunts and thrills. In the future, I shall make continued stories with the accent on the story. In the final analysis, the story is the thing. . . . We are just at the beginning of the serial era in motion pictures and the field we are entering has limitless possibilities.—Theodore Wharton, Wharton Inc.

Theodore Wharton (whose Ithaca, New York, studio had made *The Exploits of Elaine* for Pathé, along with two Elaine sequels and a number of other serials sponsored by Hearst's International Film Service and released by Pathé) went out of business just weeks after this outlook statement was printed, suggesting the degree to which the prediction of a bright future for serials was pie-in-the-sky rhetoric.[32]

* * *

To illustrate the serial's typical emphasis on blood-and-thunder melodrama, I will describe in some detail the second episode of *A Woman in Grey*, a gothic romance-adventure made in 1919–20. As mentioned in chapter 5, the serial concerns a hidden fortune whose location in the long-abandoned Amory mansion can only be discovered by matching two ancient documents. Ruth Hope, with her champion Tom Thurston, finds the codes and does battle against the villain, J. Haviland Hunter, who is trying to steal the documents and usurp the fortune. A subplot involves the mystery of Ruth's real identity: she conceals a telltale mark by a peculiar bracelet which covers the back of her left hand and is securely chained to rings on each finger. The serial's fifteen episodes unfold as a back-and-forth game of loss and repossession of the codes, as well as a series of crises in which the villain tries either to abduct and murder the heroine or wrench the bracelet off her hand.

"The Dagger of Death" (episode two) begins with a repetition of the previous episode's cliffhanger ending. Ruth, who has been abducted by the villain, jumps out of her captor's speeding car and falls hard onto the roadside. The villain stops and chases her on foot, soon catching her and, after a struggle, hurls her off a bridge above train tracks. A train passes under just at that moment, and Ruth's fall is cushioned by a coal car. She leaps off the speeding locomotive and tumbles down a steep embankment. Tom, who has pursued the abductors in a thrilling car chase, arrives at her unconscious body. Ruth revives as Tom is touching her bracelet with a look of perplexed concern. Later, Ruth drives up to the Amory mansion just in time to see the villain climb through a window. The villain steals one of the codes, but runs into Tom on the second-floor landing. While the two men engage in a turbulent brawl,

Ruth scales the outside of the mansion and enters a second-floor room with her pistol drawn. The villain manages to throw Tom over the banister and down a flight of stairs, but Ruth stalls the miscreant at gunpoint, dramatically unmasks him, and takes back the code. The villain overpowers Ruth and throws her through a closed second-floor window and then clobbers Tom again with the butt of his pistol. Ruth climbs back through the window and, kneeling down to help Tom, finds the code, which the villain accidentally has dropped. The villain returns and ransacks the place looking for the code. Ruth barricades herself in a room, but the villain finally breaks through, grabs her, and starts wrenching off her bracelet. As the episode ends, the villain takes a long dagger off a wall mount and, with Ruth splayed prone across the top of a desk, slowly brings it toward her neck.

Like the stage melodramas they replaced, American serials were an extraordinarily formulaic product. With few exceptions, the conflict between the heroine-hero team and the villain expressed itself in a back-and-forth struggle for the physical possession of the heroine (whom the villain constantly kidnaps or tries to kill) as well as for the physical possession of some highly prized object—what Pearl White, Pathé's preeminent serial queen, called the "weenie" (thus, perhaps unknowingly, becoming the world's first psychoanalytic film critic). Since none of the other words one could use for this object seem quite as apt—e.g., the talisman, the Thing, the Big Object, the fetish, the MacGuffin, the commodity, etc.—I will retain Pearl White's term. The weenie took many forms: it could be an ebony idol containing the key to a treasure trove; a blueprint for a new torpedo; a codebook needed to decipher the location of a hidden fortune; a secret document outlining the defense of the Panama Canal; a special fuel to power a machine that disintegrates people; the chemical formula for turning dirt into diamonds, and so on. Basing narrative conflict around a weenie was a convention carried over from stage melodrama. A 1909 column satirizing the 10–20–30 formula refers to "the Papahs" (i.e., the "papers," spoken with a working-class or histrionic accent): "Now, The Papahs may be the old man's will and testament, stolen by the principal bad man in order that he may substitute a forgery, or they may merely be the purloined real estate deed that will make the heroine rich beyond the dreams of avarice if only she can lay hands on it. But Papahs of some description there must be."[33]

In the serial-queen melodrama, the weenie is invariably associated with a father figure, since in almost every serial the heroine is the daughter (for some reason, often an adopted one) of a powerful man (millionaire industrialist, newspaper mogul, ambassador, attorney general, etc.) who, in the first episode, is robbed of the weenie and murdered by the villain, or in a few cases just abducted and blackmailed. With the father dead or powerless, the daughter fights for the weenie in order to gain her inheritance or to rescue her father and clear his name. This standard scenario is, needless to say, ripe for Freudian interpretation. The only exception to the formula that I have found is Mutual's *A Lass of the Lumberlands* (1916–17), which substitutes the Evil Father for the Good Father. Ruthless logging mogul Dollar Holmes abuses his wife for giving birth to a girl instead of a boy. When the wife later witnesses her husband murder a man, she fears for her life and flees with her baby girl. The serial picks up twenty years later: the girl, who for some reason controls huge tracts of timber, becomes her father's business nemesis. The father, not realizing he is battling his own daughter, orchestrates the requisite abductions, murder attempts, and weenie snatchings.[34]

The serial's bare-bones narrative structure—the repeated capture and recapture of the weenie, along with the entrapment and liberation of the heroine—afforded a sufficiently simple, predictable, and extensible framework on which to hang a series of thrills over fifteen weeks. Like earlier forms of melodrama, serials were distinguished by the simplicity and reliability of their two-stroke narrative engine, the back-and-forth movement of virtue and villainy. But the engine, to belabor the metaphor, was also intricate and peculiar in its inner design. Although simple in their basic premise of the struggle between good characters and bad characters, serial plots tended to become highly convoluted as they progressed over the weeks. An overarching narrative unmappability characterizes many serial melodramas. As a review of the 1917 serial *The Seven Pearls* stated, "There are so many conflicting parties, and so many pearls in this latest serial of Pathé's that there are times when the observer is completely mystified as to who is who, which is which, and what is what."[35] This sort of narrative unwieldiness probably resulted from several factors: from the inherent difficulty of setting up so many different situations of melodramatic crisis; from the relatively slapdash production process of early pulp cinema; and from the generic legacy of melodrama, which tolerated a high degree of narrative intricacy and discontinuity.

Although its chaotic, nonclassical structure disconcerted bourgeois critics, and studio publicity men were at pains to deny it, producers and audiences recognized as a matter of course that popular melodrama was not in the business of narrative elegance and continuity, but rather the business of graphic thrills. It has been suggested that film serials served as a kind of training ground for feature films, an intermediate step on the path toward extended stories and detailed characters.[36] While it merits further inquiry, I think the idea is essentially misleading since the serial's characters were purely stock and the causal continuity associated with classical narratives were more or less absent in both the stories contained within individual episodes and the overarching story linking the episodes.

* * *

Melodramatic series films—each one narratively complete but with continuing characters and milieux—had appeared as early as 1908, with Eclair Studio's Nick Carter series, which exploited the intertextual popularity of the famous dime novel detective.[37] The earliest serials, those made between mid-1912 and early 1914, tended to present a self-contained narrative in each episode, although an overarching premise established in the first episode (such as a conflict over the heroine's inheritance) carried over from episode to episode to motivate a series of separate adventures. From the very beginning, however, serials included a few episodes that were not self-contained. A critic complained of "A Way to the Underworld," episode nine of *What Happened to Mary*, that, "The tales continue to grow more melodramatic; this one is very lurid, and, moreover, it is incomplete, leaving the action hanging in the air." A publicity review for the fifth and sixth episodes of Selig Studio's *The Adventures of Kathlyn* (1914) declared that its "climaxes are almost exasperating, so eagerly do they leave us guessing and floundering when the 'To Be Continued' announcement flashes on the screen." It is unclear, however, whether either example may be called a real cliffhanger as the term is understood today—i.e., ending with the protagonists precariously near some sort of graphic death.[38]

Pathé's *The Perils of Pauline*, which ran between August and November 1914, can be seen as a transitional serial since some episodes presented complete adventures while others left the story, and usually the heroine, hanging until the next.[39] By late 1914 or early 1915, virtually all episodes culminated in suspenseful cliffhanger endings (fig. 7.5). With this design, serials encouraged a steady volume of return customers, tantalized and eager for the fix of narrative closure withheld in the previous installment. In this system of artificially perpetuated desire,

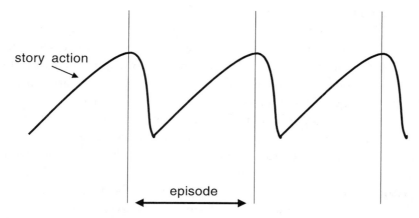

Fig. 7.5 Cliffhanger structure of serial narratives.

serials conveyed a certain acuity about the new psychology of modern consumerism. Actually, the design is slightly more elaborate (fig. 7.6), due to the cliffhanger's system of narrative overlap wherein the "next" episode briefly retraced (usually with cop-out modifications) the immediate situation leading up to the cliffhanger.

The film industry turned to serials for several reasons. First of all, it saw the commercial logic of adopting the practice of serialization, which was already a mainstay of popular magazines and newspapers. Literary models exerted a tremendous influence on the film industry because

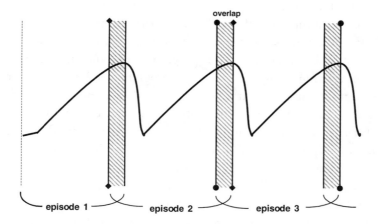

Fig. 7.6 Overlap structure of serial narratives.

popular fiction constituted the dominant entertainment medium throughout the decades surrounding the turn of the century. It is difficult for us to imagine the incredible saturation of published short fiction and serials in that era. In 1915, with the U.S. population two-fifths the size of today's, at least fifty-seven national magazines, "story papers," and syndicated Sunday newspaper supplements featured short stories and serials. (Today, only about five mass market periodicals publish fiction.) Their combined monthly circulation came to more than 79 million, four-fifths of the total population of 99 million (and this figure does not even count the fact that magazines were read by more than one person). The majority of the fiction publications featured serialized stories. The pervasiveness and popularity of fiction serials in magazines and newspaper supplements created a high degree of familiarity with the formal and generic norms of segmented and extended narratives and thus served as both a precondition and an incentive for the creation of film equivalents.[40]

Serial films also emerged in the early Teens because they represented an attractive alternative for "variety format" exhibitors and manufacturers, such as Edison, Selig, and Kalem, that were incapable or unwilling to switch over from one- and two-reel shorts to five- and six-reel feature films. During the transitional years (roughly 1912–1916), many exhibitors disliked multireel features because they were much more expensive to rent. Renting a top-rated feature for one day cost as much as an entire week's worth of single-reelers. Features also destroyed the variety format that exhibitors were accustomed to. Along with allowing individual exhibitors greater programming control over films and non-film segments of the show, the traditional variety format was considered less risky, since an unpopular short film would soon be over and could be made up for by other films in the program.[41] The audience's standard practice of arriving at any time during a program, the lack of two-projectors in most theaters, and a conception that audiences would find long stories tedious underscored exhibitors' resistance to multireel features. Perhaps most importantly, the inertia of standardized business practices predisposed both film exchanges and exhibitors against the multireel release. The well-established exchange system employed by the General Film Co. (the distribution arm of the Motion Picture Patents Company) and its independent competitors benefited from the stability and regularity of handling a fixed single-reel length (1,000 feet) based on standing orders placed by exchanges and exhibitors. The introduction of varying reel lengths meant major complications for this system.[42] Released one or two reels at a time for a dozen or so installments, serials could be pitched as "big" titles without overly daunting the studios' still relatively modest production infrastructure and entrenched system of short-reel distribution. Until as late as 1917, serials were billed as "feature" attractions—the centerpiece of short-reel or "variety" programs.[43] Later, as bona fide feature films became the main attraction, serial installments were used to fill out the program, along with a short comedies and newsreels.

* * *

What Happened to Mary, generally considered the first film serial, was released by Edison in twelve monthly "chapters" beginning in July 1912. The serial centers on the adventures of a country girl (and unknowing heiress) as she discovers the pleasures and perils of big-city life while at the same time eluding an evil uncle and sundry other villains. The story was serialized simultaneously, along with numerous stills from the screen version, in the *Ladies' World*, a mass-market woman's magazine with the third largest circulation of all monthlies in the country and a primarily working-class readership.[44] This serial was very popular at the box office, making the actress Mary Fuller (in the role of Mary Dangerfield) one of American cinema's first really big, if rather ephemeral, stars.[45] (In one of the industry's first marketing tie-ins, the back cover of *Photoplay* in September 1914 advertised Mary Fuller Perfume, "a caress from the screen.") The *New York Dramatic Mirror*'s reviewer complained that although the serial had begun with a degree of "human naturalness" and sympathetic characterization, it quickly degenerated into an "overdrawn thriller," "mere melodrama" reminiscent of the 10–20–30: "The pictures have developed into melodramas of action rather than dramas of characterization. Mary has become a mere puppet. Mary Fuller does all that is possible for the role, but, at best, Mary Dangerfield isn't very human. She is reminiscent of the heroine of the old-fashioned melodrama where the 'villain still pursued her' to the final curtain."[46]

The commercial success of *What Happened to Mary* prompted the Selig Polyscope Co. and the *Chicago Tribune* syndicate to team up in the production and promotion of *The Adventures of Kathlyn*, exhibited and published fortnightly throughout the first half of 1914. In keeping with the early star system's convention of eponymous protagonists (detailed in chapter 9), Kathlyn Williams played Kathlyn Hare, a fetching

American girl who, in order to save her kidnapped father, reluctantly becomes the Queen of Allahah, a principality in India. When it became clear that *Kathlyn* was a big hit, virtually every important studio at the time (with the notable exception of Biograph) started making action series and 12-to-15–chapter serials, running one or two reels per episode. Almost all were connected to prose-version newspaper tie-ins (also discussed in chapter 9).

Thanhouser studio had one of the silent era's biggest commercial successes with *The Million Dollar Mystery* (1914). As Terry Ramsaye reported:

The Million Dollar Mystery *swept through the motion picture theaters with a success without precedent or parallel. The twenty-three chapters of* The Mystery *played in about seven thousand motion picture theaters in a period when there were probably about eighteen thousand such houses. Production costs of* The Mystery *were in the vicinity of $125,000 [about $2,000,000 today], and the gross receipts for the picture were nearly $1,500,000 [about $25,000,000 today].*[47]

However, Thanhouser's immediate follow-up, *Zudora (The Twenty Million Dollar Mystery)*, was reportedly a huge flop. It had advance bookings totaling $750,000 (almost $12 million today), but once it was released, "exhibitors fell over each other canceling their bookings." One problem (other than the narrative awkwardness I analyze in chapter 9) was that Thanhouser made the mistake of casting the hero of *The Million Dollar Mystery* as an evil "Oriental" villain.[48]

By far the biggest producers of serials in the Teens were Universal, Mutual, Vitagraph, and the American branch of Pathé, which dubbed itself as "the house of serials" and "the small exhibitor's friend."[49] Pathé relied heavily on its successful Pearl White vehicles, almost all written and directed by George B. Seitz. *The Perils of Pauline* (1914) reportedly grossed nearly a million dollars, no doubt aided by its Hearst tie-in. *The Exploits of Elaine* (1915)—which was stretched out to thirty-six episodes by two immediate sequels, or "extenders," *The Romance of Elaine* (1915) and *The New Exploits of Elaine* (1915)—reportedly was also "a tremendous money maker," again with massive Hearst publicity. Renamed *Les Mystères de New-York* (The Mysteries of New York; see fig. 7.7), the *Elaine* series enjoyed excellent business in Europe and other parts of the world, as well.[50]

Fig. 7.7 Poster for the French release of *The New Exploits of Elaine*, 1916. (From *Manifesti del Cinema Muto*, [Turin, Italy: Museo Nazionale del Cinema, c. 1983])

Other White/Seitz Pathé serials included *The Iron Claw* (1916); *Pearl of the Army* (1916), a "preparedness" serial that capitalized on World War I as melodramatic fodder; *The Fatal Ring* (1917); *The House of Hate* (1918), which Eisenstein cited as an influence;[51] *The Lightning Raider* (1919); *The Black Secret* (1919–20); and *Plunder* (1923). In a publicity war with Mutual, which had claimed Helen Holmes was the biggest box office draw, Pathé carted out statistics indicating that the first four of these serials garnered $24,570,000 in ticket sales (the equivalent of about $320 million today).[52] However inflated that figure, there is no question that the Pearl White serials were highly successful. In a late 1916 mail-in popularity contest conducted by *Motion Picture Magazine*, Pearl White got 155,685 votes, making her the most popular female star in the business, and the second most popular star of all (Warren Kerrigan received 186,895 votes). By comparison, Lillian Gish received only 54,365 votes, making her Number 21 among the most popular female stars—a fact that highlights the degree to which our reliance on "the canon" has skewed our conception of early film history. In the same contest two years later, Pearl White again did well, coming in third, behind Mary Pickford and Marguerite Clark. Lillian Gish came in Number 35. Two years after that, in late 1920, Pearl White was third again, although the margin between her and Pickford, who was still Number 1, had increased dramatically. Gish fared considerably better, coming in eighth, but the curve was steep: Pearl White got five times as many votes as Gish, and Pickford got twenty-one times as many.[53]

Throughout the Teens, Pathé also promoted other "serial queens"—Ruth Roland, Grace Darmond, Mollie King, among others—since the studio almost always had another serial running concurrently with whatever Pearl White vehicle was out. *Neil of the Navy* (1915) privileged the hero in the title rather than the heroine played by Lillian Lorraine, but the narrative situations were probably not very different in their gender dynamic. *Patria* (1917), another preparedness serial, starred Irene Castle, a fashionable ballroom dancer (with her partner husband Vernon Castle) billed as "America's best known woman" and "New York's best dressed woman." The choice of this star suggests that Pathé was interested in the possibility of raising the serial's intertextual associations above 10–20–30 and dime novel melodramatics. The studio insisted that "there is no audience in the country too 'high class' for the right kind of picture." Trade journal publicity claimed that *Patria* could play for "one-dollar and two-dollar audiences," and that it was "booked solid" over the Proctor circuit of picture palaces. The patriotic theme, capitalizing on the country's expectancy that it would soon enter the European war, may have helped legitimize what was, for all intents and purposes, just a typical blood-and-thunder thriller, albeit with a somewhat more ladylike heroine. The plot, presumably reflecting the politics of William Randolph Hearst (whose International Film Service sponsored the production, and whose newspapers published the tie-in), centered on an attack on the United States by an allied Mexican and Japanese army. According to Kalton Lahue, after those governments protested, President Wilson asked Pathé/Hearst to eliminate the most belligerent scenes (for example, by removing shots of the flags of Mexico and Japan in order to dissimulate the enemy's identity).[54]

In a slightly different vein, Pathé also experimented with a few fourteen-episode series that, like *Patria*, covered stock melodrama with a veneer of highbrow pretense. *Who Pays?* (1915), *Who's Guilty?* (1916), and *The Grip of Evil* (1916) presented moderately lurid thrillers under the guise of edifying "problem plays that present a terrific indictment of certain present-day habits and conventions of society." These three series are distinct from the others, and from American film in general, in their consistently unhappy endings.[55]

Universal, like Pathé, had at least two serials running at any given time throughout the Teens. In the late Teens, serials reportedly made more money for Universal than any other branch of production, although the studio may not have been proud of that fact. A number of Universal serials were directed by Francis Ford (John Ford's older brother) and starred the duo of Ford and Grace Cunard: *Lucille Love, Girl of Mystery* (1914), one of the first films Luis Buñuel recalled ever seeing; *The Broken Coin* (1915); *The Adventures of Peg o' the Ring* (1916); and *The Purple Mask* (1917).[56] Among other Universal releases were *The Pursuit of Patricia* (1914—a series); *The Trey o' Hearts* (1914); *The Black Box* (1915); *The Master Key* (1914–15); *Graft* (1915); *The Mystery Ship* (1917–18); *The Gray Ghost* (1917), another serial Eisenstein mentioned; *The Red Ace* (1917–18); and *Liberty: A Daughter of the U.S.A.* (1916). *The Red Ace*, which began its run in February 1917, represents a milestone of sorts: it is the first serial, as far as I know, that began showing profuse amounts of blood during fight scenes. All previous serials were bloodless (although one does not notice the absence when watching them). The blood greatly intensified the graphic violence critics of sensational melodrama found so objectionable.

Mutual's first venture into series melodrama was with *Our Mutual Girl*, made for Mutual by the Reliance studio. It was released for fifty-two consecutive weeks beginning in 1914. Although some episodes followed the star (Norma Phillips, later Carolyn Wells) on shopping trips or meeting famous people, many incorporated typical melodrama stories. In 1916, Mutual lured away Kalem's popular stunt actress Helen Holmes (of *Hazards of Helen* fame), along with her director, J. P. McGowan. Their subsequent serials continued in the vein of railroad stunt thrillers with *The Girl and the Game* (1916), *A Lass of the Lumberlands* (1916–17), *The Lost Express* (1917), *The Railroad Raiders* (1917), and others. As Kalem had done with the original *Hazards of Helen*, Mutual generally made its serials relatively inexpensive for exhibitors to rent—a maximum of $15 a day (or about $195 in today's dollars). The price was tailored, as was the serial's melodramatic content, to small neighborhood theaters and second- or third-run downtown houses.

Vitagraph invested in serials from early on. At first, the studio claimed it was offering a "better grade" of serials for a "better class of audience." Its first serial, *The Goddess*, directed by Ralph Ince in 1915, was pitched as "The Serial Beautiful," something "light, airy, angelic, kindly, mystic—an idyllic rhapsody." The story concerns a beautiful waif raised on a desert island by rich industrialists who aim to use her as a tool for molding public opinion in favor of their self-consciously exploitative capitalist ideology. The plan goes awry when the girl, who has been raised to think she is a prophet sent from Heaven (presumably on the assumption that the rabble will therefore accept her as one), instead sets about preaching a gospel of kindness and love as "she faces the problems of anarchists, of socialists, labor questions, modern Christianity." The producers evidently aspired to some degree of highbrow appeal through the serial's sociological and humanist pretensions, as well as its "many opportunities for charming woodland settings." Unfortunately, no episodes are extant, so it is hard to know to what extent this was all window dressing for just another melodramatic thriller. Vitagraph's later serials, such as *The Secret Kingdom* (1916–17), *The Fighting Trail* (1917), *A Fight for Millions* (1918), *Man of Might* (1919), *Smashing Barriers* (1919), and *The Perils of Thunder Mountain* (1919), were no more refined than the those of its competitors.[57]

Paramount, a studio specializing in feature films for first-run theaters, put out a serial in late 1917 entitled *Who Is Number One?*

Apparently, the experiment was not as successful as Paramount had hoped, since the studio never made another serial. Strangely enough, Edison and Selig, the two studios that had pioneered the film-serial form, steered clear of serials despite their initial hits. However, after making a *Mary* sequel entitled *Who Will Marry Mary?* (1914), Edison went in big for weekly and monthly detective and plucky-girl series such as *The Chronicles of Cleek* (1913–14), *Dolly of the Dailies* (1914), *The Girl Who Earns Her Own Living* (1915), *Below the Deadline* (1915), and *Young Lord Stanleigh* (1915), along with numerous comic series. Throughout 1914, series films constituted about one third of Edison's monthly output (generally about eight of twenty-four releases per month). But the series policy did not go well for Edison, and by early 1915 the studio had dropped series altogether. The studio's executives realized that only series and serials backed by massive publicity campaigns would succeed, and Edison was not able or willing to invest in such heavy advertising. Also, exhibitors made it very clear that they did not want Edison series films, in part because it was felt that they were poorly made and lacked adequate "thrill punches."[58]

Kalem made no serials but, as mentioned earlier, after 1914 it specialized in series films, more so than any other studio. The most famous is *The Hazards of Helen*, whose success impelled the studio to launch at least five series in 1915, including *The Girl Detective*, *Mysteries of the Grand Hotel*, *The Ventures of Marguerite*, *Stingaree* (an equestrian melodrama), and a series built around the actress Alice Joyce and simply referred to as *The Alice Joyce Series*. Kalem's 1916 series included *The Girl from Frisco*, *Grant, Police Reporter*, and *The Scarlet Runner*. The studio continued its short-subject policy into 1917, making another Helen Gibson series, *A Daughter of Daring*, along with *The American Girl* series. Soon thereafter, however, Kalem ceased production, rather than braving the financial risks of producing feature films. There was still a market for shorts, to be shown before the feature, but evidently it was difficult for studios to stay afloat making only shorts.

Although when they hit they hit big, American serials had an erratic commercial history. Information on box office receipts is hard to come by, but trade journal surveys of film exchanges (rental offices) may tell us something about the serial's popularity among audiences. Between 1914 and 1917, the *Motion Picture News* conducted a number of in-depth polls of "exchangemen." In October 1914, to the question "Do serials continue popular?" 60 percent said "yes," while about 20 percent said "no" (the rest saying "fairly"). A year later, however, the no's had swelled to 70 percent. But a year after that, at the end of 1916, the serial's popularity had rallied again, with about a 65–35 percent split between yes and no responses. By the summer of 1917, the responses had leveled out to exactly fifty-fifty. One should stress that these polls are not very reliable. For example, in all eight surveys the respondent from Canton, Ohio, reported that serials were not popular, but the respondent from St. Louis reported each time that they were very popular. As tempting as it is to hypothesize regional differences in audience taste, the individual biases of particular exchange managers was probably a much stronger factor.[59]

If, in fact, serials did have mixed popularity among exhibitors and audiences, a number of factors probably came into play. At least in part, it may have reflected the growing rift between a residual "nickelodeon" cinema, geared toward small-time exhibitors and primarily lower-class audiences, and an emergent Hollywood model of middlebrow mass entertainment. It is also likely that some audiences simply tired of the serial's highly formulaic stories, not-always-so-thrilling thrills, and relatively low production values resulting from their hurried weekly release schedule.

Nevertheless, despite the fact that they represented only a fraction of the films produced every year, and despite their ambiguous commercial success, serial melodramas were commercially and culturally important in the Teens. They were extremely widespread, they represented the most coherent descendant of a popular tradition of sensational melodrama, they were controversial with respect to their lowbrow cultural status, they ushered in a new era of mass publicity, and, on a broader scale, they epitomized a new, or at least newly accentuated, cultural appetite for powerful stimuli.[60] Perhaps above all, as the following chapter explores, they were significant as expressions of a new destabilization of traditional ideologies of gender. Serials were energized by the excitement and anxiety prompted by the emergence of the New Woman.

8

Power and Peril in the
Serial-Queen Melodrama

If modernity represents an epoch marked by the "madly thoughtless shattering and dismantling of all foundations," an epoch in which all traditional belief systems "melt into air," then certainly one of the most prominent examples of modern ideological vaporization involved the destabilization of traditional ideologies of gender. Sensational melodrama was one of the prime vehicles through which the modern imagination explored a new conception of womanhood. Few, if any, popular-culture commodities in the early decades of the twentieth century showcased the novelty and dynamism of the New Woman as vividly as "the serial-queen melodrama."

The most intriguing element in the serial-queen melodramas of the Teens is their extraordinary emphasis on female heroism. Within a sensational action-adventure framework of the sort generally associated with male heroics, serials gave narrative preeminence to an intrepid young heroine who exhibited a variety of traditionally "masculine" qualities: physical strength and endurance, self-reliance, courage, social authority, and freedom to explore novel experiences outside the domestic sphere. Titles like *The Adventures of Dorothy Dare, A Daughter of Daring, The Exploits of Elaine, The Hazards of Helen, Ruth of the Rockies, Pearl of the Army, A Lass of the Lumberlands, The Girl Spy, The Girl*

Detective, The Perils of Our Girl Reporters, and so on, immediately convey their central novelty.

To shed light on the sources of this representation of female power, we need to examine the serial-queen persona on a sociological level—as a reflection of both the excitement and anxieties surrounding major transformations in the cultural construction of womanhood around the turn of the century—and also on an intertextual level, as the extension of a popular motif already pervasive in sensational melodrama.

The genre is paradoxical in that its portrayal of female power is often accompanied by the sadistic spectacle of the woman's victimization. The genre as a whole is thus animated by an oscillation between contradictory extremes of female prowess and distress, empowerment and imperilment. My explanation of this paradox focuses on the genre's function not only as an index of female emancipation, and as a wish-fulfillment fantasy of power betraying how tentative and incomplete that social emancipation actually was, but also as an index of the anxieties that such social transformations and aspirations created in a society experiencing the sociological and ideological upheavals of modernity. The serial-queen melodrama is an exemplary expression of the perennial instability and flux in modern society's most basic norms.

*   *   *

We are accustomed to thinking of the violent action-adventure thriller as a male genre, just as we classify the domestic melodrama as a woman's genre. It thus comes as something of a surprise to find a body of films that deviates so significantly from this framework of gender alignment (see fig. 8.1). It would be a mistake to classify the serial-queen melodrama strictly as a woman's genre—it certainly appealed to male spectators by virtue of its blood-and-thunder dynamism of action, its inclusion of male hero-figures, and its imagery of female victimization. Male spectators also might have allied themselves with the serial queen as a heroic agent. One could very easily adapt Carol Clover's hypothesis that the tough "final girl" in slasher movies serves as an ideal identificatory stand-in for adolescent males.[1] More generally, the serial-queen heroine exhibits a set of culturally positive behavioral traits—such as liveliness, competence, and moral fortitude—that probably prompted spectatorial allegiance and identification largely irrespective of gender. Nevertheless, it seems clear that the films go out of their way to construct a textual arena for fantasies appealing particularly to female spectators. The genre's address to women is revealed not only through textual analysis

Fig. 8.1 Trade journal ad for *A Daughter of Uncle Sam*, 1917. (*Motion Picture News*, December 29, 1917)

but also through an examination of the genre's commercial intertexts.

An important indication of a female target audience lies in the film industry's efforts to tap into the mass readership of women's popular fiction, particularly of the adventure and romance-adventure stories that had been serialized in daily newspapers and women's monthly magazines since the early 1890s and published in girls' book series (the precursors to *Nancy Drew*) since around 1905.[2] The prose-version tie-ins of a number of serials were published on the "woman's page" of daily or Sunday newspapers, as well as in national women's magazines. This practice, examined in chapter 9, began with the very first film serial— Edison's 1912–13 *What Happened to Mary*, which was "fictionalized" in the *Ladies' World*, a major national woman's magazine.

Other indications of the serial-queen melodrama's address to a female audience can be found in the films' promotional gimmicks. For example, in a contest promoting the 1915 Reliance serial *Runaway June*, forty-eight young women won a free trip to California on a train equipped with "all the luxuries you can imagine." The contest was open only to women and was publicized only in women's magazines and sewing-pattern monthlies.[3]

Further evidence of the genre's address to women is the serial-queen melodrama's promotion of "fashion interest," apparent both in the mise-en-scène of the serials and in extratextual merchandising tie-ins with fashion houses. With very few exceptions, serials placed great emphasis on luxurious fashion. Serial producers were clearly mindful of the truism expressed in a 1916 article in *Moving Picture World*: "To the feminine mind, nothing appeals so strongly as clothing, hats, or shoes—in fact finery of any kind."[4] The camera tended to linger on carefully composed views of the heroine's modish and opulent outfits—all silk frills and boas and fur. An advertisement for *The Adventures of Dorothy Dare* promoted the display of fashions on equal footing with narrative action, describing the series as "A motion picture of thrills and excitement centered around a magnificent fashion display. . . . A splendid fashion show and a vivid drama" (fig. 8.2).[5]

While the genre's emphasis on exquisite costuming may seem to have contradicted the characteristic portrayal of an intrepid heroine, the serial's address to female spectators actually interwove these distinct aspects of narcissistic pleasure in the form of two fantasies of recognition and power. The fantasy of feminine glamour situated the woman as the passive center of attention, the decorative and charming magnet of admiration, while the fantasy of female power situated her as the active center of the narrative, a heroic agent in a male environment. The female spectator was thus offered the best of both worlds: a representational structure that indulged conventionally "feminine" forms of vanity and exhibitionism while it refused the constraints of decorative femininity through an action-packed depiction of female prowess.

* * *

The clearest and most interesting indication of the genre's address to a female audience lies in its sustained fantasy of female power. Every serial-queen melodrama, without exception, placed an overt polemic about female independence and mastery at the center of its thematic design. This depiction of female power self-consciously dissolved, and sometimes even completely reversed, traditional gender positions as the heroine appropriated a variety of "masculine" qualities, competencies, and privileges. It should be stressed that the films varied considerably in their precise balance between the heroine's "masculine" assertiveness and self-reliance, on the one hand, and her "feminine" glamour, charm, and dependence on male chivalry, on the other. But at the very least, the genre portrayed the emancipated woman out in the masculine world,

Fig. 8.2 Trade journal ad for *The Adventures of Dorothy Dare*, 1916. (*Motion Picture News*, October 21, 1916)

seizing new experiences and defying the ideology of feminine domesticity. The genre celebrated the pleasures and perils of a young woman's interaction with a public sphere traditionally restricted to men. As "girl spies," "girl detectives," "girl reporters," "girl telegraphers," or as effervescent heiresses with an appetite for prenuptial adventure, heroines transgressed the conventional boundaries of female experience.

The well-known 1914 serial *The Perils of Pauline*, for example, stressed Pauline's athletic exuberance and unyielding zeal for risky experiences. The story centered on an heiress who agrees to wed an adoring suitor on the condition that she be granted a whirlwind year of adventure before settling down. Pauline's regimen of new experiences engages her in dangerous airplane races, horse jockeying, balloon flights, automobile racing, submarine exploration, and expeditions into Chinatown's criminal dens (each escapade offering the villain a new opportunity to attempt Pauline's assassination). A number of serial-queen melodramas stopped at this level, simply recounting the thrills and dangers of exploring worlds out of bounds to women. Such films tended to be the most conservative in their vision of gender positions because, while they granted their heroines vivacity and curiosity, these attributes generally increased the heroine's vulnerability in the outside world, thus necessitating a male rescue that posed a certain ambiguity about the ultimate nature of the heroine's independence.

But many serials went far beyond this level, signaling the woman as powerful in the public sphere. The genre typically granted its heroines social power in terms of conventionally male positions of professional authority. Helen in *The Hazards of Helen* is a telegraph operator on the dangerous overnight shift. In *The Girl and the Game*, Helen Holmes is in charge of an important railroad line. Ruth Ranger, in *The Haunted Valley* (Pathé, 1923), is head of an enormous dam construction project. The eponymous heroine of *Patria* (her very name a concise signifier of androgyny) owns a huge munitions factory and is commander-in-chief of a sizable private army and air force. An intertitle minces no words in telling us that Captain Donald Parr, Patria's love interest, is second in command.

The ultimate display of female power concerned the heroine's physical prowess, quick reflexes, and coordination, especially with respect to a conventionally masculine repertory of heroic stunts. Serial heroines readily brawled in fistfights with enemy thugs (fig. 8.3), and it became an absolute imperative to show the heroine's facility with a pistol at several

Fig. 8.3 Pearl White in *Plunder*, 1923. (Courtesy Museum of Modern Art Stills Archive)

points throughout a serial (figs. 8.4, 8.5, 8.6, 8.7)—as well as her agility in stunts like leaping from a speeding train into a pursuing car or jumping off a building and through an adjacent skylight three floors below.

At its most assertive, this fantasy of female prowess gravitated toward a complete reversal of gender positions. In several car chases in *The Girl and the Game*, Helen controls the wheel while her three brawny male buddies are relegated to mere passengers. Similarly, in *Pearl of the Army*, Pearl and a male ally escape artillery fire by riding double on horseback, but Pearl rides in front and controls the horse while the man holds on for dear life. Later in the episode, Pearl hops into an airplane (still a real novelty in 1916) and takes off single-handedly, leaving an assortment of less deft men on the ground. The classic positions of helplessness and chivalry were often succinctly inverted, as in "Helen's Rescue of Tom" in *A Lass of the Lumberlands* (fig. 8.8).

A synopsis provided before the last episode of Mutual's *The Girl*

Fig. 8.4 Frame still enlargement from *What Happened to Mary,* 1912–13.

Fig. 8.5 Helen Holmes in a publicity still for "The Pay Train," an episode of *The Hazards of Helen,* 1915. (*Kalem Kalander,* June 1915)

Fig. 8.6 Frame still enlargement from *A Woman in Grey*, 1919—20.

Fig. 8.7 Publicity still for *Pearl of the Army*, 1916. (From Lahue, *Bound and Gagged*)

HELEN'S RESCUE OF TOM.

Fig. 8.8 Lobby card for *A Lass of the Lumberlands*, 1916–17. (From Lahue, *Bound and Gagged*)

and the Game, a 1916 serial about the conflict between rival (and, needless to say, morally polarized) railroad factions in the Southwest, vividly illustrates the "masculinization" of the heroine that, to varying degrees and in varying ways, informed every serial-queen melodrama:

The story to date: Helen Holmes prevents collision of train carrying her father and Storm, saves Storm from death on burning train; recovers accidental duplicate map of railroad cut-off, averting withdrawal of financial support. By desperate leap, Helen recovers payroll from thieves. Kidnapped by Seagrue, Helen is rescued by Storm and Spike. She brings deputies to prevent death in rival camp's pitched battle. Helen rescues Storm, Rhinelander and Spike from runaway freight car by desperate chase in automobile, ditching car to prevent collision with limited. Rescues Spike from lynching, captures ore thieves. Saves lives of Rhinelander and Storm trapped by mine cave-in, regains money stolen by Seagrue's agents. Helen accepts Storm's proposal of marriage. After daring ride, Helen uncouples freight and prevents terrible wreck.

One is struck by the assertiveness with which this serial affirmed the heroine's "masculine" competence. Helen rescues her male allies about ten times more often than they are called upon to rescue her.

Set in western railroad yards and mining camps, *The Girl and the Game* is populated by several hundred men and literally only one woman. Many serial-queen melodramas employed this device of placing a single heroine in a social sphere where no other women (except an occasional secondary villain) were to be found. This overt demographic imbalance highlighted sexual difference, forcing recognition of the female-as-outstanding in an alien world. But it was a paradoxical accentuation, since at the same that the heroine was being showcased as an anomaly in a masculine world, the film maintained that gender had ceased to be an issue. Gender no longer dictated boundaries of behavior and experience. Helen, surrounded by buddies, is "just one of the guys." She operates among them without the erotic fetishization characteristic of later Hollywood cinema (although sadism, according to Laura Mulvey's psychoanalytic hypothesis the alternate means by which male spectators cope with the threat posed by the female body, certainly finds ample expression, as I will discuss shortly).[6] Serial-queen heroines occasionally took the appropriation of a masculine persona to an extreme by flaunting their masculinization in masquerades of cross-dressing. The heroine of *The Mystery of the Double Cross* (Pathé, 1917) spends two-thirds of her time on screen in the disguise of a man's three-piece dark flannel suit and hat. The heroine of *The Adventures of Ruth* (Pathé, 1920) goes undercover as a messenger boy and a Gloucester fisherman, and Pearl White in *The Romance of Elaine* (Pathé, 1915) disguises herself as a mustachioed toughie (fig. 8.9).

The serial-queen melodrama's spurning of the ideology of female domesticity and its aversion to the homebound realm of the sentimental or family melodrama is underscored by its total banishment of the figure of the mother—the very emblem of the Hollywood woman's film. While a benevolent father-figure was invariably established (even if only to get killed off in order to set up the central narrative conflict), the heroine was always without a mother and none was ever referred to. These films depict a world in which there simply is no such social and biological entity as a mother. This absence may not be all that rare in commercial cinema, but its imposition as an absolute generic rule suggests the determination with which the serial-queen melodrama sought to represent an antitraditional conception of womanhood, one appeal-

Fig. 8.9 Pearl White in *The Romance of Elaine,* 1915. (Courtesy Museum of Modern Art Stills Archive)

ing to a generation of young women eager to differentiate their world-view from that of their mothers.

* * *

Any attempt to account for the portrayal of female power in the serial-queen melodrama must begin by acknowledging the great extent to which this motif represented a commercial strategy to engage female spectators. The film industry recognized the economic significance of women moviegoers, perhaps of young unmarried women in particular, and sought greater or more stable profit by marketing fantasies of excitement and mastery geared to them. The serial-queen melodrama stands out as a significant index of the film industry's attempt to address a female audience at a much earlier date than generally assumed. The genre indicates the studios' perception of the economic importance of women moviegoers from the very beginning of the film industry's commercial expansion, almost a decade before the Valentino craze of the 1920s.

But over and above this economic determination, the serial-queen persona also must be seen in sociological terms as the reflection of a distinct historical moment in the cultural experience of womanhood. The serial-queen melodrama's investment in images of female power expressed women's disenchantment and frustration with conventional definitions of gender (while at the same time it celebrated tangible transformations in women's status after the turn of the century). Viewed as a utopian fantasy of female empowerment, the serial-queen melodrama suggests an escapist response to the constraints of women's experiences within patriarchal society. The fantasy of the "masculinized" heroine, as Karen Horney observed, "may be the expression of a wish for all those qualities and privileges which in our culture are regarded as masculine, such as strength, courage, independence, success, sexual freedom, right to choose a partner."[7]

To Horney's list we might add athleticism. Women were often ridiculed for lacking physical coordination. For example, it was something of a stock cultural joke in the decades around the turn of the century that women simply could not learn the right way to get on or off a moving trolley car. A comic photograph on the cover of *The Standard* in 1898 (fig. 8.10) portrayed a woman's hapless attempt to board a trolley (allowing a titillating view of her undergarments). The caption read: "Why will young women persist in boarding a moving car the wrong way? Besides making a display of legs and lingerie and blinding the conductor with her jeweled garters, she caused the poor man to lose his job." This subject of amusement reappears a decade later in a 1908 Essanay one-reel comedy entitled *Just Like a Woman*. A review in *Variety* described the film as "a collection of scenes from everyday life, showing the inconsistencies of womankind as viewed through a masculine camera." A woman who "gets off a car backwards" is one of the annoying foibles portrayed by the film. (Others included the woman's poking her parasol in pedestrians' eyes, blocking a ticket window, spending a dollar to save a cent at a bargain sale, and stealing money out of her sleeping husband's pocket.)[8] Three years later, in 1911, *The Independent* magazine featured an article called "Women and Street Cars." The author, who had lost patience with such ineptitude, approved of a plan to make lessons in getting on and off trolleys a mandatory part of the public school curriculum for girls: "That few women know how to do either is a fact attested by common observation. . . . Doubtless there are psychological reasons not yet recognized why the typical woman cannot get on

Fig. 8.10 "Stop the Car!" (*The Standard*, October 1, 1898)

or off a car unless it has come to a full stop without imminent danger of damaging the asphalt with her head, and why she can even then do either only with exasperating deliberation."[9]

Serial-queen melodramas operated as a utopian escape from such stereotypes (and, perhaps in some cases, a fantasied escape from the awkwardness of actual physical uncoordination, as well). Stunts in *The Hazards of Helen* and other railway thrillers proclaimed that women could do quite a bit more than just step hesitantly onto a stationary trolley (figs. 8.11, 8.12, 8.13, 8.14).

In a similar vein, the serial-queen melodrama's emphasis on the heroine's skill behind the steering wheel of automobiles offered an escape from another prevailing stereotype—the inept woman driver. (In this respect, they continued in the tradtion of daredevil automobile stunts pictured in figs. 3.35 and 3.36.) The stereotype of women as bad drivers hinged on a presupposition not only of women's physical unco-ordination but of their cognitive or intellectual inadequacy, as well. A 1904 article on "Why Women Are, or Are Not, Good Chauffeuses" asserted that

Fig. 8.11 Publicity still for unidentified episode of *The Hazards of Helen*, 1915. (Courtesy Academy of Motion Picture Arts and Sciences, Still no. 1307)

Fig. 8.12 Publicity still for "A Test of Courage" episode of *The Hazards of Helen*, 1915. (*Kalem Kalendar*, October 1915)

Lack of concentration is the most common failing of all among motor-women. If a woman cannot concentrate in every-day things, she cannot concentrate when she motors. The weakness that causes a woman to read the same page of a book twice to get its meaning, that makes her ask an eager question about the detail of a story which one has just carefully explained, that leads her mind on a will-of-the-wisp trip around the hem of the conversation, is the same weakness which, in motoring, keeps her looking too long at an attractive bit of scenery, or turning her attention for a moment wholly to something that has been said, or for a single instant lifting her hand from the brake. She cannot concentrate. . . . Most of the motor accidents come from carelessness that is simply due to inability to concentrate. This is a feminine fault more than a masculine.[10]

An article written five years later, in 1909, continued with this argument that an inherent feeblemindedness made women bad drivers:

The natural training of woman is not in the direction to allow her properly to manipulate an automobile in cases of emergencies. She is not trained to think of two things at once. Note her as she walks along a crowded sidewalk and suddenly desires to retrace her steps for some forgotten errand.

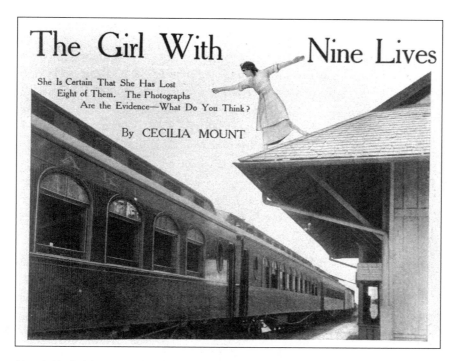

Fig. 8.13 Publicity still for "A Girl's Grit" episode of *The Hazards of Helen*, 1915. (*Motion Picture Magazine*, February 1916)

Fig. 8.14 Publicity still for "A Girl's Grit" episode of *The Hazards of Helen*, 1915. (*Kalem Kalendar*, September 1915)

Quick as a flash she will turn and bump straight into somebody approach-ing from the rear. It never occurs to her to turn to one side and then retrace her steps. If she meets a person with whom she wishes to converse, also upon the same crowded sidewalk, she will almost invariably block the traffic rather than withdraw to one side. The boy is trained [via sports] to act quickly in emergencies. . . . All his games tend to that end, and as he grows up and becomes a business man, again his training is, as it were, to think of two things at once. With few exceptions, a woman seldom reaches this particular phase of mental activity, called for time and time again in automobiling. . . . The natural hysteria of women certainly enters into this matter very strongly.[11]

In the face of such fundamental antifeminist cultural biases, the serial-queen melodrama offered women (and men) a kind of ideological holi-day. Against the stereotype of women as bad drivers impaired by their essential flighty, vapid, and hysterical nature, female spectators could relish stunts like the one displayed in *Plunder* (1923), Pearl White's last serial. The heroine (a leading Wall Street stockbroker) races her car full throttle through the rain-slicked streets of Manhattan, zooming nimbly around trolleys, cars, and pedestrians—with her eyes closed!

The serial-queen melodrama's utopian fantasy of female freedom concerned a liberation from ideologies of female passivity and weakness. It also envisioned a female liberation from conventional material or eco-nomic constraints. Consider the economic context of the time: govern-ment statistics on women wage earners in 1910 indicate that among female workers under the age of twenty-one (a key audience for serial-queen melodramas), almost 80 percent handed over their entire pay-check to the head of the household, usually the father. Only one young woman in a hundred was free to keep all her earnings.[12] Although the links between social facts such as this and cultural expression in popular amusements are never cut-and-dried and should not be oversimplified, it is tempting to hypothesize a connection between this lack of financial independence among young women and the serial-queen melodrama's stress on female agency in a fictional world suddenly divested of pater-nal power and control. With the assassination or abduction of the hero-ine's father—an absolutely essential generic element—it is a world fan-tastically free of direct patriarchal authority.

Serial-queen melodramas drew heavily and overtly on a broader feminist discourse that, propelled by the women's movement and the campaign for suffrage, was extremely prominent in the Teens. The serial-queen genre consciously tapped into the movement's polemical momentum. A sequence in an episode of the 1919 Pathé serial *The Lightning Raider*, for example, frames the heroine's aggressivity as an overtly feminist repudiation of patriarchal chauvinism. The plucky young heroine—named simply "Lightning," like a male superhero—is trying to intercept a bouquet of roses in which a villain has hidden a vial of deadly germs. The first place she searches happens to be the site of the yearly banquet of the Society for Anthropological Research. A group of gray-haired, bearded, and bespectacled scholars sits around a large table. (The contemporary viewer is struck by their visual resemblance to Freud, and the fact that the keynote speaker's name implies Jewishness makes one wonder whether a direct allusion might have been intended.) Also at the table is a younger academic with a Dutch Boy haircut, round Harold Lloyd spectacles, and effeminate mannerisms—overtly coded as homosexual. The chairman rises and announces that "Professor Absolom will now read his paper on the 'Inferiority of the Female Brain Cavity.'" Meanwhile, with ripe irony, Lightning is engaged in a treacherous climb down the side of the building with a rope. Just as the professor reads the words "From the natural timidity of the female, I deduce . . . ," Lightning blasts in through the balcony doors with her pistol drawn. As the men scramble in surprise and fear, Lightning literally heaves them out of her way, knocking over their chairs and spilling them onto the floor. She corrals them into a corner, where they stand trembling as she rips apart the flowers looking for the vial. She exits with a big grin, saying something to the effect of "So long suckers!"

A similar example of the serial-queen melodrama's employment of an overtly feminist discourse appears in *The Girl from Frisco*, a 1916 Kalem series. Barbara Brent is a spunky heiress, daughter of a western mogul. Her loving father tells her, "Some day you will be executrix of my properties—ranches, oil lands, mines." But when he learns that a brutish abutter is trying to steal the claim to his land (the deed serving as the narrative's weenie), and that the villain has mustered a mercenary army of ranch-hand renegades, the father rushes away from an elegant banquet at his city mansion (the banquet providing an opportunity for the heroine to display an exquisite silk evening dress before donning rugged masculine attire) with the stern admonition that the situation is too dangerous for his daughter to accompany him to the ranch lands. Barbara protests, but Brent hurries off without her. A U.S. congressman is the guest of honor at the banquet, and when someone asks him to give his opinion on "women's equality," he replies: "Frankly, I don't believe a woman is capable of holding down a man's job. My responsibility in making [cabinet] appointments is very grave. I would not think of using my influence to place women in important positions." Barbara intervenes: "I don't agree with Congressman Wallace. I believe a woman can do anything a man can do. Here's a case in point. I know I can help my father and am going to him in spite of his warning!" The congressman tells her, "It's foolish to rush into danger, Barbara. Besides, you can't help your father. He needs a man." The next sequence takes place at the ranch lands. Barbara discovers her father face down in dirt, unconscious from a gun wound. Following a trail of footsteps leading away from the body, Barbara tracks down the perpetrator and, with her big rifle, shoots him dead. Meanwhile, the congressman has arrived at the ranch. He immediately sprains his ankle and lies incapacitated as a brush fire begins to rage around him. Right after shooting the villain's henchman, Barbara smells smoke, races on horseback to the fire, and saves the feeble and hapless man.

The serial-queen melodrama's mythology of female power can be seen as a utopian fantasy reaction to the sexist ideology and patriarchal restrictions that women experienced in this period. But the genre is paradoxical in this respect since it not only conveyed female frustration with the cultural constraints of femininity but also encapsulated positive changes in the social reality of women around the turn of the century. Lewis Jacobs's assessment of the genre's heroines is apt: "Their exploits paralleled, in a sense, the real rise of women to a new status in society."[13] The historical spectator undoubtedly would have recognized and understood the serial-queen as a socially reflexive stereotype, and one already familiar in a variety of adjacent entertainment forms. The serial-queen persona reflected and embodied decisive transformations in the cultural construction of womanhood that accompanied America's shift to industrial capitalism and an urban consumer economy. The scope of these transformations was enormous—in one way or another they all involved the expansion of the woman's sphere of experience beyond the sheltered boundaries of the domestic circle.

Whereas few modes of public experience were acceptable for an unaccompanied woman in the Victorian era, the years between 1880 and 1920 generated a new conception of the woman's legitimate domain. Significantly lower fertility rates and the proliferation of labor-saving machines and commodities gave both lower- and middle-class women more freedom to pursue activities outside the household. Whereas only about 10 percent of women worked in paid labor in 1880, this figure had almost doubled by 1910 (or even tripled, if one looks at the urban population). By 1910, more than 40 percent of young single women worked for several years before marriage, and the figure was probably over 60 percent in urban areas.[14] The massive development of the department store made shopping a condoned activity for housewives and encouraged their presence in the public realm. Sales by department stores increased from a zero-point in 1889 to $161 million in 1899, $676 million in 1909, and $2,588 million in 1919. Entertainments eager to cater to women—music halls, amusement parks, movie theaters, and so on—also gave women places to go.[15] An unprecedented degree of independence and mobility was reinforced by the diffusion of new means of transportation—especially the electric trolley (whose miles of track increased by 245 percent in the Northeast between 1890 and 1902) and the bicycle, which in the mid-1890s took on heightened social-symbolic importance as an emblem of female emancipation.[16]

An astounding growth in the formation of women's social clubs, which served as a wellspring for feminist awareness and suffrage activism, provided a major new form of public experience for middle-class women. Even the emergence of electric streetlights played a role in expanding the world for women. In an 1896 article on "Women Bachelors in New York," Mary Humphreys wrote: "The increase in the number of women abroad at night, with no other protector than the benign beams of the electric light, affords a new and interesting manifestation of the streets. They are found in the streetcars at hours that once would have been called unseemly; they are substantial patrons of the theater."[17] The premise of this article, crystallized by the oxymoronic term "woman bachelor," was that female experience in urban modernity could be characterized in terms of a new masculinization.

Popular culture synthesized and symbolized these transformations in the social configuration of womanhood through a cultural construct dubbed the "New Woman." For years, print media and popular entertainments were preoccupied with this buzz-image, perennially attempting to define, evaluate, caricature, and mythologize its various dimensions. The remarkable cultural saturation of the New Woman stereotype stemmed from the clarity of its dialectic opposition to the "Cult of True

Womanhood," the paradigm of femininity that dominated the nine-teenth century and whose key terms, as Barbara Welter's influential essay elucidates, were "piety, purity, submissiveness and domesticity."[18] Welter quotes a passage from *The Sphere and Duties of Woman*, a typical mid-nineteenth-century handbook defining the nature of the "true woman": "She feels herself weak and timid. She needs a protector. She is in a measure dependent. She asks for wisdom, constancy, firmness and perseverance, and she is willing to repay it all by the surrender of the full treasure of her affections."[19] In sharp contrast to this ideal, a 1902 mag-azine article got to the core of the New Woman image: "The energetic, independent woman of culture is frequently caricatured as the 'New Woman.' . . . The key-note of her character is self-reliance and the power of initiation. She aims at being in direct contact with reality and forming her own judgment upon it."[20]

As America moved into modernity, an ideology of ultimate female dependence began to shift (although it would never completely yield) to a cultural image of woman as capable of standing on her own. Whereas a playwright in 1825 typically likened woman to "ivy fondly clinging to the tall oak's majestic side," a 1911 magazine essay entitled "The Masculization of Girls" spoke of "the Girl's strange metamorphosis from the clinging vine of yesterday to the near-oak of today." Echoing this theme, a film reviewer in 1911 commended the depiction of "a girl who has to fight her way instead of having it prepared for her; the kind of up-to-date heroine that American audiences admire more than the clinging vine variety."[21] Minna Thomas Antrim's essay describes "the 'Masculine Girl of today'": "She tells herself exultantly that she is man's (almost) brother. . . . She loves to walk, to row, to ride, to motor, to jump and run, not daintily with high heeled, silk-lined elegance, but as Man walks, jumps, rows, rides, motors, and runs."[22] Charles Dana Gibson's parodic illustration, "One of the Disadvantages of Being in Love with an Athletic Girl," published in *Life* in 1902 (fig. 8.15), typi-fies the mass-media's insatiable interest in this new configuration of fem-ininity and condenses the various forms of celebration, curiosity, and mild paranoia that this interest entailed.

The New Woman's trademarks—energy, self-reliance, direct contact with the extradomestic world—were clearly the terms of a revised fem-ininity celebrated and exaggerated in the serial-queen melodrama. Any consideration of the sources of this genre must stress the great extent to which it self-consciously drew upon an already codified and pervasive

Fig. 8.15 Charles Dana Gibson, "One of the Disadvantages of Being in Love with an Athletic Girl." (*Life*, May 20, 1902)

popular discourse around the New Woman.

More specifically, the serial-queen melodrama developed out of several interrelated popular entertainments that had already transposed the figure of the New Woman into action-oriented narratives aimed primarily at working-class readers and theatergoers. In the last decades of the nineteenth century, dime novels, story papers, popular newspapers, and popular-priced melodramas all developed subgenres built around the exploits and perils of working-girl heroines. One sees scattered instances of climactic female agency in stage melodramas as early as the mid-1860s. In Augustin Daly's *Under the Gaslight* (1867), for example, the heroine hacks her way out of a locked woodshed and saves a man tied to the railroad tracks (directly anticipating "Helen's Rescue of Tom" shown in fig. 8.8). (See fig. 8.16.) The rescued man declares, "Victory! Saved! Hooray! And these are the women who ain't to have a vote!"[23]

Climaxes such as this in which the heroine rescues the hero became a common motif in 10–20–30 stage melodrama. As noted earlier, in Joseph Arthur's *Blue Jeans* (1890) the heroine smashes through a locked door to rescue the hero from an unpleasant bifurcation by a buzz saw (see figs. 6.8, 6.9, 6.10). In *In Old Kentucky* (1893; revival in 1907) the heroine swings by rope across a stage chasm in order to save her hero, who is about to be blown to bits by dynamite. Later she rescues a rac-

Fig. 8.16 Stock poster for *Under the Gaslight,* c. 1870. (Courtesy Harvard Theatre Collection)

ing filly from a burning stable and then rides the horse to victory in the Ashland Oaks derby. In Charles Blaney's *The Factory Girl* (1903), the heroine smashes through a large window to save the hero from being decapitated by some kind of industrial guillotine. The heroine again rescues the hero in the nick of time just as his canoe is swept over a waterfall in Charles Taylor's *Through Fire and Water* (1903), and in *A Woman's Pluck* (1905), "the heroine dons the gloves and gives the villain a startling insight into her boxing accomplishments." In *The Girl and the Detective* (1908), the heroine saves the prone hero from being seared and mashed by a white-hot slab of iron under a steam hammer (a reviewer noted that "the girl has business enough to keep six actresses busy"). And in *No Mother to Guide Her* (1905), the plucky-as-ever young heroine (named "Bunco") "throughout the whole play is the bravest of the brave, is sufficiently cunning, and rescues everybody and everything to the satisfaction of an audience that is boisterously fond of melodrama."[24] Sensational plays such as these provided an immediate prototype for the serial-queen melodrama. Audiences viewing serial-queen melodramas understood this intertextual lineage: they were well aware that the serials (and a number of nonserial film precursors) were basically 10–20–30 plays rendered in a new medium. (See fig. 8.17.)

Representations of dynamic New Women also featured important-

Fig. 8.17 Poster for the stage melodrama *My Tom-Boy Girl*, c. 1905. (Courtesy Museum of the City of New York)

ly in metropolitan newspapers by the mid-1890s, corresponding to the onset of "the volcanic school of journalism."[25] The popular newspaper, an entertainment form through and through, combined vibrant lithographs and sensationalistic accounts of curiosities, disasters, scandals, stunts, and accidents. Women readers were crucial to this new form of mass entertainment largely because of its dependence on revenue from department store advertising aimed at female consumers. The necessity to cater to women merged with the policy of sensationalism in two forms: columns devoted to brave or unconventional exploits by actual women, and "plucky girl reporter" features.

In the *New York World* of Monday, March 23, 1896, the lead article on the front page concerned a Jersey City housewife who had battled relentlessly with a burglar and won. The customary plethora of headlines and subheadlines (all before getting to the actual text of the article) read: "She Held a Burglar / Little Mrs. Gilligan Rolled Downstairs with Him in Her Grip / Then They Fought on the Floor / Once He Got Away by Slipping Off His Coat, but She Sprang on Him Again / Husband Came After She Had Him Safe."

The "Plucky Girl Nabs Thief" item congealed into something of a newspaper staple during this period (see fig. 8.18). An item in an 1896 *New York Sunday World* column entitled "Woman's Record During the Week" exemplifies the formula:

It is pleasant to turn . . . to the excellent record of Mrs. Bloomer, who well deserves her name. Mrs. Bloomer is a lady of high standing in Port Jervis, N.Y. She follows the usual careful housewife's habit of looking under the bed for a man, and her vigilance was rewarded by the discovery of a man there several evenings ago. Did Mrs. Bloomer shriek and faint? She did not. She seized a revolver, dragged the man ignominiously forth, took his revolver from him, made him empty his pockets before her, and finally gave him into the willing arms of the law—all without assistance and in the coolest possible manner.[26]

A syndicated "news" item appearing on the front page of the *Newark Daily Advertiser* on March 9, 1895, entitled "Met a Woman with Nerve," provides another example of the cultural interest in female fearlessness. It is particularly interesting in that, but for its last clause, one could very easily mistake it for a synopsis of a Griffith Biograph film from fifteen years later.

Fig. 8.18 "Burglars Are Pie for Her" (detail from cartoon, "What the New Woman Is Coming To"). (*New York World*, March 29, 1896)

Duluth, Minn.,—Shortly before midnight, Mrs. Richards, the Northern Pacific agent at Kimberly, a small station near Brainard, overheard two men outside her window planning to rob the eastbound express. One of them wanted to throw ties on the track, but the other was of the opinion that the best plan would be to wreck the train at the east end of the bridge. It could be done in such a way that the express car would not fall into the river. Just as they had settled on this plan, the woman got out of her bed to give the alarm. Before she touched the telegraph key, one of the robbers proposed to go inside the station and await the train, which was not due for some time. At the same time they tried to smash the door in. Instantly the woman grabbed her revolver and put several bullets through the door, causing the surprised desperadoes to flee. Word was telegraphed along the line, but no trace of the men was found.[27]

A regular column comprised of such items began in the *New York Sunday World* in August 1895. Its most frequent heading was "The

Fig. 8.19 "Saved Two Men from an Angry Lion" (*New York World*, May 3, 1896)

'New Woman' in Everyday Life: Various Interesting Manifestations of the Emancipated Female's Foibles and Freaks, and her Curious Interests, Powers and Exploits."[28] Along with accounts of bravery—women snaring burglars or rescuing people from fire, drowning, or even angry lions (fig. 8.19)—the most common subjects in these New Woman columns related to women at work in traditionally male jobs like steamboat engineer, deputy marshal, bank president, coroner, coal miner, grist mill operator, bicycle mechanic, itinerant photographer, carpenter, marble cutter, lawyer, dentist, physician, and insurance broker.

The second prominent newspaper form that emerged alongside the New Woman articles in the mid 1890s constitutes what I call "stunt articles"—recounted exploits contrived by daring women reporters. Telling of their adventures in first-person narration, a small group of "plucky girl reporters" became familiar, consistent personalities, much like serial queens. The sole objective of these women reporters was to seek out "novel and thrilling experiences" that extended the experiential sphere of women. Stunt articles vivified places and experiences that were out of reach to women, restricted by virtue of either their danger or their indelicacy. Which is to say, these articles explored for women areas of activity normally designated as culturally proper only to men.

Many stunt articles focused on the intrepid pursuit of physical peril and kinesthetic excitement: plucky girl reporter Kate Swan scales the Harlem River Bridge just for the thrill of it, conquering "a Spot No Woman's Foot Ever Before Trod" (fig. 8.20); she kayaks through a mad whirlpool in the East River at midnight; she struggles in a bout with a champion wrestler; she works as a stoker, heaving coal into the fiery furnace of a North River ferryboat; she drives a locomotive through the B&O tunnel at 75 mph, becoming the first woman ever to run an electric engine. Dorothy Dare, becoming "the first woman to take a spin through the streets of New York in a horseless carriage," drives at the dizzying speed of 30 mph; Sallie Madden shoots a perilous mountain chute on a frail railroad car (fig. 8.21). Other articles, while involving less physical action, were nevertheless daring and similarly took women to places outside their traditional zone of experience—opium dens, mass burials, leper colonies, execution chambers, insane asylums, gambling dens, police patrols, mortuaries, flop houses, and freak shows. In perhaps the most telling stunt of all, Dorothy Dare simply dresses up in men's clothing to explore New York at liberty. The serial-queen melodrama's intertextual link to both the New Woman column and these stunt articles is direct and self-evident. The connection is made explicitly in titles like Mutual's 1917 *The Perils of Our Girl Reporters* (fig. 8.22) and in the resurrection of Dorothy Dare as a series heroine in International's *The Adventures of Dorothy Dare* (1916).

A variation on the girl-reporter articles were items about supposedly aristocratic female adventure-seekers. In 1904, Hearst newspapers syndicated an account of the daring Mme. de Gast. The headline and subheadings read, "The Most Remarkable Woman on Earth: How the Very Rich Mme. de Gast, Who Was Dragged from Under her Motor Boat Half-Drowned the Other Day, Spends Her Time and Money Seeking Hair-Breadth Escapes from Death." Photographs showed the French woman "Driving Her Mile-a-Minute Racing Car"; "In Her Balloon"; and "At the Tiller of Her Racing Boat."[29]

The serial-queen melodrama clearly extended an image already con-

Kate Swan, at a Dizzy Height.

PLUCKILY CLINGING TO A ROPE, SHE WAS SWIFTLY LIFTED TO THE TOP BRIDGE GIRDER.

Fig. 8.20 "Kate Swan at a Dizzy Height." (*New York World*, April 12, 1896, 29)

A WOMAN'S WILD RIDE DOWN A MOUNTAIN.

Her Thrilling Experience Shooting a Perilous Pennsylvania Chute a Half Mile Long on a Frail Railroad Handcar.

FANCY shooting a chute half a mile long with a vertical descent of four hundred feet! This thrilling ride was made down an incline with a pitch steeper than the roof of an old-fashioned house. It was down Mahanoy Plane, in Pennsylvania, that the writer took a ride like no ride ever taken by another woman since railroads came into existence. She would not repeat it for untold wealth. Mahanoy Plane is one of the relics of a past era in railroading, when engineering skill was far less advanced than at present.

This plane was built years ago in order to get traffic over the Broad Mountain, and it is to-day in active operation, pulling long trains of loaded coal cars from the valley beneath to the top of the mountain, where the regular railroad begins again and runs to Pottsville and Philadelphia.

The plane is cut through the living rock in the mountain side, and describes a great curve in its descent—that is, the slope is not uniform but dish-shaped, being steeper near the top than at the bottom. From the top the valley below seems miles away. The at the foot had promised plane slopes away from one's feet. So dangerous is this place that the company forbids under the severest penalty any employee riding on the cars moving up and down the incline.

THRILLING RIDE ON A HANDCAR.

Yes! I not only rode down the plank, but rode on a little light four-wheel car, such as track laborers use, commonly known as a "truck," a feat the most foolhardy railroader would declare impossible.

The time chosen was midnight of a recent Saturday. There was a double reason for this, one being that the feat would be impossible at any other time because of the working of the plane; the other being that at that hour the locality was temporarily deserted by employees and villagers alike. I had two confederates, one at the top, the other at the foot of the incline.

The little car was poised on the brink.

"Are you ready?" I was asked.

"Yes," I said.

A push, a start, a sudden tilt of the platform as the car reached the slope; here almost 75 degrees, or more than three-quarters perpendicular—a quick realization when too late of the stupendous feat—and then drop, drop, drop, farter and faster, until the very breath refused to come.

WILD DASH DOWN A MOUNTAIN.

The keen wintry air cut me like a knife, though I was clad in the heaviest garments, and my tightly bound hair was torn loose with a feeling akin to scalping. Talk about a falling elevator! If you can imagine yourself on a bare platform freight "lift," dropping not fifty feet nor one hundred feet, but three thousand feet, you may be able to faintly realize my situation.

Sparks flew in a steady stream from the rails, and each separate wheel hummed like a buzz-saw, louder and louder, until the noise seemed to rend my brain.

Then a sudden horror into my consciousness. Suppose the switches should be set wrong at the bottom. I should be dashed into the valley below a train! True, my ally seems miles away. The at the foot had promised to see to all that; but suppose he should have overlooking some trifling detail! The fear was overpowering.

A flash of light shot past me, another and another, then a rumble and roar growing louder and louder, drowning the noise of my vehicle, a sensation of warmth as the chilling wind grew less fierce, a quick gasp of life-saving breath into my poor lungs, a cheery hail, and a gradual checking of the car.

I was down, and half a mile away from the foot of the plane on a long empty siding, while a heavy coal train rumbled alongside in the darkness.

The time of the descent was fifteen seconds, or a speed equal to something over one hundred miles an hour. Somebody else can complete the remaining ninety-nine and a half miles if they desire. I've had enough.

SALLIE MADDEN.

SPARKS FLEW FROM THE RAILS AS THE FRAIL CAR WHIZZED DOWN THE INCLINE.

Fig. 8.21 "A Woman's Wild Ride Down a Mountain." (*New York World*, February 14, 1897)

Fig. 8.22 Advertisement for *The Perils of Our Girl Reporters*, 1917. (*Motion Picture News*, January 13, 1917)

structed in the urban mythology of popular entertainment. It is important to underscore that this discourse was rhetorically polyvalent in nature. The genre's portrayal of the New Woman, like that of its intertextual precursors, suggests a complex mixture of social reflection, utopian fantasy, and simple curiosity. First of all, as I have suggested, the genre documented and celebrated concrete sociological changes in the cultural construction of womanhood. There was a tangible link, in other words, between social facts and cultural representation. Society represented itself to itself with a certain degree of fidelity. But, as I have also argued, the genre functioned on the level of female fantasy and escapism. The utopian image of female prowess and emancipation tells us as much about the continuing cultural restrictions on female experience as it does about her new exposure to the public sphere. The genre's focus on female heroic agency both memorialized an actual expansion of women's sphere of experience and, as vicarious fantasy, suggested the ongoing constraints of conventional definitions of gender.

Finally, I think it cannot be stressed too much that the image of the New Woman captured the attention of both men and women at the turn of the century by virtue of its sheer novelty and curiosity. Beyond any coefficient of social reflection or utopian fantasy (and inseparable from either), the widespread cultural fascination with the New Woman suggests the appeal of simply playing around with gender for its own sake. Helen Holmes's extraordinary daredevil stuntwork in *The Hazards of Helen*, for example, may have had less to do with an earnest stake in a progressive ideology of female emancipation than with the utter novelty and curiosity value of a spectacle based on the "category mistake" of a woman taking death-defying physical risks, getting filthy, brawling with crooks in muddy riverbanks—in short, of a woman acting like a man.

* * *

Female power constitutes a central theme in the serial-queen melodrama, but it would be very misleading to characterize the genre as a one-dimensional exposition of Amazonian prowess. There was another aspect that, while it did not surface in all serial-queen melodramas, played an extremely pronounced role in those films in which it did appear. This strain involved the lurid victimization of the heroine by male villains who exploit their greater size, strength, and sadistic guile to render her powerless and terrified. All serial-queen narratives, by definition, placed the heroine in positions of danger—it was a necessary part of her emancipation and "masculine" agency. But a number of serial-queen films went much further and amplified an extremely graphic spectacle of female distress, helplessness, and abject terror. In films like *The Perils of Pauline*, *The Exploits of Elaine*, *The Fatal Ring*, and *A Woman in Grey*, the heroine systematically would be assaulted, bound

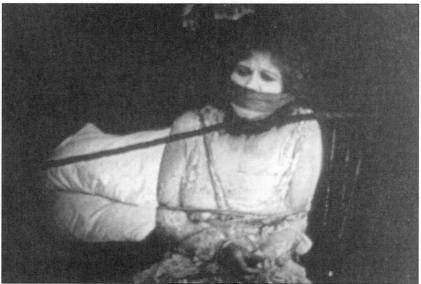

Fig. 8.23 Frame still enlargements for *A Woman in Grey*, 1919—20.

and gagged, terrorized by instruments of torture and dismemberment, hurled out windows or off bridges, and threatened with innumerable means of assassination. The genre thus coupled an ideology of female power with an equally vivid exposition of female defenselessness and weakness (fig. 8.23).

It is telling that stills from serials (albeit later ones) pop up in adult catalogs of bondage photos.[30] The serial-queen melodrama—at least this variation of the genre—can be regarded as one of the first systematic explorations and exploitations of a strain of perverse stimulus that would later shape the psycho-killer crime thriller, the slasher film, and S&M pornography—to mention only the most overt instances within a dominant cinema that many feminist critics have regarded as inherently male-oriented. The serial's spectacle of misogynistic sadism is certainly a prime candidate for psychoanalytic interpretation. But much more than male sadism is at issue in the serial-queen melodrama. The genre is a particularly fascinating text for psychoanalytic exegesis because it is structurally capable of accommodating a complex interplay of disparate psychic fantasies and anxieties relating to both male and female subjectivity.

Spelled out most simply, the serial-queen melodrama prompts questions such as: What explains the female spectator's interest in a fantasy of a masculinized woman? What explains her interest in viewing female victimization? And likewise, what explains the male spectator's interest in female prowess and in victimization? Psychoanalysis offers a number of compelling hypotheses about these spectatorial phenomena, and about their paradoxical combination within a psychic/textual economy. One could draw parallels between the serial-queen melodrama, as it separately engages both male and female subjectivity, and psychoanalytic theories of sadism, masochism, penis envy, phallic narcissism, the disavowal of sexual difference, and the fantasies and anxieties of both male and female oedipal trajectories. It would take us too far afield to elaborate further on the psychoanalytic undercurrents in the serial-queen melodrama, but I do want to underscore the idea that a historical "contextualist" approach is not necessarily at odds with—and indeed may never be really adequate without—a parallel consideration of other kinds of forces shaping cultural texts.

In this case, however, the inverse is even more obvious: a purely psychoanalytic approach by itself would be blind to crucial intertextual and sociological sources behind the display of female imperilment. The seri-

al-queen melodrama's fixation on female imperilment stemmed immediately and unequivocally from the basic iconographic formula of sensational melodrama in its various lowbrow stage and dime novel manifestations. At the very core of virtually all sensational melodramas, from
1800 onward, one finds the persecution of a virtuous heroine by a dia-
bolical villain (fig. 8.24). Essayists and critics writing near the turn of
the century had no difficulty stereotyping this classic configuration of
villainy and victimization as it appeared in 10–20–30 melodrama:

*The villain, without provocation, punched the heroine in the nose or
kicked her feet from under her. (1903)*

*The villain, who has learned that he is next of kin and so will inherit
millions—millions—millions in the event of the death of the girl whom
he has quite given up hope of winning, tries upon the heroine and her sole
defender every known, and some unknown, ways of inducing physical disintegration. (1909)*

*You could enter any one of a dozen or fifteen New York temples of art con-
fident of seeing a lady sawed, blown up, poisoned, electrocuted, strangled,
smothered, choked, gouged, shot, maimed, drowned and hurled from the
Brooklyn Bridge. (1909)*

*Just when the heroine is about to be disintegrated by the sausage machine,
or reduced to longitudinal sections by the buzz-saw, or run over by the
express-train as she lies bound across the rails, or blown to bits by the pow-
der-barrel as the fuse sputters nearer and nearer, then . . . in jumps the
hero. (1909)*

*You may lock the heroine in a lion's cage, throw her off of the Brooklyn
Bridge, tie her to the subway tracks, and dangle her by a rope from the
windy summit of the Singer tower. (1911)*[31]

The spectacle of abduction and violent imperilment was a crucial
element in the sensational melodrama's generic iconography (along with
the corollary spectacle of escape or chivalrous intervention). This image
of female victimization in the serial-queen melodrama clearly con-
formed to a formula already firmly codified by the serial's intertextual
matrix.

Female victimization may have become such a central generic con-

Fig. 8.24 Stock poster for *Colleen Bawn*, c. 1870. (Courtesy Harvard Theatre Collection)

vention in sensational melodrama in the first place because of the clarity with which it could function in terms of social allegory. Thomas Elsaesser has argued, for example, that the inherently melodramatic tragedies and sentimental novels of Samuel Richardson, Johann Schiller, and Gotthold Lessing hinged on "a metaphorical interpretation of class-conflict as sexual exploitation and rape" and thus express "the struggle of a morally and emotionally emancipated bourgeois consciousness against the remnants of feudalism" (as discussed in chapter 5).[32] American popular melodrama at the turn of the century continued to use crises of female victimization to stress themes of class stratification and injustice, although its contrasts and clashes were adjusted downward a stratum to counterpose not a villainous aristocracy and virtuous bourgeoisie, but rather a corrupt bourgeoisie and poor-but-noble working class.[33]

The serial-queen melodrama marks an interesting shift in this vein of social allegory, since the films almost never directly addressed issues of social injustice or posed the characters as symbolic stand-ins for entire socioeconomic classes. The heroine and hero invariably were depicted as belonging to either a blithe upper or solidly professional middle class.

Serials dispensed with the stage melodrama's glorification of "only a working girl" and completely avoided the pathos of stoic poverty sometimes attached to her victimization (in serials, there were no sick mothers or blind sisters for the heroine to provide for). The serial-queen melodrama also had no place for the stage melodrama's typical "blue shirt lead" (the working-man good guy) or its retinue of comic street-life characters. The benevolent wino messengers, soubrettes, bootblacks, and immigrant peddlers—ennobled by their street smarts, moral fortitude, and impudence in the face of social elitism—were entirely omitted.

The serial-queen melodrama's allegorical shift was decisive: it metaphorized the social dynamics not of class but of gender. The films charted the social instability and oppressiveness feared not by a "morally and emotionally emancipated" underclass, but rather by the similarly emancipated New Woman in the public sphere. The genre captured the basically paradoxical nature of female experience at a pivotal phase of modernity. With its repudiation of domesticity and its fantasy of empowerment, the serial-queen melodrama celebrated the excitement of the woman's attainment of unprecedented mobility outside the confines of the home. But, correspondingly, in its imagery of female victimization the genre also envisioned the dangers of this departure. Its scenes of

Fig. 8.25 Frame still enlargement from *The Perils of Pauline,* 1914.

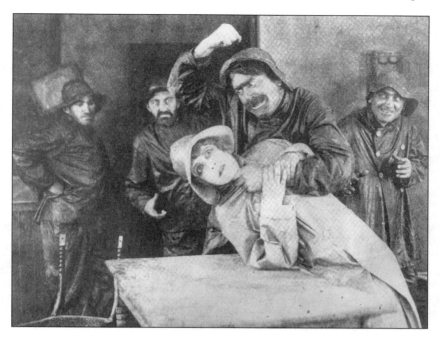

Fig. 8.26 Publicity still for *The Perils of Pauline*, 1914. (Courtesty Museum of Modern Art Stills Archive)

assault, abduction, torture, and intimated rape suggested the worst-case scenario of woman's entry into the mixed-sex, mixed-class, and mixed-ethnicity chaos of the modern urban milieu (figs. 8.25, 8.26).

Popular magazines in this period began to describe a general disintegration of public civility coinciding with the greater independence of women in an urbanized America no longer protected by Victorian strictures of social decorum. Eleanor Gates's 1906 article in *Cosmopolitan Magazine* entitled "The Girl Who Travels Alone" describes a new social problem, particularly severe in New York but existing in all the country's urban centers—namely, the harassment of unaccompanied women in the form of relentless unwanted advances by strange men; rude calls in Central Park by ethnic packs (especially native-born "foreigner's sons"); "forced kissing" on the subway by college rowdies; lewd calls by wagon-drivers, a type that "flourishes by the thousands in New York, calling out obscenities to young girls as he rattles past, purposely driving close to young women who are alone and saying whatever insolent thing occurs to him"; or ultimately even physical harm, as in the case of "Dr. S—," a young woman physician: "As she approached a subway entrance at

Fig. 8.27 Publicity still for *Plunder*, 1923. (Courtesy Museum of Modern Art Stills Archive)

Forty-second Street, carrying her satchel, a man whom she had never seen before took her by the arm. What he said was so infamous that she struck him. He struck back at her, tore her dress, and knocked her down the flight of steps. A crowd gathered, but no bystander offered aid (fig. 8.27)."[34] Gates stated that her examples, which "could be multiplied by the thousands," left out those which "would not bear publication"— presumably a reference to rape. All these problems arose from the novel convergence of the anonymity, heterogeneity, and mobility of the modern city and, as Gates put it, "the social conditions in this country which admit the widest liberty to women."

The venerable Harvard psychologist Hugo Münsterberg, in a 1913 *New York Times* essay, encapsulated a fundamental ambivalence about the new "American position of the woman outside of the family circle." "Her contact with men," he wrote, "has been multiplied, her right to seek joy in every possible way has become the counterpart of her new independence, her position has become more exposed and more dangerous."[35] Münsterberg's assessment could almost stand as a synopsis of

Fig. 8.28 "A Typical Scene on the Bowery" in lower Manhattan, c. 1899. (From Zeisloft, ed., *The New Metropolis*, 1899)

a serial like *The Perils of Pauline*, with which it almost precisely coincided (*Pauline* was probably being shot while Münsterberg was writing his essay). Like the controversial wave of "white slavery" films also appearing at this time (depicting the abduction, imprisonment, and forced prostitution of innocent women in the cities), the serial-queen genre gave shape to a pervasive social anxiety—one felt by both men and women—about the consequences of woman's emancipation and independence in the heterosocial public sphere (fig. 8.28).[36]

Modernity granted women a new freedom of social circulation—or rather, it might be more accurate to say that modernity *required* it. Female mobility was necessary for the sake of modern capitalism. As cheap labor in unskilled, semiskilled, and clerical occupations, women contributed greatly to the expansion of factory-based mass production and bureaucratic rationalization. As shoppers (and, again, as low-paid "shopgirls" in department stores and other commercial concerns), women fueled the consumer economy on which capitalism depended. Female participation in modern capitalism energized society, but it also entailed exposure to new varieties and intensities of risk. The serial-queen's oscillation between agency and vulnerability expressed the paradoxes and ambiguities of women's new situation in urban modernity.

9

Marketing Melodrama:
Serials and Intertextuality

One of the defining aspects of modern culture, one that sets it apart from earlier epochs, is the abundance and intricacy of textual intersections and interactions. Just as the rise of the metropolis involved an infinitely busier and more varied arena of human interaction, so too did the rise of modernity involve a much more active and complex network of interconnections among texts. This is not to suggest that intertextuality has not always informed the visual arts, theater, music, and literature (think of the Bible's influence over the last 1,500 years), but there is something epochally extraordinary about the pervasiveness of textual interaction in modern capitalist society. The phenomenon is an outgrowth of, among other things, the expansion of media technology, communications networks, and the commercialization of amusement, and it is central to what I described in chapter 1 as the increased mobility and circulation of all "social things." Needless to say, this aspect of modernity has continued to escalate over the last century (a fact that might call into question the "postness" of postmodernity, since this facet of contemporary society does not represent a break with modernity, but rather a kind of "modernity plus").

While it would be overreaching to assert that melodrama was somehow more profoundly intertextual than other cultural forms, it is fair to say that sensational melodrama was probably unsurpassed in this regard, particularly in the case of early serial films. On the most basic level, serials were intrinsically intertextual: each episode was tied to the one before and the one after, and with the cliffhanger overlap structure, the episodes actually incorporated parts of one another. The structure encouraged a mental matching-up of separate texts. More broadly, as earlier chapters discussed, serial films were shaped by close intertextual links to 10–20–30 stage melodrama (as well as dime novels, story papers, and other kinds of popular fiction, particularly serialized fiction), which consequently also enmeshed serials in the textual web of critical discourse on the aesthetic and social status of cheap melodrama. The serial-queen melodrama, further, drew upon a specific sort of sensational-newspaper stunt article, and more generally upon widespread cultural motifs surrounding the New Woman and the rise of feminism. On the broadest level, a discourse on sensationalism and hyperstimulus hovered over serial melodrama, and over cinema in general.

This chapter explores another dimension of sensational melodrama's intertextual context by focusing on a range of publicity texts that surrounded film serials. I am particularly interested in fiction tie-ins, a form of intense direct intertextuality through which movies and short stories were bound together as two halves of what might be described as a larger, multimedia, textual unit.

* * *

Serials played a leading role in ushering the film industry into the era of modern consumerism. More than any other early film product, serials introduced a business model founded on extensive marketing. As early film critic Robert Grau observed in 1915, "Serials . . . have created a demand for publicity experts to such an extent that the advertising department of the modern film concern has become almost as important as that of production."[1] This was, of course, a paradigm that was emerging in all sectors of the economy in the decades around the turn of the century. By that time, no longer was capitalism just about the production of goods for sale; it was just as much about the production of appetites for goods.

In the mid-Teens, the film industry was beginning to recognize the importance of aggressive "exploitation," but it was still frustrated by brief exhibition runs that kept advertising relatively inefficient. In 1916 only one theater in thirty-three ran its programs for a full week. The average number of changes per week was five, and one theater in three changed films six times a week. Contrary to what one might expect, a report three years later found short runs even more prevalent: only one theater in a hundred ran films for an entire week, and over four-fifths changed films daily.[2] Such rapid turnovers restricted the cost-effectiveness of advertising and also reduced the influence of ancillary publicity such as word-of-mouth and newspaper reviews. A 1916 article in *McClure's Magazine* highlighted the problem:

A single photodrama is a perishable quantity. It is here today and there tomorrow, and no matter how good it is and how big it is, the entire receipts from its production do not justify the producer in investing several hundred thousand dollars, as is so often done with the serials, in educating the public as to the nature and subject matter of a single photoplay that cannot possibly earn for him the amount of money he would have to spend in advertising.

As this writer indicated, serials solved the problem. They were ideal vehicles for massive publicity, since any given title would stay at the same theater for three or four months.[3]

Producers and exhibitors of serials invested heavily in advertising using newspapers, magazines, trade journals, billboards, streetcars, sheet music, novelty giveaways, prize contests, coupons, postcards, and so on. Pathé reportedly spent $500,000 (the equivalent of about $7.7 million today) on newspaper and billboard advertising for its five serial releases of 1916.[4] Pathé claimed to have put out fifty-two billboards for *The Perils of Pauline* in New York City alone (fig. 9.1). For their first (and last) serial, *Who Is Number One?* (1917), Paramount boasted of "a comprehensive billboard campaign [that] will cover one hundred and fifty cities, and will include sections that have a population totaling fifty million persons—half the people in the United States." For *The Fighting Trail* (1917), Vitagraph carried out an enormous billboard campaign with 12,000 "twenty-four sheets" and another 12,000 to follow up a month later. The interest in billboards as a vehicle for serial publicity corresponded to the extremely rapid growth of this form of advertising in the Teens.[5] Already by 1915, as a cartoon in *Puck* showed (fig. 9.2), billboards advertising serial melodramas had become a stereotypical component of urban blight in the poorer areas of cities.

Prize contests provided a common form of serial publicity. The sums of money at stake made them highly impressive exploitation gimmicks. Pathé and the Hearst syndicate began a trend by offering

Fig. 9.1 Billboard for *The Perils of Pauline*, Brooklyn, New York, 1914. (*Motion Picture News*, June 13, 1914)

$25,000 (about $385,000 today) in prize money in conjunction with *The Perils of Pauline*: viewers had to speculate on items of narrative anticipation—for example, "What did the mummy say?" Thanhouser ran a contest, conducted by the *Chicago Tribune* syndicate, offering $10,000 (about $165,000 today) for a 100-word story ending to be

Fig. 9.2 "Aesthetic U.S.A.—Being a Panorama of Approach to the Average American Town or City": Cartoon parody of Serial-Film Billboard Advertising. (*Puck*, May 15, 1915)

used in the last chapter of *The Million Dollar Mystery* (1914). The *Tribune* and the American Film Manufacturing Company followed with a $10,000 scenario contest for a 30-installment serial, produced as *The Diamond from the Sky* (1915). Film historian Terry Ramsaye, who at the time was a *Tribune* editor and judge for the contest, reported that 19,003 scenario ideas were submitted. The winner was announced at the end of the first episode, thus assuring plenty of prerelease publicity. Then, to motivate moviegoers to stick with the serial over its unusually long run of seven and a half months, the producers offered another $10,000 for the best idea on how to end the serial. The *Tribune* and American later offered $5,000 (or $83,550 today) for the best concept for a sequel to *The Diamond from the Sky*. According to Kalton Lahue, that tidy sum was awarded to a certain Terry Ramsaye—a scam (assuming Lahue is not mistaken) that, needless to say, was not mentioned in *A Million and One Nights*.[6]

Sheet music afforded another common mode of publicity for serial films. Tapping into the popularity of recitals and sing-alongs as forms of recreation both in the home and at movie and vaudeville theaters, film publicists hooked up with sheet music producers to publish songs about the adventures of Mary, Pauline, Lucille Love, Zudora, Runaway June, Romantic Ruth, Helen, and other serial heroines. The sheet music's cover always featured a large portrait of the film heroine. Presumably, the songs played as part of the programs in which the serials were shown.[7]

The star system—the practice of promoting stars rather than studios, genres, directors, or some other potential marker of product differentiation as the most important element in a film—was central to the marketing methods that emerged in the Teens. Only around 1910 did studios begin to furnish the names of their actors. That initiated what could be called the "picture personality" system, to use Richard deCordova's term. The star system proper, as deCordova has documented, involved two further phenomena—first, efforts to blur the boundaries between the real actor's personality and fictional screen persona, thus encouraging fans to regard the two as one and the same; and second, the creation of a publicity apparatus to disseminate tidbits of "information" not only about an actor's current professional activities but about his or her supposedly real-life activities as well. Whereas publicity at the beginning of the decade might have focused on the role an actor was playing and suggest some ways in which the actor's biography made him or her particularly well suited to the role, publicity features in the mid-Teens and beyond included items about the star's ostensible private life, romances, taste in home decor, favorite fashion and beauty tips, vacation activities, and so on.[8]

Serials were ideally suited to the star system because their extended release period, spanning months instead of days, allowed so many more opportunities for the concoction of publicity features in fan magazines and other promotional venues. It is no coincidence that in a 1916 star popularity poll in *Motion Picture Magazine*, three of the top five highest female vote-getters worked solely in serials, and a fourth occasionally worked in that format.[9] Moreover, the fact that in serials the same actress appeared in the same role week after week greatly facilitated the process of fixing in place the star's persona and promulgating the myth that the actress and her role were essentially one and the same. One very common strategy toward that end was to use the star's name for that of the protagonist. Mary Fuller played Mary Dangerfield in *What Happened to Mary* (Edison, 1912–13); Kathlyn Williams played Kathlyn Hare in *The Adventures of Kathlyn* (Selig, 1914); Florence La Badie played Florence Gray in *The Million Dollar Mystery* (Thanhouser, 1914); Marguerite Courtot played the eponymous heroine in *The Ventures of Marguerite* (Kalem, 1915); Ruth Roland played Ruth Reading in *The Timber Queen* (Pathé, 1922), and Ruth Ranger in both *The Haunted Valley* (Pathé, 1923) and *Ruth of the Range* (Pathé, 1923), as well as other heroines named Ruth in *The Adventures of Ruth* (Pathé, 1920) and *Ruth of the Rockies* (Pathé, 1920); Pearl White played Pearl Dare in *Pearl of the Army* (Pathé, 1916), Pearl Standish in *The Fatal Ring* (Pathé, 1917), and Pearl Travers in *Plunder* (Pathé, 1923); Beverly Bayne played Beverly Clarke in *The Great Secret* (Metro, 1917); Helen Holmes played the heroine Helen in *The Hazards of Helen* (Kalem, 1913–17) and *The Lost Express* (Mutual, 1917), and indeed, in *A Lass of the Lumberlands* (Mutual, 1916–17) and *The Girl and the Game* (Mutual, 1916), Helen Holmes's character was actually named "Helen Holmes." After Holmes left Kalem, the studio substituted an actress named Ellen Gibson, but only after first changing her name to Helen Gibson.

* * *

Perhaps the most important mode of publicity for serials, at least until around 1917, came through prose-version tie-ins published simultaneously in newspapers and national magazines that invited consumers to

"Read It Here in the Morning; See It on the Screen Tonight!" While reaffirming the film serial's origins in cheap fiction, tie-ins saturated the entertainment marketplace to a much greater degree than dime novels and feuilletons ever could have hoped to. Since they were syndicated, the prose tie-ins appeared in hundreds (the studios claimed thousands) of newspapers across the country, as well as in mass-circulation popular magazines, reaching a potential readership well into the tens of millions. Tie-ins appeared in virtually every major newspaper across the country. This system exploded the scope of film publicity, which just a few years before had been limited to lobby cards, screen slides, and occasionally small newspaper notices, and contributed to the cinema's development into a mass medium as we understand it today. Tie-ins were one of the first examples of the mega-publicity marketing paradigm that would soon characterize the Hollywood system.

Most of us have a general sense of the degree to which film and television has superseded reading as a means of entertainment, but few recognize how enormously important cheap short fiction was as a popular amusement in the decades around the turn of the century. It is difficult for us to imagine the utter saturation of short stories in this period. As I noted in chapter 7, while today only a few general periodicals publish fiction, in 1915 almost sixty major national magazines, "story papers," and Sunday supplements published short stories and serialized novels. Their combined monthly circulation came to about eighty million, almost equivalent to the country's total population. Many metropolitan newspapers also published short stories as a regular daily feature—an attraction that brought millions more in circulation. Short fiction was a deeply ingrained part of everyday life at a time when the cinema was trying to expand its hold on the popular market. It is not surprising, therefore, that both film manufacturers and cheap fiction publishers saw the commercial logic of forming cross-media alliances to help them compete with their immediate same-medium competitors. With tie-ins, film manufacturers gained national publicity, and newspapers and magazines gained "copy" material and circulation boosters.

Tie-ins clearly served to maximize publicity for film serials (and, as we will see, for other short films as well). The rest of this chapter considers another possible function. Perhaps tie-ins tell us something about the difficulties directors encountered during the "transitional period" of the early Teens. Cinema's shift from "primitive" to classical narrative modes was by no means an instantaneous and unproblematic metamorphosis. As any one who has viewed a fair sampling of films made between roughly 1908 and 1916 will attest, films from this period often leave one somewhat confused about exactly what has happened in the story and why. There is no reason to think that the original spectators had significantly greater powers of narrative comprehension.[10]

The question is whether early spectators read tie-ins as a way of compensating for a film-narrative language that was still having trouble making itself fully understood. Did spectators use tie-ins to make sense of film narratives they found baffling? Did filmgoers—and filmmak-ers—rely on tie-ins as a means to ease the proto-classical cinema's semi-otic growing pains? This question is an elusive one, particularly since we have no way of knowing how many spectators actually read tie-ins before going to the movies and how these readers used the prose ver-sions. A look at the scope of the tie-in system, and an analysis of a par-ticularly difficult tie-in duo (film and short-story versions of an episode of the 1914–15 serial *Zudora*) may shed some light on the issue.

J. Stuart Blackton, Vitagraph's cofounder and president, was, as far as I have been able to determine, the first to implement the fiction tie-in idea. In February 1911 he launched *The Motion Picture Story Magazine*, which has the distinction of being America's first movie fan magazine (fig. 9.3). Published monthly out of Brooklyn, each issue con-tained as many as twenty (but usually around fifteen) "photoplay sto-ries," running about ten pages apiece including numerous movie-still illustrations (fig. 9.4). For the first six months, the magazine did not identify the studios that produced the films being "storyized," no doubt because Blackton was reluctant to promote Vitagraph's competitors. It ultimately became clear that the magazine only published stories based on "licensed" films (i.e., those released by the General Film Co., the dis-tribution arm of the Motion Picture Patents Company). *The Motion Picture Story Magazine* was a commercial success and by 1913 reached a circulation of 215,000, a figure that *Photoplay* (which today we tend to think of as the preeminent fan magazine in this period) did not top until 1920.[11] It changed its name to *Motion Picture Magazine* in 1915, reflect-ing a transformation into a more general fan magazine with greater focus on star personalities, Hollywood gossip, and special-interest fea-tures.[12] Gradually, it scaled down its use of tie-in fiction, running three or four photoplay stories per issue in 1918, and one or two per issue into the 1920s.

Fig. 9.3 Front cover for April issue of *The Motion Picture Story Magazine*.

The IRON STRAIN

by NORMAN BRUCE

·K·B· TRIANGLE

This story was written from the Photoplay of C. GARDNER SULLIVAN

"YOU TALK," observed Adele Van Ness with cold fury, "like a stock farmer instead of the head of a great house." Her delicate nostrils contracted fastidiously, and a network of nerve-etched wrinkles that careful massage could not wholly eradicate sprang web-like across her skin.

Her father laughed grimly. "It is as the head of a family that I would keep great that I speak, daughter," he said; "the Whitney blood is thin-

ning out, and we need a newer, sturdier fluid in our veins. Octavia is the last of my race. God help her children if she marries one of those brainless, spineless misfits that I saw at your ball tonight."

"Octavia," said Octavia's mother coldly, "is not an animal. She is, I am happy to say, quite sensible of her duty in marrying a refined, educated gentleman of her own station in life. I am afraid, father, that your Alaska experiences have hardly fitted

39

Fig. 9.4 Fiction tie-in for *The Iron Strain* (*The Motion Picture Story Magazine*, December 1913)

Following the lead of *Motion Picture Magazine*, most movie fan magazines in the early and mid-Teens featured tie-in fiction, among them *Movie Pictorial* (1913–1916) and *Motion Picture Classic* (1915 onward).[13] *Photoplay*, published monthly out of Chicago beginning in 1911, originally was also designed as an all tie-in magazine, featuring about a dozen stories per issue. All of *Photoplay*'s stories were based on two- and three-reelers made by independent (non-MPPC) studios. Like *Motion Picture Magazine*, as the Teens progressed it placed less and less emphasis on tie-in fiction. It featured about seven photoplay stories per issue in 1915, and only about two per issue in 1917.

Probably the most abundant source of photoplay story tie-ins was the weekly magazine *Moving Picture Stories* (not to be confused with *The Motion Picture Story Magazine*, which, to make matters worse, was sometimes issued as *Moving Picture Story Magazine*). Published out of New York by Frank Tousey (a prominent publisher of pulp fiction magazines), *Moving Picture Stories* (fig. 9.5), at least in its first few years, used stories exclusively from Mutual's stable of independent producers. Running six photoplay stories a week, the magazine printed almost five thousand fiction tie-ins from its first issue of January 3, 1913, to 1929, when it ceased publication.[14]

These fan magazines reached a niche market of diehard movie buffs, but it was in syndicated newspaper features and mass-market magazines that tie-ins reached a mass public. The *Chicago Sun Tribune* led the way: beginning on January 7, 1912, its Sunday edition devoted a full page to "film-stories" based on movies made by the main Chicago studios (Selig Polyscope, Essanay, and American). These tie-ins are distinctive in their emphasis on film-still illustrations. As many as sixteen stills might accompany a relatively brief text, thus achieving a kind of photo-novella effect (fig. 9.6). For reasons that are not clear, the newspaper discontinued the series after ten weeks, although the *Tribune* would later return to fiction tie-ins with the rise of the serial film.[15]

Another Chicago paper, the *Record-Herald* (later just called the *Herald*), ran an extensive tie-in series throughout 1914, drawn exclusively from two- and three-reelers released by Universal. The *Record-Herald*'s "picture stories" appeared daily, except Sunday, and covered about one-third of a full newspaper page, including two or three stills. A sidebar listed local theaters where the movie would be screened that day. The newspaper syndicated its stories to other papers around the country.

MOVING PICTURE STORIES

PRICE 5 CENTS

A WEEKLY MAGAZINE

DEVOTED TO PHOTO-PLAYS AND PLAYERS

HARRY BID IRENE FAREWELL.   "The Coward's Atonement."

Fig. 9.5 Front cover for *Moving Picture Stories* (March 14, 1913).

Fig. 9.6 Tie-in for Essanay's *Love Versus Genius*, 1912 (*Chicago Sun Tribune*, February 25, 1912)

A few mass-market magazines published tie-ins based on discrete short films.[16] However, it was the emergence of the film serial in 1912 that began the tie-in's phase of truly massive exposure. For *What Happened to Mary* (1912–13), Edison teamed up with the *Ladies' World* (the country's fourth largest monthly, with a circulation of 1.1 million) and released the film installments monthly to correspond with the magazine's schedule. Both concerns reportedly benefited greatly from the arrangement: Edison got massive well-targeted publicity, making the serial a major hit, and the magazine significantly boosted its circulation.

Motivated in part by the success of *Mary*, Selig and the *Chicago Tribune* collaborated on a tie-in for *The Adventures of Kathlyn*, which ran for six months beginning around January 1, 1914. When Pathé and the Hearst organization followed suit in April with *The Perils of Pauline* and, at the same time, the *Chicago Herald* incorporated a tie-in for *Lucille Love, Girl of Mystery* into its already-running series of Universal tie-ins, the trend was set (figs. 9.7, 9.8). Virtually every American serial before 1917 was packaged with a tie-in that ran its duration, generally twelve to fifteen weeks.

Any given serial tie-in would appear in about fifty to one hundred

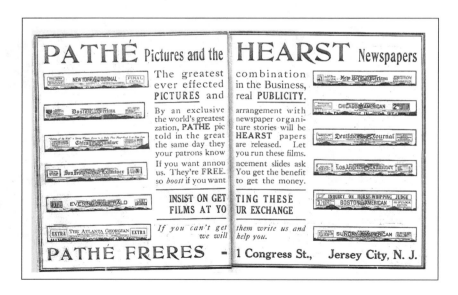

Fig. 9.7 Advertisement for Pathé-Hearst collaboration. (*Moving Picture World*, February 28, 1914)

Fig. 9.8 Fiction tie-in for *The Perils of Pauline*, 1914. (Hearst syndicate, November 22, 1914)

newspapers across the country (although some film trade journal ads were audacious enough to claim as many as five thousand newspapers—well above the total number of newspapers in the entire country). For a few years, serial tie-ins were everywhere. In 1915 six of the seven major New York newspapers were featuring tie-ins in their daily or Sunday editions, or both, and all four of Boston's major papers carried them.[17] According to Pathé, twenty million people a week read the *Perils of Pauline* tie-in. Considering the size of the Hearst network, as well as the array of smaller newspapers that picked up the syndicated tie-in, that figure might not have been too gross an exaggeration (at least, of the number of potential readers). In the theaters, lobby posters, slides, and titles at the beginning and end of each episode all encouraged spectators to read the tie-in in their local paper.

For all its tremendous exposure, the heyday of the serial tie-in was quite brief. They had all but disappeared by 1918. Originally, newspapers had been eager to get tie-ins. The *Chicago Tribune* actually paid Selig $12,000 (about $200,000 today) in 1913 for the rights to publish the tie-in for *The Adventures of Kathlyn*, primarily because it hoped to stimulate advertising from Selig and local exhibitors. Within a few months, however, film producers were all too happy to provide the story texts to newspapers at no cost in hope of free publicity. Newspapers recognized that they had the upper hand: in some cases they received 25 percent of the net profits from local theaters screening the serial, and they began requiring that producers and distributors do a certain amount of display advertising. Their charge for that advertising quickly increased to the point that the film concerns were almost paying ad-space rates for the tie-in columns. With little to gain from this arrangement, most producers discontinued tie-ins in favor of conventional advertisements.[18]

There was also some feeling among producers and exhibitors that tie-ins simply did not succeed in increasing viewer interest, and that they may in fact hurt ticket sales since they gave away the story in advance. A September 1917 article in *Motion Picture News* summed up the situation:

At the start of the serial game, Universal provided for the publication of the stories of the various chapters of the serial in leading newspapers throughout the country, but this plan has been abandoned and Universal now takes the stand that this publication does not help the serial over. The same attitude is taken by Mutual, which now makes no effort to secure the publication of the chaptered story. Vitagraph supplies the [story] of the episodes to the exhibitor and leaves it to him to secure their publication if he desires. . . . . Some theater managers claim that it weakens the pulling power of the story to have it published in advance of the showing, and at least one of the producers declares that he has had greater success with serials that have not been fictionized.[19]

Moreover, with the shortage and price inflation of white paper during

World War I, newspapers cut back their consumption of newsprint and it became harder for studios, producers, or exhibitors to convince newspapers to run tie-ins.

In some cases, Mutual published its own mock tabloid newspapers for exhibitors to hand out in the theater. Louis Feuillade's *Les Vampires* (Gaumont, 1915; American release, 1917) was read in this form (fig. 9.9). Because of its close alliance with the Hearst organization, Pathé was able to get its tie-ins published until mid-1918. Thereafter, until 1923, Hearst papers ran tie-ins based on discrete feature films released by Paramount and the International Film Service (Hearst's own company, specializing in Marion Davies vehicles). The switch no doubt arose from Hearst's priorities, but Pathé also may have stopped supplying tie-in text for serials, deeming the expense of writing it no longer worthwhile.

* * *

Another factor may have played a role in the decline of tie-ins in both newspapers and fan magazines in the late Teens. Perhaps tie-ins simply were not needed anymore. As the classical Hollywood style developed, and filmmakers gained a better command of its codes of filmic narration (and a better understanding of its limitations), perhaps tie-ins were no longer important as narrative guides. As movies became more intelligible, and longer, filmmakers and spectators had less need of ancillary texts to elucidate subtleties of plot, motivation, and psychology. But in the period during which filmmakers were still struggling to internalize the conventions of classical narration and were still constrained by the brevity of two reels, filmmakers and spectators alike might have relied on tie-ins to compensate for the limitations of cinematic storytelling. Interviewed in a promotional article for *The Perils of Pauline*, Pathé vice president L. P. Bonvillain makes this point overtly:

We can now, through the medium of all these newspapers, which cover so large a portion of the more thickly settled sections of the country, tell the story of the picture in a satisfactorily complete form. We can do fully what the sub-titles try to do: we can make intelligible all the happenings of the play; we can analyze character, explain motives—we can, if you will, amplify the action and set forth those things which cannot be shown on the screen.[20]

One must not forget that this is press agent talk, but nevertheless it may express at least one aspect of the studio's view of the tie-in's function.

Fiction tie-ins were well suited to be used by spectators as a tool to

Fig. 9.9 Trade journal advertisement for Mutual's in-house tie-in for *Les Vampires*, 1915 (American release, 1917). (*Motion Picture News*, March 3, 1917)

assure narrative comprehension, since they followed the movies very closely. The usual method for writing tie-ins was designed to minimize discrepancies between short story and movie: a writer would "storyize" a movie by viewing the finished film on the screen and working from the film scenario.[21] From our historical distance, it is difficult to know how tie-ins were actually used by spectators. Some people may have used tie-ins to enhance narrative comprehension, while others may have read them for other reasons (e.g., for the cognitive pleasure of drawing links between the two versions or simply as just a short story like any other) and, certainly, many people saw movies without ever encountering their tie-ins. As Shelley Stamp has shown in a marvelous example of empirical hypothesis-testing, no single pattern of coordination between tie-ins and film-viewings could have prevailed, since in the multiple-run exhibition system smaller outlying theaters might show a serial episode several weeks, even months, after its first run and accompanying tie-in publication. Moreover, some subsequent-run theaters occasionally chose to bundle episodes together, showing a number back-to-back on the same bill.[22]

Nevertheless, when one looks at particular examples of films with tie-ins, it seems almost inconceivable that spectators could have made any sense of the film without an elucidating intertext, and perhaps filmmakers assumed their audience would have the benefit of such a supplementary guide. One such example is the two-reel film "The Mystery of the Dutch Cheese Maker," the third episode of Thanhouser's 1914–15 serial *Zudora*. The film is absolutely baffling without its tie-in (fig. 9.10). The following extended comparison suggests that the film did not stand on its own and was indeed dependent on the print version to convey the story.

To begin with, "The Mystery of the Dutch Cheese Maker" provides no introduction to the story situation or main characters. Without seeing the serial's first episode, where presumably this basic information was established, the viewer is at a loss to understand the dynamic between Zudora, the heroine, and Hassam Ali, a sinister-looking older man with whom she lives.

The newspaper tie-in, on the other hand (summarized in brackets below for comparison with the film), sets up the story with this synopsis:

Zudora is left an orphan at an early age. Her father is killed in a gold mine he has discovered. Half an hour after learning of the death of her

Fig. 9.10 Fiction tie-in for *Zudora*, 1914–15. (*Chicago Sun Tribune* syndicate, December 15, 1915)

husband, Zudora's mother—a tight rope walker with a circus—is seized with vertigo, falls, and is killed. Zudora and the fortune from the mine, which grows to be worth $20,000,000, are left in the guardianship of Frank Keene, a circus man, Zudora's mother's brother. Zudora, giving promise of great beauty, reaches the age of eighteen. The uncle, who has set himself up as a Hindu mystic and is known as Hassam Ali, decides in his greed that Zudora must die before she can have a chance to come into possession of her money, so that it may be left to him, the next of kin, and he prevails upon the girl to leave her money in his hands three years longer and say nothing to any one about the fortune. Hassam Ali sees an obstacle to his scheme in the person of John Storm, a young lawyer, for whom Zudora has taken a fancy, and he commands the girl to put the man out of her mind. Storm comes to ask Hassam Ali for the hand of his niece. At first the crystal gazer will not listen to the proposal, but Zudora insists that if she cannot marry Storm, she will marry no one. "Well, well," says Hassam Ali, "if you take such a stand, I'll compromise. Solve my next twenty cases and you can marry him; fail in a single case and you must renounce him."[23]

At the beginning of "The Mystery of the Dutch Cheese Maker," we see a bizarre-looking old man (clearly coded to suggest a Jew) working excitedly over a makeshift scientific instrument in a dingy basement workshop. An intertitle identifies him as "The Diamond Manufacturer." He places a large diamond on a cupboard shelf along with six or seven others and then sits on his bed.

[The tie-in clues us in to what the diamond manufacturer is thinking about on the bed: he is excited that he has discovered a way to make synthetic diamonds and that he will become a phenomenally rich man, but he is worried that if he tries to sell his gems, he will be arrested as a thief or smuggler since the diamonds are not registered. At the same time, he fears that if he tells the truth about his invention, it might become public property and he would be ruined. (Presumably, either he is ignorant of patent law or he anticipates that synthetic diamonds would have no value if everyone knew how easy it was to make them.) He decides he needs a partner to unload the gems, and resolves to ask Ali.]

An intertitle then reads, "Hassam Ali disguises himself to watch Zudora," and we see Zudora leave her mansion and Ali enter a secret room where he proceeds to apply makeup, a false beard, and different clothes. [The tie-in elaborates on Ali's greed and evil scheming, giving the character psychological depth.]

Zudora meets her lover John Storm. [In the story, Storm asks Zudora probing questions about Ali. He cannot understand why she is so devoted to him, and is on the verge of articulating his suspicion that Ali may be trying to rub him out.] Ali shows up and spies on them from a distance. We have no way of knowing why he is trailing the couple. [The tie-in explains that Ali wants to know if the young lovers plan to get married clandestinely, so that he can kill them both right away.]

We see a man enter a cheese shop. Ali walks past and looks into the shop window. (The man, it turns out, is Storm, and Ali is trailing him. This is confusing, since no passage of time is indicated in the transition from the previous shot). Storm chats cordially with the cheese maker and his family. We then see the diamond maker lock up his rooms and depart. He evidently lives in quarters below the cheese shop. As he walks past, Ali taps him on the shoulder, makes a pointing gesture and says something, while the diamond maker strokes his beard, wrings his hands, and nods. This strikes one as a curious interchange since the two appear to be strangers. Ali gives the diamond maker his business card. [In the story version, Ali and the diamond maker already know each other.] An intertitle reads, "Bengal, the Diamond Maker, seeks a confederate to help dispose of his diamonds." After some inscrutable wild gesturing by Bengal, the two enter the building and go down to the basement workshop. Bengal shows Ali the furnace and gives a demonstration of his diamond-making system. There is more indecipherable head-shaking and gesturing by Ali, and intense querying and hand-wringing by Bengal. Ali nods, places the newly made diamond in a handkerchief, and leaves. Bengal remains, clutching his hands with a thrilled look on his face.

Ali goes to a diamond expert, who certifies the diamond's purity. Back in the workshop again, Bengal and Ali discover that two of the diamonds that had been locked in the cupboard are missing. Bengal becomes hysterical and falls to his knees in front of Ali, groping wildly at his coat. Ali takes Bengal by the neck, shakes him violently, and strangles him until he is limp. But he is not dead, and Ali soon lets Bengal get back up on his feet. The two walk out of the room, as if nothing has happened. This scene is perplexing. [In the tie-in, Bengal, in his agitation, screams that the cheese maker upstairs must be robbing him through some hole in the wall. Ali shakes him to shut him up, saying,

"If he is guilty and hears you, good-bye to your gems!"]

Soon an unknown man arrives, sets a bear trap in the workshop, and then leaves an unrecognizable wired instrument under a pillow. [The tie-in informs us that Ali and Bengal have decided to catch the culprit by installing a "dictagraph."]

An intertitle reads "That night." Storm walks into the cheese shop. Ali follows, in disguise, and watches Storm from the hallway. Ali yells, "Fire! Fire! Fire!" Everyone from the cheese shop and sundry panicking tenants dash into the hallway. Storm gesticulates and says something to the crowd, which soon calms down and disperses. In the mayhem, Storm drops the package of cheese he has just bought. Ali picks it up after Storm leaves. Bengal suddenly comes up, bug-eyed and frantic, groping desperately at Ali's lapel.

This scene is totally incomprehensible: Why does Ali yell "Fire!"? What does Storm say to the crowd? What does Ali want with Storm's package of cheese? Why is Bengal so agitated? [The tie-in explains that Ali causes the commotion in order to clear the cheese shop so that he can search it for clues that its owner is the diamond thief. He didn't expect Storm to be there, but when he sees Storm drop the package, he picks it up on the principle that anything belonging to Storm might eventually prove useful. Earlier in the story, he had thought about possibly poisoning Storm. Bengal's agitation apparently is supposed simply to convey that he is in poor health. In the story version, he pants, "It is making me ill. My heart is bad."]

In the basement workshop, Bengal and Ali discover that more diamonds are missing. After more frantic pawing at his lapels by Bengal, Ali suddenly decides (for no apparent reason) to look inside Storm's package. He is amazed to find the missing diamonds embedded in the cheese. Meanwhile, Storm realizes he has lost his cheese and returns to the shop to buy some more. When Ali and Bengal spot Storm in the cheese shop, Bengal runs out and hails two policemen. He then gestures frantically, and everyone calmly walks out of the shop. Although it is unclear at first, Storm, the cheese maker, and some of his family have all been arrested. They are taken to the police station. Storm telephones Zudora.

Zudora sneaks out of her house. Ali (who has somehow managed to get back home and out of his disguise) sees her leave and follows. Zudora goes to the diamond maker's workshop. Bengal, who for some reason has been standing under the stairs in wait, attacks her from behind. But Ali appears from another room and Bengal lets her free (although, according to the story's logic, Ali should want Zudora to come to harm). She flees without seeing Ali. [This scene is not in the tie-in].

In the next scene, Zudora again sneaks out of her house past Ali and returns to the diamond maker's den. It is unclear why she would go right back after what she has just been through. This time, inexplicably, Bengal sits calmly on his bed as Zudora snoops around the workshop. He even unhitches the bear trap so that she can enter the adjacent furnace room. Suddenly, however, he runs amuck and cries, "You have discovered my secret!" He lunges at her and they struggle near the furnace. An anticipatory intertitles reads, "Bengal strives to kill Zudora. She is saved by his accidental fall." Bengal's "fall" is confusing since it looks very much more like a suicide: he seems to leap right into the open furnace like a trained dog going through a hoop. Zudora runs out of the room in distress. Hassam happens to be right there and comforts her. [The tie-in handles this scene more simply and logically. Bengal attacks Zudora as soon as she appears and dies of a heart attack, which was already foreshadowed in the story. Ali is not there.]

The next day, Zudora, Ali, and an inspector return to the workshop. Zudora discovers still more diamonds missing from the cupboard. Hearing a faint sound, she opens the cupboard once more and finds a rat with a diamond stuck on its nose. She has found the culprit! They go up to the cheese shop to show the owner's wife. An intertitle reads, "How the mice got the gluey cheese on their noses." The film ends with what is surely one of the weirdest and most surreal moments in early cinema. The inspector takes a huge mixing bowl filled with cottage cheese off the shelf. Zudora places the rat in the bowl, and it tramps around in the cottage cheese while everyone (including the cheese maker and his wife, who evidently don't mind having rat hair in their merchandise) pets the squirmy rodent and laughs heartily.

Daniel Carson Goodman, the director of "The Mystery of the Dutch Cheese Maker," was clearly no Griffith, and Thanhouser was no Biograph. It is probably fair to say that even for its day the movie displays a below-average grasp of the rudiments of filmic narration, which might help explain why *Zudora* was a box-office flop.[24] But very few directors told stories as clearly as Griffith, and it is misleading to regard him as a yardstick for the standardization of film language. The codes of classical narration developed unevenly. Many filmmakers, and many spectators, struggled with narrative unintelligibility throughout the Teens.

The example of "The Mystery of the Dutch Cheese Maker" suggests that fiction tie-ins may have constituted more than simply an innovative mode of publicity. Perhaps both filmmakers and spectators relied on them as a key to narrative comprehension. Recent scholars have emphasized that, unlike primitive cinema's heavy dependence on spectatorial foreknowledge (viewers were already familiar with the skits and tales early films drew upon), films after around 1908 became more autonomous, more adept at telling complete, comprehensible stories on their own, solely through images and limited intertitles. Fiction tie-ins prompt one to reassess that generalization.

Conclusion

———

In 1920, Siegfried Kracauer wrote an essay attempting to describe the methodology guiding the works of Georg Simmel. "The core principle of Simmel's thought," he suggested, "might be formulated something like this":

All expressions of spiritual/intellectual life are interrelated in countless ways. No single one can be extricated from this web of relations, since each is enmeshed in the web with all such other expressions. . . . There is no individual being or individual event that can be extracted from the totality . . . such that it can then be explained by itself and observed in itself. . . . One of Simmel's fundamental aims is to rid every spiritual/intellectual phenomenon of its false being-unto-itself and show how it is embedded in the larger contexts of life. In this way, his manner of thinking functions both to connect and to dissolve: the former in that he reveals connections everywhere between seemingly separate things, the latter insofar as he makes us aware of the complexity of many supposedly simple objects and problems. . . . Simmel ties together what is separated, collects into large bundles what is scattered, and draws aside the veil that . . . usually obscures the linkages of things. . . . He recognizes that a boundless plenitude of qualities inhabits each phenomenon, and that each is subject to widely different laws. But the more he becomes aware of the many-sidedness of things, the more it becomes possible for him to relate them to each other. Among the many determinations of some phenomenon that are unveiled to him, one of these can also be attributed to another phenomenon: everywhere he looks, relations between phenomena impose themselves upon him. . . . What is always at stake . . . is the liberation of the thing from its isolation. He turns it this way and that way, until we recognize in it the fulfillment of a lawfulness that is simultaneously embodied in many other places, and we can thereby weave it into an extensive net of relations.[1]

One cannot help but be struck by how contemporary this sounds. With its talk of intricate webs and nets of relations, of the polyvalence of things, of the fallacy of perceiving anything as a "being-unto-itself," Kracauer's take on Simmel seems presciently poststructuralist. At the same time, however, one might be justified in saying that the basic idea borders on the banal. There is nothing particularly revelatory in the commonplace that, ultimately, everything is (or can be) related to everything else—a sort of expansion on the six-degrees-of-separation notion to include all "spiritual/intellectual" (or what we will just call cultural) phenomena.

What *does* appear to be exceptional is the degree of emphasis Simmel and Kracauer place on a methodologically self-conscious process of recognizing interrelationships among very disparate phenomena or clusters of phenomena. This focus on mapping configurations of interrelated items, properties, ideas could be called a "contextualist" approach, and a number of metaphorical terms ("constellational," "molecular," etc.) might also be apt. It is an approach with built-in pitfalls stemming from the fact that, with some ingenuity in turning things "this way and that way," one can manage to find at least some resemblance between just about any phenomena. But it is also an approach that can yield a much fuller understanding of the structural organization and historical embeddedness of whatever phenomenon is being explored.

The main phenomenon studied in this book is a cultural object called melodrama, which, analyzed as a genre, is itself a complex cluster of elements. Many generic breakdowns are possible, but I have proposed one highlighting five key elements—strong pathos, heightened emotionality, nonclassical narrative mechanics, moral polarization, and spectacular sensationalism—which combine in varying configurations to form different kinds of melodrama. While there are no doubt exceptions, in general what is thought of as Hollywood melodrama—family melodrama and women's films—accentuates the first two and eschews the last two. The other major configuration of melodrama—blood-and-thunder or sensational melodrama—potentially combines all five elements, but absolutely requires moral polarization and sensational effects.

The phenomenon of melodrama can also be broken down with respect to different media or cultural forms in which it materializes. My study has tried to shed light on crucial interrelationships and interactions between 10–20–30 stage melodrama and early film melodrama, concerning, for example, their common status as lowbrow pariahs, their shared reservoir of narrative motifs (most notably the portrayal of female heroics and victimization), and their mutual stress on violent action and spectacular diegetic realism. I have concentrated on serial films of the Teens in part because of a desire to fill in a largely unwritten passage in our historical narrative of American cinema.

That passage is worth writing because the film serial was arguably the most direct descendant of a major tradition of popular-priced melodramatic theater. Studying serials is rewarding for precisely the reason expressed by Eisenstein in my epigraph quotation from "Dickens, Griffith, and Film Today":

It is always pleasing to recognize again and again the fact that our cinema is not altogether without parents and without pedigree, without a past, without the traditions and rich cultural heritage of the past epochs. It is only very thoughtless and presumptuous people who can erect laws and an esthetic for cinema, proceeding from premises of some incredible virginbirth of this art![2]

Studying melodrama's transition from stage to screen is particularly interesting since, to belabor Eisenstein's metaphor, it was a flagrant case of matricide. Film melodrama killed off stage melodrama with stunning rapidity during the nickelodeon boom. In trying to understand why the demise of the 10–20–30 was so quick and complete, the challenge is to assess the relative importance of economic versus aesthetic factors (and perhaps others that I have overlooked). Aesthetic factors are stressed in Nicholas Vardac's argument that stage melodrama went bust because movies simply beat it at its own game by providing much more impressive and convincing spectacular illusions of reality. My research into period sources has shown that many people who observed the transition firsthand also espoused that explanation. Period comments lend support to Vardac's argument, but I have also argued that the aesthetic explanation requires qualification. Contrary to Vardac's characterization, theatrical melodrama was not just a botched proto-cinema, trying, but failing miserably, to do on stage what could really only be done on screen (that is, show explosions, floods, tornadoes, locomotive crashes, races-to-the-rescue, etc.). Many reports from the period indicate that 10–20–30 audiences often found such effects extremely thrilling on stage. More important, the 10–20–30's frank theatricality and spectatorial boisterousness suggests that sensational melodrama's main operative aesthetic may not have been a variety of realist illusionism at all, but rather a form of gleeful, interactive anti-illusionism. Sensational melodrama offered pleasures that ran counter to diegetic absorption. It may be an oversimplification, therefore, to argue that cinema's more convincing realism brought about the extinction of 10–20–30 melodrama. This qualification moves economic explanations toward center stage.

This book has also tried to highlight a number of relationships between melodrama and another broad and complex cluster of phenomena grouped under the term *modernity*. While, again, any number of conceptual breakdowns is possible, I have proposed a model based on six aspects shaping modernity—the socioeconomic developments labeled modernization; the centrality of instrumental rationality; the condition of cultural discontinuity; the dynamism of social mobility and circulation; the hegemony of competitive individualism; and the intensification of sensory stimuli.

This last facet of modernity lies at the heart of a debate over the plausibility of a causal connection between the environment of urban modernity and the emergence of sensational amusements—amusements like blood-and-thunder melodrama on stage and screen, and like cinema in general viewed as a medium of powerful fleeting impressions, kinetic rapidity, constant juxtaposition, and visceral stimulation. I have documented a turn-of-the-century discourse in the illustrated press and elsewhere on the phenomenology of the new metropolis as "a series of shocks and collisions." This discourse cannot be taken at face value as an impartial, unembellished record of metropolitan experience—it certainly involved some degree of rhetorical posturing and commercially motivated bombast—but it did not come out of nowhere; it was not fabricated out of thin air. However mediated or refracted it may have been, the discourse pointed to a recognized dimension of subjective experience in the modern metropolis. There is no question, further, that popular amusements in the 1890s underwent an extraordinary turn toward sensationalism, with the intensification of exciting spectacle in existing amusements like stage melodrama and vaudeville, and the introduction of new pastimes—like amusement-park rides, daredevil displays, and cinema—with an inherent tendency toward powerful sensory stimulation.

The crucial question is whether the similarities between urban sensation and popular sensationalism were more than simply superficial and coincidental. The modernity thesis rests on the notion that the metropolis brought about changes in the prevailing "mode of perception," which then somehow prompted corresponding changes in the formal qualities of cinema and other popular amusements. Although it may be taken for granted that cultural expressions cannot help but reflect the social context in which they were produced, there is nothing at all given about the notion that something as fundamental as human perception can change as a result of short-term social-environmental situations, or that such perceptual changes, assuming they could occur, would then have a tangible impact on film style. The modernity thesis is indeed a speculative argument, but I have tried to show that it is not a hopelessly implausible one. There are a number of viable ways to understand the idea of short-term perceptual change, based on neurological, experiential, cognitive, and physiological perspectives. It is not unreasonable to infer that there may be at least some degree of causal connection behind apparent correlations between the perceptual qualities of urban experience and formal-stylistic elements of early cinema (even an early cinema undergoing significant aesthetic changes). Questions remain about the precise mechanisms involved in the translation from social-environmental experience to cultural expression (I have presented several hypotheses sketched by the first generation of modernity theorists, but these need further scrutiny and other hypotheses may be called for), and more work needs to be done in order to understand how these mechanisms combined with other, perhaps more immediate, factors shaping cinema (economics, industry practices, reception, etc.). But comparisons between early cinema and the sensory environment of urban modernity are nevertheless compelling—at least compelling enough to merit further inquiry.

Concerning melodrama more specifically, a line of inquiry that has received considerable attention in recent scholarship, and one that is largely responsible for the genre's rehabilitation (or just habilitation) as a legitimate topic of investigation, proposes another sort of link to modernity, focusing not on sensory experience but on sociopsychological dimensions of the modern order. The emergence of melodrama mirrors the emergence of modern capitalism and the corresponding erosion of traditional social systems and worldviews governed by religious and feudal authority. The popularity of melodrama, while reflecting many causes, derived in part from its capacity to capture the sense of upheaval and vulnerability experienced by the masses in a world of unprecedented cultural discontinuity and social atomization. While melodrama expressed modern anxieties, it also served an ameliorative function, providing reassurance of ultimate divine protection and fortifying faith in simple, immutable moral verities. Melodrama was thus both dystopian, portraying worst-case scenarios of the victimization of innocents and competitive individualism run rampant, and utopian, offering a comforting affirmation of moral oversight and inevitable poetic justice.

Like most examples of symptomatic interpretation, this approach to melodrama is difficult to prove and wide open to criticism. It might be objected, for example, that stories of conflict between virtue and villainy with happy endings are hardly specific to nineteenth- and twentieth-century industrial societies; that symptomatic interpretation relies on selective reading that highlights conceptual matches and brushes contradictions under the rug; and that it ignores narratives from the same period that might have very different motifs leading to incompatible interpretations. Such objections are very important to bear in mind, but until researchers in the humanities are willing to concede that cultural artifacts are completely impervious to the social, historical, and ideological states-of-affair surrounding their creators and their receivers, or until conventional interpretive strategies are revised by much better understanding of the mechanisms and vagaries of social reflection, it is worthwhile observing apparent connections between narrative motifs, social contexts, and intended audiences. The correspondences between the motifs of melodrama, the transformations of modernity, and the situation of the masses under modern capitalism are important to recognize, and no doubt will continue to invite analysis.

So, too, judging from several important recent works in film studies, will the situation of women during the social and ideological transformations of modernity.[3] The image of a new kind of independent, energetic woman—the New Woman—fascinated turn-of-the-century America like few other novelties of modern life. It was a multilayered fascination, conveying the simple attraction of novelty but also wrapped up with emotions of celebration, wish-fulfillment, and apprehension. The depth of interest was a measure of the extent to which the New

Woman, both as a cultural symbol and as a real flesh-and-bones social entity, encapsulated several key facets of modernity. The New Woman represented a destabilization of the traditional ideology of gender, and in this respect constituted a particularly striking example of modernity's characteristic cultural discontinuity. As in most if not all such instances, this manifestation of cultural discontinuity was closely linked to concrete developments in socioeconomic and technological modernization. Women became active in public space as never before due to, among other things, the emergence of an urban consumer economy, an emphasis on women as primary purchasers, increased mobility via expanded transportation systems, employment of low-paid female factory and clerical workers, the introduction of labor-saving housekeeping devices, the trend toward smaller families, and the rise of mass entertainments catering to women, which both brought women into the public space of the theater and provided an iconology of popular feminism.

Popular melodrama had, from the start, focused on the vicissitudes of women out in the world. Pathetic melodrama often chronicled the suffering of women cast out in the world by forces of injustice, intolerance, and coercion. As modernity became increasingly dynamic near the turn of the century, the focus appears to have shifted to an emphasis on women venturing out into the world voluntarily, with a capacity for heroic agency, and sometimes a zeal for risky adventure. To some extent, the spectacle of female pluckiness operated as a kind of utopian wish-fulfillment, betraying the gap that remained between the feminist imagination and the actual circumstances of modern society. Nevertheless, the motif was also socially reflective of real changes in the experience of women in America. Women's increased freedom of circulation and mobility granted them new powers and pleasures. Serial-queen melodramas of the Teens, like earlier 10–20–30 melodramas, showcased and celebrated these changes. At the same time, however, they also conveyed new perils and apprehensions associated with it. As the motif of female pluckiness increased, so too did the spectacle of violent female victimization. Sensational melodrama was built around the oscillation between empowerment and imperilment. In this respect, it expressed the fact that in an increasingly heterosocial and ideologically unstable modern world, excitement and anxiety were intimately connected.

If unprecedented dynamism of mobility and circulation characterized the social environment of urban modernity, this affected the movements and intersections not just of people, but of all social things, including all sorts of textual objects. Intertextual linkages proliferated in modernity. This dimension was epitomized by the eclectic publicity strategies surrounding film serials, especially the system of close cross-media intertextuality involving prose-fiction tie-ins. Tie-ins illustrated the pervasive textual interconnectedness of the modern cultural milieu, and indicated the emergence of a new model of mass-publicity adopted by the film industry. This volume has posed the question of whether they also may have served a practical narrational purpose by helping viewers make sense of confusing films. Whether or not this was a deliberate rationale, comparing the narrative clarity of the newspaper prose versions with their cinematic counterparts reminds us that the dissemination of cinematic techniques of classical storytelling was a slow and uneven process that lasted at least into the late Teens.

In a work dealing with two such expansive topics as melodrama and modernity, many questions and connections invariably remain unaddressed. For example, would the models of melodrama and modernity I have presented be equally applicable for studying Hollywood family melodrama and the woman's film (and televisual variations), or melodramas from India and Egypt, or different genres altogether? What are the relationships between the contemporary action-adventure thriller and the kinds of sensational melodrama I have examined? How has the genre changed over the decades, and how directly do these changes reflect their different historical contexts? Is it necessary to shift the terms of an analysis of contemporary sensationalism from modernity to postmodernity? What would such a change entail? Whether or not future scholars choose to pursue such questions, my hope is that this study will prove useful both for its concrete historical information on 10–20–30 melodrama and a prominent vein of early cinema, and for its models of modernity and melodrama—models that might be adaptable to other lines of research exploring the dynamics of cinema and society.

Notes

———

Introduction

1. Christopher Strong, "Good-by, Melodrama," *Green Book* 8.3 (September 1912): 435–39.
2. Garff B. Wilson, *Three Hundred Years of American Drama and Theatre*, 104–105.
3. Linda Williams quotes some recent examples in *"Playing the Race Card."*
4. For an analysis of this aspect of criticism on Sirk and melodrama, see Barbara Klinger's excellent work, *Melodrama and Meaning: History, Culture, and the Films of Douglas Sirk.*
5. My study does not attempt to provide a review of this literature, since my focus lies elsewhere, and good overviews can be found in the introductions, essays, and bibliographies of two anthologies: Christine Gledhill, ed., *Home Is Where the Heart Is: Studies in Melodrama and the Woman's Film,* and Marcia Landy, ed., *Imitations of Life: A Reader in Film and Television Melodrama.* A helpful brief discussion of the trajectory of the melodrama in cinema studies is in Rick Altman, *Film/Genre,* 70–78 (although I think it mischaracterizes my own findings).
6. David A. Cook, *A History of Narrative Film* (1981). The 1996 second edition differs very little in its coverage of the Teens decade.
7. For a more detailed year-by-year enumeration of American film releases in this period, see my essay "Retracing the Transition: A Statistical Overview of the Emergence of Feature Films and Picture Palaces, 1908–1920," in Charles Keil and Shelley Stamp, eds., *Cinema's Transitional Era: Audiences, Institutions, Practices* (forthcoming).
8. The Edison Manufacturing Company's "Chart for Judging Motion Pictures" evaluated films in these eight genres according to Subject, Characterization, Conflict, Brevity, Coherency, Woman Interest, Comedy Relief, Suspense, Thrill, Climax Well Placed, Incidental Business. See Edison Archives, Edison National Historic Site, West Orange, N.J., Document File: "Motion Picture—General (3 of 3)."

9. Review of *Lucille Love: Girl of Mystery*, episode nine, in *New York Dramatic Mirror*, June 3, 1914, 35.

10. Russell Merritt, "Melodrama: Postmortem for a Phantom Genre," *Wide Angle* 5.3 (1983): 24–31; Gledhill, ed., *Home Is Where the Heart Is*, 354.

11. Williams, "*Playing the Race Card.*"

12. A typical turn-of-the-century tourist guidebook for Manhattan listed theaters with information on theater name, location, and "character of performance usually to be found on their boards." The last column categorized theaters as offering Drama, Melodrama, Musical Comedy, Vaudeville, or Burlesque. Several theaters were listed as presenting both musical comedy and drama, but melodrama theaters (along with burlesque and vaudeville houses) were devoted exclusively to their own specific genre. Harry J. Doyle, *The Tourist's Hand-Book of New York* (New York: Historical Press, 1906), 46.

13. Williams is in agreement on this. She writes, "I am sympathetic to the historical need to specify the actual emergence and development of a theatrical genre called melodrama, rather than the vaguer application . . . of the adjectival 'melodramatic.'" She points out, correctly, that defining melodrama as a genre is more problematic for cinema than for theater, owing to the relative narrowness with which film genres have been demarcated. Rather than being tied specifically to the woman's picture and family drama, melodrama should rightly subsume a number of film genres (e.g., the western, courtroom drama, detective story, action-adventure, etc.). Williams, "*Playing the Race Card.*".

14. Walter Benjamin, "The Work of Art in the Age of Mechanical Reproduction" (1936), in Hannah Arendt, ed., *Illuminations*, 250n19, 222.

15. David Bordwell, *On the History of Film Style*, 141–46.

16. "35 Melodramas in 35 Years." *Boston Sunday Globe*, n.d. (clipping, Harvard Theatre Collection, "Lincoln Carter" file).

17. Despite the label, admission to 10–20–30 plays generally cost between 20 and 50 cents around the turn of the century.

1. Meanings of Modernity

1. Jürgen Habermas notes that Hegel uses this tripartite historical division in his 1825–26 *Lectures on the History of Philosophy*. Habermas, *The Philosophical Discourse of Modernity*, 5. Another example is Georg Simmel, "The Metropolis and Mental Life," in *The Sociology of Georg Simmel*, 417.

2. Katherine Bregy, *From Dante to Jeanne d'Arc: Adventures in Medieval Life and Letters*, 137.

3. Habermas, *Philosophical Discourse*, 5.

4. Giddens, *The Consequences of Modernity*, 1.

5. Barrett, *Death of the Soul: From Descartes to the Computer*, xiv.

6. Kumar, *The Rise of Modern Society: Aspects of the Social and Political Development of the West*, 3.

7. Nordau, *Degeneration* (1895), 37.

8. Freeman, *Social Decay and Degeneration*, 141.

9. Kern, *The Culture of Time and Space, 1880–1918*, 1.

10. See, for example, the essays in Leo Charney and Vanessa R. Schwartz, eds., *Cinema and the Invention of Modern Life.*

11. Clement Greenberg, "Modernist Painting," in *The Collected Essays and Criticism* 4:86, ed. John O'Brien.

12. Stuart Hall et al., eds., *Modernity: an Introduction to Modern Societies.* Kracauer is not even given an index entry, although his name appears, with no discussion, on page 606.

13. Max Weber, *The Protestant Ethic and the Spirit of Capitalism*, 17.

14. Ronald Inglehard, *Modernization and Postmodernization: Cultural, Economic, and Political Change in 43 Societies* (Princeton: Princeton University Press, 1997); Anthony McGrew, "A Global Society?" in Hall et al., eds., *Modernity*, 466–503; Arjun Appadurai, *Modernity at Large: Cultural Dimensions of Globalization* (Minneapolis: University of Minnesota Press, 1996).

15. Franz M. Wuketits, *Evolutionary Epistemology and Its Implications for Humankind*, ch. 5.

16. The wording for this definition is derived from Alan Sica, *Weber, Irrationality, and Social Order*, 5.

17. L. Urwick, *The Meaning of Rationalisation*, 154.

18. Weber, *Economy and Society* 1:637.

19. Simmel, "The Metropolis and Mental Life," 422.

20. Among the many dozens of secondary works dealing with the rationalist theory of modernity are Melvin L. Adelman, "Modernization Theory and Its Critics." in Cayton, Gorn, and Williams, eds., *Encyclopedia of American Social History* 1:347–58; Rogers Brubaker, *The Limits of Rationality: An Essay on the Social and Moral Thought of Max Weber*; David Ingram, *Habermas and the Dialectic of Reason*; Henry Jacoby, *The Bureaucratization of the World*; Lawrence A. Scoff, *Fleeing the Iron Cage: Culture, Politics, and Modernity in the Thought of Max Weber*; Sica, *Weber, Irrationality, and Social Order*; and Alain Touraine, *Critique of Modernity*.

21. Alfred de Musset, quoted by Lews Coser, *Men of Ideas* (New York: Free Press, 1965), 101, and by Krishan Kumar, *Prophecy and Progress: the Sociology of Industrial and Post-Industrial Society*, 95.

22. Quoted in P. Abrams, "The Sense of the Past and the Origins of Sociology," *Past and Present* 55 (May 1972): 22; and in Kumar, *Prophecy and Progress*, 58.

23. Giddens, *The Consequences of Modernity*, 39.

24. Georg Lukács, *The Theory of the Novel* (1920) (rpt., Cambridge: MIT Press, 1971, 121.

25. Friedrich Nietzsche, *Untimely Meditations*, quoted in David Frisby, *Fragments of Modernity: Theories of Modernity in the Work of Simmel, Kracauer, and Benjamin*, 28.

26. Karl Marx and Friedrich Engels, *The Communist Manifesto*, 39.

27. Dozens of period articles comment on this phenomenon. Typical are Lazare Weiller, "The Annihilation of Distance," in *La Revue des Deux Mondes*, reprinted in *The Living Age* 219 (October 15, 1898): 163–78; and "The Shrinkage of the World," *The Spectator* 99 (October 19, 1907): 557–58. Contemporary analyses of transformations of time and space in modernity include Giddens, *The Consequences of Modernity*, esp. 17–28; and David Harvey, *The Condition of Postmodernity* (Oxford: Blackwell, 1990), 201–326.

28. Pitirim Sorokin, *Social Mobility*, 389.

29. Sorokin, *Social Mobility*, 392.

30. Nordau, *Degeneration*, 38.

31. Sorokin, *Social Mobility*, 390.

32. Nordau, *Degeneration*, 36.

33. Marx and Engels, *The Communist Manifesto*, 38.

34. Sorokin, *Social Mobility*, 394, 409.

35. Karl Marx, *Capital* 1:165.

36. Simmel, *The Philosophy of Money*, section excerpted as "Money and the Style of Modern Life" in a collection of Simmel's writings edited by Nicholas J. Spykman, *The Social Theory of George Simmel*, 243.

37. Simmel, "Money and Individual Liberty" (again, from *The Philosophy of Money*) in Spykman, ed., ibid., esp. 221–24.

38. Because capitalism tended to do away with direct contact between producer and end-user, it diminished awareness of the commodity as a product of human labor. Detached from the human context of its creation and defined solely in terms of its exchange value—in other words, in its relation to other commodities—the commodity seemed to take on an objective identity of its own. Marx, *Capital* 1 (ch. 1, sec. 4).

39. Adna Ferrin Weber, *The Growth of Cities in the Nineteenth Century: A Study in Statistics*, 431.

40. Among other important nineteenth-century works offering binary models of traditional versus modern capitalist society are those by Herbert Spencer, Henry Maine, and Émile Durkheim, surveyed briefly in Kumar, *Prophecy and Progress*, 58–60. On Tönnies, with some comparison to similar theories, see Charles P. Loomis and John C. McKinney, "Introductory Essay," in Tönnies, *Community and Society*, 1–11; Arthur Mitzman, *Sociology and Estrangement: Three Sociologists of Imperial Germany*; Werner J. Cahnman, ed., *Ferdinand Tönnies: A New Evaluation—Essays and Documents*.

41. Tönnies, *Community and Society*, 77.

42. Simmel, "The Metropolis and Mental Life," 415.

43. John A. Hobson, *The Evolution of Modern Capitalism: A Study of Machine Production*, 340.

44. Mike Featherstone, "Theories of Consumer Culture," *Consumer Culture and Postmodernism*, 24.

2. Meanings of Melodrama

1. Steve Neale, "Melo-Talk: On the Meaning and Use of the Term 'Melodrama' in the American Trade Press," *Velvet Light Trap* 32 (Fall 1993): 66–89.

2. Alan Dale, "The Tear-Drenched Drama," *Cosmopolitan Magazine* 48.2 (January 1910): 199–205 (quotation from 200).

3. Ibid. The play was based on the 1906 novel by Margaret Deland. It was turned into a five-reel film in 1916. See *American Film Institute Catalogue: Feature Films, 1911–1920*, 40.

4. A more pragmatic explanation would be that the term *melodrama* was deliberately avoided, particularly in publicity materials, because of the genre's lowbrow connotations. As drama critic Clayton Hamilton noted in 1911, "In the vocabulary of theatre-goers, no word has suffered more from . . . iniquitous degeneration than the adjective 'melodramatic.' Careless writers are now accustomed to call a play melodramatic when they wish to indicate that it is bad. . . . The very word melodrama has so fallen into disrepute that nowadays when a man puts forth a melodrama he usually pretends that it is something else and writes in a few extraneous passages to justify his press agent in advertising it as a social study or a comedy." Hamilton, "Melodrama, Old and New," *The Bookman* 33.3 (May 1911): 310.

5. Nowell-Smith, "Minnelli and Melodrama," *Screen* 18.2 (Summer 1977): 113–18. The theme of excess also gained currency with the publication of Peter Brooks's book *The Melodramatic Imagination: Balzac, Henry James, Melodrama, and the Mode of Excess*.

6. Linda Williams discusses melodrama with respect to bodily excess, drawing comparisons between melodrama and other "body genres" like horror and pornography, in "Film Bodies: Gender, Genre, and Excess," *Film Quarterly* 44.4 (Summer 1991): 2–13. Peter Brooks also discusses melodrama in relation to the body, although he is more concerned with dramatic representations of bodily danger than the spectator's bodily responses: "Melodrama, Body, Revolution," in Jacky Bratton et al., eds., *Melodrama: Stage, Picture, Screen*, 11–24.

7. Ludwig Lewisohn, "The Cult of Violence," *The Nation* 110.2847 (January 24, 1920): 118.

8. Lea Jacobs, "The Woman's Picture and the Poetics of Melodrama," *Camera Obscura* 31 (1993): 121–47. Jacobs's ideas in this essay are integrated into her book coauthored with Ben Brewster, *Theatre to Cinema: Stage Pictorialism and the Early Feature Film* (Oxford: Oxford University Press, 1997), esp. ch. 2 ("Situations").

9. Harry James Smith, "The Melodrama," *Atlantic Monthly* 99 (March 1907): 324, 326.

10. Arthur Ruhl, "Ten-Twenty-Thirty," in *Second Nights: People and Ideas of the Theater Today*, 145.

11. "Melodrama: By a Touring Manager," *The Stage* (October 2, 1919): 8.

12. I should clarify that establishing such a generalization is not Jacobs's stated objective. In *Theatre to Cinema* she and Brewster simply state that, "Our concern here is to demonstrate the extent to which playwriting technique, and later script construction

for films, made use of a conception of plot as a series of situations" (22).

13. Jacobs, "The Woman's Picture," 124.

14. Thomas Elsaesser, "Tales of Sound and Fury: Observations on the Family Melodrama," in Christine Goldhill, ed., *Home Is Where the Heart Is*, 64; originally in *Monogram* 4 (1972): 2–15.

15. On the cluster-concept model, see Max Black, "Definition, Presupposition, and Assertion," in *Problems of Analysis: Philosophical Essays*, 28; and Black, "How Do Pictures Represent?" in E. H. Gombrich, Julian Hochberg, and Max Black, eds., *Art, Perception, and Reality*, 128.

16. William S. Dye, *A Study of Melodrama in England from 1800 to 1840* (published Ph.D. diss.: see entry in bibliography). Despite the fact that State College is the location of Penn State University, the title page states that the dissertation was presented to the faculty of the University of Pennsylvania.

17. Dye lists "terror, horror; illogical ending; supernatural elements, chance and accident as preventing [delaying] the working out of that seldom-found poetic justice; exceptional scenery and stage effects; appeal to the emotion rather than to the intellect; a struggle invariably between vice and virtue; a visual representation of everything that is of importance (real melodrama, for example, would show the murder of Duncan by Macbeth); a play of types that are usually exaggerated and sometimes even caricatured; little or no growth of character; sudden twists and turns in personality without much apparent reason; a play usually with 'moral' written large upon it; a play full of exciting incidents—a 'thriller.' . . . In addition, the method of speech is much strained. The characters often use grandiloquent phrases and give voice to sentiments not in keeping with their personalities. The musical element in the later melodrama does not occupy so important a place as formerly, although we still find tremulo music on the violins as the villain appears or in places where the situation rises to more than ordinary height." To this list, Dye later adds, "A tendency to lay greater stress on situation than on character, together with a corresponding exaggeration intended to heighten the effect." Dye, *A Study of Melodrama*, 10, 11.

18. Aristotle, quoted in S. H. Butcher, *Aristotle's Theory of Poetry and Fine Art*, 237.

19. Eric Bentley, "Melodrama," in *The Life of the Drama*, 198.

20. Henry Albert Phillips, *The Photodrama*, 154.

21. Phillips, *The Photodrama*, 154.

22. Smith, "The Melodrama," 321.

23. "Melodrama: By a Touring Manager," 8.

24. Smith, "The Melodrama," 321.

25. My quotation condenses two reviews: " 'Wolves of New York' at the Boston," *Boston Post*, May 19, 1891, and "Boston Theatre: 'The Wolves of New York,' " *Boston Evening Transcript*, May 19, 1891.

26. Rollin Lynde Hartt, *The People at Play: Excursions in the Humor and Philosophy of Popular Amusements*, 187.

27. Smith, "The Melodrama," 324.

28. "Melodrama: By a Touring Manager," 8.

29. Henry Tyrell, "Drama and Yellow Drama," *The Theatre* 4.42 (August 1904): 193.

30. Hartt, *The People at Play*, 187–88.

31. Smith, "The Melodrama," 327.

32. Frederic Taber Cooper, "The Taint of Melodrama and Some Recent Books," *The Bookman* 22.6 (February 1906): 630.

33. Strong, "Good-by, Melodrama," 438. "St. Vitus's dance," also know as "chorea," is a nervous disorder marked by spasmodic movements of limbs and facial muscles.

34. Montrose J. Moses, "Concerning Melodrama," *Book News Monthly* 26.11 (July 1908): 846.

35. W. T. Price, "The Technique of the Drama: The Bowery Theaters," *Harper's Weekly*, May 10, 1890, 368–72 (quotation from 370).

36. "Statement of Mr. Ellis P. Oberholtzer," *Report of the Chicago Motion Picture Commission* (Chicago, September 1920): 105.

37. Dye, *A Study of Melodrama*, 8.

38. It should be noted that there is a critical tradition that contrasts naturalism and realism, rather than seeing them as synonymous. For Georg Lukács, realism was a literary mode in which the portrayal of characters exposed the social dynamics of a period; characters had descriptive relevance beyond themselves, conveying common types and tendencies. Naturalism, which Lukács criticized, was an attempt to reproduce surface appearances with no such generalizing aspiration. See Eugene Lunn, *Marxism and Modernism: An Historical Study of Lukács, Brecht, Benjamin, and Adorno* (Berkeley: University of California Press, 1982), ch. 3.

39. Tyrell, "Drama and Yellow Drama," 193. The term "yellow drama" is intended to disparage melodrama as resembling sensational "yellow journalism."

40. Strong, "Good-by, Melodrama," 436.

41. "The Corse Payton Engagement." Newspaper clipping, probably from Springfield, Mass., paper, August 5, 1902 (Harvard Theatre Collection, "Corse Payton" file).

42. "Melodrama: By a Touring Manager," 8.

43. Cooper, "The Taint of Melodrama," 630.

44. "America's Oldest Dramatist" (pre-1895), n.d. (Clipping, Harvard Theatre Collection, "Charles Foster" file; Foster died in 1895.)

45. "Risks Life for Realism," *Moving Picture World* (May 6, 1916): 190.

46. Alan Dale, "Boom of 'Mellerdrama,' " *New York Journal*, February 12, 1899, 26.

47. " 'A Nutmeg Match' at Jacob's," *Newark Daily Advertiser*, March 27, 1894, 4.

48. Elsaesser, "Tales of Sound and Fury," 49.

49. Bentley, "Melodrama," 205–206, 215–17 (emphasis in original).

50. Hamilton, "Melodrama, Old and New," 310, 312, 313.

51. Elsaesser, "Tales of Sound and Fury," 48.

52. Hartt, *The People at Play*, 185–86.

53. Reference to Sirk's statement in Elsaesser, "Tales of Sound and Fury," 52.

54. Williams, *"Playing the Race Card,"* "Introduction."

55. Alan Reynolds Thompson, "Melodrama and Tragedy," *Publication of the Modern Language Association of America* 43 (1928): 823.

56. Richard Steele, *The Tatler* 181 (June 6, 1710), quoted in Thompson, ibid., 830.

57. Just as action melodrama need not feature pathos, I also do not think pathetic melodrama must incorporate action, in the normal sense in which action is understood as the basis of action melodrama. Williams offers as an example of action in pathetic melodrama the fact that "Stella Dallas throws herself quite actively into the self-sacrificial task of alienating her daughter's affections [and] in the film's pathos-filled ending she also physically pushes through the crowd in order to see her daughter's wedding." I find this unconvincing, since it waters down the term to mean something very different than melodramatic action as it was normally understood. Melodramatic action must be perilous, extraordinary, exciting, sensational, not something as banal (even if dramatically charged) as smoking cigarettes, pretending to be callous, or moving through a crowd.

58. Williams has a very interesting section on the importance of time—both "too late" and "in the nick of time," drawing on work by Franco Moretti and Steve Neale.

59. Thompson, "Melodrama and Tragedy," 835; Clayton Hamilton, "Melodrama and Farces," *The Forum* 41.1 (January 1909): 23–27.

60. Robert B. Heilman, "Tragedy and Melodrama: Speculations on Generic Form," *Texas Quarterly* 3.2 (Summer 1960): 36–50.

3. Sensationalism and the World of Urban Modernity

1. Population statistics in U.S. Bureau of the Census, "Number of Inhabitants: U.S. Summary," Table 3, *1980 Census of the Population*; statistics on gross national product in U.S. Bureau of the Census, *Historical Statistics of the United States, Colonial Times to 1957*, 139. Miles of electric-trolley tracks in the North Atlantic region increased from 2,952 in 1890 to 10,175 in 1902. In the United States as a whole, coverage rose 178 percent in those years, from 8,123 to 22,589 miles of track (statistics in U. S. Bureau of the Census, *Special Reports, Street and Electric Railways* [1903], 34). The Outdoor Advertising Association of America estimated that expenditures for outdoor advertising escalated from $2 million a year in 1900 to $4 million in 1912, $15 million in 1917, and $35 million in 1921 (statistics cited in Alfred M. Lee, *The Daily Newspaper in America: The Evolution of a Social Instrument*, 366).

2. Simmel, "The Metropolis and Mental Life," 410.

3. Good compilations of film footage of Manhattan around 1900 can be found in episode seven of the PBS video series *Heritage: Civilization and the Jews* and in episode four of the *PBS* video series *New York: A Documentary Film*. The screening list of the DOMITOR conference, "Cinema Turns 100" (New York, 1994), included numerous street scenes from the 1896–1902 period held by major film archives in Europe and North America. DOMITOR is an international association for scholars interested in cinema before 1915. More information can be found on its web site: http://cri.histart.umontreal.ca/DOMITOR.

4. J. H. Girdner, "The Plague of City Noises," *North American Review* 163.478 (September 1896): 297.

5. Henry Adams, *The Education of Henry Adams* (1917), 494–95.

6. Howard B. Woolston, "The Urban Habit of Mind," *American Journal of Sociology* 17.5 (March 1912): 602, 604.

7. Michael M. Davis, *The Exploitation of Pleasure*, 33, 36.

8. Stephen Kern offers an eclectic survey of the period's literary and artistic discourses on speed, fragmentation, and modernity (such as the Cubist and Futurist manifestos) in *The Culture of Time and Space*, esp. ch. 5. On neurasthenia, see Kern, ch. 5; Tom Lutz, *American Nervousness, 1903: An Anecdotal History*; James B. Gilbert, *Work Without Salvations: America's Intellectuals and Industrial Alienation, 1880–1910*, 31–43. George Beard's *American Nervousness* (1881) is generally considered the seminal discussion of neurasthenia.

9. Walter Lippmann, "More Brains, Less Sweat," *Everybody's Magazine* 25 (1911): 827–28, quoted in John Tipple, *The Capitalist Revolution: A History of American Social Thought, 1890–1919*, 103.

10. It is no coincidence that social theorists began focusing on mob psychology around the turn of the century. Two key works, among many popularizations, were Gustave Le Bon's *Psychologie des Foules* (1895, translated as *The Crowd*) and Gabriel Tarde's *Opinion and the Crowd* (1901). A representative popularization is Gerald Stanley Lee, *Crowds: A Study of the Genius of Democracy and the Fear, Desires, and Expectations of the People*. Quotation from Walter Benjamin, "On Some Motifs in Baudelaire" (1939), in Arendt, ed., *Illuminations*, 174.

11. "New York City: Is it Worth It?" appeared in *Life* on May 6, 1909. Picasso held the first exhibition of Cubist paintings at Ambroise Vollard's gallery a bit later, in the summer of 1909. Cubism did not emerge as a bona fide movement (at least not one that a mainstream illustrator in New York might catch wind of) until the 1911–1914 period. The Armory Show, in which eleven hundred works of modern art were exhibited in New York (and then Chicago and Boston) and which was America's first real exposure to modern art, took place in February 1913. Herbert Read, *A Concise History of Modern Painting*, 117.

12. "Ground to Pieces on the Rail," *Newark Daily Advertiser*, May 9, 1894, 7.

13. A wealth of municipal government data on the numbers of trolley and road accidents and deaths has survived. Some statistics are presented in "Highway Accidents in New York City During 1915," *Journal of American Statistical Association* 15 (September 1916): 318–23; Roger Lane, *Violent Death in the City: Suicide, Accident, and Murder in Nineteenth-Century Philadelphia*.

14. "The Spectator," *The Outlook* 66 (September 15, 1900): 153.

15. Benjamin, "On Some Motifs in Baudelaire," 175.

16. "Whirled to Instant Death: His Body Caught in Rapidly Revolving Belts and Crushed Against the Ceiling at Every Revolution," *Newark Daily Advertiser*, May 29, 1891, 1; and "Horrible Death of a Street-Cleaner: His Head Twisted Almost Off by a Sweeping

Machine," *Newark Daily Advertiser*, May 18, 1891, 1.

17. "A Little Girl's Peculiar Death," *Newark Daily Advertiser*, May 26, 1891, 1.

18. Deaths by falling might also have had a particular resonance for first-generation immigrants, many of whom came from rural agrarian cultures with no tall buildings. Perhaps these images spoke to their sense of disquiet in the strange spatial coordinates of the vertical modern metropolis.

19. José Ortega y Gasset, *The Revolt of the Masses*, 31.

20. On amusement parks, roller coasters, and other rides and spectacles, see Robert Cartmell, *The Incredible Scream Machine: A History of the Roller Coaster*; John F. Kasson, *Amusing the Million: Coney Island at the Turn of the Century*; Richard Snow, *Coney Island: A Postcard Journey to the City of Fire*; Judith A. Adams, *The American Amusement Park Industry: A History of Technology and Thrills*; Andrea Stulman Dennett and Nina Warnke, "Disaster Spectacles at the Turn of the Century," *Film History* 4 (1990): 101–111.

21. "A Hundred Ways of Breaking Your Neck," *Scientific American* (October 14, 1905): 302–303.

22. "The Dime Museum Drama," *New York World*, April 16, 1893, 22.

23. "An Eighth Avenue Thriller." *New York Sun*, December 8, 1903 (clipping, Harvard Theatre Collection).

24. Vachel Lindsay, *The Art of the Moving Picture*, 39–40.

25. Gabriele Buffet, article from *391* digested as "The Superiority of American to European Films as Explained by a French Critic," *Current Opinion* 63.4 (October 1917): 250–51.

26. Marinetti et al., "The Futurist Cinema," in R. W. Flint, ed., *Marinetti: Selected Writings*, 131.

27. Benjamin, "The Work of Art," 238.

28. Both Phillipe Soupault and Jean Epstein recalled the thrill of seeing *The Exploits of Elaine* in Paris in 1915. Soupault wrote: "We dashed into the movie house and realized that all was changed. Pearl White's smile appeared on the screen, that almost ferocious smile announcing the upheavals of the new world. We finally understood that the cinema was not just a mechanical toy, but the terrible and magnificent flag of life. Wide eyed, we [saw] crimes, departures, phenomena, nothing less than the poetry of our age." Soupault, "Cinema, U.S.A." (1923), reprinted in Paul Hammond, ed., *The Shadow and Its Shadow: Surrealist Writings on Cinema*, 32.

   Jean Epstein similarly declared, "These popular, foolish (that goes without saying), penny dreadful-ish, incredible, blood-and-thunder films such as *The Exploits of Elaine* mark an epoch, a style, a civilization no longer lit by gas, thank God." Jean Epstein, "Le Sens 1Bis," in *Bonjour Cinema*, trans. Stuart Liebman in his Ph.D. diss., "Jean Epstein's Early Film Theory, 1920–1922" (1980). An alternate (and I think somewhat less apt) translation by Tom Milne is in *Afterimage* 10 (Autumn 1981): 9–16, reprinted in Abel, *French Film Theory and Criticism*, vol. 1.

29. Sergei Eisenstein, "The Problem of the Materialist Approach to Form" (1925), trans.

Roberta Reeder, in P. Adams Sitney, ed., *The Avant-Garde Film* (New York: NYU Press, 1978), 15–21 (quote from 21).

30. Robert Wagner, "You—At the Movies," *American Magazine* 90.6 (December 1920): 42–44; excerpted as "A Movie of the Movie Fan at the Movies" in *Literary Digest* 68 (February 26, 1921): 46.

31. John Kasson discusses the new middle class and its looser attitudes toward entertainment in *Amusing the Million.*

32. Hermann Kienzl, "Theater und Kinematograph," *Der Strom* 1 (1911–12): 219ff.; quoted in Anton Kaes, "The Debate About Cinema: Charting a Controversy (1909–1929)," *New German Critique* 40 (Winter 1987): 12.

33. Davis, *Exploitation of Pleasure*, 33, 36.

34. Burton Rascoe, "The Motion Pictures–an Industry, Not an Art." *The Bookman* 54.3 (November 1921): 194.

35. Siegfried Kracauer, "The Cult of Distraction: On Berlin's Picture Palaces" (1926), *The Mass Ornament: Weimar Essays*, ed. and trans. Thomas Y. Levin, 323–28 (quotation from 326). Levin's translation was earlier published in *New German Critique* 40 (Winter 1987): 91–96. There are several valuable essays on Kracauer and Benjamin in that issue of *New German Critique*, particularly Miriam Hansen's "Benjamin, Cinema, and Experience," Heide Schlupmann's "Kracauer's Phenomenology of Film," Patrice Petro's "Discourse on Sexuality in Early German Film Theory," and Sabine Hake's "Girls and Crisis: The Other Side of Diversion."

36. Benjamin, "The Work of Art," 250.

37. Benjamin, "On Some Motifs in Baudelaire," 175.

4. Making Sense of the Modernity Thesis

1. Luigi Pirandello, *Shoot! The Notebooks of Serafino Gubbio, Cinematograph Operator* (1915), trans. C. K. Scott Moncrieff, 10–11.

2. In chronological order of publication: Miriam Hansen, "Benjamin, Cinema, and Experience: The Blue Flower in the Land of Technology," 179–224 (1987); Tom Gunning, "An Aesthetics of Astonishment: Early Film and the (In)credulous Spectator," *Art and Text* 34 (Spring 1989): 31; Gunning, "Heard Over the Phone: *The Lonely Villa* and the De Lorde Tradition of Terrified Communication," *Screen* 32.2 (Summer 1991): 184–96; Hansen, "Decentric Perspectives: Kracauer's Early Writings on Film and Mass Culture," *New German Critique* 54 (Fall 1991): 47–76; Bruno, Giuliana. *Streetwalking on a Ruined Map: Cultural Theory and the City Films of Elvira Notari* (1993); Anne Friedberg, *Window Shopping: Cinema and the Postmodern* (1993); Gunning, "The Whole Town's Gawking: Early Cinema and the Visual Experience of Modernity," *Yale Journal of Criticism* 7.2 (Fall 1994): 189–201; Gunning, "The World as Object Lesson: Cinema Audiences, Visual Culture, and the St. Louis World's Fair," *Film History* 5.4 (Winter 1994): 422–44; Charney and Schwartz, eds., *Cinema and the Invention of Modern Life* (1995) (and which includes, among other essays, Gunning, "Tracing the Individual Body: Photography,

Detectives, and Early Cinema"; Hansen, "America, Paris, and the Alps: Kracauer (and Benjamin) on Cinema and Modernity"; and Ben Singer, "Modernity, Hyperstimulus, and the Rise of Popular Sensationalism" [an early version of ch. 3, this volume]); Lynne Kirby, *Parallel Tracks: The Railroad and Silent Cinema* (1997); Lauren Rabinovitz, *For the Love of Pleasure: Women, Movies, and Culture in Turn-of-the-Century Chicago* (1998); Leo Charney, *Empty Moments: Cinema, Modernity, and Drift* (Durham, N.C.: Duke University Press, 1998). A useful brief survey of this literature is in Gunning, "Early American Film," in John Hill and Pamela Church Gibson, eds., *The Oxford Guide to Film Studies*, 266–68. Two noncinema books that speculate on perceptual changes in modernity and have had an influence on the above works are Wolfgang Schivelbusch, *The Railway Journey: The Industrialization of Time and Space in the Nineteenth Century* (Berkeley: University of California Press, 1977; paperback, New York: Urizen, 1979); and Jonathan Crary, *Techniques of the Observer: On Vision and Modernity in the Nineteenth Century* and *Suspensions of Perception: Attention, Spectacle, and Modern Culture* (this last book appeared after this chapter was completed).

3. Bordwell, *History of Film Style*, 141–46.

4. Gunning, "The Whole Town's Gawking," 194, 196.

5. Ibid., 195.

6. Benjamin, "The Work of Art," 222, 250.

7. Bordwell calls it the "history-of-vision thesis." Although most work in this vein has focused on vision, for my purposes it will be more accurate to refer to the "history of perception," since much more than vision is at issue when Benjamin and others describe the subjective consequences of urban modernity.

8. Gunning's side of the discussion is presented by Bordwell in quotations from a correspondence Gunning sent to Bordwell, presumably in response to a manuscript draft of *On the History of Film Style*.

9. In lieu of a causal argument, one would be obliged to offer a specific explanation for why a causal argument would be mistaken. One might argue, for example, that the animals' long necks stem from different adaptive imperatives: perhaps the giraffe's long neck evolved because of a need to feed on high foliage whereas the ostrich's long neck evolved because of a need to spot predators over tall grasses.

10. Bordwell, *History of Film Style*, 142.

11. Ibid.

12. While the modernity thesis literature no doubt has its share of hyperbole and sloppy exposition (Jonathan Crary, for example, writes, "If vision can be said to have any enduring characteristic within twentieth-century modernity, it is that it has no enduring features" [Crary, "Dr. Mabuse and Mr. Edison," *Hall of Mirrors: Art and Film Since 1945*, 264]), Bordwell offers no quotations or even notes to illustrate that proponents of the modernity thesis have actually embraced a Lamarckian position. This may be because he is writing in a hypothetical-conditional mode to establish some givens before moving on to more promising hypotheses (i.e., Bordwell is saying some-

thing to the effect that, "If one *were* to argue that hard-wiring can change rapidly, then it would be wrong"). However, it is easy to get the impression that Bordwell is going after a straw man; as Gunning demurred, "Bordwell is aware that no theorist of modernity could responsibly claim a transformation in the perceptual hard wiring of human beings, so some of his objections seem to be based on a disingenuous *reductio ad absurdum*" (Gunning, "Early American Film," 267).

In any event, it probably would not be too difficult to find passages in recent articulations of the modernity thesis that sound more or less similar to Bordwell's paraphrase: "There is not only a history of ideas, beliefs, opinions, attitudes, tastes, and the like but also a history of how people take in the world through their senses . . . [involving] some fundamental reorganization of perception."

13. Tomaso Poggio, "Vision and Learning," in Robert A. Wilson and Frank C. Keil, eds., *The MIT Encyclopedia of the Cognitive Sciences*, 863–64.

14. Ehud Zohary et al., "Neuronal Plasticity That Underlies Improvement in Perceptual Performance," *Science* 263.5151 (March 4, 1994): 1289–93 (quotation from 1289).

15. Other consequences of enriched conditions include increases in neuron size, neuron density, dendritic branching, size of synaptic contact, and volume of glial cells that facilitate impulse conduction and protection of the neuron. Brian Kolb, *Brain Plasticity and Behavior*, esp. ch. 2; Marian Cleeves Diamond, *Enriching Heredity: The Impact of the Environment on the Anatomy of the Brain*.

16. Kolb, *Brain Plasticity*, 28–32; Charles Gilbert writes, "Training a monkey to do a texture discrimination task with a particular digit will increase the area of primary somatosensory cortex representing that digit. . . . Some of the initial evidence for cortical plasticity in the adult came from changes in somatotopic maps following digit amputation. Amputation of a body part or transection of a sensory nerve causes the area of cortex initially representing that part to be remapped toward a representation of the adjacent body parts. Gilbert, "Neural Plasticity," in Wilson and Keil, eds., *MIT Encyclopedia*, 598–601.

17. Gilbert, "Neural Plasticity," 599–600; see also Diamond, *Enriching Heredity*, chs. 5 and 10, and Kolb, *Brain Plasticity*, 31–32.

18. A summary of this research is in Michael J. Renner and Mark R. Rosenzwieg, *Enriched and Impoverished Environments: Effects on Brain and Behavior*, ch. 4. Other chapters offer an accessible overview of the neurobiology of differential experience.

19. Gilbert, "Neural Plasticity," 599.

20. Simmel, "The Metropolis and Mental Life," 410.

21. Nels Anderson and Eduard C. Lindeman, *Urban Sociology: An Introduction to the Study of Urban Communities*, 203–205.

22. Mary F. Asterita, *The Physiology of Stress, with Special Reference to the Neuroendocrine System*; John R. Hubbard and Edward A. Workman, *Handbook of Stress Medicine: An Organ System Approach*; Gary W. Evans and Sheldon Cohen, "Environmental Stress," in Daniel Stokols and Irwin Altman, eds., *Handbook of Environmental Psychology*, 571–610; S. Clare Stanford and Peter Salmon, eds., *Stress: From Synapse to Syndrome*;

George S. Everly and Robert Rosenfeld, *The Nature and Treatment of the Stress Response: A Practical Guide for Clinicians*; Ronald C. Simmons, *Boo! Culture, Experience, and the Startle Reflex*; Carney Landis and William A. Hunt, *The Startle Pattern*; Robert M. Sapolsky, *Why Zebras Don't Get Ulcers: A Guide to Stress, Stress-Related Diseases, and Coping*.

23. Hans Selye, *The Physiology and Pathology of Exposure to Stress*; W. B. Cannon and D. Paz, "Emotional Stimulation of Adrenal Gland Secretion," *American Journal of Physiology* 28 (1911): 64–70; Cannon, "The Emergency Function of the Adrenal Medulla in Pain and the Major Emotions," *American Journal of Physiology* 33 (1914): 356–72.

24. Gunning, "The Whole Town's Gawking," 194.

25. Levi studied adrenalin secretion in twenty subjects who watched four emotionally different films: Kubrick's *Paths of Glory* (which subjects described as making them feel agitated, angry, uneasy, and despondent); a Mario Brava gruesome horror film *The Mask of Satan* (agitated, uneasy, and frightened); the comedy *Charlie's Aunt* (amused and laughing); and a bland natural-scenery film produced by the Swedish National Railway Company (tired and bored). Adrenalin was raised markedly by all three of the fiction films—suspense-melodrama, horror, and comedy alike—but was affected little by the travelogue. Lennart Levi, "Sympathoadrenomedullary Responses to 'Pleasant' and 'Unpleasant' Psychosocial Stimuli," in Levi, ed., *Stress and Distress in Response to Psychosocial Stimuli*, 55–74. Figure 4.1 is adapted from a diagram in "Introduction: Psychosocial Stimuli, Psychophysiological Reactions, and Disease," in ibid., 13.

26. See Y. N. Sokolov, *Perception and the Conditioned Reflex*. A valuable summary of the Soviet research is Richard Lynn, *Attention, Arousal, and the Orientation Reflex*.

27. D. E. Berlyne, *Aesthetics and Psychobiology*; D. E. Berlyne et al., "Novelty, Complexity, Incongruity, Extrinsic Motivation, and the GSR [Galvanic Skin Response]," *Journal of Experimental Psychology* 63.6 (1963): 560–67; D. E. Berlyne and George H. Lawrence, "Effects of Complexity and Incongruity Variables on GSR, Investigatory Behavior, and Verbally Expressed Preference," *Journal of General Psychology* 71 (1964): 21–54; Garry Baker and Robert Franken, "Effects of Stimulus Size, Brightness, and Complexity upon EEG Desynchronization," *Psychonomic Science* 7 (1967): 289–90; David Gibson et al., "Effects of Size-Brightness and Complexity of Non-Meaningful Stimulus Material on EEG Synchronization," *Psychonomic Science* 8 (1967): 503–504; D. E. Berlyne et al., "Effects of Auditory Pitch and Complexity on EEG Desynchronization and on Verbally Expressed Judgements," *Canadian Journal of Psychology* 21.4 (1967): 346–57; D. E. Berlyne, *Conflict, Arousal, and Curiosity*.

28. Bordwell, *History of Film Style*, 301–302.

29. Bordwell begins: "The history-of-vision proponent may reply [in response to the Lamarckian objection] that biological evolution is irrelevant to claims about the new modes of perception in modernity." My question is, why would anyone trying to distance themselves from a quasi-Lamarckian position wish to deny the relevance or

validity of *all* hypotheses involving evolutionary biology? That would be like demonstrating one's rejection of phrenology—another great debacle in nineteenth-century biology—by denying the legitimacy of all scientific study of the human brain. Perhaps Bordwell had in mind as his imaginary interlocutor an orthodox Culturalist opposed to anything that might sound even remotely transhistorical. Evolutionary biology, with its emphasis on how current behavior is tied to hard-wiring that has evolved over millions of years, does not fit well at all with the prevailing dogma that all identity—including "the body"—is socially constructed and contingent upon immediate, politically determined contexts. History-of-perception arguments are definitely strongly Culturalist in that they posit major subjective transformations caused by rapid historical changes like the onset of urban modernity. It would be myopic, however, for any Culturalist argument to ignore the rudimentary fact that any historical variability can take place only within the biological parameters that have evolved in the human organism. I consider the stress/arousal version of the history-of-perception argument an example of the compatibility between Culturalist and "Biologist" approaches. On the relationship between biological evolution and "cultural evolution," see Wuketits, *Evolutionary Epistemology*, ch. 6.

30. Girdner, "The Plague of City Noises," 297.

31. Ludwig Wilheim Weber, "Grossstadt und Nerven," *Deutsches Rundschau* (December 1918): 391–407. I am grateful to Skadi Loist for her translation.

32. Neil D. Weinstein, "Community Noise Problems: Evidence Against Adaptation," *Journal of Experimental Psychology* 2 (1982): 87–97; Gary W. Evans et al., "Chronic Noise and Psychological Stress," *Psychological Science* 6.6 (November 1995): 333–38; Evans et al., "Chronic Noise Exposure and Physiological Response: A Prospective Study of Children Living Under Environmental Stress," *Psychological Science* 9.1 (January 1998): 75–77.

33. Robert D. Kaminoff and Harold M. Proshansky, "Stress as a Consequence of the Urban Physical Environment," in Leo Goldberger and Shlomo Breznitz, eds., *Handbook of Stress: Theoretical and Clinical Aspects*, 380–409; Gary W. Evans and Sybil Carrere, "Traffic Control, Perceived Control, and Psychophysiological Stress Among Urban Bus Drivers," *Journal of Applied Psychology* 76.5 (1991): 658–63. On the variability of individual appraisal of stress, see Randolph J. Paterson and Richard W. J. Neufeld, "Clear Danger: Situational Determinants of the Appraisal of Threat," *Psychological Bulletin* 101.3 (1987): 404–16; Richard S. Lazarus and Judith Blackfield-Cohen, "Environmental Stress," in Irwin Altman and Joachim F. Wohlwhill, eds., *Human Behavior and the Environment: Advances in Theory and Research* 2:89–127.

34. Simmel, "The Metropolis and Mental Life," 409. First part of quotation blends slightly different translations by Wolff and by Frisby in *Fragments of Modernity*, 73. The last two lines are from Simmel's *Philosophy of Money*, quoted in Frisby, ibid., 72, 74.

35. Woolston, "The Urban Habit of Mind," 602. Anderson and Lindeman also state that even after "working hours [are] over, the city people who pass along the great avenues still retain to some degree the intensity of countenance and rapidity of pace which

marked their working period," implying that the intensity and rapidity carry over into recreation. Anderson and Lindeman, *Urban Sociology*, 206.

36. Benjamin, "On Some Motifs in Baudelaire," 175.

37. Sheo D. Singh, "Effect of Urban Environment on Visual Curiosity Behavior in Rhesus Monkeys," *Psychonomic Science* 11.3 (1968): 83–84. The sample was small—eight adult female monkeys—so further research would be needed to confirm the hypothesis. The article's bibliography lists five similar studies by Singh. The research was conducted in India.

38. Simmel, *Der Krieg und die Geistigen Entschenidungen* (Munich, 1917), 27; quoted in Frisby, *Fragments of Modernity*, 75.

39. Nordau, *Degeneration*; quotation combines excerpts from pages 39, 41, 42.

40. Simmel, "The Metropolis and Mental Life," 414.

41. Selye, *Physiology and Pathology of Exposure*, 54.

42. Woolston, "The Urban Habit of Mind," 602.

43. Rascoe, "Motion Pictures," 194.

44. Simmel, "Metropolis and Mental Life," 410.

45. Rascoe, "Motion Pictures," 194.

46. Sorokin, *Social Mobility*, 518.

47. Sigmund Freud, "Beyond the Pleasure Principle" (1920), in vol. 18 of the *Standard Edition of the Complete Psychological Works*, 7–64 (quotation combines passages from pages 13 and 162).

48. Benjamin's fullest discussion of Freud's theory of protective anxiety is in "On Some Motifs in Baudelaire," 161–63. The first sentence of my quotation is taken from "Baudelaire" (162), the rest from "The Work of Art" (250). The last sentence is from the second, untranslated version of the latter essay, as quoted in Kracauer, *The Mass Ornament*, 353. For similar interpretations of this aspect of Benjamin's framework, see Susan Buck-Morss, "Aesthetic and Anaesthetics: Walter Benjamin's Artwork Essay Reconsidered," *New Formations* 20 (Summer 1993): 123–43; and Wolfgang Schivelbusch's discussion of the "stimulus shield" in *The Railway Journey*, 159–71.

49. Kracauer, "The Cult of Distraction," 325.

50. "Berliner Gewerbe-Ausstellung," *Die Zeit* 8 (Vienna) (July 25, 1896); quoted in Frisby, *Fragments of Modernity*, 94.

51. Kracauer, "The Cult of Distraction," 325.

52. Weber, "Grossstadt und Nerven," 397–98. At the end of the passage, Weber is quoting from Lamprecht.

53. Pirandello, *Shoot!*, 5–6. Very similar arguments were made in 1895 by Nordau, *Degeneration*, 41, and later by a British journalist named Arnold Smith in "The Ethics of Sensational Fiction," *Westminster Review* 162 (August 1904): 190.

54. Bordwell, *History of Film Style*, 141; Charlie Keil, " 'Visualised Narratives,' Transitional Cinema, and the Modernity Thesis," in Clair Dupré la Tour, André Gaudreault, and Roberta Pearson, eds., *Le Cinéma au Tournant du Siècle / Cinema at the Turn of the Century*, 133–47. I have embellished the argument: Bordwell's and

Keil's texts are not quite so cynical. It should be noted that Keil dislikes the modernity thesis not only because it is blind to year-by-year developments in early film style but also because, in his view, it privileges certain tangential connections between cinema and noncinematic forms possessing attributes associated with modernity (for example, film and the mail-order catalog) at the expense of other connections (such as film and magic lantern mini-narratives) that are more important to cinema's genealogy but may not necessarily invite comparison to modernity.

55. Tom Gunning, "The Cinema of Attractions: Early Film, Its Spectator, and the Avant-garde," in Elsaesser, ed., *Early Cinema*, 134.

56. Cf. Gunning, "Early American Film," 267–68.

57. Keil, " 'Visualised Narratives,' " 137.

58. Cf. Gunning, "Early American Film," 267–68.

5. Melodrama and the Consequences of Capitalism

1. A detailed account of the dramatic forms and terminology leading up to melodrama is in James Frederick Mason, *The Melodrama in France from the Revolution to the Beginning of Romantic Drama, 1791–1830*. An early reference to *A Tale of Mystery* as the first English-language play described as a melodrama is in "Melodrama," *All the Year Round* (November 9, 1878): 436–42. The article is anonymous, but every page of the magazine bears the heading "Conducted by Charles Dickens." Other informative sources on the development of melodrama are Dye, *A Study of Melodrama*; Lewin A. Goff, "The Popular-Priced Melodrama in America, 1890 to 1910, with Its Origins and Development to 1890" (Ph.D. diss., Western Reserve University, 1948); Michael Booth, *English Melodrama*; and David Grimsted, *Melodrama Unveiled: American Theater and Culture, 1800–1850*.

2. England's Licensing Act of 1737 imposed the same restriction: three "patent" theaters charged with the responsibility of upholding English dramatic tradition enjoyed a monopoly on spoken drama. (It is from this system the term *legitimate theater* is derived: the serious drama we describe today as "legitimate" corresponds to the kind produced in the legitimate—i.e., patent-holding—theaters.) The theatrical patent-privilege law was not rescinded until 1843, but by then producers already had been taking greater liberties with the law for several decades. Booth, *English Melodrama*, 52–53.

3. Mason, *Melodrama in France*, 7–16.

4. "Déclaration des Droits de l'Homme et du Citoyen" (1789), translated in a bicentennial commemorative booklet issued by the U.S. Congress: *The French Declaration of the Rights of Man and of the Citizen and the American Bill of Rights*, Senate Document 101–9 (1988). An engaging short account of the social and political dynamics of the French Revolution is in Robert C. Solomon, *Bully Culture: Enlightenment, Romanticism, and the Transcendental Pretence, 1750–1850* (ch. 5), originally published as *History and Human Nature: A Philosophical Review of European Philosophy and Culture*.

5. Elsaesser, "Tales of Sound and Fury," 45.

6. Brooks, *The Melodramatic Imagination* (1976), earlier version of relevant material published in *Partisan Review* 39.2 (1972); Bentley, *The Life of the Drama*, 195–218; Robert B. Heilman, "Tragedy and Melodrama," 36—50; Heilman, *Tragedy and Melodrama: Versions of Experience*; David Grimsted, "Melodrama as Echo of the Historically Voiceless," in Tamara K. Hareven, ed., *Anonymous Americans: Explorations in Nineteenth-Century Social History*, 80–98; Elsaesser, "Tales of Sound and Fury"; Martha Vicinus, "'Helpless and Unfriended:' Nineteenth-Century Domestic Melodrama, *New Literary History* 13.1 (Autumn 1981): 127–43; Laura Mulvey, "Melodrama In and Out of the Home," in Colin MacCabe, ed., *High Theory/Low Culture: Analysing Popular Television and Film* (Manchester, Eng.: Manchester University Press, 1986), 80–100; Christine Gledhill, "The Melodramatic Field: An Investigation," in Gledhill, ed., *Home Is Where the Heart Is*, 5–39; Judith R. Walkowitz, *City of Dreadful Delight: Narratives of Sexual Danger in Late-Victorian London.*

7. Grimsted, "Melodrama as Echo," 80–98 (quotation from 84).

8. Walkowitz, *City of Dreadful Delight*, 86.

9. Brooks, *The Melodramatic Imagination*, 14–15.

10. Ibid., 20.

11. Hamilton, "Melodrama, Old and New," 310, 312, 313.

12. "The Decay of Melodrama," *The Nation* 6.23 (British) (March 5, 1910): 877–78; reprinted in *The Living Age* 265.3432 (April 16, 1910): 182–84.

13. Hartt, *The People at Play*, 188, 190.

14. Friedrich Engels, *The Condition of the Working Class in England* (1844), trans. and ed. W. O. Henderson and W. H. Chaloner, 31.

15. Marx and Engels, *The Communist Manifesto* (1848), 37.

16. Tönnies, *Community and Society* (*Gemeinschaft und Gesellschaft*): quotations, as ordered in my presentation, are from 77, 65, 170, 227.

17. Hobson, *The Evolution of Modern Capitalism*, 340.

18. Vicinus, "Helpless and Unfriended," 128.

19. Desmond MacCarthy, "Melodrama," *The New Statesman* 3 (June 27, 1914): 4.

20. C. H. C. Wright, *A History of French Literature*, 696.

21. "Princess Theater." *San Francisco Weekly*, c. February 12, 1911: n.p. (clipping, Harvard Theatre Collection, "Chinatown" file).

22. Porter Emerson Browne, "The Mellowdrammer," *Everybody's Magazine* 21.3 (September 1909): 347.

23. Ibid., 348. A few months before writing this article, Browne's play *A Fool There Was* premiered in New York. He later wrote the screen adaptation for the famous 1916 Fox production starring Theda Bara—the film that began the vamp craze.

24. Hartt, *The People at Play*, 155. According to the *Oxford English Dictionary*, a "general" was a colloquial term for a maid or general servant.

25. Ruhl, "Ten-Twenty-Thirty," 143. The chapter undoubtedly appeared as a magazine

article previous to 1914.

26. Strong, "Good-by, Melodrama," 435.

27. "Melodrama: By a Touring Manager," 8.

28. Harry James Smith, "The Melodrama," 320.

29. Hartt, *The People at Play*, 182.

30. Walter Prichard Eaton, "Is 'Melodramatic Rubbish' Increasing?" *American Magazine* 82.6 (December 1916): 34.

31. See Michael R. Booth, *Victorian Spectacular Theatre, 1850–1910*.

32. Siegfried Kracauer, *Theory of Film: The Redemption of Physical Reality* (Oxford: Oxford University Press, 1960), 288.

6. Ten-Twenty-Thirty Melodrama: Boom and Bust

1. Horace Kallen, "The Dramatic Picture versus the Pictorial Drama: A Study of the Influences of the Cinematograph on the Stage," *Harvard Monthly* 50.1 (March 1910): 23.

2. H. Barton Baker, "The Old Melodrama," *Belgravia* 50.199 (May 1883): 331. See also Michael R. Booth, *Victorian Spectacular Theatre*, esp. chs. 1 and 3, and Booth's introduction to *Hiss the Villain: Six English and American Melodramas*.

3. Archibald Haddon, "Sensational Melodrama: Extreme Popularity of the Drama of Crime," *London Daily Express*, August 28, 1905.

4. My quotation combines a Boston and Providence notice about the same touring production: "Grand Opera: Queen of the White Slaves," *Boston Transcript*, March 28, 1905; and "Queen of the White Slaves" (review), *Providence Journal*, March 21, 1905, n.p. (clipping, Harvard Theatre Collection).

5. MacCarthy, "Melodrama," 4.

6. "Stage Notes: 'The Eye Witness,' " *Brooklyn Daily Eagle*, February 24, 1907, sec. 4, p. 2. I am indebted to Prof. Lewin A. Goff of the University of Kansas for directing me to this Brooklyn newspaper. Goff's unpublished dissertation, "The Popular-Priced Melodrama in America," is a very valuable resource.

7. "Bertha, the Sewing Machine Girl," ads and reviews in the *Brooklyn Daily Eagle*: September 2, 1906, 9; September 4, 1906, 4; September 23, 1906, sec. 3, p. 10; October 6, 1906, sec. 2, pp. 8–9.

8. " 'The Girl and the Detective' Again," *Brooklyn Daily Eagle*, October 31, 1909, sec. 2, p. 9. The buzz-saw thrill, in which the villain attempts to bifurcate the hero tied to a log, dates at least as far back as Augustin Daly's 1869 melodrama *The Red Scarf*. It was made famous, however, by Joseph Arthur's 1890 thriller *Blue Jeans*, discussed later in this chapter.

9. "Theaters: 'Edna, the Pretty Typewriter,' " *Brooklyn Daily Eagle*, September 1, 1907, sec. 3, p. 7.

10. "Lincoln J. Carter's Genius Runs to Scenic Effects," *New York Morning Telegraph* (January 28, 1906), n.p.. For clarity I have also inserted a few clauses from another article in which Carter describes the production: "Realism on the Stage," *Pittsburgh*

Post, January 28, 1906, n.p.

11. Charles Dalton, *Evening World* (city no determined), January 25, 1906, n.p.

12. Review in the *Toledo Blade,* April 15, 1907, n.p. (clipping, Robinson Locke Collection, New York Public Library, catalogued "NAFR Ser. 2.26": scrapbook page 95).

13. Owen Davis, *I'd Like to Do It Again,* 90. My calculations of current money values are based on comparison of the August 1999 consumer price index (current indexes available monthly from the U.S. Bureau of Labor Statistics, at http://stats.bls.gov/blshome.htm) with figures in U.S. Department of Labor, Bureau of Labor Statistics, "Consumer Price Indexes and Purchasing Power of the Consumer Dollar, 1913–1988," *Handbook of Labor Statistics* (August 1989): table 113, p. 475; and U.S. Department of Labor, Bureau of Labor Statistics, "The Consumer Price Index, 1800–1974," *Handbook of Labor Statistics* (Reference Edition, 1975): table 122, p. 313. Money equivalences can be only approximate since the bushel of goods and services used to chart costs has changed considerably since the early 1900s.

14. Interview with Owen Davis in Charles Estcourt, Jr., "New York Skylines," syndicated newspaper column (February 2, 1941). Davis, class of 1893, misremembered the name as "Munsterberger."

15. M. B. Leavitt, *Fifty Years in Theatrical Management,* 569, and the *Brooklyn Dramatic Eagle,* May 13, 1903, 3 (both cited in Goff, "The Popular-Priced Melodrama in America," 248); Owen Davis, "Why I Quit Writing Melodrama," *American Magazine* 78.3 (September 1914): 28–31, 77–80; Davis, *I'd Like to Do It Again,* 83–90; Davis, *My First Fifty Years in the Theatre,* 22–49.

16. "What Is the Cause? A Great Falling Off in Patronage of the Popular-Price Theatres," *New York Dramatic Mirror,* April 18, 1908, 5; "An Absorbing Problem: The Cause of the Decline in Patronage of the Popular-Price Theatres," ibid., April 25, 1908, 3; "Good and Bad Melodrama: The Decline in Patronage of the Popular-Price Theatre from a New Viewpoint," ibid., May 9, 1908, 2; "The Popular-Price Theatre: Still Another Producing Manager Gives His Views of Conditions," ibid., May 16, 1908, 8; "The Melodrama Theatre: The Discussion as to Its Decline in Popularity and Its Needs Continued," ibid., June 6, 1908, 3. I learned of this series of articles in Roberta Pearson's *Eloquent Gestures: The Transformation of Performance Style in Griffith Biograph Films.*

17. "Popular-Price Drama Waning," *New York Dramatic Mirror,* November 28, 1908, 8.

18. Eaton, "The Canned Drama," *American Magazine* 68 (September 1909): 500.

19. Glenmore Davis, "The Moving-Picture Revolution," *Success Magazine* 13.192 (April 1910): 238–40.

20. For example: Roy L. McCardell, "The Chorus Girl Deplores the Moving Picture's Triumph Over Drama," *Moving Picture World,* April 11, 1908, 321; Amy Leslie, "Actors, Farm Hands," *Chicago News,* April 18, 1908, 88; John Collier, "Cheap Amusements," *Charities and the Commons* 20 (April 11, 1908): 73–78; Montrose J. Moses, "Where They Perform Shakespeare for Five Cents," *Theatre Magazine* 8.92 (October 1908): 264–65, xi–xii; "Downfall of Melodrama," *New York Sun,* February

10, 1909, 7; "A Theatre with a 5,000,000 Audience," *World's Work* 20.1 (May 1910): 12876; Kallen, "The Dramatic Picture," 22–31; William Inglis, "Morals and Moving Pictures," *Harper's Weekly*, July 30, 1910, 12; W. Dayton Wegefarth, "The Decline of Lurid Melodrama," *Lippincott's Monthly Magazine* 88 (September 1911): 427–28; Robert Grau, "The Moving-Picture Show and the Living Drama," *American Review of Reviews* 45.3 (March 1912): 329–36; "The New Owen Davis," *New York Dramatic Mirror*, October 22 ,1913, 1, 10; Clayton Hamilton, *Studies in Stagecraft*; Walter Prichard Eaton, "Class Consciousness and the Movies," *Atlantic Monthly* 115.1 (January 1915): 49–56; H. O. Stechhan, "Stage versus Screen," *The Theatre* 21.169 (March 1915): 126–30, 144; Eaton, "Is 'Melodramatic Rubbish' Increasing?" 34, 114, 116; "Are the Movies a Menace to the Drama?" *Current Opinion* 62.5 (May 1917): 331.

21. Goff, "The Popular-Priced Melodrama in America," 171.

22. Jack Poggi, *Theater in America: The Impact of Economic Forces, 1870–1967*, 30–31.

23. On provincial melodrama in the Teens, see Eaton, "Is 'Melodramatic Rubbish' Increasing?" The situation was essentially the same in England. On melodrama's commercial difficulty in London in the early Teens, see ""Drury Lane's Director Talks of Melodrama" (interview with Arthur Collins), unknown newspaper, c. 1912, n.p. (clipping, Harvard Theatre Collection, "Melodrama, General," file 3); on its provincial vestiges, see "Melodrama: By a Touring Manager," 8.

24. "Lincoln J. Carter and His Big Stage Effects," *Columbus Journal*, October 15, 1911 (clipping, Robinson Locke Collection, New York Public Library, catalogued "NAFR Ser. 2.26": scrapbook page 101).

25. On superspectacles, see newspaper clippings in the "Lincoln Carter" file of the Harvard Theatre Collection; "Stair and Havlin Trying at Popular-Priced Vaudeville," *Variety*, March 27, 1909, 1; reference to A. H. Woods in Burns Mantle, "What's What in Theater," *Green Book* (June 1918): 114, and Walter Prichard Eaton, "The Latest Menace of the Movies," *North American Review* 212.776 (July 1920): 83; Barry Witham, "Owen Davis, America's Forgotten Playwright," *Players Magazine* 46.1 (October-November 1970): 30–35; and Owen Davis, "Why I Quit Writing Melodrama," 28–31, 78–80.

26. Brady, "Melodrama—What It Is and How to Make It," *Green Book* 14 (August 1915): 310–313.

27. Hamilton, "Melodrama, Old and New," 314.

28. George Jean Nathan, "The Hawkshavian Drama," *Mr. George Jean Nathan Presents*, 25. For more on the switch to drawing room melodrama, see Eaton, "Is 'Melodramatic Rubbish' Increasing?" 34, 114, 116, and an interview with Al Woods: "Producing Spine-Thrillers," *Literary Digest* 45.6 (August 10, 1912): 222–23. Like Nathan, Olivia Howard Dunbar reassessed old-time melodrama nostalgically in "The Lure of the Films," *Harper's Weekly*, January 18, 1913, 20, 22.

29. Phelps added, "As a matter of fact, in the five-cent performance you are at a great advantage because you don't have to hear the voices." According to Phelps's survey of

New York theatrical offerings, there were ten to fifteen melodramas at any one time in 1900, but only three in 1916. Phelps, "The Drama of Today," *Journal of the National Institute of Social Sciences* 3 (January 1917): 17–33.

30. Eaton, "Is 'Melodramatic Rubbish' Increasing?" 114.

31. Poggi, *Theater in America.*

32. Bennett Musson and Robert Grau, "Fortunes in Film: Moving Pictures in the Making," *McClure's Magazine* 40 (December 1912): 193–202.

33. A. Nicholas Vardac, *Stage to Screen: Theatrical Origins of Early Film—David Garrick to D. W. Griffith*, xxv. Subsequent page numbers will be cited in the text.

34. "A Unique Stage Effect." *Pittsburgh Sun*, December 5, 1906 (clipping, Robinson Locke Collection, New York Public Library, catalogued "NAFR Ser. 2.26": scrapbook page 94).

35. "American—Bertha, the Sewing Machine Girl." Unknown New York trade journal, 1906 (n.d., n.p.) (clipping, Harvard Theatre Collection, "Bertha, the Sewing Machine Girl" file).

36. "An Eighth Avenue Thriller." *New York Sun*, December 8, 1903 (clipping, Harvard Theatre Collection).

37. Harry James Smith, "The Melodrama," 325.

38. Browne, "The Mellowdrammer," 353.

39. Heywood Broun in the *New York Tribune*, syndicated in the *Boston Transcript*, April 4, 1918, n.p. (clipping, Robinson Locke Collection, New York Public Library, catalogued "NAFR Ser. 2.26": scrapbook page 103).

40. "The Drama of the People," *The Independent* 69.3226 (September 29, 1910): 713–15.

41. Ibid. The last line of this quotation is particularly interesting in its anticipation of Münsterberg's mentalistic theory of film that appeared six years later.

42. Barton W. Currie, "The Nickel Madness," *Harper's Weekly*, August 24, 1907, 1246–47.

43. Lucy France Pierce, "The Nickelodeon," *The World Today* 25.4 (October 1908): 1052–57.

44. "Spectator's Comments," *New York Dramatic Mirror*, May 22, 1909, 17.

45. C. H. Claudy, "The Degradation of the Motion Picture," *Photo-Era* 21.4 (October 1908): 162. Another description of intense diegetic immersion is in Mary Heaton Vorse, "Some Picture Show Audiences," *The Outlook* 98 (June 24, 1911): 445.

46. George Bernard Shaw, "What the Films May Do to the Drama," *Metropolitan Magazine* 42 (May 1915): 23.

47. Brian Hooker, "Moving-pictures: A Critical Prophecy," *The Century* 93.6 (April 1917): 857–68.

48. Walter Prichard Eaton, "Making Scenarios for the Movies," *Boston Evening Transcript*, November 13, 1916, 15.

49. Eaton, "The Theater: A New Epoch in the Movies," *American Magazine* 78.4 (October 1914): 95.

50. In addition to the passages I have quoted, typical discussions of the film's advantages over theater in terms of diegetic realism and scenic diversity can be found in Montrose

J. Moses, "Where They Perform Shakespeare for Five Cents," 264–65 and xi–xii; "Spectator's Comments," *New York Dramatic Mirror*, May 14, 1910, 18; Hamilton, *Studies in Stagecraft*, 233; Eleanor Gates, "Best Seller Drama," *Harper's Weekly*, June 6, 1914, 20; "The Moving Picture of Tomorrow," *The Outlook* 107 (June 27, 1914): 444.

51. Hooker, "Moving-pictures," 868.

52. Hartt, *The People at Play*, 183.

53. Browne, "Mellowdrammer," 354.

54. Ibid.

55. Davis, interviewed in anonymous article, "Ahaah! Baffling the Villain—Currrses [*sic*]," *New York Herald*, October 3, 1909, n.p. (clipping, New York Public Library, "Owen Davis" file).

56. Hollinshead quoted in Erroll Sherson, *London's Lost Theatres of the Nineteenth Century*, 13.

57. Dunbar, "The Lure of the Films," 20–22.

58. "Brunswick's Letter: The Buzz-Saw Drama—Agnes Huntington and Her Operetta—Personal." *Boston Transcript*, October 11, 1890: n.p. (clipping, Harvard Theatre Collection). Joseph Arthur's obituary in the *New York Dramatic Mirror* (March 3, 1906, n.p.) states that he "may be said to have originated the modern melodrama of mechanical devices."

59. "Producing Spine-Thrillers" (interview with Al Woods), 222–23.

60. "Risks Life for Realism," *Moving Picture World*, May 6, 1916, 190.

61. Harold Cary, "Life to the Wind for the Movies," *Technical World Magazine* 20.6 (February 1914): 866—71; "Risky Realism for the Movies," *Literary Digest* 48.16 (April 18, 1914): 954—59; "Pearl White Injured," *New York Dramatic Mirror*, May 6, 1914, 28; William Lord Wright, "Perils of the Motion Picture," *Motion Picture Magazine* 9.3 (April 1915): 95; Cecelia Mount, "The Girl with Nine Lives," *Motion Picture Magazine* 11.1 (February 1916): 121—25; Burr C. Cook, "Realism: The New Word in the Movies," *Motion Picture Magazine* 11.6 (July 1916): 49—54; Orson Meriden, "A Chat with Pearl White," *The Theatre* (July 1916): 61; "Risks Life for Realism," ibid.; "Flirting with the Great Unknown," *Motion Picture Magazine* 12.7 (August 1916): 64—66; "She Discusses Realism," *New York Dramatic Mirror*, November 4, 1916, 35; Mary B. Mullett, "The Heroine of a Thousand Dangerous Stunts," *American Magazine* 92.3 (September 1921): 32–34.

62. Reinhold E. Becker, "The Principle of Suggestion in Art as Applied to the Photoplay," *The Editor* 46.11 (September 12, 1917): 323–25.

7. "Child of Commerce! Bastard of Art!": Early Film Melodrama

1. Letter from G. Day Smith of Duluth, Minnesota, published in *Moving Picture World*, December 23, 1910, 1301.

2. *New York World* excerpts, and rebuttal, in "Pictures Need No Censoring," *New York Dramatic Mirror*, August 13, 1910, 25.

3. Harry James Smith, "The Melodrama," 323; see also Booth, *English Melodrama*, 35–36.

4. According to Harold Stearns, writing in 1915, "The histrionic standard of the movies has been raised immeasurably in the last three years. Gone are the old nervous fidgeting, the exaggerated emphasis, the perpetual restlessness; the value of restraint has been learned, together with the imaginative power of quiet methods, the force of few gestures." Stearns, "Art in Moving Pictures," *The New Republic*, September 25, 1915, 208. Roberta Pearson details the transformation of early film acting styles in *Eloquent Gestures*.

5. Richard Abel, *The Ciné Goes to Town: French Cinema, 1896–1914*, 97; see also "Downfall of Melodrama," *New York Sun*, February 10, 1909, 7.

6. Screened at the British Film Institute conference, "Melodrama: Stage—Picture—Screen," London, July 1992. The connection to *The Heart of Maryland* is mentioned in the screening notes by Jim Cook and Christine Gledhill. Belasco's play is described in Booth,.ed., *Hiss the Villain*, 36.

7. On the popularity of "turf melodramas," see Frank Rahill, *The World of Melodrama*, 218. Vardac mentions the play *A Race For Life* (but not Porter's film) in *Stage to Screen*, 57; Charles Musser notes the connection between the play and the film in *Before the Nickelodeon: Edwin S. Porter and the Edison Manufacturing Company* (407), but mistitles the play as *A Race for a Wife*. That title was used for a 1906 Vitagraph parody.

8. *Variety*, February 2, 1907. Unless page numbers are provided, the reference can be found in a comprehensive chronological collection entitled *Variety Film Reviews*, vol. 1, *1907–1920*.

9. *Variety*, April 27, 1907. The review does not identify the producer.

10. *Biograph Bulletins, 1908–1912*, introduction by Eileen Bowser (New York: Octagon Books, 1973), 3.

11. Ibid., 11.

12. Tom Gunning, *D. W. Griffith and the Origins of the American Narrative Film*, 143–62.

13. *Kalem Kalendar*, March 1, 1913, 3. Similar films include *The Pony Express Girl* (released November 6, 1912), *A Race with Time* (released December 7, 1912), *A Desperate Chance* (released January 18, 1913), *The Flying Switch* (released July 14, 1913), *The Railroad Inspector's Peril* (released October 1, 1913), *The Railroad Detective's Dilemma* (released October 1, 1913).

14. Similar titles include *The Girl Scout* (released November 6, 1909), *The Tide of Battle* (released March 7, 1912), *The Drummer Girl of Vicksburg* (released May 15, 1912), *The Colonel's Escape* (released June 1, 1912), *The Soldier Brothers of Susanna* (released July 1, 1912), *Saved from Court Martial* (released August 30, 1912), *The Darling of the C.S.A.* (released September 6, 1912), *The Filibusters* (released June 15, 1912).

15. Ellis Paxson Oberholtzer, *The Morals of the Movies*, 57.

16. Frank Bruner, "The Modern Dime Novel," *Photoplay* 16 (January 1919): 118.

17. Review of *Lucille Love: Girl of Mystery* in the *New York Dramatic Mirror*, June 3, 1914, 35.

18. *New York Dramatic Mirror*, September 9, 1916, 29.

19. "Statement of Mr. Ellis P. Oberholtzer," 106.

20. "Laemmle Explains 'Diploma System' for His Directors and Cameramen," *Moving Picture World*, February 14, 1920, 1104. The assertion that serials were Universal's most lucrative product appeared in Alfred A. Cohn, "Harvesting the Serial," *Photoplay* 11.3 (February 1917): 25. However, one should treat this claim skeptically without further research.

21. George B. Seitz, "The Serial Speaks," *New York Dramatic Mirror*, August 19, 1916, 21.

22. Oberholtzer, *Morals of the Movies*, 55.

23. *Variety*, August 18, 1916. *The Yellow Menace* was an independent production by the Edwin Sales Corporation.

24. In his excellent study of early film exhibition in Lexington, Kentucky, Gregory Waller found three theaters that relied quite heavily on serials. The Colonial was a small, albeit relatively respectable, downtown nickelodeon between 1911 and 1917, screening films from 10 A.M. to 11 P.M. Except for a few unsuccessful attempts to switch over to feature films (which proved too expensive for a theater with relatively low volume), the Colonial filled its bills with serials, one-reel comedies, and other shorts. The Gem was a theater catering solely to black audiences and under black management. Before its demise sometime around 1917, the Gem primarily screened short action films and comedies, with only an occasional feature film. Serials figured prominently: in November 1915, for example, the Gem was running three different serials each week: *The Perils of Pauline* on Tuesdays, *The Broken Coin* on Thursdays, and *The Phantom Extra* on Sundays. The Orpheum was a small, 300-seat nickelodeon opened in early 1912 in Lexington's central business district. Like the Colonial, it ran short "variety programs" from 10 A.M. to 11 P.M. By the late Teens, it had settled into its niche as a "second-rank" house, still changing programs daily and running continuous short programs of serial episodes, newsreels, comedies, and two- or three-reel westerns. Even into the early 1920s, the Orpheum sometimes ran as many as five different serials each week. Waller, *Main Street Amusements: Movies and Commercial Entertainment in a Southern City, 1896–1930*, 86–95, 197–98.

25. Ernest A. Boyd, "The 'Movie Fan,' " *The New Statesman* 10 (March 30, 1918): 617.

26. "Statement of Mr. Ellis P. Oberholtzer," 106.

27. Advertisement for *The Fatal Ring* (1917), *Motion Picture News*, October 27, 1917, 2838.

28. Miriam Hansen has suggested, for example, that the spectator's sense of belonging to a specific communal audience was diminished by the rise of classical narration, since the feature film "mandated prolonged attention and absorption" and was therefore "an effective step in minimizing awareness of the theater space." This is a compelling argument, but the serials highlight a need for further qualification. Hansen, *Babel and Babylon: Spectatorship in American Silent Film*, ch. 2.

29. Bruner, "The Modern Dime Novel," 48.

30. *Motion Picture News*, December 2, 1916, 3379.

31. Fred C. Quimby, "A Standard Feature," *Wid's Year Book* (1919–20): 71.

32. "What of the Serial?" *Wid's Year Book* (1919–20): 67–71; "Outlook for Serials," *Wid's Year Book* (1920–21): 72–3. On Kalem, see entry in Anthony Slide, *The American Film Industry: A Historical Dictionary*.

33. "Downfall of Melodrama," *New York Sun*, February 10, 1909, 7.

34. Synopses of *A Lass of the Lumberlands* can be found in Mutual's publicity magazine *Reel Life*, beginning October 14, 1916.

35. Peter Milne, "The Seven Pearls," *Motion Picture News*, November 3, 1917, 3132.

36. See, for example, Kristin Thompson and David Bordwell, *Film History: An Introduction*, 61.

37. Richard Abel discusses the Nick Carter series in *The Ciné Goes to Town*, 196–98.

38. Review of "A Will and a Way," *New York Dramatic Mirror*, March 12, 1913, 32; "The Adventures of Kathlyn," *Moving Picture World*, February 21, 1914, 926.

39. Readers should be warned that the existing prints and videos of *The Perils of Pauline*, ostensibly representing nine episodes, are an abridgment and reordering of the original twenty episodes. The current prints and videos not only lack over half the episodes but also combine parts of different episodes, in certain cases eradicating the cliffhanger structure. The original sequence of episodes is also reshuffled. I had originally thought that the bastardization derived from the compilation of extant fragments from a print released by Pathé for showing at home or clubs with the "Pathé Baby" small-gauge projector. However, Rudmer Canjels, a graduate student in Film and Television Studies at the University of Utrecht who is writing a dissertation on serial exhibition in Holland, informs me that when *The Perils of Pauline* was released in Holland in 1916 (with a print probably imported from France), theaters screened nine single episodes corresponding exactly to the ones that we have today. This suggests that Pathé condensed and reordered the serial deliberately for European release. The reasons for this are not entirely clear. Presumably, European exhibitors preferred shorter runs for serials. Canjels has found that American serials screened in Holland usually ran for only five or six weeks, with two or three episodes shown back-to-back each week.

40. The five mass circulation magazines currently publishing fiction that I can think of are *The New Yorker*, *The Atlantic Monthly*, *Cosmopolitan*, *Playboy*, and *Omni*. Information on fiction-publishing periodicals in 1915 was derived, and aggregate circulation figures calculated, from *American Newspaper Annual and Directory: 1915*. The U.S. Census population statistic for 1910 is 91,972,266; for 1920: 105,710,620. Assuming a constant rate of growth between these two censuses, the 1915 population would be 99,125,000. Many magazines used a standardized format found, for example, in the original *Cosmopolitan Magazine* (a general interest monthly with circulation of one million). Each issue carried two serials, five or six short stories, and three nonfiction articles, besides department pieces on the theater, current events, etc. The *Ladies' World*, similarly, included each month two or three serials, three romance short stories, and sundry items in departments on advice, floral arrangement, food preparation, fashion, health, etc.

41. This rationale was expressed in "Single Reel Biographs," *Motion Picture News*, September 4, 1915, 1671.

42. At a convention in New York in June 1914, exhibitors passed a resolution in which they "expressed their disapproval of the production of reels of 1000 feet and upward." For an articulation of these sentiments from the standpoint of producers, see William Selig, "Present Day Trend in Film Lengths," *Moving Picture World*, July 11, 1914, 181, and Carl Laemmle, "Doom of Long Features Predicted," in ibid., 185; see also "Edison Touches Popular Chord," *Moving Picture World*, January 3, 1914, 28–29.

43. In October 1916 publicity articles, Kalem called its *Grant, Police Reporter* a "short length feature" series. In September 1916, a Universal press release announced, "The feature of the week will be the fifth two-reel episode of *Liberty*." A 1915 issue of *Motion Picture News* (*MPN*) similarly includes a two-reel episode of Pathé's *The Exploits of Elaine* on a page devoted to "Feature Releases—Current and Coming." "Series Idea Means Cumulative Advertising," *MPN*, October 21, 1916, 2552; "Twenty-six Reels a Week . . . from Universal," *MPN*, September 16, 1916, 1698; "Feature Releases—Current and Coming," *MPN*, April 3, 1915, 78–83.

44. Circulation figures are from the *American Newspaper Annual and Directory*. Characterization of the *Ladies' World* readership appears in Ellen Gruber Garvey, *The Adman in the Parlor: Magazines and the Gendering of Consumer Culture, 1880s to 1910s*, 9.

45. The serial's popularity is indicated in comments by exhibitors that were gathered by Edison agents who visited about 150 theaters across the country. "1914 Moving Picture General (4 of 6)," Edison Archives, Edison National Historic Site, West Orange, N.J.

46. Reviews of episodes "A Will and a Way," *New York Dramatic Mirror*, March 12, 1913, 32, and "The High Tide of Misfortune," *New York Dramatic Mirror*, May 7, 1913, 30.

47. Terry Ramsaye, *A Million and One Nights: A History of the Motion Picture Through 1925*, 666.

48. Cohn, "Harvesting the Serial," 22.

49. In the survey of titles that follows, I have chosen not to provide narrative synopses. Unless otherwise noted, they all follow the melodramatic plucky-heroine-and-weenie formula discussed above. Kalton Lahue provides a somewhat random overview of a number of serial narratives, along with release dates, casts, and episode titles, in *Continued Next Week: A History of the Moving Picture Serial*. Other synopses of serial episodes can be found in the many short trade journal publicity reviews listed in the bibliography.

50. The financial successes of the *Pauline* series and the *Elaine* series are mentioned in Cohn, "Harvesting the Serial." Also, "Pathé's Own Convention," *New York Dramatic Mirror*, July 14, 1915, 21, reports on a banquet "to celebrate the reaching of $1 million mark for Elaine."

51. Eisenstein, "Dickens, Griffith, and Film Today," in Leyda, ed., *Sergei Eisenstein: Film*

Form, 203.

52. "Pathé Claims Pearl White Greatest Drawing Card," *Motion Picture News*, April 28, 1917, 2655.

53. See *Motion Picture Magazine* 12.11 (December 1916): 15; ibid., 16.11 (December 1918): 12; and ibid., 20.11 (December 1920): 94.

54. Lahue, *Continued Next Week*, 48–49. See also comments per various publicity articles and reviews of *Patria* appearing in *Motion Picture News* (*MPN*), December 2, 1916, 40; *MPN*, December 9, 1916, 3668; *MPN*, February 3, 1917, 735; *MPN*, February 17, 1917, 1061 and 1075; *MPN*, March 19, 1917, 1363; and *MPN*, April 14, 1917, 2365.

55. See publicity articles and reviews in *Moving Picture World*, May 13, 1916, 1146; ibid., July 8, 1916, 262; *New York Dramatic Mirror*, July 22, 1916, 27; ibid., November 4, 1916, 34; and *Motion Picture News* (*MPN*), June 10, 1916, 3549; *MPN*, July 1, 1916, 4033.

56. On Francis Ford, see Tag Gallagher, "Brother Feeney," *Film Comment* 12.6 (November-December 1976): 12–18. Also, see Luis Buñuel, *My Last Sigh*, 32. Buñuel gets things a bit mixed up. He refers to "Lucilla Love . . . pronounced Lové in Spanish," as a popular actress, rather than as a character.

57. "Vitagraph's First Serial," *Moving Picture World*, May 1, 1915, 710; see also advertisement, ibid., May 15, 1915, 1042.

58. Studio memos and reports: "1914 Moving Pictures General (4 of 6)"; "Moving Picture Info" (files A—C, box 1); "1915 Moving Pictures—General (1 of 3)"—all found in the Edison Archives, Edison National Historic Site, West Orange, N.J.

59. "The Motion Picture News Chart of National Film Trade Conditions," *Motion Picture News* (*MPN*), October 31, 1914, 20–21; "Second Motion Picture News Chart," *MPN*, March 13, 1915, 32–35; "Third Motion Picture News Chart," *MPN*, May 22, 1915, 38–41; "Fourth Motion Picture News Chart," *MPN*, August 28, 1915, 39–40; "Fifth Motion Picture News Chart," *MPN* 12.22 (December 4, 1916): 56, 58; "Sixth Motion Picture News Chart," *MPN*, June 10, 1916, 3556–3557; "Seventh Motion Picture News Chart," *MPN*, December 30, 1916, 4192; "Eighth Motion Picture News Chart," *MPN*, July 28, 1917, 656–57.

60. For a concise history of serial films from 1913 to the mid-1950s, when their production ceased, and of serials made by non-American studios, see my entry entitled simply "Serials" in Geoffrey Nowell-Smith, ed., *The Oxford History of World Cinema*, 105–11.

8. Power and Peril in the Serial-Queen Melodrama

1. Carol Clover, *Men, Women, and Chainsaws: Gender in the Modern Horror Film*.

2. On the girls' adventure book series, see Nancy Tillman Romalov, "Unearthing the Historical Reader, or Reading Girls' Reading," in Larry E. Sullivan and Lydia Cushman Schurman, eds., *Pioneers, Passionate Ladies, and Private Eyes: Dime Novels, Series Books, and Paperbacks*, 87–101.

3. *Ladies Home Journal* (May 1915): 91 (advertisement).

4. C. D. Crain, "Fights for Men, Finery for Women," *Moving Picture World*, July 29, 1916, 818.

5. Advertisement in *Motion Picture News*, October 21, 1916, 2490. Although this ad does not indicate a specific tie-in, the film itself probably announced one in a title card. At the end of each episode of *The Ventures of Marguerite*, for example, an inter-title reads, "The exclusive creations worn by Miss Marguerite Courtot in this series furnished by Russek, of Fifth Avenue, New York City." Fashion tie-ins were usually promoted as a big asset. A publicity article in *Motion Picture News* for Pathé's series *Who's Guilty?* announces that "all of Miss Nilsson's gowns in the *Who's Guilty?* series were made especially for her by Hickson, the Fifth Avenue modiste. The striking blonde beauty that is one of Miss Nilsson's chiefest charms is admirably set off by the queenly sweep of the frocks that Hickson has furnished her. There seldom are fewer than four Hickson gowns to each *Who's Guilty?* photo-novel, but in one Miss Nilsson is seen in fourteen of the smartest costumes that Hickson could turn out" (" 'Who's Guilty?' Series Will Come from Pathé May 8," *Motion Picture News*, April 22, 1916, 23).

    Charles Eckert's article, "The Carole Lombard in Macy's Window" (*Quarterly Review of Film Studies* 3.1, Winter 1978: 1–22), describes the pervasiveness in the 1930s of the use of movies to advertise particular fashion lines. It is evident from series and serial fashion tie-ins that this practice had already been fully implemented by the mid-teens.

6. Laura Mulvey, "Visual Pleasure and Narrative Cinema," *Screen* 16.3 (Autumn 1975): 6–18.

7. Karen Horney, *New Ways in Psychoanalysis*, 108.

8. Frank Wiesberg, "Review of 'Just Like a Woman,' " *Variety*, July 11, 1908.

9. "Women and Street Cars," *The Independent* 71.3271 (August 10, 1911): 330–32 (quotation from 331).

10. "Why Women Are, or Are Not, Good Chauffeuses," *Outing Magazine* 44.2 (May 1904): 154–59 (quotation from 156–57).

11. Montgomery Rollins, "Women and Motor Cars," *The Outlook* 92 (August 7, 1909): 859–60. For a dissenting view from a woman's perspective, see Mrs. Andrew Cuneo, "Why There Are So Few Women Automobilists," *Country Life in America* 13.5 (March, 1908): 515–16.

12. Statistics on female earnings contributions in "Report on Conditions of Women and Child Wage Earners in the United States," reprinted in part in The Commonwealth of Massachusetts, *Report of the Commission on Minimum Wage Boards* (Boston: January 1912): 260–61, 288–89, 318–19.

13. Lewis Jacobs, *The Rise of the American Film: A Critical History* (1939), 270; reprinted in 1969.

14. For information on marriage and fertility rates between 1880 and 1920, see Margaret Gibbons Wilson, *The American Woman in Transition: The Urban Influence,*

1870–1920, 174. Concerning changes in the nature of housework, see Ruth Schwartz Cowan, "The 'Industrial Revolution' in the Home: Household Technology and Social Change in the 20th Century," *Technology and Culture* 17 (January 1976): 1–23; reprinted in Martha M. Trescott, ed., *Dynamos and Virgins Revisited: Women and Technological Change in History*, 205–232. Information about female participation in extradomestic work is in Alba M. Edwards, *Comparative Occupation Statistics for the United States, 1870–1940*, 99, and Joseph A. Hill, *Women in Gainful Occupation, 1870–1920*, 23; both are cited in Elyce Rotella, *From Home to Office: U.S. Women at Work, 1870–1930* (see tables 2.2, 2.4, and 2.8).

15. Department store figures are found in Harold Barger, *Distribution's Place in the American Economy Since 1869*, 148–49, cited in Wilson, *The American Woman in Transition*, 174. Concerning involvement in public entertainments, see Kathy Peiss, *Cheap Amusements: Working Women and Leisure in Turn-of-the-Century New York*; Rabinovitz, *For the Love of Pleasure*; and Shelley Stamp, *Movie-Struck Girls: Women and Motion Picture Culture After the Nickelodeon*.

16. Miles of tracks in the Northeast increased from 2,952 in 1890 to 10,175 in 1902. In the United States as a whole, coverage rose 178 percent, from 8,123 to 22,589. U.S. Department of Commerce and Labor, *Special Reports: Street and Electric Railways* (1903): 34; table broken down by region reproduced in Wilson, *The American Woman in Transition*, 27.

    Throughout 1895, Sunday editions of the more popular newspapers, such as the *New York World* and the *New York Journal*, were full of articles and illustrations concerning the appropriation of the bicycle by women. These items clearly demarcate the bicycle as the nexus of a social debate between the New Woman, enjoying a new athleticism and mobility, and conservative forces denouncing the compromise of gentility and specifically condemning the appearance of "bloomers" as a clothing for feminine outdoor activity. See, for example, Ida Trafford Bell, "The Mission of the Bicycle for Women: Women's Fight for Liberation," *New York Sunday World*, August 18, 1895, 33; and "Around the World on a Bicycle: Nellie Bly, Jr. Makes the Most Extraordinary Journey Ever Undertaken by a Woman," *New York Sunday World*, October 20, 1895, 29. For a contemporary discussion, see "Reframing the Bicycle: Magazines and Scorching Women," ch. 4 in Garvey, *The Adman in the Parlor*, 109–134.

17. Mary Humphreys, "Women Bachelors in New York," *Scribner's* 19.5 (November 1896): 635.

18. Barbara Welter, "The Cult of True Womanhood: 1820–1860," *American Quarterly* 18 (Summer 1966): 151–74.

19. George Burnap, *The Sphere and Duties of Woman* (1854), 47; cited in Welter, "The Cult of True Womanhood," 159.

20. Boyd Winchester, "The New Woman," *Arena* (April 1902): 367; cited in Wilson, *The American Woman in Transition*, 3. A recent book on the new woman, with a British emphasis, is Sally Ledger, *The New Woman: Fiction and Feminism at the Fin de Siècle*.

21. Samuel Woodworth, *The Widow's Son; Or, Which Is the Traitor?* (New Yor,k, 1825), 64 (cited in Grimsted, *Melodrama Unveiled*, 175); Minna Thomas Antrim, "The Masculization of Girls," *Lippincott's Monthly* 88, no. 526 (October, 1911): 564. The 1911 film reviewer was Louis Reeves Harrison, "Superior Plays: 'The Reform Candidate' (Edison)," *Moving Picture World*, September 30, 1911, 957. Gaylyn Studlar discusses the compensatory reaction to this conception of female masculinization (and male feminization) in her impressive analysis of the discourses surrounding the stardom of Douglas Fairbanks (Studlar, *This Mad Masquerade: Stardom and Masculinity in the Jazz Age*, ch. 1).

22. Antrim, "The Masculization of Girls," 565.

23. The play is anthologized in Booth, ed., *Hiss the Villain*.

24. See review of *In Old Kentucky* in the *New York Tribune*, October 24, 1893, 7, and in "Stage Notes: 'The Eye Witness,' " *Brooklyn Daily Eagle*, February 24, 1907, sec. 4, p. 2; review of *The Factory Girl* in the *New York Tribune*, October 24, 1893, 7; review of *Through Fire and Water* in the *Brooklyn Daily Eagle*, October 4, 1903, 8; reference to *A Woman's Pluck* in Archibald Haddon, "Sensational Melodrama," *London Daily Express*, August 28, 1905; " 'Girl and Detective' Again," *Brooklyn Daily Eagle*, October 31, 1909, sec. 2, p. 9.; review of *No Mother to Guide Her* in newspaper clipping from some time in 1905, no source or date (Harvard Theatre Collection, "No Mother to Guide Her" file).

25. Ramsaye, *A Million and One Nights*, 653.

26. "Woman's Record During the Week," *New York Sunday World*, April 19, 1896, 21.

27. "Met a Woman with Nerve," *Newark Daily Advertiser*, March 9, 1895, 1.

28. A variety of titles headed these columns. One that is particularly interesting in its feminist sarcasm is "Frail Woman's Achievements: New and Startling Records Made by Her During the Week—Some Extraordinary Freaks and Fashions of the Season," *New York Sunday World*, April 12, 1896, 31.

29. *Boston American*, June 22, 1904, 10.

30. *Bizarre Katalog: Cartoon and Model Parade* (1979), vol. 1, 172–73.

31. Extracts in order of quotation are from (1) an editorial in the *Chicago Republic*, December 28, 1903, 6; (2) Porter Emerson Browne, "The Mellowdrammer," *Everybody's Magazine* 21.3 (September 1909): 347–54; (3) "Downfall of Melodrama," *New York Sun*, February 10, 1909, 7;(4) Hartt, *The People at Play*, 166; (5) Hamilton, "Melodrama, Old and New," *The Bookman* 33.3 (May 1911): 309–14.

32. Elsaesser, "Tales of Sound and Fury."

33. William A. Brady, an important theatrical producer, complained that American melodrama's use of bourgeois rather than aristocratic villains put it at a disadvantage against the greater moral extremes allowable in British melodrama. Brady, "Melodrama—What It Is and How to Make It," 313.

34. Eleanor Gates, "The Girl Who Travels Alone: An Inquiry into a Distinctly American Problem That Has Been Created by the Social Conditions in This Country Which Admit The Widest Liberty to Women," *Cosmopolitan Magazine* 42.2 (December

1906): 163–72. In the next month's issue, Gates discusses similar problems of sexual harassment as they relate specifically to working women: "Making Her Way in the World," ibid. (January 1907): 308–15.

35. Hugo Münsterberg, "Muensterberg Vigorously Denounces Red Light Drama," *New York Times*, September 14, 1913, n.p.

36. On white slavery films, see Shelley Stamp, *Movie-Struck Girls*, 41–101; Janet Staiger, *Bad Women: Regulating Sexuality in Early American Cinema*, 116–46.

9. Marketing Melodrama: Serials and Intertextuality

1. Robert Grau, "Motion Picture Publicity from the Standpoint of a Famous Critic," *The Editor and Publisher and the Journalist* 48.24 (November 20, 1915): 634.

2. Figures for 1916 film schedule changes are published in L. C. Moen, "Statistics of the Motion Picture Industry," *Motion Picture News*, November 25, 1922, 2655. Figures for 1919 appear in William M. Seabury, *The Public and the Motion Picture Industry*, 277; cited in Richard Koszarski, *An Evening's Entertainment: The Age of the Silent Feature Picture, 1915–1928*, 35.

3. "Movies of the Future: A Review and Prophecy," *McClure's Magazine* 47 (October 1916): 14–15, 87 (quotation from 14). See also E. Lanning Masters, "Marketing the Movies," *Harper's Weekly*, January 1, 1916, 24; "Series Idea Means Cumulative Advertising," *Motion Picture News*, October 21, 1916, 2552; "Series Backed by Big Magazine Publicity," *Motion Picture News*, January 6, 1917, 97; and Quimby, "A Standard Feature," 71.

4. Cited, without reference, in Lahue, *Continued Next Week*, 38. For details on how I calculated money equivalences, see ch. 6, n. 14, above.

5. Pathé's claim appears in "The Growth of Eclectic in a Year," *Motion Picture News*, June 13, 1914, 69; Paramount's in "Paramount Announces Details of Vast Advertising Campaign on First Serial," *Motion Picture News*, October 6, 1917, 2342. For Vitagraph reference, see "Problems and Power of Serials," *Motion Picture News*, September 22, 1917, 1984, 1989.

   On billboards: according to the Outdoor Advertising Association of America, expenditures for outdoor advertising escalated from $2 million a year in 1900 to $4 million in 1912, $15 million in 1917, and $35 million in 1921. Statistics cited in Alfred M. Lee, *The Daily Newspaper in America*, 366.

6. Ramsaye describes the first *Tribune* contest in *A Million and One Nights*, 669. Ramsaye as winner of *Diamond* sequel noted, unfortunately without citations, in Lahue, *Continued Next Week*, 6 and 46 (Lahue misses the connection). Other serial contests are discussed in Shelley Stamp, *Movie-Struck Girls*, 120–22, and mentioned in *Continued Next Week*, 6, and in Lahue, *Bound and Gagged*, 125. On the sequel-plot contest, see "Four-Chapter Sequel to 'The Diamond from the Sky,'" *Motion Picture News*, December 2, 1916, 3479; and advertisement, *Moving Picture World*, March 27, 1915, 1882–83. These prize-contest figures in today's dollars sound rather high to me. The conversion may not always be very reliable, since the makeup of the bushel of

goods and services used in the consumer price index has changed considerably over time.

7. Lahue, *Bound and Gagged*, 139.

8. Richard deCordova, *Picture Personalities: The Emergence of the Star System in America*.

9. "Popular Player Contest," *Motion Picture Magazine* 12.11 (December 1916): 15. On the rise of the star system, fan magazines, and fandom, see Kathryn H. Fuller, *At the Picture Show: Small-Town Audiences and the Creation of Movie Fan Culture*. For a discussion of these topics with respect to serials and female moviegoers in particular, see Stamp, *Movie-Struck Girls*, ch. 3.

10. For an exhaustive analysis of the characteristics and techniques of early narrative cinema, see Charlie Keil, *Early American Cinema in Transition: Story, Style, and Filmmaking, 1907–1913*.

11. Throughout this chapter, circulation figures are taken from various yearly editions of the *American Newspaper Annual and Directory*, which despite its title contains statistics for thousands of magazines and trade journals as well as newspapers.

12. Fuller discusses *Motion Picture Story Magazine* as an arena for fan participation in *At the Picture Show*, ch. 6.

13. An article in the *New York Dramatic Mirror* (January 10, 1912, 30) mentions a photoplay-story magazine called *Moving Picture Tales*, published by the *Motion Picture News*. I have found no trace of such a publication.

14. The superabundance of tie-ins in *Moving Picture Stories* underscores the fact that, although almost completely overlooked so far as a research tool, tie-ins offer scholars a glimpse at the plots and themes of many thousand lost films. They provide more information than the synopses found in trade journals and studio bulletins, and most include several production stills.

15. All the tie-ins were on page seven of the "Special Features Section" (sec. 7) of the *Chicago Tribune*. These tie-ins included "Paid Back: A Photoplay in Story Form" (Selig Polyscope; 16 stills), *Chicago Tribute*, January 7; "The Prosecuting Attorney" (Selig Polyscope; 12 stills), ibid., January 14; "The Melody of Love" (Essanay; 9 stills), ibid., January 21; "The Real Estate Fraud" (American Film Mfg. Co.; 16 stills), ibid., January 28; "The Hospital Baby" (Essanay; 12 stills), ibid., February 4; "The Test" (Selig Polyscope; 12 stills), ibid., February 11; "An Interrupted Romance," by Amanda Buckman (Essanay; 8 stills), ibid., February 18; "Love Versus Genius" (Essanay; 12 stills), ibid., February 25 (see also fig. 9.6, this volume); "An Assisted Elopement" (American Film Mfg. Co.; 10 stills), ibid., March 3; "The Loan Shark" (Essanay; 12 stills), ibid., March 10.

16. For example, the *Popular Magazine* (circulation 400,000) storyized American's two-reeler *Her Big Story* in April 1913. The *Ladies' World* ran a number of Edison and Essanay tie-ins between late 1913 and early 1915 (the following information is somewhat incomplete since it comes from various trade journal articles and ads): *Peg o' the Movies* (Edison, 2 reels, released December 12, 1913); *A Romany Spy* (3 reels, c. March 18, 1914); *The Greater Love* (2 reels, c. March 25, 1914); *The Tell-Tale Hand* (Essanay,

November 18, 1914); *The Plum Tree* (Essenay); *The Glare of the Lights* (Essenay); *Poison* (2 reels, c. March 17, 1915). The *Associated Sunday Magazine*, a Sunday newspaper supplement (circulation 1.5 million), published a photoplay story of Edison's two-reeler *Sheep's Clothing*, released September 18, 1914.

17. The New York papers included the *American*, the *Globe and Commercial Advertiser*, the *Journal*, the *Mail*, the *Sun*, the *Times*, the *Tribune*, and the *World*. Only the *New York Times* eschewed fictionalization tie-ins. The Boston papers included the *American*, the *Globe*, the *Herald and Traveler*, and the *Post*. I am defining a major newspaper as one having over 150,000 circulation.

18. "Kathlyn, Popular Queen," *New York Dramatic Mirror*, January 21, 1914, 31; Frank Leroy Blanchard, "Photo-Play Makers Are Spending a Million a Year in Newspapers," *The Editor and Publisher and the Journalist* 48.21 (October 30, 1915): 529; "Problems and Power of Serials," *Motion Picture News*, September 22, 1917, 1984, 1989; and "Keeping Up Interest in Serials," *Motion Picture News*, October 6, 1917, 2336, 2341.

19. Quotation combines passages from "Problems and Power of Serials" and "Keeping Up Interest in Serials," ibid.

20. "Boosting Pathé Pictures," *Moving Picture World*, March 14, 1914, 1392.

21. "On the Photoplay Serial: An Interview with Eustice Hale Ball," *The Editor*, April 7, 1917, 294–96; Fred J. Balshofer and Arthur C. Miller, *One Reel a Week*, 102–104.

22. Stamp, *Movie-Struck Girls*, 115–20.

23. *Chicago Sunday Tribune*, December 13, 1914, part 5 (color section).

24. Cohn, "Harvesting the Serial," 22.

Conclusion

1. Siegfried Kracauer, "Georg Simmel" in *The Mass Ornament*, ed. and trans. Thomas Y. Levin, 225–58.

2. Quotation from Eisenstein, "Dickens, Griffith, and Film Today" (1944), in Leyda, ed., *Sergei Eisenstein: Film Form*, 195–255.

3. Janet Staiger, *Bad Women: Regulating Sexuality in Early American Cinema*; Lauren Rabinovitz, *For the Love of Pleasure: Women, Movies, and Culture in Turn-of-the-Century Chicago*; Jennifer M. Bean, "Bodies in Shock: Gender, Genre, and the Cinema of Modernity" (Ph.D. diss., University of Texas, Austin, 1998; forthcoming published version in progress); Shelley Stamp, *Movie-Struck Girls*. Stamp's book appeared too late for me to integrate its findings adequately into my exposition. The chapter entitled "Ready-Made Customers: Female Movie Fans and the Serial Craze" (ch. 3, pp. 102–153) contains superb research that complements, and in places qualifies, the material I present in my chapters 7, 8, and 9.

Bibliography

Abel, Richard. *The Ciné Goes to Town: French Cinema, 1896–1914*. Berkeley: University of California Press, 1994.

——. *French Cinema: The First Wave, 1915–1929*. Princeton: Princeton University Press, 1984.

——. *French Film Theory and Criticism: A History/Anthology, 1907–1939*, vol. 1. Princeton: Princeton University Press, 1988.

——. *Silent Cinema*. New Brunswick, N.J.: Rutgers University Press, 1995.

Abercrombie, Nicholas, Stephen Hill, and Bryan S. Turner. *Sovereign Individuals of Capitalism*. London: Allen and Unwin, 1986.

Adams, Henry. *The Education of Henry Adams* (1917). Rpt., New York: Modern Library, 1931.

Adams, Judith A. *The American Amusement Park Industry: A History of Technology and Thrills*. Boston: Twayne, 1991.

Adelman, Melvin L. "Modernization Theory and Its Critics." In Mary Kupiec Cayton, Elliott J. Gorn, and Peter W. Williams, eds., *Encyclopedia of American Social History* 1:347–58. New York: Scribner's, 1993.

"All International Films to Be Released Through Pathé." *Motion Picture News*, January 13, 1917, 227.

Altman, Rick. "Dickens, Griffith, and Film Theory Today." *South Atlantic Quarterly* 88.2 (1989): 321–59. Reprinted in Jane Gaines, ed., *Classical Hollywood Narrative: The Paradigm Wars*, 9–47. Durham, N.C.: Duke University Press, 1992.

——. *Film/Genre*. London: British Film Institute, 1999.

American Film Institute Catalog: Feature Films, 1911–1920. Berkeley: University of California Press, 1988.

American Newspaper Annual and Directory (various issues). Philadelphia: N. W. Ayer, 1915 (and various).

Ames, Hector. "Helen Gibson, the Kalem Madcap." *Motion Picture Magazine* 13.5 (June 1917): 114–17.

"Among the Gods: The Boys Who Fill the Gallery." *New York Daily Tribune*, November 1, 1896, 5.

Anderson, Nels and Eduard C. Lindeman. *Urban Sociology: An Introduction to the Study of Urban Communities*. New York: Knopf, 1928.

Antrim, Minna Thomas. "The Masculization of Girls." *Lippincott's Monthly Magazine* 88.526 (October 1911): 564.

"Are the Movies a Menace to the Drama?" *Current Opinion* 62.5 (May 1917): 331.

Asterita, Mary F. *The Physiology of Stress, with Special Reference to the Neuroendocrine System.* New York: Human Sciences Press, 1985.

"At Brooklyn Theaters." *Brooklyn Daily Eagle*, October 6, 1907, sec. 2, p. 8.

"At Brooklyn Theatres." *Brooklyn Daily Eagle*, December 22, 1907, sec. 4, p. 2.

Atoji, Yoshio. *Sociology at the Turn of the Century: On G. Simmel in Comparison with F. Tonnies, M. Weber, and E. Durkheim.* Translated by Y. Atoji, K. Okazawa, and T. Ogane. Tokyo: Dobukan, 1984.

Baker, Garry and Robert Franken. "Effects of Stimulus Size, Brightness, and Complexity upon EEG Desynchronization." *Psychonomic Science* 7 (1967): 289–90.

Baker, H. Barton. "The Old Melodrama." *Belgravia* 50.199 (May 1883): 331–39.

Balides, Constance. "Scenarios of Exposure in Everyday Life: Women in the Cinema of Attractions." *Screen* 34.1 (Spring 1993): 19–31.

Balshofer, Fred J. and Arthur C. Miller. *One Reel a Week.* Berkeley: University of California Press, 1967.

Barbour, Alan G. *Cliffhanger: A Pictorial History of the Motion Picture Serial.* Secaucus, N.J.: Citadel, 1977.

Bardedne, Maurice and Maurice Brasillach. *The History of Motion Pictures.* Translated and edited by Iris Barry. New York: Norton, 1938.

Barger, Harold. *Distribution's Place in the American Economy Since 1869.* Princeton: Princeton University Press, 1955.

Barnes, Earl. "The Feminizing of Culture." *Atlantic Monthly* 109.6 (June 1912): 770–76.

Barr, Amelia E. "Discontented Women." *North American Review* 162.471 (February 1896): 201–209.

Barrett, William. *Death of the Soul: From Descartes to the Computer.* Garden City, N.Y.: Anchor/Doubleday, 1986.

Bean, Jennifer M. "Bodies in Shock: Gender, Genre, and the Cinema of Modernity." Ph.D. diss., University of Texas, Austin, 1998 (forthcoming published version in progress).

Beard, George. *American Nervousness.* New York, 1881.

Becker, Reinhold E. "The Principle of Suggestion in Art as Applied to the Photoplay." *The Editor* 46.11 (September 12, 1917): 323–25.

Beckman, Frank J. "The Vanished Villains: An Exercise in Nostalgia" (unpublished typescript). New York: New York Public Library, Theater College, c. 1950.

Bell, Ida Trafford. "The Mission of the Bicycle for Women: Women's Fight for Liberation." *New York Sunday World*, August 18, 1895, 33.

Benjamin, Walter. "On Some Motifs in Baudelaire" (1939). In Hannah Arendt, ed., *Illuminations*, 155–200. Translated by Harry Zohn, New York: Schocken, 1968. (The original sources of Benjamin's essays are listed on page 266 of this collection.)

——. "The Work of Art in the Age of Mechanical Reproduction" (1936). In Arendt, ed., *Illuminations*, 217–51. New York: Schocken, 1968.

Bentley, Eric. *The Life of the Drama.* New York: Atheneum, 1964.

Berlyne, D. E. *Aesthetics and Psychobiology.* New York: Appleton-Century-Crofts, 1971.

——. *Conflict, Arousal, and Curiosity.* New York: McGraw-Hill, 1960.

Berlyne, D. E. and George H. Lawrence. "Effects of Complexity and Incongruity Variables on GSR, Investigatory Behavior, and Verbally Expressed Preference." *Journal of General Psychology* 71 (1964): 21–54.

Berlyne, D. E. et al. "Effects of Auditory Pitch and Complexity on EEG Desynchronization and on Verbally Expressed Judgements." *Canadian Journal of*

Psychology 21.4 (1967): 346–57.

——. "Novelty, Complexity, Incongruity, Extrinsic Motivation, and the GSR [Galvanic Skin Response]." *Journal of Experimental Psychology* 63.6 (1963): 560–67.

"Bertha at Folly" (review). *Brooklyn Daily Eagle*, September 4, 1906, 4.

"Bertha, the Sewing Machine Girl." *Brooklyn Daily Eagle*, October 6, 1906, sec. 2, pp. 8–9.

Bizarre Katalog: Cartoon and Model Parade, vol. 1. New York: Belier Press, 1979.

Black, C. E. *The Dynamics of Modernization: A Study of Contemporary History.* New York: Harper and Row, 1966.

Black, Max. "Definition, Presupposition, and Assertion." *Problems of Analysis: Philosophical Essays*, 24–45. Ithaca: Cornell University Press, 1954.

——. "How Do Pictures Represent?" In E. H. Gombrich, Julian Hochberg, and Max Black, eds., *Art, Perception, and Reality*, 95–129. Baltimore: Johns Hopkins University Press, 1972.

Blackbeard, Bill. "Pulps." In M. Thomas Inge, ed., *Concise Histories of American Popular Culture.*, 289–307. Westport, Conn.: Greenwood, 1982.

Blanchard, Frank Leroy. "Photo-play Makers Are Spending a Million a Year in Newspapers." *The Editor and Publisher and the Journalist* 48.21 (October 30, 1915): 529.

Bonner, Geraldine. "Women and the Unpleasant Novel." *The Critic* 48 (February 1906): 172–75.

Booth, Michael R. *English Melodrama.* London: Herbert Jenkins, 1965.

——. *Victorian Spectacular Theatre, 1850–1910.* Boston: Routledge and Kegan Paul, 1981.

Booth, Michael R., ed. "Introduction." *Hiss the Villain: Six English and American Melodramas.* New York: Benjamin Bloom, 1964; London: Eyre and Spottiswoode, 1964.

Bordwell, David. *On the History of Film Style.* Cambridge: Harvard University Press, 1997.

Bordwell, David, Janet Staiger, and Kristin Thompson. *The Classical Hollywood Cinema: Film Style and Mode of Production to 1960.* New York: Columbia University Press, 1985.

"Boston Theatre: 'The Wolves of New York,' " May 19, 1891. (Clipping, Harvard Theatre Collection. Journal is probably the *Boston Evening Transcript*, not the *Boston Herald*, the *Boston Advertiser*, or the *Boston Post*.)

Bottomore, Tom. *Theories of Modern Capitalism.* London: Allen and Unwin, 1985.

"Bowery Amusements." *Annual Report* (New York City, 1899), 14–19.

Boyd, Ernest A. "The 'Movie Fan.' " *The New Statesman* 10 (March 30, 1918): 617.

Brady, William A. "Melodrama Revivals." *New York Times*, May 7, 1911, 2.

——. "Melodrama—What It Is and How to Make It." *Green Book* 14 (August 1915): 310–13.

Bregy, Katherine. *From Dante to Jeanne d'Arc: Adventures in Medieval Life and Letters.* Port Washington, N.Y.: Kennikat Press, 1933.

"Brief Review of Serial(s)." *Variety*, August 18, 1916, n.p.

"Bringing Serial Profits Home." *Motion Picture News*, September 29, 1917, 2152, 2212.

Brooks, Peter. "Melodrama, Body, Revolution." In Jacky Bratton et al., eds., *Melodrama: Stage, Picture, Screen.* London: British Film Institute, 1994.

——. *The Melodramatic Imagination: Balzac, Henry James, Melodrama, and the Mode of Excess* (1976). New York: Columbia University Press, 1985.

Brooks, Sydney. "The American Yellow Press." *Fortnightly Review* 96 (December 1911): 1126–37.

Browne, Porter Emerson. "The Mellowdrammer." *Everybody's Magazine* 21.3 (September 1909): 347–54.

Brubaker, Rogers. *The Limits of Rationality: An Essay on the Social and Moral Thought of Max Weber.* London: Allen and Unwin, 1984.

Bruner, Frank. "The Modern Dime Novel." *Photoplay* 16 (January 1919): 48–49, 118.

Bruno, Giuliana. *Streetwalking on a Ruined Map: Cultural Theory and the City Films of Elvira Notari.* Princeton: Princeton University Press, 1993.

Buck-Morss, Susan. "Aesthetic and Anaesthetics: Walter Benjamin's Artwork Essay Reconsidered." *New Formations* 20 (Summer 1993): 123–43.

Buffet, Gabriele. "The Superiority of American to European Films as Explained by a French Critic." *Current Opinion* 63.4 (October 1917): 250–51.

Buñuel, Luis. *My Last Sigh.* Translated by Abigail Israel. New York: Vintage, 1984.

Burnap, George. *The Sphere and Duties of Woman.* 5th ed. Baltimore, 1854. Cited in Barbara Welter, "The Cult of True Womanhood: 1820–1860," *American Quarterly* 18 (Summer 1966): 151–74.

Burnstein, Jules. "An Exchange Man's Views." *New York Dramatic Mirror*, January 27, 1915, 43.

Bush, W. Stephen. "The Added Attraction." *Moving Picture World*, November 18, 1911, 533.

——. "Facing an Audience." *Moving Picture World*, September 16, 1911, 771.

——. "Signs of a Harvest." *Moving Picture World*, August 5, 1911, 272.

" 'The Business of Smash' Coins Term: 'Canned Holocausts.' " *Photoplay* 7.5 (April 1915): 57–63.

Butcher, S. H. *Aristotle's Theory of Poetry and Fine Art* (1895). 4th ed. London: Macmillan, 1927.

Cahnman, Werner J., ed. *Ferdinand Tönnies: A New Evaluation—Essays and Documents.* Leiden, Netherlands: E. J. Brill, 1973.

Cahoon, Haryot Holt. "Women in Gutter Journalism." *Arena* 17 (March 1897): 568–74.

Cail, Harold. "On Owen Davis." [Unknown Boston newspaper, 1939, n.p.] (clipping, Harvard Theatre Collection).

Cannon, W. B. "The Emergency Function of the Adrenal Medulla in Pain and the Major Emotions." *American Journal of Physiology* 33 (1914): 356–72.

Cannon, W. B. and D. Paz. "Emotional Stimulation of Adrenal Gland Secretion." *American Journal of Physiology* 28 (1911): 64–70.

Carpenter, Niles. *The Sociology of City Life.* New York: Longmans, Green, 1932.

Cartmell, Robert. *The Incredible Scream Machine: A History of the Roller Coaster.* Bowling Green, Ohio: Bowling Green State University Press, 1987.

Cary, Harold. "Life to the Wind for the Movies." *Technical World Magazine* 20.6 (February 1914): 866–71.

Cecil, Mirabel. *Heroines in Love, 1750–1974.* London: Michael Joseph, 1974.

Chandler, Tertius and Gerald Fox. *3000 Years of Urban Growth.* New York: Academic Press, 1974.

Charney, Leo and Vanessa R. Schwartz, eds. *Cinema and the Invention of Modern Life.* Berkeley: University of California Press, 1995.

"Chinatown Charlie." *New York Dramatic Mirror*, 1906 (n.d., n.p.) (clipping, Harvard Theatre Collection).

"Chinatown Trunk Mystery." *Boston Globe*, August 9, 1910, n.p.

Claudy, C. H. "The Degradation of the Motion Picture." *Photo-Era* 21.4 (October 1908): 161–65.

Clover, Carol. *Men, Women, and Chainsaws: Gender in the Modern Horror Film.* Princeton: Princeton University Press, 1992.

Cohen, Jan. *Romance and the Erotics of Property: Mass Market Fiction for Women.* Durham, N.C.: Duke University Press, 1988.

Cohn, Alfred A. "Harvesting the Serial." *Photoplay* 11.3 (February 1917): 19–26.

Collier, John. "Cheap Amusements." *Charities and the Commons* 20 (April 11, 1908): 73–78.

Colquhoun, Ethel. "Modern Feminism and Sex Antagonism." *Living Age* 278 (September 6, 1913): 579–94.

Commonwealth of Massachusetts. *Report of the Commission on Minimum Wage Boards.* Boston: January 1912.

"Concerning the New Woman and Her Doings." *New York World*, May 24, 1896, 24.

Cook, David A. *A History of Narrative Film.* New York: Norton, 1981; 2d ed., 1996.

Cook, Burr C. "Realism: The New Word in the Movies." *Motion Picture Magazine* 11.6 (July 1916): 49–54.

"Cool Reception for Melodrama." *New York Dramatic Mirror*, October 14, 1916, n.p.

Cooper, Frederic Taber. "Feminine Unrest and Some Recent Novels." *The Bookman* 30 (December 1909): 382–88.

——. "The Taint of Melodrama and Some Recent Books." *The Bookman* 22.6 (February 1906): 630–35.

Corbin, John. "How the Other Half Laughs." *Harper's New Monthly Magazine* 98.583 (December 1898): 30–48.

Cowan, Ruth Schwartz. "The 'Industrial Revolution' in the Home: Household Technology and Social Change in the 20th Century." In Martha M. Trescott, ed., *Dynamos and Virgins: Women and Technological Change in History*, 205–232. Methuen, N.J.: Scarecrow Press, 1979. Originally published in *Technology and Culture* 17 (January 1976): 1–23.

Craig, Patricia and Mary Cadogan. *The Lady Investigates: Women Detectives and Spies in Fiction.* New York: St. Martin's, 1981.

Crain, C. D. "Fights for Men, Finery for Women." *Moving Picture World*, July 29, 1916, 818.

Crary, Jonathan. "Dr. Mabuse and Mr. Edison." *Hall of Mirrors: Art and Film Since 1945*, 262–79. Los Angeles: Museum of Contemporary Art and Monacelli Press, 1996.

——. *Suspensions of Perception: Attention, Spectacle, and Modern Culture.* Cambridge: M.I.T. Press, 1999.

——. *Techniques of the Observer: On Vision and Modernity in the Nineteenth Century.* Cambridge, Mass.: MIT Press, 1990.

Cuneo, Mrs. Andrew. "Why There Are So Few Women Automobilists." *Country Life in America* 13.5 (March 1908): 515–16.

Currie, Barton W. "The Nickel Madness." *Harper's Weekly*, August 24, 1907, 1246–47.

Dale, Alan. "Boom of 'Mellerdrama,' " *New York Journal*, February 12, 1899, 26.

——. "The Tear-Drenched Drama." *Cosmopolitan Magazine* 48.2 (January 1910): 199–205.

Dalton, Charles. *Evening World* (city not determined), January 25, 1906, n.p. (clipping, Robinson Locke Collection, New York Public Library, catalogued "NAFR Ser. 2.26": scrapbook page 87).

"A Daring Woman's Perilous Promenade / A Woman's Giddy Walk / She Walks Around the Ledge of the Lofty American Surety Building and Writes to the Sunday World About Her Feelings." *New York World*, May 17, 1896, 27.

"Davis Talks of His Plays." [Unknown publication], December 7, 1924, n.p. (clipping, Harvard Theatre Collection).

Davis, Glenmore. "The Moving-Picture Revolution." *Success Magazine* 13.192 (April 1910): 238–40, 271.

Davis, Michael M. *The Exploitation of Pleasure.* New York: Russell Sage Foundation, 1911.

Davis, Owen. *I'd Like to Do It Again.* New York: Farrar and Rinehart, 1931.

——. *My First Fifty Years in the Theatre.* Boston: Walter H. Baker, 1950.

——. "Wherein Owen Davis Recalls Days of Puritan Stage." *New York Herald Tribune*, March 2, 1941, n.p.

——. "Why I Quit Writing Melodrama." *American Magazine* 78.3 (September 1914): 28–31, 77–80.

"A Day with Bellevue's Insane/The 'New Woman' Present at the Examination by the Visiting and House Physicians." *New York World*, September 29, 1895, 35.

"The Decay of Melodrama." *The Nation* 6.23 (British) (March 5, 1910): 877–78. Reprinted in *The Living Age* 265.3432 (April 16, 1910): 182–84.

deCordova, Richard. *Picture Personalities: The Emergence of the Star System in America.* Urbana: University of Illinois Press, 1990.

Deland, Margaret. "The Change in the Feminine Ideal." *Atlantic Monthly* 105.3 (March 1910): 289–302.

Dennett, Andrea Stulman and Nina Warnke. "Disaster Spectacles at the Turn of the Century." *Film History* 4 (1990): 101–11.

"Dens of Chinatown Explored by a Woman/Steve Brodie Takes Her to See a 'Chink' Play, an Opium Joint and the Joss-House." *New York World*, May 10, 1896, 27.

Diamond, Marian Cleeves. *Enriching Heredity: The Impact of the Environment on the Anatomy of the Brain.* New York: Free Press, 1988.

"The Dime Museum Drama." *New York World*, April 16, 1893, 22.

"Doings, Ambitions, and Fashions of the New Woman." *New York World*, May 17, 1896, 24.

"Dorothy Dare on the Street in Boy's Clothes." *New York World*, April 12, 1896, 29.

"Dorothy Dare's Wild Night on a Lightship/In the Recent Storm when Even Stout Hearts of Sea-Faring Men Beat with Alarm." *New York World*, March 8, 1896, 25.

"Down in the Depths/Miss Margaret Leland Explores the Bottom of the Sea/The Daring Young Woman of the World Staff Risks the Dangers of a Diver." *New York World*, March 15, 1896, n.p.

"Drama Exploits Fiendish Crimes." [Unknown San Francisco newspaper, n.p. (clipping, Harvard Theatre Collection).

"Drama for West Siders." *New York Sun*, January 6, 1895, 4 (clipping, Harvard Theatre Collection, "Melodrama, General," file 3).

Dunbar, Olivia Howard. "The Lure of the Films." *Harper's Weekly*, January 18, 1913, 20, 22.

Dye, William S. *A Study of Melodrama in England from 1800 to 1840.* State College, Penn.: Nittany Printing, 1919.

Eaton, Walter Prichard. "The Canned Drama." *American Magazine* 68 (September 1909): 493–500.

——. "Class Consciousness and the Movies." *Atlantic Monthly* 115.1 (January 1915): 49–56.

——. "How to Write Plays." [Unknown publication], February 8, 1931, n.p. (clipping, Harvard Theatre Collection, "Owen Davis" file).

——. "Is 'Melodramatic Rubbish' Increasing?" *American Magazine* 82.6 (December 1916): 34, 114, 116.

——. "The Latest Menace of the Movies." *North American Review* 212.776 (July 1920): 80–87.

——. "The Theater: The Menace of the Movies." *American Magazine* 76.3 (September 1913): 55–60.

——. "The Theater: A New Epoch in the Movies." *American Magazine* 78.4 (October 1914): 44, 93, 95.

——. "Wanted—Moving Picture Authors." *American Magazine* 81.3 (March 1916): 67–73.

——. " 'Why Do You Fear Me, Nellie?' The Melodramas of Forty Years Ago." *Harper's* 183 (July 1941): 164–70.

Eckert, Charles. "The Carole Lombard in Macy's Window." *Quarterly Review of Film Studies* 3.1 (Winter 1978): 1–22.

Edwards, Alba M. *Comparative Occupation Statistics for the United States, 1870–1940.* U.S. Bureau of the Census, Washington, D.C.: GPO, 1943.

Egarth, Howard E. and Steven Yantis. "Visual Attention: Control, Representation, and Time Course." *Annual Review of Psychology* 48 (1997): 269–98.

Eisenstein, Sergei. "Dickens, Griffith, and Film Today" (1944). In Leyda, ed., *Sergei Eisenstein: Film Form*, 195–255.

——. "The Problem of the Materialist Approach to Form" (1925). In Richard Taylor, ed. and trans., *S. M. Eisenstein: Selected Works*, vol. 1, *Writings, 1922–34*, 59–64. Bloomington: Indiana University Press, 1988.

"Elliott's Dramatic Page." *Binghamton Chronicle*, n.d., 4 (clipping, Harvard Theatre Collection).

Elsaesser, Thomas. "Tales of Sound and Fury: Observations on the Family Melodrama." *Monogram* 4 (1972): 2–15. Reprinted in Christine Goldhill, ed., *Home Is Where the Heart Is: Studies in Melodrama and the Woman's Film*, 43–69. London: British Film Institute, 1987.

Elsaesser, Thomas, ed. *Early Cinema: Space, Frame, Narrative.* London: British Film Institute, 1990.

Engels, Friedrich. *The Condition of the Working Class in England* (1844). Translated and edited by W. O. Henderson and W. H. Chaloner. Oxford: Blackwell, 1958; rpt., Stanford: Stanford University Press, 1968.

Epstein, Jean. "Le Sens 1Bis." In *Bonjour Cinema*. Paris: Éditions de la Sirene, 1921. Translated by Stuart Liebman in his Ph.D. diss., "Jean Epstein's Early Film Theory, 1920–1922" (New York University, 1980). Also translated by Tom Milne in *Afterimage* 10 (Autumn 1981): 9–16; reprinted in Abel, *French Film Theory and Criticism*, vol. 1.

Erenberg, Lewis A. *Steppin' Out: New York Nightlife and the Transformation of American Culture, 1890–1930.* Chicago: University of Chicago Press, 1981

Estcourt, Charles, Jr. "New York Skylines" (syndicated newspaper column), from Springfield, Mass., paper, February 2, 1941 (clipping, Harvard Theatre Collection, "Owen Davis" file).

Evans, Gary W. et al. "Chronic Noise and Psychological Stress." *Psychological Science* 6.6 (November 1995): 333–38.

Evans, Gary W. et al. "Chronic Noise Exposure and Physiological Response: A Prospective Study of Children Living Under Environmental Stress." *Psychological Science* 9.1 (January 1998): 75–77.

Evans, Gary W. and Sheldon Cohen. "Environmental Stress." In Daniel Stokols and Irwin Altman, eds., *Handbook of Environmental Psychology*, 571–610. New York: Wiley, 1987.

Evans, Gary W. and Sybil Carrere. "Traffic Control, Perceived Control, and Psychophysiological Stress Among Urban Bus Drivers." *Journal of Applied Psychology* 76.5 (1991): 658–63.

Everly, George S. and Robert Rosenfeld. *The Nature and Treatment of the Stress Response: A Practical Guide for Clinicians.* New York: Plenum, 1981.

Everson, William K. "The Silent Serial." *Screen Facts* 1.1 (1963): 2–14.

"Exploits of the New Woman: The Emancipated Female's Latest Foibles and Freaks." *New York World*, November 10, 1895, 33.

"Failures on Stage: Merits That Were Overwhelmed by Ruinous Faults." *New York Sun*, February 23, 1894, n.d. (clipping, Harvard Theatre Collection, "Melodrama, General," file 3).

"The Fatal Wedding . . . at Grand Opera House." *Brooklyn Daily Eagle*, September 20, 1903, 8.

Featherstone, Mike. *Consumer Culture and Postmodernism.* London: Sage, 1991.

Fell, John L. *Film and the Narrative Tradition.* Berkeley: University of California Press, 1974.

——. *Film Before Griffith.* Berkeley: University of California Press, 1993.

"The Feuilleton." *Living Age* 229.2964 (April 27, 1901): 260–61.

Finck, Henry T. "Are Womanly Women Doomed?" *The Independent* 53.2722 (January 31, 1901): 267–71.

——. " 'Only a Girl.' " *The Independent* 53.2736 (May 9, 1901): 1061–64.

Firkins, O. W. "The Source of Pleasure in Familiar Plays." *North American Review* 197 (May 1913): 692–700.

Fitch, Walter M. "The Motion Picture Story Considered as a New Literary Form." *Moving Picture World*, n.d., n.p.

"A Flag of Truce." *Newark Daily Advertiser*, November 3, 1894, 4.

Foster, Rhea Dulles. *America Learns to Play: A History of Popular Recreation, 1607–1940.* New York: Appleton-Century, 1940.

Franklin, Barnett. "The Decline of the Stage Villain." *Overland Monthly* 53.3 (March 1909): 175–79.

Freedman, Estelle B. "The New Woman: Changing Views of Women in the 1920s." *Journal of American History* 61.2 (1974): 372–93.

Freeman, R. Austin. *Social Decay and Degeneration.* London: Constable, 1921.

Friedberg, Anne. *Window Shopping: Cinema and the Postmodern.* Berkeley: University of California Press, 1993.

Freud, Sigmund. "Beyond the Pleasure Principle" (1920). In vol. 18 of the *Standard Edition of the Complete Psychological Works*, 7–64. Edited by James Strachey. Translated by James Strachey, and others. London: Hogarth Press, 1953–1974.

Freuler, John R. "A Year of Picture History." *Reel Life*, January 1, 1916, 1.

Frisby, David. *Fragments of Modernity: Theories of Modernity in the Work of Simmel, Kracauer, and Benjamin.* Cambridge, Mass.: MIT Press, 1986.

——. *Simmel and Since: Essays on George Simmel's Social Theory.* London: Routledge, 1992.

Fuller, Kathryn H. *At the Picture Show: Small-Town Audiences and the Creation of Movie Fan Culture.* Washington, D.C.: Smithsonian Institution Press, 1996.

Gabin, Nancy F. "Women and Work." In Mary Kupiec Cayton, Elliott J. Gorn, and Peter W. Williams, eds., *Encyclopedia of American Social History* 2:1541–55. New York: Scribner's, 1993.

Gaddis, Pearl. "He, She, or It." *Motion Picture Magazine* 13.6 (July 1917): 27–33.

Gallagher, Tag. "Brother Feeney: Tag Gallagher on the Career of Francis Ford." *Film Comment* 12.6 (November-December 1976): 12–18.

Garvey, Ellen Gruber. *The Adman in the Parlor: Magazines and the Gendering of Consumer Culture, 1880s to 1910s*. New York: Oxford University Press, 1996.

Gates, Eleanor. "Best Seller Drama." *Harper's Weekly*, June 6, 1914, 20.

———. "The Girl Who Travels Alone: An Inquiry into a Distinctly American Problem That Has Been Created by the Social Conditions in This Country Which Admit the Widest Liberty to Women." *Cosmopolitan Magazine* 42.2 (December 1906): 163–72.

———. "Making Her Way in the World." *Cosmopolitan Magazine* 42.3 (January 1907): 308–15.

Gazzaniga, Michael S. et al. *Cognitive Neuroscience: The Biology of the Mind*. New York: Norton, 1998.

"George K. Spoor Urges Varied Program Use." *Motion Picture News*, August 25, 1917, 1262.

Gerould, Daniel and Jeanine Parisier, eds. *Melodrama*. Vol. 7. New York: New York Literary Forum, 1980.

Gevison, Alan. "The Birth of the American Feature Film." In Paolo Cherchi Usai and Lorenzo Codelli, eds., *The Path to Hollywood, 1911–1920*, 154. [City not available]: Edizioni Biblioteca dell'Imagine, 1988.

Gibson, David et al. "Effects of Size-Brightness and Complexity of Non-Meaningful Stimulus Material on EEG Synchronization." *Psychonomic Science* 8 (1967): 503–504.

Gibson, James J. *The Senses Considered as Perceptual Systems*. Boston: Houghton Mifflin, 1966.

Giddens, Anthony. *The Consequences of Modernity*. Stanford, Calif.: Stanford University Press, 1990.

Gilbert, Charles. "Neural Plasticity." In Robert A. Wilson and Frank C. Keil, eds., *The MIT Encyclopedia of the Cognitive Sciences*, 598–601. Cambridge, Mass.: MIT Press, 1999.

Gilbert, James B. *Work Without Salvations: America's Intellectuals and Industrial Alienation, 1880–1910*. Baltimore: Johns Hopkins University Press, 1977.

Girdner, J. H. "The Plague of City Noises." *North American Review* 163.478 (September 1896): 297.

Glanz, Rudolph. *Jew and Italian: Historic Group Relations and the New Immigration, 1881–1924*. New York: Ktav, 1970.

Gleber, Anke. *The Art of Taking a Walk: Flanerie, Literature, and Film in Weimar Culture*. Princeton, N.J.: Princeton University Press, 1999.

Gledhill, Christine, ed., *Home Is Where the Heart Is: Studies in Melodrama and the Woman's Film*. London: British Film Institute, 1987.

———. "The Melodramatic Field: An Investigation." In Gledhill, ed., *Home Is Where the Heart Is*, 5–39.

Goff, Lewin A. "The Popular-Priced Melodrama in America, 1890 to 1910, with Its Origins and Development to 1890." Ph.D. diss., Western Reserve University, 1948.

Goodman, Jules Eckert. "The Lure of Melodrama." [Unknown publication, n.d.]: 180–92 (clipping, Harvard Theatre Collection).

Gorky, Maxim. "Gorky on the Films, 1896." In Herbert Kline, ed., *New Theatre and Film, 1934 to 1937: An Anthology*, 227–33. New York: Harcourt Brace Jovanovich, 1985.

Grau, Robert. "Motion Picture Publicity from the Standpoint of a Famous Critic." *The Editor and Publisher and the Journalist* 48.24 (November 20, 1915): 634.

———. "The Moving-Picture Show and the Living Drama." *American Review of Reviews*

45.3 (March 1912): 329–36.

Greenberg, Clement. "Modernist Painting." In *The Collected Essays and Criticism* 4:85–93. Edited by John O'Brien. Chicago: University of Chicago Press, 1993.

Greusel, John Hubert. "In the Glare of Melodrama." *Associated Sunday Magazine*, November 8, 1908, 7–8.

Grimsted, David. "Melodrama as Echo of the Historically Voiceless." In Tamara K. Hareven, ed., *Anonymous Americans: Explorations in Nineteenth-Century Social History*. Englewood Cliffs, N.J.: Prentice-Hall, 1971.

——. *Melodrama Unveiled: American Theater and Culture, 1800–1850*. Chicago: University of Chicago Press, 1968.

Gunning, Tom. "An Aesthetics of Astonishment: Early Film and the (In)credulous Spectator." *Art and Text* 34 (Spring 1989): 31–45. Reprinted in Linda Williams, ed., *Viewing Positions: Ways of Seeing Film*, 114–33. New Brunswick, N.J.: Rutgers University Press, 1994.

——. "The Cinema of Attraction: Early Film, Its Spectator, and the Avant-garde." *Wide Angle* 8 (Fall 1986): 63–70. Reprinted as "The Cinema of Attractions" in Elsaesser, ed., *Early Cinema*, 56–62.

——. *D. W. Griffith and the Origins of the American Narrative Film*. Urbana: University of Illinois Press, 1991.

——. "Early American Film." In Hill and Gibson, eds., *The Oxford Guide to Film Studies*, 255–71.

——. "Heard Over the Phone: *The Lonely Villa* and the De Lorde Tradition of Terrified Communication." *Screen* 32.2 (Summer 1991): 184–96.

——. "The Whole Town's Gawking: Early Cinema and the Visual Experience of Modernity." *Yale Journal of Criticism* 7.2 (Fall 1994): 189–201.

——. "The World as Object Lesson: Cinema Audiences, Visual Culture, and the St. Louis World's Fair." *Film History* 5.4 (Winter 1994): 422–44.

Habermas, Jürgen. *The Philosophical Discourse of Modernity*. Cambridge, Mass.: MIT Press, 1987.

Haddon, Archibald. "Sensational Melodrama: Extreme Popularity of the Drama of Crime." *London Daily Express*, August 28, 1905, n.p. (clipping, Harvard Theatre Collection).

Hagedorn, Roger. "Technology and Economic Exploitation: The Serial Form of Narrative Presentation." *Wide Angle* 10.4 (1988): n.p.

Hake, Sabine. "Girls and Crisis: The Other Side of Diversion." *New German Critique* 40 (Winter 1987): n.p.

Hall, Stuart, David Held, Don Hubert, and Kenneth Thompson, eds. *Modernity: An Introduction to Modern Societies*. Oxford: Blackwell, 1996.

Halliday, E. M. " 'Curses, Foiled Again.' " *American Heritage* 15 (December 1963): 12–23.

Hamilton, Clayton. "Melodrama, Old and New." *The Bookman* 33.3 (May 1911): 309–14.

——. "Melodramas and Farces." *The Forum* 41.1 (January 1909): 23–27.

——. *Studies in Stagecraft*. New York: Holt, 1914.

Hamlyn, D. W. *Sensation and Perception: A History of the Philosophy of Perception*. New York: Humanities Press, 1961.

Handy, Truman B. "So Many Per! Serials, the Thrilling Fiction of the Cinema." *Motion Picture Magazine* 20.8 (September 1920): 70–71, 110–11.

Hansen, Miriam. "America, Paris, and the Alps: Kracauer (and Benjamin) on Cinema and

Modernity." In Charney and Schwartz, eds., *Cinema and the Invention of Modern Life*, 362–402.

——. *Babel and Babylon: Spectatorship in American Silent Film*. Cambridge: Harvard University Press, 1991.

——. "Benjamin, Cinema, and Experience: The Blue Flower in the Land of Technology." *New German Critique* 40 (Winter 1987): 179–224.

——. "Decentric Perspectives: Kracauer's Early Writings on Film and Mass Culture." *New German Critique* 54 (Fall 1991): 47–76.

Harmon, Jim and Donald F. Glut. *The Great Movie Serials: Their Sound and Fury*. Garden City, N.Y.: Doubleday, 1972.

Harris, William E. "A Chat with Owen Davis." *The Writer* (August 1931): n.p.

Harrison, Louis Reeves. "Over Their Heads." *Moving Picture World*, November 11, 1911, 449.

——. "Superior Plays: 'The Reform Candidate' (Edison)." *Moving Picture World*, September 30, 1911, 957.

——. "What's New?" *Moving Picture World*, November 22, 1913, 344.

Hartt, Rollin Lynde. *The People at Play: Excursions in the Humor and Philosophy of Popular Amusements*. Boston: Houghton Mifflin, 1909.

Harvey, Charles M. "The Dime Novel in American Life." *Atlantic Monthly* 100 (July 1907): 37–45.

Haskell, Mary. "The American Peril: Its Remedy." *The Forum* 42 (August 1914): 144–46.

Hayes, R. M. *The Republic Chapterplays: A Complete Filmography of the Serials Released by Republic Pictures Corporation, 1934–1955*. Jefferson, N.C.: McFarland, 1991.

Hedges, H. M. "A Laocoon for the Movies." *The Play-book* 2.8 (January 1915): 20–23.

Heilman, Robert. "Tragedy and Melodrama: Speculation on Generic Form." *Texas Quarterly* 3.2 (Summer 1960): 36–50.

——. *Tragedy and Melodrama: Versions of Experience*. Seattle: University of Washington Press, 1968.

Heller, Adele and Lois Rudnick, eds. *1915—The Cultural Moment: The New Politics, the New Woman, the New Psychology, the New Art, and the New Theatre in America*. New Brunswick, N.J.: Rutgers University Press, 1991.

Hemery, Gertrude. "The Revolt of the Daughters." *Westminster Review* 141 (June 1894): 679–81.

Henderson, John M. and Andrew Hollingworth. "High-Level Scene Perception." *Annual Review of Psychology* (1999): 243–61.

Hill, Joseph A. *Women in Gainful Occupation, 1870–1920*. U.S. Census Monographs, 9. Washington, D.C.: GPO, 1929.

Hill, John and Pamela Church Gibson, eds. *The Oxford Guide to Film Studies*. Oxford: Oxford University Press, 1998.

Hisham, Jon. "The Reorientation of American Culture in the 1890s." In John Weiss, ed., *The Origins of Modern Consciousness*, 25–48. Detroit: Wayne State University Press, 1965.

Hobson, John A. *The Evolution of Modern Capitalism: A Study of Machine Production*. London: Walter Scott, 1894.

"Hodkinson Organizes $9,000,000 Company." *Motion Picture News*, November 25, 1916, 3273.

"Hodkinson Urges Abolition of Daily Program Policy." *Motion Picture News*, March 10, 1917, 1527.

Hoekstra, Ellen. "The Pedestal Myth Reinforced: Women's Magazine Fiction,

1900–1920." In Russel B. Nye, ed., *New Dimensions in Popular Culture*, 43–58. Bowling Green, Ohio: Bowling Green University Popular Press, 1972.

Hofstadter, Beatrice. "Popular Culture and the Romantic Heroine." *American Scholar* 30 (Winter 1960): 98–116.

Hooker, Brian. "Moving-pictures: A Critical Prophecy." *The Century* 93.6 (April 1917): 857–68.

Horney, Karen. *New Ways in Psychoanalysis*. New York: Norton, 1939.

"How Motion Pictures Are Made." *New York Dramatic Mirror*, March 6, 1912, n.p.

Howard, Clifford. "Ways of the Hour: The Masculization of Girls." *Lippincott's Monthly Magazine* 88.526 (October 1911): 564–67.

Hubbard, John R. and Edward A. Workman. *Handbook of Stress Medicine: An Organ System Approach*. Boca Raton: CRC Press, 1990.

Humphrey, Nicholas. *A History of the Mind: Evolution and the Birth of Consciousness*. New York: Harper Perennial, 1992.

Humphreys, Mary. "Women Bachelors in New York." *Scribner's* 19.5 (November 1896): 626–36.

Huxley, Aldous. *The Doors of Perception*. New York: Harper and Row, 1954.

"Industry Answers 'News' Appeal for Longer Runs." *Motion Picture News*, February 17, 1917, 1035.

Inglis, William. "Morals and Moving Pictures." *Harper's Weekly*, July 30, 1910, 12–13.

Ingram, David. *Habermas and the Dialectic of Reason*. New Haven: Yale University Press, 1987.

"International Starts Third Year." *Motion Picture News*, January 6, 1917, 94.

"Is Woman Making a Man of Herself?" *Current Literature* 52.6 (June 1912): 682–84.

Jacobs, Lea. "The Woman's Picture and the Poetics of Melodrama." *Camera Obscura* 31 (1993): 121–47.

Jacobs, Lewis. *The Rise of the American Film: A Critical History*. New York: Teachers' College Press, 1969 (originally published in 1939 by Harcourt Brace, New York).

Jacoby, Henry. *The Bureaucratization of the World*. Berkeley: University of California Press, 1973.

Jenks, George C. "Dime Novel Makers." *The Bookman* 20 (October 1904): 108–14.

Johnston, Wm A. "Small House and Short Film." *Motion Picture News*, October 21, 1916, 1.

Kaes, Anton. "The Debate About Cinema: Charting a Controversy (1909–1929)." *New German Critique* 40 (Winter 1987): 12.

Kallen, Horace. "The Dramatic Picture versus the Pictorial Drama: A Study of the Influences of the Cinematograph on the Stage." *Harvard Monthly* 50.1 (March 1910): 22–31.

Kaminoff, Robert D. and Harold M. Proshansky. "Stress as a Consequence of the Urban Physical Environment." In Leo Goldberger and Shlomo Breznitz, eds., *Handbook of Stress: Theoretical and Clinical Aspects*, 380–409. New York: Free Press, 1982.

Kasson, John F. *Amusing the Million: Coney Island at the Turn of the Century*. New York: Hill and Wang, 1978.

"Kate Swan a Fairy Bareback Rider / Thrilling Experiences in the Tan-Bark Ring / Poised on a Trained, Galloping Steed." *New York World*, March 8, 1896, 25.

"Kate Swan Rides with Life-Savers / Covered with Ice and Nearly Frozen, She Shares Danger with the Crew of Seabright Station." *New York World*, February 23, 1896, 24.

"Kate Swan Scales Harlem River Bridge: A Dizzy, Difficult Ascent to a Spot No Woman's Foot Ever Trod Before." *New York World*, April 12, 1896, 29.

"Kate Swan as a Snake Charmer." *New York World*, March 29, 1896, 23.

"Kate Swan at Table with Women Convicts." *New York World*, March 1, 1896, 17.

"Kate Swan Visits New York's Leper Colony." *New York World*, September 27, 1896, 17.

"Kate Swan at Women's Policy Shop [illegal gambling den]." *New York World*, March 15, 1896, 24.

"Kate Swan's Night on Ellis Island." *New York World*, April 12, 1896, 29.

"Kate Swan's Pirate Hunt/An Enlivening Midnight Prowl on a Police Boat in Jamaica Bay to Capture the Daring Thieves That Loot Rich Oyster Beds." *New York World*, October 11, 1896, 17.

"Kate Swan's Rescue/She Falls in the Raging Surf at Coney Island, to Be Snatched from Death by an Up-to-Date Life-Saver." *New York World*, June 28, 1896, 17.

"Kate Swan's Two Views of Death [burial and cremation]." *New York World*, March 22, 1896, 17.

"Kate Swan's Visit to a Fiery Stoke-Hole/The Ferry-boat Cincinatti's Furnace Room Is Hotter Than Any Turkish Bath in the World/Kate Swan Works as a Stoker/Heaving Coal in the Fire-Room of the North River Ferry-boat." *New York World*, April 5, 1896, 17.

"Kate Swan's Wrestling Bout with Champion Leonard." *New York World*, October 18, 1896, 31.

Keil, Charlie. *Early American Cinema in Transition: Story, Style, and Filmmaking, 1907–1913*. Madison: University of Wisconsin Press, 2001.

——. " 'Visualised Narratives': Transitional Cinema and the Modernity Thesis." In Clair Dupré la Tour, André Gaudreault, and Roberta Pearson, eds., *Le Cinéma au Tournant du Siècle/ Cinema at the Turn of the Century*. 133–47. Lausanne/Québec: Éditions Payot Lausanne/Éditions Nota Bene, 1999.

Keil, Charles and Shelley Stamp, eds. *Cinema's Transitional Era: Audiences, Institutions, Practices* (forthcoming).

Kern, Stephen. *The Culture of Time and Space, 1880–1918*. Cambridge: Harvard University Press, 1983.

Kienzl, Hermann. "Theater und Kinematograph." *Der Strom* 1 (1911–12): 219ff.; quoted in Anton Kaes, "The Debate About Cinema," 12.

Kingsley, Sherman C. "The Penny Arcade and the Cheap Theatre." *Charities and the Commons* 18.10 (June 8, 1907): 295–97.

Kinnard, Roy. *Fifty Years of Serial Thrills*. Metuchen, N.J.: Scarecrow Press, 1983.

Kirby, Lynne. *Parallel Tracks: The Railroad and Silent Cinema*. Durham, N.C.: Duke University Press, 1997.

Kitses, Jim. *Horizons West—Anthony Mann, Budd Boettcher, Sam Peckinpah: Studies of Authorship Within the Western*. Bloomington: Indiana University Press, 1970.

Klinger, Barbara. *Melodrama and Meaning: History, Culture, and the Films of Douglas Sirk*. Bloomington: Indiana University Press, 1994.

Kolb, Brian. *Brain Plasticity and Behavior*. Mahwah, N.J.: Lawrence Erlbaum Associates, 1995.

Koszarski, Richard. *An Evening's Entertainment: The Age of the Silent Feature Picture, 1915–1928*. New York: Scribner's, 1990.

Kracauer, Siegfried. "The Cult of Distraction: On Berlin's Picture Palaces" (1926). In *The Mass Ornament*, 323–28.

"Georg Simmel" (1920–21). In *The Mass Ornament*, 225–58.

——. *The Mass Ornament: Weimar Essays*. Edited and translated by Thomas Y. Levin. Cambridge: Harvard University Press, 1995.

——. *Theory of Film: The Redemption of Physical Reality.* Oxford: Oxford University Press, 1960.

Krutch, Joseph. "What Is Melodrama?" *The Nation* 138 (May 9, 1934): 544.

Kumar, Krishan. *Prophecy and Progress: The Sociology of Industrial and Post-Industrial Society.* New York: Penguin Books, 1978.

——. *The Rise of Modern Society: Aspects of the Social and Political Development of the West.* Oxford: Blackwell, 1988.

Laemmle, Carl. "Doom of Long Features Predicted." *Moving Picture World,* July 11, 1914, 185.

Lahue, Kalton C. *Bound and Gagged: The Story of the Silent Serials.* South Brunswick, N.J.: A. S. Barnes, 1968.

——. *Continued Next Week: A History of the Moving Picture Serial.* Norman: University of Oklahoma Press, 1964.

Landis, Carney and William A. Hunt. *The Startle Pattern.* New York: Farrar and Rinehart, 1939.

Landy, Marcia, ed. *Imitations of Life: A Reader in Film and Television Melodrama.* Detroit: Wayne State University Press, 1991.

Lane, Roger. *Violent Death in the City: Suicide, Accident, and Murder in Nineteenth-Century Philadelphia.* Cambridge: Harvard University Press, 1979.

Lash, Scott. *Sociology of Postmodernism.* London: Routledge, 1990.

Lash, Scott and Jonathan Friedman. *Modernity and Identity.* Cambridge: Blackwell, 1992.

Lash, Scott and Sam Whimster. *Max Weber, Rationality, and Modernity.* London: Allen and Unwin, 1987.

Lauritzen, Eisnar and Gunnar Lundquist. *American Film Index.* Stockholm: [Publisher unavailable], 1984.

Lavoisier, Madam Therese. "The Latest Fashions in Moving Pictures: A Review of Dainty Gowns Worn by Studio Stars." *Motion Picture Magazine* 9.6 (July 1915): 117–20.

Lawrence, Peter. *Georg Simmel: Sociologist and European.* New York: Harper and Row, 1976.

Lazarus, Richard S. and Judith Blackfield-Cohen. "Environmental Stress." In Irwin Altman and Joachim F. Wohlwhill, eds., *Human Behavior and the Environment: Advances in Theory and Research* 2:89–127. New York: Plenum, 1977.

Leavitt, M. B. *Fifty Years in Theatrical Management.* New York: Broadway Publishing, 1912.

Le Bon, Gustave. *The Crowd.* New York: Viking, 1960 (originally published in 1895 as *Psychologie des Foules*).

Leacock, Stephen. "A Plain Man at the Play." *The Rotarian* 43.4 (October 1933): 20–21, 55–56.

Ledger, Sally. *The New Woman: Fiction and Feminism at the Fin de Siècle.* Manchester: Manchester University Press, 1997.

Lee, Alfred M. *The Daily Newspaper in America: The Evolution of a Social Instrument.* New York: Macmillan, 1947.

Lee, Gerald Stanley. *Crowds: A Study of the Genius of Democracy and the Fear, Desires, and Expectations of the People.* London: Methuen, 1913.

Leslie, Amy. "Actors, Farm Hands." *Chicago News,* April 18, 1908 (clipping, Robinson Locke Collection, New York Public Library, catalogued "NAFR Ser. 2.26": scrapbook page 88).

Levi, Lennart. "Sympathoadrenomedullary Responses to 'Pleasant' and 'Unpleasant' Psychosocial Stimuli." In Levi, ed., *Stress and Distress in Response to Psychosocial Stimuli,*

55–74. Oxford: Pergamon, 1972.

Lewisohn, Ludwig. "The Cult of Violence." *The Nation* 110.2847 (January 24, 1920): 118.

Leyda, Jay. *Kino: A History of the Russian and Soviet Film.* New York: Collier, 1973.

Leyda, Jay, ed. *Sergei Eisenstein: Film Form—Essays in Film Theory.* San Diego: Harvest/Harcourt Brace Jovanovich, 1949.

Liebersohn, Harry. *Fate and Utopia: 1870–1923.* Cambridge, Mass.: MIT Press, 1988.

Liebman, Stuart E. "Jean Epstein's Early Film Theory." Ph.D. diss., New York University, 1980.

"Limitations of Heroines in Fiction." *The Independent* 54.2789 (May 1902): 1198–99.

"Lincoln J. Carter's Genius Runs to Scenic Effects." *New York Morning Telegraph,* January 28, 1906, n.p. (clipping, Robinson Locke Collection, New York Public Library, catalogued "NAFR Ser. 2.26": scrapbook page 83).

Lindsay, Vachel. *The Art of the Moving Picture.* New York: Macmillan, 1915; rev. ed., 1922.

Lippmann, Walter. "More Brains, Less Sweat." *Everybody's Magazine* 25 (1911): 827–28; quoted in Tipple, *The Capitalist Revolution,* 103.

Loomis, Charles P. and John C. McKinney. "Introductory Essay." In Tönnies, *Community and Society,* 1–11. Translated and edited by Loomis. East Lansing: Michigan State University, 1957.

Lutz, Tom. *American Nervousness, 1903: An Anecdotal History.* Ithaca: Cornell University Press, 1991.

Lynn, Richard. *Attention, Arousal, and the Orientation Reflex.* Oxford: Pergamon, 1966.

MacCarthy, Desmond. "Melodrama." *The New Statesman* 3 (June 27, 1914): "Dramatic Supplement," 4.

"Making Snowballs During the Heat Plague/Last Tuesday with the Mercury at 96, Kate Swan Picked Icicles in the Heart of New York." *New York World,* August 16, 1896, 24.

Mantle, Burns. "What's What in Theater." *Green Book* (June 1918) (clipping, Robinson Locke Collection, New York Public Library, catalogued "NAFR Ser. 2.26": scrapbook page 114).

Marcus, Judith and Zoltan Tar, eds. *Foundations of the Frankfurt School of Social Research.* London: Transaction Books, 1984.

Marinetti. Filippo Tommaso et al. "The Futurist Cinema." In R. W. Flint, ed., *Marinetti: Selected Writings,* 131. New York: Farrar, Straus and Giroux, 1971.

Marx, Karl. *Capital.* Vol. 1 (1867). Translated from the 3d German edition by Samuel Moore and Edward Aveling (1906 translation). London: Lawrence and Wishart, 1970.

Marx, Karl and Friedrich Engels. *The Communist Manifesto* (1848). London: Verso, 1998.

Mason, James Frederick. *The Melodrama in France from the Revolution to the Beginning of Romantic Drama, 1791–1830.* Baltimore: J. H. Furst, 1912 (originally, a Ph.D. diss., Johns Hopkins University).

Masters, E. Lanning. "Marketing the Movies." *Harper's Weekly,* January 1, 1916, 24.

Masterson, Kate. "The Monster in the Car: A Study of the Twentieth-Century Woman's Passion for the Motor Speed-Mania and Its Attendant Evils and Vagaries." *Lippincott's Monthly Magazine* 86.512 (August 1910): 204–11.

Matthaei, Julie A. *An Economic History of Women in America.* New York: Schocken, 1982.

McBurney, Donald H. and Virginia B. Collings. *Introduction to Sensation/Perception.* 2d ed. Englewood Cliffs, N.J.: Prentice-Hall, 1984.

McCardell, Roy L. "The Chorus Girl Deplores the Moving Pictures' Triumph Over Drama." *Moving Picture World,* April 11, 1908, 321.

McCracken, Elizabeth. "The Playground and the Gallery." *Atlantic Monthly* 89.534 (April 1902): n.p.

"The Melancholy of Women's Pages." *Atlantic Monthly* 97.4 (April 1906): 574–75.

"Melodrama as a Business." [Unknown publication], April 7, 1918, n.p. (clipping, Harvard Theatre Collection).

"Melodrama: By a Touring Manager." *The Stage* (October 2, 1919): 8.

"Melodrama Commended." *The Castle Square Theater Program Magazine* (n.d.) (clipping, Harvard Theatre Collection).

Mendelson, Alan. "The Rise of Melodrama and the Schematization of Women in England, 1760–1840." Ph.D. diss., Stanford University, 1977.

Meriden, Orson. "A Chat with Pearl White." *Theatre Magazine* (July 1916): 61 (clipping, Robinson Locke Collection, New York Public Library, catalogued Ser. 2 v306).

Merritt, Russell. "Melodrama: Postmortem for a Phantom Genre." *Wide Angle* 5.3 (1983): 24–31.

Meyer, Annie Nathan. "The Snap-Shot and the Psychological Novel." *The Bookman* 15 (May 1902): 260–63.

Mitchell, Sally. "Sentiment and Suffering: Women's Recreational Reading in the 1890s." *Victorian Studies* 21.1 (Autumn 1977): n.p.

Mitzman, Arthur. *Sociology and Estrangement: Three Sociologists of Imperial Germany.* New York: Knopf, 1973.

"Modern Mannish Maidens." *Blackwood's Magazine* (Edinburgh) 147.892 (February 1890): 252–64.

Moen, L. C. "Statistics of the Motion Picture Industry." *Motion Picture News*, November 25, 1922, 2655.

Monahan, Michael. "The American Peril." *The Forum* 51 (June 1914): 878–82.

Morehouse, Ward. "Broadway After Dark: Owen Davis Man of Forty Pencils and 300 Plays." *New York Sun*, February 6, 1933, n.p.

——. "Broadway After Dark: Those Owen Davis Plays—They Total 103, Says Johnson Briscoe." *New York Sun*, February 18, 1933, n.p. (clipping, Harvard Theatre Collection).

Moses, Montrose J. *The American Dramatist.* Boston: Little, Brown, 1911.

——. "Concerning Melodrama." *Book News Monthly* 26.11 (July 1908): 843–47.

——. "Where They Perform Shakespeare for Five Cents." *Theatre Magazine* 8.92 (October 1908): 264–65, xi–xii.

"The Motion Picture Hall of Fame." *Motion Picture Magazine* 16.11 (December 1918): 12–14.

Mott, Frank Luther. *A History of American Magazines.* Cambridge: Belknap Press of Harvard University Press, 1957.

Mount, Cecilia. "The Girl with Nine Lives." *Motion Picture Magazine* 11.1 (February 1916): 121–25.

"Movies Once More." *The Outlook* 108 (October 28, 1914): 449.

"Moving Picture Tales, a photoplay-story magazine, published by the Motion Picture News." *New York Dramatic Mirror*, January 10, 1912, 30.

"Moving Pictures Ad Nauseam." *American Review of Reviews* 38.6 (December 1908): 744.

Mullett, Mary B. "The Heroine of a Thousand Dangerous Stunts." *American Magazine* 92.3 (September 1921): 32–34.

Mulvey, Laura. "Visual Pleasure and Narrative Cinema." *Screen* 16.3 (Autumn 1975): 6–18.

Munich, Adrienne Auslander. *Andromeda's Chains: Gender and Interpretation in Victorian*

Literature and Art. New York: Columbia University Press, 1989.

Münsterberg, Hugo. "Muensterberg [*sic*] Vigorously Denounces Red Light Drama." *New York Times*, September 14, 1913, n.p.

Mussell, Kay, ed. *Women's Gothic and Romantic Fiction: A Reference Guide.* Westport, Conn.: Greenwood, 1981.

Musser, Charles. *Before the Nickelodeon: Edwin S. Porter and the Edison Manufacturing Company.* Berkeley: University of California Press, 1991.

Musson, Bennett and Robert Grau. "Fortunes in Films: Moving Pictures in the Making." *McClure's Magazine* 40 (December 1912): 193–202.

Nathan, George Jean. *Mr. George Jean Nathan Presents* (1917). Rpt., Cranbury, N.J.: Associated University Presses, 1971.

——. *The Popular Theatre.* Cranbury, N.J.: Associated University Presses, 1971 (originally published in 1918 by Knopf).

Neale, Steve. "Melo-Talk: On the Meaning and Use of the Term 'Melodrama' in the American Trade Press." *Velvet Light Trap* 32 (Fall 1993): 66–89.

"Nellie Bly as an Elephant Trainer/Novel and Thrilling Experience with the Immense Animals in Their Winter Home/Perilous Ride on the Ivory Tusks of Fritz." *New York World*, February 23, 1896, 17.

"Nellie Bly Proposes to Fight for Cuba/Women Have More Courage Than Men and Would Make Better Officers/Ready to Recruit Volunteers for Her First Regiment." *New York World*, March 8, 1896, 24.

"Nellie, the Beautiful Cloak Model." *Brooklyn Daily Eagle*, January 24, 1907, sec. 3, p. 4.

"The New Owen Davis." *New York Dramatic Mirror*, October 22, 1913, 1, 10.

"The New Woman in a Life-Saver's Boat/She Goes with the Hell Gate Heroes and Helps Them Rescue Two Lives from the Seething Wives." *New York World*, June 23, 1895, 29.

"The 'New Woman' in Everyday Life: Various Interesting Manifestations of the Emancipated Female's Foibles and Freaks, and Her Curious Interests, Powers, and Exploits." *New York Sunday World* (1895). Featured as a regular Sunday column in 1895: see, e.g., *New York Sunday World*, August 11, p. 32; August 18, p. 32; September 20, p. 38; October 6, p. 36; October 31, p. 21; and October 20, p. 35.

"A 'New Woman' Mail Clerk." *New York World*, November 10, 1895, 27.

"The New Woman—What She Is Doing, Wearing, and Saying." *New York World*, May 10, 1896, 27.

"The New Woman's Night in Greenwood [Cemetery]/Gruesome Adventures Among the Solitary Tombs and Receiving Vaults." *New York World*, August 11, 1895, 26.

"New Women—Their Efforts, Follies, and Fashions." *New York World*, May 3, 1896, 21.

"New Women—Their Efforts and Their Interests." *New York World*, May 31, 1896, 24.

"New York's Catacomb of Frozen Dead/Refrigerated Corpses Kept by the Hundred in a Columbia College Vault for Dissecting-Room Use [Kate Swan visits]." *New York World*, August 23, 1896, 19.

" 'News' Campaign for Longer Runs Succeeding Nationally." *Motion Picture News*, February 10, 1917, 869.

"News of Brooklyn Theaters." *Brooklyn Daily Eagle*, September 13, 1903, 8.

Nisbet, Robert A. *The Sociological Tradition.* New York: Basic Books, 1966.

Noel, Mary. *Villains Galore: The Heyday of the Popular Story Weekly.* New York: Macmillan, 1954.

Nordau, Max. *Degeneration* (1895). Translated by George L. Mosse. New York: Howard Fertig, 1968.

"The Novellete and the Superwoman." *Living Age* 260 (January 16, 1909): 183–85.

Nowell-Smith, Geoffrey. "Minnelli and Melodrama," *Screen* 18.2 (Summer 1977): 113–18. Reprinted in Marcia Landy, ed., *Imitations of Life*, 268–74, and in Christine Gledhill, ed., *Home Is Where the Heart Is*, 10–14.

Nowell-Smith, Geoffrey, ed. *The Oxford History of World Cinema*. Oxford: Oxford University Press, 1996.

"Now the Woman Contractor." *New York World*, November 10, 1895, 25.

Oberholtzer, Ellis Paxson. *The Morals of the Movies*. Philadelphia: Penn Publishing, 1922.

——. "Statement of Mr. Ellis P. Oberholtzer." *Report of the Chicago Motion Picture Commission* (10th session). Chicago, September 1920: 105.

Obituaries

——. Arthur, Joseph: "Joseph Arthur." *New York Dramatic Mirror*, March 3, 1906, n.p.

——. Carter, Lincoln J.: "Lincoln J. Carter." *Boston Transcript*, July 13, 1926, n.p. (clipping, Harvard Theatre Collection).

——. Carter, Lincoln J.: "Lincoln J. Carter." [Unknown newspaper], July 14, 1926, n.p. (clipping, Harvard Theatre Collection).

——. Carter, Lincoln J.: "Lincoln J. Carter." [Unknown London newspaper], August 3, 1926, n.p. (clipping, Harvard Theatre Collection).

——. Foster, Charles: "Charles Foster." *New York Dramatic Mirror*, August 24, 1895, n.p.

——. Davis, Owen: "Owen Davis." *New York Times*, October 15, 1956, n.p.

"On a $3,000 Bicycle/Kate Swan the First Woman to Ride a Monster Sextet/Describes Thrilling Sensation/Faster Than Any Woman EverRode Before." *New York World*, July 26, 1896, 11.

Ortega y Gasset, José. *The Revolt of the Masses* (1929). New York: Norton, 1932 (uncredited authorized translation); also available in a different translation by Anthony Kerrigan (Notre Dame, Ind.: University of Notre Dame Press, 1985).

"Owen Davis." [Unknown publication], April 6, 1924, n.p. (clipping, Harvard Theatre Collection).

"Owen Davis—the Abou ben Adhem of American Playwrights." *American Magazine* (March: n.d.): n.p. (clipping, Harvard Theatre Collection, "Owen Davis" file).

Pam, Dorothy S. "Exploitation, Independence, and Solidarity: The Changing Role of American Working Women as Reflected in the Working-Girl Melodrama." Ph.D. diss., New York University, 1980.

Paterson, Randolph J. and Richard W. J. Neufeld. "Clear Danger: Situational Determinants of the Appraisal of Threat." *Psychological Bulletin* 101.3 (1987): 404–16.

"Pathé: A Word That Has Come to Mean News, Entertainment and Education to Millions—From the Oldest Producing Company in the Business." *Moving Picture World*, March 26, 1927, 398, 417.

Pearson, Roberta. *Eloquent Gestures: The Transformation of Performance Style in Griffith Biograph Films*. Berkeley: University of California Press, 1992.

Peiss, Kathy. *Cheap Amusements: Working Women and Leisure in Turn-of-the-Century New York*. Philadelphia: Temple University Press, 1986.

Peterson, Joyce Shaw. "Working Girls and Millionaires: The Melodramatic Romances of Laura Jean Libbey." *American Studies* 24 (Spring 1983): 19–35.

Petro, Patrice. "Discourse on Sexuality in Early German Film Theory." *New German Critique* 40 (Winter 1987): n.p.

Phelps, William Lyon. "The Drama of Today." *Journal of the National Institute of Social Sciences* 3 (January 1917): 17–33.

Phillips, Henry Albert. *The Photodrama*. Larchmont, N.Y.: Stanhope-Dodge, 1914.

Pierce, Lucy France. "The Nickleodeon." *The World Today* 25.4 (October 1908): 1052–57.

Pirandello, Luigi. *Shoot! The Notebooks of Serafino Gubbio, Cinematograph Operator* (1915). Translated by C. K. Scott Moncrieff. New York: Dutton, 1926.

"A Plucky Girl Nabs a Thief." *New York World*, January 6, 1894, 9.

Poggi, Jack. *Theater in America: The Impact of Economic Forces, 1870–1967.* Ithaca: Cornell University Press, 1968.

Poggio, Tomaso. "Vision and Learning." In Robert A. Wilson and Frank C. Keil, eds., *The MIT Encyclopedia of the Cognitive Sciences*, 863–64. Cambridge, Mass.: MIT Press, 1999.

"The Point of View." *Scribner's* 46.1 (July 1909): 121–22.

"Popularity Contest Closes." *Motion Picture Magazine* 20.11 (December 1920): 94.

"The Popularity of the Serial Photoplay." *Pathé* 2.8 (February 25, 1916): n.p.

Price, W. T. "The Technique of the Drama: The Bowery Theaters," *Harper's Weekly*, May 10, 1890, 370.

"Producing Spine-Thrillers" (interview with Al Woods). *Literary Digest* 45.6 (August 10, 1912): 222–23. Excerpted from an article by A. H. Woods in the *Associated Sunday Magazine*.

"Prolific Writer of Thrilling Melodramas." [Unknown publication], April 28, 1918, n.p. (clipping, Harvard Theatre Collection, "Lincoln Carter" file).

Putnam, Nina Wilcox. "Fashion and Feminism." *The Forum* 52 (October 1914): 580–84.

Quimby, Fred C. "A Standard Feature." *Wid's Year Book* (1919–20): 71.

Quinn, Arthur Hobson. "In Defense of Melodrama." *The Bookman* 61.4 (June 1925): 413–17.

Rabinovitz, Lauren. *For the Love of Pleasure: Women, Movies, and Culture in Turn-of-the-Century Chicago.* New Brunswick, N.J.: Rutgers University Press, 1998.

Rahill, Frank. *The World of Melodrama.* University Park: Pennsylvania State University Press, 1967.

Rahn, Carl. "The Relation of Sensation to Other Categories in Contemporary Psychology." *Psychological Monographs* 16.1 (December 1913): 1–131.

——. "Sensation and Its Physiological Conditions." *Psychological Monographs* 21.4 (June 1916): 55–79.

Ramsaye, Terry. *A Million and One Nights: A History of the Motion Picture Through 1925.* New York: Simon and Schuster, 1926.

Rascoe, Burton. "The Motion Pictures—an Industry, Not an Art." *The Bookman* 54.3 (November 1921): 193–99.

——. *We Were Interrupted.* Garden City, N.Y.: Doubleday, 1947.

Read, Herbert. *A Concise History of Modern Painting.* New York: Praeger, 1959.

"Realism on the Stage." *Pittsburgh Post*, January 28, 1906, n.p. (clipping in Robinson Locke Collection, New York Public Library, catalogued "NAFR Ser. 2, 26," scrapbook page 94).

"Record-Breaking Ride on an Electric Engine/Kate Swan Drives a Motor Through the B. and O. Tunnel at 75 Miles an Hour/First Electric Engine Ever Run by a Woman." *New York World*, May 31, 1896, 25.

Renner, Michael J. and Mark R. Rosenzweig. *Enriched and Impoverished Environments: Effects on Brain and Behavior.* New York: Springer-Verlag, 1987.

"Report on Conditions of Women and Child Wage Earners in the United States." Reprinted in The Commonwealth of Massachusetts, *Report of the Commission on Minimum Wage Boards* (Boston: January 1912): 260–61, 288–89, 318–19.

"Risks Life for Realism." *Moving Picture World*, May 6, 1916, 190 (clipping, Robinson Locke Collection, New York Public Library, catalogued Ser. 2 v47).

Roberts, Robin. "The Female Alien: Pulp Science Fiction's Legacy to Feminists." *Journal of Popular Culture* 21.2 (1987): 33–52.

Robinson, David. *The History of World Cinema*. New York: Stein and Day, 1973.

Rollins, Montgomery. "Women and Motor Cars." *The Outlook* 92 (August 7, 1909): 859–60.

Romalov, Nancy Tillman. "Unearthing the Historical Reader, or Reading Girls' Reading." In Larry E. Sullivan and Lydia Cushman Schurman, eds., *Pioneers, Passionate Ladies, and Private Eyes: Dime Novels, Series Books, and Paperbacks*, 87–101. New York: Haworth, 1996.

"The Romance of a Great Business." *Education* 36 (February 1916): 395–98; originally published in *Moving Picture World* (uncited in *Education*).

Rotella, Elyce. *From Home to Office: U.S. Women at Work, 1870–1930*. Ann Arbor: UMI Research Press, 1981.

Ruhl, Arthur. "Ten-Twenty-Thirty." *Second Nights: People and Ideas of the Theater Today*, 141–63. New York: Scribner's, 1914.

Ryan, Mary P. *Womanhood in America*. New York: New Viewpoints, 1975.

Sapolsky, Robert M. *Why Zebras Don't Get Ulcers: A Guide to Stress, Stress-Related Diseases, and Coping*. New York: W. H. Freeman, 1994.

Sayer, Derek. *Capitalism and Modernity: An Excursus on Marx and Weber*. London: Routledge, 1991.

Schlupmann, Heide. "Kracauer's Phenomenology of Film." *New German Critique* 40 (Winter 1987): n.p.

Schmidt, Emile. "The Bowery! The Bowery!" *Players Magazine* 45 (June-July 1970): 223–27.

Schutz, Wayne. *The Motion Picture Serial: An Annotated Bibliography*. Metuchen, N.J.: Scarecrow Press, 1992.

Scoff, Lawrence A. *Fleeing the Iron Cage: Culture, Politics, and Modernity in the Thought of Max Weber*. Berkeley: University of California Press, 1989.

Seabury, William M. *The Public and the Motion Picture Industry*. New York: Macmillan, 1926.

Sedgwick, Ruth. "Those Dear Dead Days of Melodrama." *The Stage* (August 1935): 38 (clipping, Harvard Theatre Collection).

Seitz, George B. "The Serial Speaks." *New York Dramatic Mirror*, August 19, 1916, 21.

Selig, William. "Present Day Trend in Film Lengths." *Moving Picture World*, July 11, 1914, 181.

Selye, Hans. *The Physiology and Pathology of Exposure to Stress*. Montreal: Acta Medical, 1950.

"Sensation and Plenty of It: The Late Charles Foster's Efforts to Serve Highly Spiced Plays to the Bowery." [Unknown publication], n.d., n.p. (clipping, Harvard Theatre Collection, "Charles Foster" file).

"Sensational Melodrama." *London Daily Express*, August 28, 1905, n.p. (clipping, Harvard Theatre Collection).

"The Serial Speaks." *New York Dramatic Mirror*, August 19, 1916, 21.

"Serials Versus Novels." *The Dial* 57.677 (September 1): 125–27.

Shaw, George Bernard. "What the Films May Do to the Drama." *Metropolitan Magazine* 42 (May 1915): 23.

"She Held a Burglar: Little Mrs. Gilligan Rolled Downstairs with Him in Her Grip/Then

They Fought on the Floor/Once He Got Away by Slipping Off His Coat, but She Sprang on Him Again." *New York World*, March 23, 1896, 1.

Sherson, Erroll. *London's Lost Theatres of the Nineteenth Century*. London: John Lane the Bodley Head, 1925.

"The Shrinkage of the World." *The Spectator* 99 (October 19, 1907): 557–58.

Showalter, Elaine. "Desperate Remedies: Sensation Novels of the 1860s." *Victorian Newsletter* 46 (Spring 1976): n.p.

Sica, Alan. *Weber, Irrationality, and Social Order*. Berkeley: University of California Press, 1988.

Simmel, Georg. "The Metropolis and Mental Life." *The Sociology of Georg Simmel*. Translated and edited by Kurt H. Wolff. Glencoe, Ill.: Free Press, 1950. (For other translations of Simmel's essays, see entries below for Nicholas Spykman and Kurt H. Woolf.)

——. *On Individuality and Social Forms*. Edited by Donald Levine. Chicago: University of Chicago Press, 1971.

——. *The Philosophy of Money* (1900). Translated by Tom Bottomore and David Frisby. London: Routledge and Kegan Paul, 1978.

Simmons, Ronald C. *Boo! Culture, Experience, and the Startle Reflex*. New York: Oxford University Press, 1996.

Singh, Sheo D. "Effect of Urban Environment on Visual Curiosity Behavior in Rhesus Monkeys." *Psychonomic Science* 11.3 (1968): 83–84.

Slide, Anthony. *The American Film Industry: A Historical Dictionary*. Westport, Conn.: Greenwood, 1986.

Smith, Arnold. "The Ethics of Sensational Fiction." *Westminster Review* 162 (August 1904): 190.

Smith, Frederick James. "The Evolution of the Motion Picture: The Feature Picture and Exhibiting Methods." *New York Dramatic Mirror*, September 3, 1913, 25.

Smith, Harry James. "The Melodrama." *Atlantic Monthly* 99 (March 1907): 320–28.

Smith, John Leslie. *Victorian Melodramas: Seven English, French, and American Melodramas*. Totowa, N.J.: Rowman and Littlefield, 1976.

Snow, Richard. *Coney Island: A Postcard Journey to the City of Fire*. New York: Brightwaters Press, 1984.

Sokolov, Y. N. *Perception and the Conditioned Reflex*. Translated by Stefan W. Waydenfeld. Oxford: Pergamon, 1963.

Solomon, Robert C. *Bully Culture: Enlightenment, Romanticism, and the Transcendental Pretence, 1750–1850*. Lanham, Md.: Rowman and Littlefield, 1993 (originally published in 1979 by Harcourt Brace Jovanovich as *History and Human Nature: A Philosophical Review of European Philosophy and Culture, 1750–1850*).

Sorokin, Pitirim. *Social Mobility*. New York: Harper, 1927.

Sorokin, Pitirim and Carle C. Zimmerman. *Principles of Rural-Urban Sociology*. New York: Holt & Co., 1929.

Soupault, Phillipe. "Cinema, U.S.A." (1923). In Paul Hammond, ed., *The Shadow and Its Shadow: Surrealist Writings on Cinema*, 32. London: British Film Institute, 1978.

"The Spectator." *The Outlook* 66 (September 15, 1900): 153.

——. *The Outlook* 68 (August 17, 1901): 905–6.

——. *The Outlook* 103 (January 25, 1913): 230–31.

" 'Spectator's' Comments." *New York Dramatic Mirror*, June 19, 1909, 16.

——. *New York Dramatic Mirror*, January 29, 1910, 16.

——. *New York Dramatic Mirror*, May 8, 1912, 24.

Spigel, Lynn and Denise Mann. "Women and Consumer Culture: A Selective Bibliography." *Quarterly Review of Film and Video* 11 (1989): 85–105.

Spykman, Nicholas. *The Social Theory of George Simmel.* Chicago: University of Chicago Press, 1925; rpt., New York: Russel and Russel, 1964.

Staiger, Janet. *Bad Women: Regulating Sexuality in Early American Cinema.* Minneapolis: University of Minnesota Press, 1995.

Stamp, Shelley. *Movie-Struck Girls: Women and Motion Picture Culture After the Nickelodeon.* Princeton: Princeton University Press, 2000.

Stanford, S. Clare and Peter Salmon, eds. *Stress: From Synapse to Syndrome.* London: Academic Press, 1993.

Stedman, Raymond William. *The Serials: Drama and Suspense by Installment.* 2d ed. Norman: University of Oklahoma Press, 1977.

Stearns, Harold. "Art in Moving Pictures." *The New Republic,* September 25, 1915, 207–208.

Stechhan, H. O. "Stage versus Screen." *Theatre Magazine* 21.169 (March 1915): 126–30, 144.

"Strenuous Davis, Who Has Written Seventy-Six Plays." *Chicago Inter-Ocean,* August 18, 1907, n.p.

Strong, Christopher. "Good-by, Melodrama." *Green Book* 8.3 (September 1912): 435–39.

"Swam Tandem Through Swirling Hell Gate/Kate Swan Takes a Midnight Ride Through the Mad Whirlpool." *New York World,* May 17, 1896, 31.

Studlar, Gaylyn. *This Mad Masquerade: Stardom and Masculinity in the Jazz Age.* New York: Columbia University Press, 1996.

Tarbell, Ida M. "Making a Man of Herself." *American Magazine* 73.4 (February 1912): 427–30.

——. "The Uneasy Woman." *American Magazine* 73.3 (January 1912): 259–62.

Tarde, Gabriel. *Opinion and the Crowd* (1901; no further information available).

Taylor, Charles A. "Earned $1,250 a Week in 1892" (obituary). *New York Times,* March 22, 1942, 48.

Tazelaar, Marguerite. "Owen Davis Looks at His Record." *New York Herald Tribune,* March 30, 1938, n.p.

"The Sensational Serial: An Enquiry." *Living Age* 230.2975 (July 13, 1901): 129–32.

"30 Miles an Hour in a Horseless Carriage/Dorothy Dare's Exciting Ride/The First Woman to Take a Spin Through the Streets of New York in a Horseless Carriage." *New York World,* May 3, 1896, 18.

Thompson, Alan R. "A Study of Melodrama as a Dramatic Genre." Ph.D. diss., Harvard University, 1926.

——. "Melodrama and Tragedy." *Publications of the Modern Language Association* 43 (1928): 810–35.

Thompson, Kristin, and David Bordwell. *Film History: An Introduction.* New York: McGraw-Hill, 1994.

Tickner, Lisa. *The Spectacle of Women: Imagery of the Suffrage Campaign, 1907–1914.* Chicago: University of Chicago Press, 1988.

Tipple. John. *The Capitalist Revolution: A History of American Social Thought, 1890–1919.* New York: Pegasus, 1970.

Tönnies, Ferdinand. *Community and Society* (*Gemeinschaft und Gesellschaft,* 1887). Translated and edited by Charles P. Loomis. East Lansing: Michigan State University Press, 1957.

"The Tornado at Miner's." *Newark Daily Advertiser,* April 17, 1894, 4.

Turner, Bryan S. *Max Weber: From History and Modernity.* London: Routledge, 1992.

Turner, Stephen P. and Regis A. Factor. *Max Weber and the Dispute Over Reason and Value: A Study in Philosophy, Ethics, and Policy.* London: Routledge and Kegan Paul, 1984.

Touraine, Alain. *Critique of Modernity.* Oxford: Blackwell, 1995.

Tyrell, Henry. "Drama and Yellow Drama." *Theatre Magazine* 4.42 (August 1904): 193.

"Uncle Sam on the New Woman." *New York World*, June 23, 1895, 22.

Urwick, L. *The Meaning of Rationalisation.* London: Nisbet, 1929.

U.S. Bureau of the Census. *Historical Statistics of the United States, Colonial Times to 1957.* Washington, D.C.: GPO, 1960.

——. "Number of Inhabitants: U.S. Summary," Table 3. *1980 Census of the Population.* Washington, D.C.: GPO, 1980.

——. *Special Reports, Street and Electric Railways.* Washington, D.C.: GPO, 1903.

U.S. Bureau of National Affairs. "Consumer Price Index." *Labor Relations Expediter no. 696 LRX 430:713* (September 29, 1991): 7.

U.S. Congress. *The French Declaration of the Rights of Man and of the Citizen and the American Bill of Rights.* Senate Document 101–9. Washington, D.C.: GPO, 1988.

U.S. Department of Commerce and Labor. *Special Reports: Street and Electric Railways.* Washington, D.C.: Bureau of the Census, 1903.

U.S. Department of Labor, Bureau of Labor Statistics. "The Consumer Price Index, 1800–1974." *Handbook of Labor Statistics*, Bulletin no. 1865 (Reference Edition, 1975): 313.

——. "Consumer Price Indexes and Purchasing Power of the Consumer Dollar, 1913–1988." *Handbook of Labor Statistics*, Bulletin no. 2340 (August 1999): 475.

Vance, Carole S. "Pleasure and Danger: Toward a Politics of Sexuality." In Vance, ed., *Pleasure and Danger: Exploring Female Sexuality*, 1–5. Boston: Routledge and Kegan Paul, 1984.

Van de Water, Frederic F. "Books and So Forth." *New York Herald Tribune*, January 24, 1924, n.p. (clipping, Harvard Theatre Collection, "Chinatown Charley" file).

Vann, J. Don. *Victorian Novels in Serial.* New York: Modern Language Association of America, 1985.

Vardac, A. Nicholas. *Stage to Screen: Theatrical Origins of Early Film—David Garrick to D. W. Griffith.* Cambridge: Harvard University Press, 1949. Subsequent editions by De Capo Press and the University of California Press.

Variety Film Reviews, vol. 1, *1907–1920.* New York: Garland, 1983.

Vicinus, Martha. "Helpless and Unfriended: Nineteenth-Century Domestic Melodrama." *New Literary History* 13.1 (Autumn 1981): 127–43.

Vorse, Mary Heaton. "Some Picture Show Audiences." *The Outlook* 98 (June 24, 1911): 441–47.

Wagner, Robert. "You—At the Movies." *American Magazine* 90.6 (December 1920): 42–44, 210–12; excerpted in *Literary Digest* 68 (February 26, 1941): 46.

Walkowitz, Judith R. *City of Dreadful Delight: Narratives of Sexual Danger in Late-Victorian London.* Chicago: University of Chicago Press, 1992.

Waller, Gregory. *Main Street Amusements: Movies and Commercial Entertainment in a Southern City, 1896–1930.* Washington, D.C.: Smithsonian Institution Press, 1995.

"Wanted, a Chivalry for Women." *The Spectator* 66 (April 11, 1891): 506–507.

Warner, Sam B. *Streetcar Suburbs: The Process of Growth in Boston, 1870–1900.* Cambridge: Harvard University Press, 1962.

Watson, Elmo Scott. *A History of Newspaper Syndicates in the United States, 1864–1935.* Chicago: [Publisher unavailable], 1936.

Weber, Adna Ferrin. *The Growth of Cities in the Nineteenth Century: A Study in Statistics* (1899). Ithaca: Cornell University Press, 1963.

Weber, Ludwig Wilheim. "Grossstadt und Nerven," *Deutsches Rundschau* (December 1918): 391–407 (translation for author by Skadi Loist).

Weber, Max. *Economy and Society: An Outline of Interpretive Sociology.* Edited by Guenther Roth and Claus Wittich. 2 vols. Berkeley: University of California Press, 1978.

———. *The Protesant Ethic and the Spirit of Capitalism* (1904–1905). Rpt., New York: Scribner's, 1958.

Wegefarth, W. Dayton. "The Decline of Lurid Melodrama." *Lippincott's Monthly Magazine* 88 (September 1911): 427–28.

Weinstein, Neil D. "Community Noise Problems: Evidence Against Adaptation." *Journal of Experimental Psychology* 2 (1982): 87–97.

"Weird Powers Claimed by Woman Pow-Wow/Mysterious Voodoo Rites Practiced by Pennsylvania Woman to Cure Any and All Diseases/Kate Swan with a Wizard of Disease." *New York World*, August 2, 1896, 22.

Weiller, Lazare. "The Annihilation of Distance." *Living Age* 219 (October 15, 1898): 163–78 (originally published in *La Revue des Deux Mondes*).

Welter, Barbara. "The Cult of True Womanhood: 1820–1860." *American Quarterly* 18 (Summer 1966): 151–74.

"What Is Melodrama?" *The Nation* 138.3592 (1934): 545–46.

"Where the Pauper Dead of New York Are Buried/Kate Swan Watches the Unhallowed Burial of New York's Nameless Dead." *New York World*, September 20, 1896, 22.

"Whirled to Instant Death: His Body Caught in Rapidly Revolving Belts and Crushed Against the Ceiling at Every Revolution." *Newark Daily Advertiser*, May 29, 1891, 1.

"Why the Movies and the Drama Must Take Different Roads." *Current Opinion* 58.5 (1915): 333.

Wiesberg, Frank. "Review of 'Just Like a Woman.' " *Variety*, July 11, 1908.

Wilcox, Ella Wheeler. "The Restlessness of the Modern Woman." *Cosmopolitan Magazine* 31.3 (July 1901): 314–17.

Wilcox, Susanne. "A Typical Uneasy Woman." *The Independent* 74.3351 (February 20, 1913): 398–403.

"A Wild Night Ride on a Cable Snow Plough/ Dorothy Dare's Thrilling Trip Through the Storm on a Whirling Roaring Rotary Sweeper." *New York World*, March 22, 1896, 21.

Williams, Linda. "Film Bodies: Gender, Genre, and Excess." *Film Quarterly* 44.4 (Summer 1991): 2–13.

———. *"Playing the Race Card": Melodramas of Black and White from Uncle Tom to O. J. Simpson.* Princeton: Princeton University Press, 2001.

Wilson, Garff B. *Three Hundred Years of American Drama and Theatre: From Ye Bear and Ye Cubb to Hair* (1973). 2d ed. Englewood Cliffs, N.J.: Prentice-Hall, 1982.

Wilson, Margaret Gibbons. *The American Woman in Transition: The Urban Influence, 1870–1920.* Contributions in Women's Studies, 6. Westport, Conn.: Greenwood, 1979.

Winchester, Boyd. "The New Woman." *Arena* 27 (April 1902): 367.

Winston, Ella W. "Foibles of the New Woman." *The Forum* 21 (April 1896): 186–92.

Witham, Barry. "Owen Davis, America's Forgotten Playwright." *Players Magazine* 46.1 (October-November 1970): 30–35.

Wolff, Kurt H. *Essays on Sociology, Philosophy, and Aesthetics by Georg Simmel et al.* New York: Harper Torchbooks, 1965 (originally published in 1959 by the Ohio State University Press under the title *Georg Simmel, 1858–1918*). (This volume also includes Wolff's translation of Simmel's essay "The Metropolis and Mental Life.")

"A Woman in the Death Chair/The Experience and Torture of Bat Shea Repeated in the

Investigation of Kate Swan, Plucky Woman Reporter of the World." *New York World*, February 16, 1896, 17.

"A Woman to the Rescue: Mrs. Howard Interferes in a Saloon Fight in Behalf of the Weaker One." *New York World*, March 29, 1896, 1.

"Womanliness and Womanishness." *The Spectator* 71 (November 25, 1893): 742–43.

"Woman's Latest Feats and Fancies." *New York World*, April 12, 1896, 31.

"Women and Bad Books." *The Independent* 63.3077 (November 21, 1907): 1260–61.

"Women in the Rush Line [women's football team]." *New York World*, March 17, 1895, 22.

Woodworth, Samuel. *The Widow's Son; Or, Which Is the Traitor?* New York, 1825. Cited in Grimsted, *Melodrama Unveiled*, 175.

Woolston, Howard B. "The Urban Habit of Mind." *American Journal of Sociology* 17.5 (March 1912): 602–14.

"World Pictures Ready Seven Months in Advance." *Motion Picture News* 14.16 (1916): 2552.

Wright, C. H. C. *A History of French Literature*. New York: Oxford University Press, 1925.

Wright, William Lord. "Dame Fashion and the Movies." *Motion Picture Magazine* 8.8 (September 1914): 107–11.

——. "Perils of the Motion Picture." *Motion Picture Magazine* 9.3 (April 1915): 95.

Wuketits, Franz M. *Evolutionary Epistemology and Its Implications for Humankind*. Albany: State University of New York Press, 1990.

Zeisloft, E. Idell, ed. *The New Metropolis: Memorable Events of Three Centuries, 1600–1900*. New York: Appleton, 1899.

Zohary, Ehud et al. "Neuronal Plasticity That Underlies Improvement in Perceptual Performance." *Science* 263.5151 (March 4, 1994): 1289–93.

Index of Names and Subjects

Index of Titles
